7-17-74

Plate I

GREY FRIARS' BELFRY, KING'S LYNN

FRANCISCAN ARCHITECTURE IN ENGLAND

BY

A. R. MARTIN, F.S.A.

WITH

A PREFACE BY

SIR CHARLES PEERS

C.B.E., LITT.D., D.LIT., P.P.S.A., F.B.A.

MANCHESTER: THE UNIVERSITY PRESS

1937

Republished in 1966 by Gregg Press Limited,
1 Westmead, Farnborough, Hants., England

Printed in England.

TO
MY MOTHER

CONTENTS

TEXT FIGURES

PLATES

xi

FOLDING PLANS

PREFACE

A COMPREHENSIVE account of the buildings of the Mendicant Orders in Britain has hitherto been lacking, and Mr. Martin's book on Franciscan building will go far towards meeting the want. The story of the Friars has often been told, and with the personality of many members of the various Orders the world is familiar. The need of a bridge between monastic and secular life, which might combine the excellences of both, had never been more apparent than in the eleventh and twelfth centuries, when the monastic ideal was at its height. And the need produced the solution. The Friars took their place in the order of things, and for a while the enthusiasm which attends on a new enterprise carried them forward till they were to be found in every part of Europe. But their very success brought them enemies. They invaded on the one hand the privileges of the parochial clergy, and on the other the vested interests of the regulars. The writings of contemporaries are for the most part hostile to them ; the greed and duplicity of the friar are common themes, and now that the men themselves have long vanished from among us, their memory cannot but suffer from the volume of adverse record.

For reasons too well known to be dwelt upon here, they have not left behind them, as have the Benedictines, the Cistercians and others, the splendid architectural monuments which must ever command our admiration for the societies which produced them. It is one of the functions of Mr. Martin's book to redress this balance, and to show that our debt to the Friars is a very real one after all, in this matter of architecture. The type of church which was evolved to suit their requirements was both noble and spacious. Though the greatest of such churches, that of the London Franciscans, is gone, we can see in the Dominican church in Norwich, shorn as it is of all its colour and ornament, how impressive such a building could be. In one respect, indeed, the English province can claim real distinction ; that is, by the invention of the slender bell turret over the passage separating nave from choir, which was characteristic of friars' churches in this country, but is not to be found anywhere on the Continent. The delightful example at King's Lynn which forms the frontispiece to this book shows how attractive this feature could be. Of other buildings than the churches not much can be said : there was no such regularity in the planning of a friars' cloister as is to be found in the claustral buildings of the Monastic Orders, and it is to be remembered that friars' houses were not the places where the whole life of the members of the community was normally spent. They were rather the resting-places between journeys, the sleeping-places of men whose activities took them incessantly outside their precincts, and while rich foundations might find themselves able to provide costly lodgings, in the vast majority of cases nothing of the sort was possible.

For the rest it remains to note that of the sixty-one Franciscan houses which existed at the suppression only thirteen are now represented by appreciable relics of building. Of these, and of all the rest which are now little more than a memory, this book provides a careful, thorough and scholarly record, representing the labour of many years, and a collation of all available evidence. It is a work of permanent value, and I wish it all the success it deserves.

CHARLES PEERS.

September, 1936.

AUTHOR'S NOTE

A FEW words are perhaps necessary to explain the scope of this book. I have attempted to describe all the Franciscan buildings now surviving in the English province and to supplement this where possible with some account of those that have disappeared in recent years or of which the plan is capable of reconstruction from other sources. Franciscan architecture as a typological expression is in some respects a misnomer, as the distinctive and highly individual characteristics of the friars' buildings in this country were in no important feature peculiar to the Grey Friars. On purely architectural grounds therefore there is perhaps little justification for limiting the survey to the buildings of a single branch of the Mendicant Orders, and thereby excluding such a building as the Dominican church at Norwich, undoubtedly the finest example of a friars' church now surviving in England. Historically however the Order of St. Francis was probably the most important as it was certainly the most popular, while, apart from practical considerations of space and cost, there are obvious advantages in restricting the scope of such a work to the product of a single historical movement.

The surviving examples of Franciscan building in this country are few and for the most part of comparatively late date, and it is therefore only with the aid of documentary records that the early architectural history of the province can be studied and the full extent of the Franciscan achievement realized. For this reason I have prefaced the purely architectural description of each house with an historical account intended not only to assist in a proper understanding of the existing buildings but where possible to throw some light on those that preceded them. At the same time full use has been made of the Dissolution records which have perhaps in the past received less attention than those of the earlier periods and which often afford valuable details concerning the site and its buildings at that date. The method of treatment adopted inevitably results in a series of monographs on individual houses rather than in a con-

nected story of Franciscan architecture, but an attempt
has been made in an introductory chapter to review the
characteristics of the friars' buildings generally and those
of the Franciscans in particular.

Much work still remains to be done in the exploration of
certain sites, while a systematic survey of the Irish Franciscan houses would probably yield further evidence bearing
on the architectural history of the English province. In
the meantime it is hoped that the present work may serve
to some extent to fill a gap in English Franciscan literature
and perhaps to throw some further light on one of the most
remarkable phases of religious enthusiasm which the world
has ever seen.

It should perhaps be pointed out that it has not been
found practicable to reproduce all the plans on a uniform
scale, but as some compensation for this defect a comparative plan of the principal Franciscan churches has
been added.

While writing this book I have met with much kindness.
First I must express my indebtedness to Dr. A. G. Little,
not only for having read the proofs, but for many additions
and corrections and for constant advice throughout. I also
wish to thank Mr. P. B. Chatwin, F.S.A., F.R.I.B.A., for
looking through my accounts of the Coventry and Lichfield
houses and for kindly supplying a note on the Lichfield
tiles, and Mr. E. J. Highley for furnishing me with an
account and plan of his excavations at Bridgwater.

In regard to illustrations my obligations are numerous
and these are acknowledged in their appropriate place, but
I would here express my special indebtedness to Mr. A. W.
Clapham, F.S.A., for the use of his plan of Ware, to Mr.
F. C. Elliston Erwood, F.S.A., for his plan and photographs
of Winchelsea, and for the loan of his notes on the building,
to Mr. W. H. Godfrey, F.S.A., for the plan of the building
at Dunwich, to Mr. W. M. Woodhouse for kindly preparing
the plan of Denny Abbey, to Miss V. M. Dallas for permission to use her plans of Gloucester, to the Borough
Surveyor of Lichfield for the plan of Lichfield, and to Mr.
W. N. Henman for permission to use his photographs of
the destroyed buildings at Bedford.

A. R. MARTIN.

BLACKHEATH,
September, 1936.

LIST OF ABBREVIATIONS

Ann. Mon. . . .	*Annales Monastici*, ed. H. R. Luard (Rolls Series), 5 vols., 1864–69.
Arch.	*Archæologia.*
Archiv. Franc. Hist..	*Archivum Franciscanum Historicum* (Quaracchi).
Arch. Journ.. . .	*Archæological Journal.*
B.M.	British Museum (Manuscripts).
B.S.F.S.	British Society of Franciscan Studies.
Bull. Franc.. . · .	*Bullarium Franciscanum*, ed. Sbaralea and Eubel, 7 vols., Rome, 1759–1904.
C.C.R.	Calendar of Close Rolls.
C.Ch.R.	,, ,, Charter Rolls.
C.F.R.	,, ,, Fine Rolls.
C.Lib.R.	,, ,, Liberate Rolls.
C.Pap.L.	,, ,, Papal Letters.
C.Pap.Pet. . . .	,, ,, Papal Petitions.
C.P.R.	,, ,, Patent Rolls.
C.Inq.p.m. . . .	,, ,, Inquisitions post mortem.
C. & Y. Soc. . .	Canterbury and York Society for the publication of Episcopal Registers.
Cat. Anc. Deeds. .	*Descriptive Catalogue of Ancient Deeds preserved in the Public Record Office*, vols. I–VI.
D.K.R.	Reports of the Deputy Keeper of the Public Records.
D.N.B.	*Dictionary of National Biography.*
Eccleston	*Tractatus Fr. Thomae vulgo dicti de Eccleston De Adventu Fratrum Minorum in Angliam* edidit. . . . A. G. Little (Collection d'Études et de Documents sur l'histoire religieuse et littéraire du moyen âge tome VII), Paris, 1909.
Eccleston, trans. Salter.	*The Coming of the Friars Minor to England and Germany*, E. Gurney Salter, London, 1926.
E.E.T.S.	Early English Text Society.
E.H.R.	*English Historical Review.*
R.C.H.M.(Eng.) . .	Inventories of the Royal Commission on Historical Monuments (England).
Hist. MSS. Com. . .	Reports of the Historical Manuscripts Commission.
Inq. a.q.d. . . .	Inquisitions ad quod damnum (P.R.O.).
L. and P. Hen. VIII.	Letters and Papers foreign and domestic of the reign of Henry VIII.
Leland Itin. . . .	*Leland's Itinerary in England and Wales*, ed. Lucy Toulmin Smith, 5 vols., 1907–10.
Leland Coll. . . .	*Leland's Collectanea*, ed. Thos. Hearne, second edition, 6 vols., 1770–74.

Monasticon . . . W. Dugdale, *Monasticon Anglicanum*, ed. Caley, Ellis and Bandinel, 6 vols. in 8 (1846).

Mon. Franc. . . . *Monumenta Franciscana* (Rolls Series), 2 vols., 1858 and 1882.

P.C.C. . . . . . Prerogative Court of Canterbury Wills.

P.R.O. . . . . . Public Record Office.

Rec. Com. . . . Record Commission.

R.S. . . . . . Rolls Series, Chronicles and Memorials (etc.), published under the direction of the Master of the Rolls.

Test. Vet. . . . . *Testamenta Vetusta*, ed. Sir Harris Nicolas, 2 vols., 1826.

V.C.H. . . . . . *Victoria History of the Counties of England.*

Val. Eccles. . . . *Valor Ecclesiasticus temp Henrici VIII*, ed. J. Caley and J. Hunter, 6 vols., 1825–34.

Wadding . . . . *Wadding Annales Minorum*, Romae, 1731, etc.

Worcester Itin. . . *Itineraria (S. Simeonis et), Willelmi de Worcestre*, ed. Nasmith, 1778.

Wright, Suppression. *Letters relating to the Suppression of the Monasteries*, ed. Thomas Wright (Camden Society, vol. 26), 1843.

BIBLIOGRAPHY

THE following list contains the principal works dealing generally with the English Franciscan Province, as distinct from those treating of individual houses which will be found in Appendix V. Works containing only occasional or passing references to the subject are generally excluded, while manuscript sources and texts and calendars of official documents are also omitted. For the latter as well as for a useful list of books dealing with Franciscan subjects generally including Franciscan art, reference should be made to Dr. A. G. Little's *Guide to Franciscan Studies* (S.P.C.K., 1920).

William Dugdale, *Monasticon Anglicanum*, edited by Caley Ellis and Bandinel (1846), vol. 6, part 3, pp. 1509-55.

A[thony] P[arkinson], *Collectanea Anglo-Minoritica or a collection of the Antiquities of the English Franciscans or Friers Minors commonly call'd Grey Friars* (1726).

Luke Wadding, *Annales Minorum*, 2nd edition, 20 vols., 1731-94.

Itinerary of William of Worcester, edited by J. Nasmith (1778).

Thomas Tanner, *Notitia Monastica*, edited by J. Nasmith (1787).

Monumenta Franciscana, edited by J. S. Brewer and R. Howlett (Rolls Series), 2 vols., 1858 and 1882.

A. G. Little, " Chronology of the Provincial Ministers of the Friars Minor in England," *Eng. Hist. Rev.*, vol. VI (1891), pp. 743-51.

A. Jessopp, *The Coming of the Friars*, 1889.

Father Cuthbert, *The Friars and how they came to England*, 1903.

W. Moir Bryce, *The Scottish Grey Friars*, 2 vols., 1909.

Tractatus Fr. Thomae vulgo dicti de Eccleston. De Adventu Fratrum Minorum in Angliam, edited by A. G. Little. (Collection d'Etudes et de Documents sur l'histoire religieuse et litteraire du moyan âge, tome vii.) Paris, 1909.

A. W. Clapham, F.S.A., " The Friars as Builders," *Some Famous Buildings and their Story* (N.D.) (c. 1913), pp. 241-67.

A. G. Little, " Records of the Franciscan Province of England." *Collectanea Franciscana*, (B.S.F.S.), vol. 1 (1914), pp. 141-53.

John Sever, *The English Franciscans under Henry III*, 1915.

A. G. Little, *Studies in English Franciscan History*, 1917.

E. Gurney Salter, *The Coming of the Friars Minor into England and Germany being the Chronicles of Brother Thomas of Eccleston and Brother Jordan of Giano*, translated from the critical editions of A. G. Little and H. Boehmer, 1926.

A. F. C. Bourdillon, *The Order of Minoresses in England*, 1926.

Edward Hutton, *The Franciscans in England*, 1926.

E. Hermitage Day, *St. Francis and the Greyfriars* (1926), pp. 103-29.

G. G. Coulton, *Five Centuries of Religion*, vol. 2, " The Coming of the Friars and the Dead Weight of Tradition, 1200-1400," 1927.

G. G. Coulton, *Life in the Middle Ages*, vol. IV. "Monks, Friars and Nuns," 1930.

For the Irish Province the following are the principal works :

Mervyn Archdall, *Monasticon Hibernicum*, 1786 (another edition, 2 vols., 1873-76).

Charles Patrick Meehan, *The Rise and Fall of the Irish Franciscan Monasteries in the Sixteenth Century*, 5th edition, 1877.

E. B. Fitzmaurice and A. G. Little, *Franciscan Province of Ireland* (Brit. Soc. Franc. Studies), 1920.

CHAPTER I

INTRODUCTORY

WHILE the general history of the friars and of the followers of St. Francis in particular has received considerable attention, it is only in comparatively recent years that the importance of their buildings in the development of Gothic architecture has come to be realized.[1] This somewhat tardy recognition is perhaps not surprising in view of the comparative scarcity and fragmentary character of the surviving buildings which in a general survey of English medieval ecclesiastical architecture might almost pass unnoticed among the numerous and imposing monuments of the earlier monastic orders. The reason for the almost total disappearance of the enormous architectural output of the English mendicants is not far to seek. The aims of the friars generally rendered it essential that their convents should be placed in or near to the great towns. At the Dissolution the sites were soon acquired for other purposes and the presence of a convenient quarry of worked stones resulted in the rapid spoliation of the buildings. The survival of any portion of these has therefore been largely a matter of chance, while the presence of later buildings which usually encumber the site has with few exceptions prevented any systematic excavation from being carried out. In spite of this, however, the ground plans of several friars' houses have been recovered and there remains sufficient of their work still standing to show that their buildings must have formed a group remarkable at once for their individuality of plan and design and for the uniformity with which the type when once established was adopted throughout the province.

Before proceeding to discuss the principal characteristics of these buildings as illustrated by the surviving Franciscan examples, it is desirable at the risk of repeating what is well known to give a brief account of the origin and aims of the Order itself and the circumstances connected with its introduction into this country.

[1] See article by A. W. Clapham, F.S.A., on " The Friars as Builders " in *Some Famous Buildings and their Story* (c. 1913).

It was about the year 1206 that Francis, the son of a wealthy merchant of Assisi, after an early life of dissipation, determined to retire from the world and seek a new life in absolute poverty. The process of his conversion was gradual, but we are told that it was in the little church of St. Damian outside the walls of Assisi that he first heard a voice saying, " Go, Francis, and repair my house which as thou seest is falling into ruin." From that hour the Legend of the Three Companions says " his heart was melted by the remembrance of the Lord's Passion," and after some delay, discarding all his worldly possessions he clothed himself in the coarse woollen tunic of a peasant and went forth into the country around Assisi exhorting the people to penance, brotherly love and peace. At first he had no thought of founding a new order, and it was not until 1209, some eight years before St. Dominic obtained Papal confirmation of his order, that St. Francis journeyed to Rome with a small band of followers calling themselves Penitents of Assisi, to seek Papal approval for their order or "way of life " as he would probably have called it.

After some hesitation Pope Innocent III gave his formal sanction to the Order whose members were to be called Friars Minor as a perpetual reminder of their humility. In 1217 or 1219 a general chapter of the Order which met outside Assisi was held, and it was resolved to extend the mission beyond the borders of Italy.

About the same time the second order of St. Francis had been put on a permanent footing by the granting of its first detailed Rule between August 1218 and July 1219. It was early in the year 1212 that St. Clare had escaped from her father's home in Assisi and made her vow before St. Francis in the little chapel of the Portiuncula. At first she was placed by him under the care of the Benedictine nuns, but after a short stay first at their convent of Bastia and then at that of St. Angelo, where she was joined by her sister Agnes, she was given the little church and house of St. Damian half a mile below Assisi, where she remained for forty-two years until her death in 1253. St. Clare, like St. Francis, came of a wealthy local family, and like him regarded the ideal of absolute poverty as the first essential of her Order. Perhaps as early as 1214 Francis had drawn up for her and her companions a " form of life " based on his own Rule of 1209, but from the first the Benedictine type of enclosed life seems to have been adopted by the

Claresses or Damianites, as they were called in the lifetime of their founder. The Rule of 1219 is stricter than the contemporary Benedictine Rule on the question of enclosure, and although slightly modified by the Rule drawn up by Innocent IV in 1247 in an attempt to impose uniformity on the Order, no laxity in this respect was ever permitted. As early as 1241, however, there were Franciscan women who were not bound by any rule of enclosure, as a Papal bull of that year forbade such wandering women the privileges and habit of the order of St. Damian, " as they were not of it being not enclosed." We hear of this un-authorized movement again in connection with the earliest evidence of Franciscan women in England, but in this country at least they appear to have died out before the arrival of the regular nuns of the second order.

The decision to send a Franciscan mission to Britain was taken in the last General Chapter at which St. Francis himself was present, which was held at Assisi in 1224. Friar Agnellus, the first custodian of Paris, was appointed its leader and with him went eight other friars. The story of their arrival in England is well known from the account given by Eccleston.[1] In the year of Our Lord 1224, he tells us, on the third day in the week after the Feast of the Nativity which in that year fell on a Sunday (i.e. 10 October 1224) the Friars Minor first arrived in England. The party consisting of four clerks and five lay brothers were so poor that their passage had been paid by the monks of Fécamp in Normandy. They landed at Dover and proceeded at once to Canterbury, where they were entertained for two days at the Priory of the Holy Trinity or Christchurch. From there four of their number went on to London, while the remainder, after a brief sojourn in the Poor Priests Hospital in Stour Street, are stated [2] to have made use of a small room under a schoolhouse as their first home on English soil. From London two of the four who had set out from˙ Canterbury went on to Oxford, where the third house was founded before the end of October 1224. The rapidity ˙of the spread of the Order is remarkable. Three houses were founded within the first two months of their arrival in England and by 1230 sixteen houses had been established. Soon after 1240 the rate of expansion became less rapid, though by the end of the century there were fifty-four houses in England and four in Scotland, while

---

[1] Eccleston, pp. 3–8 ; *ibid.* (ed. Salter), pp. 6–13.   [2] *Ibid.*, p. 8.

Ireland had been established as a separate province as early as 1230. The foundation of new houses in these early days was of course a very simple matter. No church was necessary and no elaborate conventual buildings. A small chamber in the schoolhouse at Canterbury, a house in Cornhill, and even a cellar in one instance, sufficed for their first temporary homes.

With the close of the thirteenth century the Order had already passed its zenith, and subsequent foundations are few. Only four new houses were established in England in the fourteenth century—at Walsingham, Ware, Plymouth and Aylesbury—and in each case the step was taken at the instance of a single private benefactor rather than from the pressure of popular demand. In this respect the later foundations bear a closer resemblance to those of the Franciscan nuns who had arrived in England in 1293–94 than to the spontaneous settlements of the previous century. The story of the introduction of the second order into England is referred to in a subsequent chapter. It forms a curious contrast to that of the first Franciscan mission, for their arrival was in response to no widespread enthusiasm, but was rather the culmination of long-delayed plans which had in one case at least proved abortive.[1] Like the Observants at a later date, the English minoresses never seem to have secured more than a limited local popularity, for the plant was a forced growth which failed to take root and accordingly disappeared almost as unnoticed as it came. In connection with the English nuns of St. Clare, it is interesting to note that there are occasional and somewhat vague references to Franciscan women in this country long before the foundation of the houses at London and Waterbeach. As early as 1250 a bull of Innocent IV ordered the English bishops not to allow certain women who called themselves " sorores minores " to build houses except with the consent of the Provincial minister of the Friars Minor,[2] while in 1252 there were five sisters minor living an apparently conventual life at Northampton.[3] The status of these early Franciscan sisters is, however, never clearly defined and it is possible that they may have been more akin to the Franciscan tertiaries than to the regular nuns of the second order.

[1] An attempt to found a house of Claresses at Newcastle-on-Tyne in 1286 failed, as did a later effort to establish one at Kingston-upon-Hull.

[2] *Register of Archbishop Giffard*, Surtees Soc., vol. 109, p. 93.

[3] Liberate Roll, 36 Hen. III, m. 2.

Hitherto reference has only been made to the first and second orders of St. Francis. Each of the four great mendicant orders, however, was triple, the third order or Penitents, as they were called, being composed of men and women who, while continuing their secular vocations, undertook to devote themselves to pious works in accordance with the teaching of their founder. A Rule for the Franciscan Tertiaries was composed in 1221, but information concerning them, especially in England, is extremely scanty. In Scotland there appear to have been three Tertiary congregations in existence about 1384, and a little more than a century later another had been formed in Brechin under the influence of the Observants of Aberdeen. In Ireland the Observantine revival of the fifteenth century was responsible for some of the Tertiary communities being organized on conventual lines with regular houses for each sex, and the remains of some of these buildings are still surviving. Under the same influence two houses of female Tertiaries [1] were founded in Scotland at Aberdour in Fife about 1486, and at Dundee in 1502. In England the documentary evidence for the existence of any tertiary communities in the fourteenth or fifteenth century is lacking, except an isolated reference to four " congregations " in 1385, and it seems probable therefore that in this country the movement was largely superseded by the system of letters of confraternity, the granting of which became a regular practice in many Franciscan houses from the close of the thirteenth century onwards.[2]

The conditions under which the early Franciscan settlements were established frequently had an important bearing on the ultimate choice of the site. The new Order had little in common with the older orders of monks and canons. Their work was not within the precinct but among the laity of whom they came, and in particular among the very poorest classes in the towns and the lepers who were entirely outside the sphere of any existing ecclesiastical influence. Even within the convent their mode of life was very different to that of the monks. Changes from friary to friary were frequent, while many friars would be absent from their house for long periods together. As mission-preachers they made periodical tours of the countryside, particularly at Lent and Advent, hearing confessions, enjoining penances

[1] There were apparently no regular houses of male tertiaries in Scotland.
[2] *Archæologia*, vol. 75 (1925), pp. 19–60, and vol. 79 (1929), pp. 179–216.

and distributing indulgences to the faithful, so that many friaries served rather as centres of organization than as permanent self-supporting homes. Moreover, the settlement of the friars had frequently to be carried out in the face of considerable opposition, as the older orders generally tended to regard the newcomers with suspicion which often developed into active hostility. Not only do they appear to have feared encroachments on their established privileges and the diversion of local bequests from their own houses, but the way of life of the mendicants was of course directly opposed to earlier monastic ideals. Their attitude is perhaps nowhere better shown than at Scarborough, where as early as 1240 the settlement of the Franciscans was opposed by the Cistercians, who appealed to Rome against the intruders. The friars had the support of the King and the Bishop of Lincoln received Papal authority to hear the parties and settle the dispute. After the inquiry had proceeded for two days, however, the friars renounced their claim on the grounds that to proceed in face of the opposition of the monks would be inconsistent with Franciscan principles. This example of humility appears to have made a deep impression both on the bishop and the monks present who were disposed thereby to allow the friars to remain.[1] The decision, however, lay with the Abbot of Citeaux, who refused his consent, and the friars had to go. It was not until some thirty years later that they returned to Scarborough, only to face the same opposition again, and for some fifteen years there ensued a bitter struggle between the monks and friars in which Archbishop Peckham, himself a Franciscan, energetically intervened on behalf of the latter.[2] Similar instances of opposition from established houses could easily be multiplied. The Benedictines of Bury St. Edmunds three times forcibly expelled the Franciscans from that town and razed their buildings to the ground, while the Canons of the Augustinian priories at Dunstable and Walsingham made determined but unsuccessful attempts to prevent the settlement of the Dominicans and Franciscans respectively in these towns. The abbot of Reading was more cautious and sought, by providing the Franciscans with a site outside the town, to obtain a strict and effective

[1] *Mon. Franc.* (R.S.), vol. 1, p. 406 ; *Grosseteste Epist.* (R.S.), pp. 321–3.
[2] *Reg. J. Peckham* (R.S.), pp. 214–16, 246–8, 284. For a fuller account of these incidents, see Little, *Studies in English Franciscan History*, pp. 93–5.

control over their activities. Occasionally opposition came from other and less expected sources. The friction between the friars and the secular clergy reached its height at a period later than that of the foundation of the majority of the English Franciscan houses, but there are occasional instances at an early date of ill feeling and jealousy between the two principal orders of mendicants themselves. It was probably at the instance of the Dominicans of Chester that Alexander of Stavensby [1] opposed the settlement of the Franciscans there, and the establishment of a house of Austin Friars at Chichester was successfully opposed on the ground that it would encroach on the privileges of the Franciscans. In contrast to this attitude, it is interesting to note that the nunneries appear to have regarded the friars with less hostility than the male orders and there are several instances of their providing a newly founded house of friars with food or other necessaries. Thus the Franciscans and Dominicans of York received a fortnightly dole of loaves from the nunnery of St. Clement, and the Franciscans also received bread and ale from the nunnery of Moxby, [2] while we find the prioress of the small Benedictine nunnery of Markyate near Luton helping the Dominicans of Dunstable on their arrival with a daily gift of loaves " out of pure charity." [3]

From what has been said already it will be seen that the aims of the friars limited the choice of sites in the first instance to the principal centres of the medieval population. Occasionally when a site had been chosen the opposition of local vested interests proved too strong, but generally with the support of the king or Papal and episcopal sanction the friars won the day. As comparatively late-comers to the crowded towns, however, they had often to be content

[1] This is perhaps the only instance of episcopal opposition to the Friars Minor in England. There are on the other hand frequent examples of the partiality of the bishops for the mendicant orders, particularly in the selection of friars as diocesan penitencers and in the fact that many of the suffragan bishops with titular sees *in partibus* were themselves friars. Grosseteste of Lincoln, Richard Poore of Salisbury, St. Richard de Wyche of Chichester and Archbishop Peckham, himself a Franciscan, were among the more prominent of the early supporters of the Friars Minor , while even Alexander of Stavensby welcomed if he did not actually establish the Franciscans in Lichfield (see p. 163). The favour shown to the friars by the English bishops is the more remarkable in view of the fact that the friars' exemption from episcopal authority must have proved a source of frequent embarrassment.
[2] Cf. Eileen Power, *Medieval English Nunneries* (1922), p. 199.
[3] Matthew Paris, *Gesta Abbatum* (R.S.), vol. 1, p. 387.

with sites that were both cramped and insanitary, a fact which accounts in many cases for their subsequent abandonment in favour of new sites in the more open suburbs.[1] The position chosen was no doubt frequently selected from a necessity for economy not only in the initial cost of the site which was often raised by public subscription, but in the amount expended on building.[2] The early sites were with few exceptions all within the walls, and it seems to have been a frequent practice for them to be so placed that a large section of the town wall could be made to serve as the precinct boundary, thus effecting a substantial saving in building material. In towns of Roman origin the rectangular plan facilitated this, and it can scarcely have been entirely coincidence that the Franciscan houses at Colchester, Chichester, Lincoln, Gloucester and elsewhere, were placed in one corner of the town with the town walls forming the precinct boundary on two sides. This very practice, however, repeatedly led to difficulties, as the existence of the town wall effectively barred any extension into the more open land outside, while there are numerous instances of encroachments on the town's defences, leading to friction with the local authorities.[3] Occasionally permission was ultimately obtained to extend into the suburbs by demolishing a portion of the intervening wall, but more frequently in such cases a new site was obtained outside the walls. In many instances, however, the abandonment of the first site was due not so much to its cramped position as to its dampness or liability to floods. That this was a common defect is suggested by Bishop Grosseteste's warning to the friars against low-lying sites. It is expressly stated to have been the reason for the removal from the early sites at Worcester and Reading, and was also a source of trouble at Oxford, Lincoln, Boston and elsewhere. Occasionally, as at Exeter,

---

[1] There is no evidence, as Dr. Little has pointed out (*Studies in English Franciscan History*, p. 10), for the suggestion that the poorest and meanest parts of the town were deliberately chosen as a token of humility. In the average medieval town and notably in London there was no clearcut distinction between the quarters of the rich and those of the poor.

[2] In order to comply with the Franciscan rule against the ownership of property, various methods were adopted. The most usual way for the site to be vested in the community of the town for the use of the friars, but occasionally the ownership remained in the original donor or was transferred to named trustees on the friars'. behalf. In course of time these legal fictions sometimes became lost sight of or survived only in the right of the founder's heirs to certain privileges such as hospitality within the precinct.

[3] Cf. Lincoln *infra*.

the insanitary position of the early site is given as the reason for the move. At York similar complaints were made at a later date, but the question of transfer was not raised, and at Cambridge the annoyance caused by the proximity of the town gaol was removed by its incorporation in the friary buildings. At Dunwich and Winchelsea the first sites had to be abandoned owing to encroachments by the sea, while the removal from Bury to Babwell was, as we have seen, directly due to the violence of the opposition of the monks of Bury.

Before passing to a consideration of the buildings themselves, something must be said of the precinct which enclosed them. The area was almost invariably small. At Grimsby the Friars Minor owned 3 acres, at Newcastle 3½ acres, at Lincoln 4 acres, at Shrewsbury not more than 3 or 4 acres, at Oxford 8 or 9 acres, at Richmond (Yorks) about 16 acres, and at Canterbury about 18 acres, while at York they owned a single acre only. Even in the important house in London, the precinct never extended to more than 4 acres. There were of course exceptions, but it is to be noted that it was not the large and important town houses that owned the greatest amount of land, but the small and poorer houses in rural districts where voluntary alms were less plentiful, and the friars had to supplement these with a certain amount of agricultural operations. Thus at Llanfaes in Anglesea, one of the smallest friaries, the area was at least 30 acres, while the Franciscans of Babwell owned no less than 43 acres, the largest area recorded. Apart from their actual precincts the English Franciscan houses seldom held any landed property. Where this did exist it was usually of late origin and held as the endowment of a particular chantry, or for the maintenance of specified obits.[1] Occasionally, as at Exeter and Dunwich, the original site was retained after the removal to new quarters and let by the friars, but in spite of these and other instances of the ownership of property by the Franciscans, there is in England no real evidence of any serious breach of the vow of poverty in regard to the permanent endowments of the order.[2] In richness and size of their buildings, however, a considerable relaxation of the primitive teach-

---

[1] The rents referred to in the Minister's accounts, though sometimes of this nature, were frequently derived from leases, granted shortly before the suppression of land or buildings within the precinct.

[2] The evidence of the Dissolution records relating to the friaries is in fact one of almost universal poverty.

ing must be admitted, and to this subject we must now turn our attention.

The humility and love of poverty which was characteristic of the Franciscan order generally in the earlier years of its existence seems to have found its most obvious expression in the deliberate avoidance of all show in their buildings which were to be kept as mean and humble as possible. This was of course no new phenomenon, as it was practised in varying degrees by most of the earlier reformers. Both the Cistercians and the Premonstratensian Canons favoured a severely simple type of building, while the Order of Grandmont probably came nearest to the true Franciscan ideal of poverty in buildings. It was left, however, to the early followers of St. Francis to carry the theory of genuine poverty in building to its furthest practical limit. The teaching of their founder was quite clear on this point. They were to build poor little houses of mud and wood, and small churches, as these would prove better sermons than words. In the first instance St. Francis probably never even contemplated the necessity for permanent convents at all, and certainly any system based on the conventual arrangements of the older monastic orders was far from his mind. The rigors of the English climate, however, necessitated something more permanent in the way of buildings than was necessary in Italy, and although the first ministers of the Order strove hard to adhere to the early ideal, their efforts were successful only for a time. Under Agnellus only one instance is mentioned by Eccleston of an infringement of the rule of poverty in buildings, but Albert of Pisa, the second provincial minister, had already to contend with the generosity of devout benefactors coupled probably with some relaxation of the primitive teaching within the Order itself. The case of Reading, referred to in a subsequent chapter, is perhaps typical of the difficulties encountered, though as yet the growth in the size and splendour of buildings was far from general. In course of time, however, it was realized that some modification of the early ideal was necessary, and we accordingly find William of Nottingham, the third provincial minister, admitting that it was wise to make buildings fairly large lest the brethren in future times should make them larger still.[1]

In the second half of the thirteenth century there are frequent denunciations of the excessive luxury of the friars'

[1] Eccleston, p. 57.

buildings, though there seems little to justify the assertion of Matthew Paris that they rivalled royal palaces.[1] " All who beheld them," he writes of the buildings of the Franciscans of Bury, " were struck with amazement at the sudden expenditure of so much money by those poor brethren, persons who professed voluntary poverty." [2] The danger was recognized by the leaders of the order, and in the General Constitutions of 1260, it was ordered that " elaboration of buildings in pictures, canopies, windows, pillars, and so forth or excess in length, breadth and height—the importance of the place being taken into account—shall be strictly avoided . . . churches shall not be vaulted except the main chapel—the campanile shall in future nowhere be made in the shape of a tower ; painted glass windows shall not be introduced, except that in the principal window behind the high altar of the quire there may be images of the Crucifix, the Blessed Virgin, St. John (the Evangelist), St. Francis and St. Anthony." [3] This order was aimed primarily at the continental houses, where the primitive simplicity of the Franciscan ideal had already been far surpassed. In England the great building period which lasted from about 1270 to 1320 was yet to come.

The reason for the enormous expansion of building during this period is not apparent at first sight. The increase in the number of friars was scarcely a sufficient cause in itself. Dr. Little has shown [4] that in 1256 the average number of friars in each house of the English Franciscan province was about twenty-five, while some eighty years later this had increased to an average of about thirty-five friars. These figures are based on those houses for which records have survived. Of the nineteen houses for which there are no details, the majority were of less importance, so that the actual average for the whole province was probably nearer thirty. In other words, at a date shortly before the Black Death, when the friars were numerically at their strongest, the total number of Franciscans in the English Province must have been somewhat less than 2,000. One must therefore look to other reasons for the increase of building towards the close of the thirteenth century and it is possible to point to three main causes. In the first place, with the growing popularity of the friars the rule of

[1] *Chronica Majora* (R.S.), vol. 4, p. 280.   [2] *Ibid.*
[3] *A.L.K.G.*, vol. 6, pp. 94–5.
[4] *Studies in English Franciscan History*, p. 68.

c

poverty in buildings enforced by the early provincial ministers proved an ideal increasingly difficult to maintain in
the face of the generosity of devout citizens. Not only
were new sites, as we have seen, frequently provided in
ampler surroundings, but as at London and Richmond a
single benefactor would sometimes assume responsibility
for the greater part of the cost of new buildings, and so
come to be regarded as the second founder of the house.
In the second place, in a country where regular open-air
preaching was impractical, it was soon found that the
narrow aisleless naves of the early churches were totally
inadequate to hold the increasing congregations attracted
by the popular preaching which formed an important part
of the duties of all the mendicant orders alike. Finally,
one may suspect that the growing popularity of burial
within a Franciscan church and the valuable pecuniary
advantages derived by the friars from this source led at
an early date to a demand for an increase of the space
available. Whatever the causes, however, there is evidence
for the rebuilding or enlargement of the great majority of
the English houses at this period. For the most part the
records refer only to the church, but it is clear that the
domestic buildings were not infrequently included in the
general scheme of rebuilding. Dr. Little has noted evidence
of enlargement or rebuilding in thirty-four of the English
Franciscan friaries between 1270 and 1320.[1] The consecration of new Franciscan churches is recorded at Bedford
(1295), Southampton (1287), York (1303), Nottingham
(1303), Bodmin (1322) and Canterbury (1325), while those
at London, Winchelsea, Chichester, Reading, Grantham,
Exeter, Colchester, Dunwich, Worcester, Lichfield, Beverley,
Scarborough, Carlisle and probably at Salisbury and Ipswich, were rebuilt during the same period.

This mass of building was scarcely finished when the
Black Death swept the country, carrying off many of the
friars and inflicting a blow which seems to have hastened
the decay that had perhaps already begun with the failure
of mendicancy. There are no means of judging exactly
how far the friaries were affected. In a few instances as
at Bridgwater and Yarmouth, we know the losses were
heavy, and it is probable that from this date the accommodation in many of the houses proved greater than the
needs demanded. In any case, there is no evidence of any

[1] *Studies in English Franciscan History*, p. 73.

general renewal of building activity in the English province after the middle of the fourteenth century. A certain amount of new building became necessary in connection with the late foundations, while destruction of the older work by fire was responsible for such buildings as the great fifteenth-century church of the Dominicans at Norwich. Generally speaking, however, the building activities of this period seem to have been confined to additions such as the erection of chantry chapels or the insertion of bell towers and to the carrying out of general repairs. Work on the scale of the reconstruction of the great cloister in London and the building of the new library there was probably exceptional at this date. There is, however, some evidence of a certain revival of building activity on the eve of the Suppression which is somewhat difficult to explain. Thus the church at Gloucester was rebuilt about 1520, while other work of the early sixteenth century survives at Walsingham and Shrewsbury. There is also documentary evidence that building was either recently finished, in hand or contemplated at the time of the Suppression at Lincoln, Lichfield, Salisbury and elsewhere.

Turning now to consider the buildings themselves, it will be convenient to deal first with the church and then with the domestic buildings separately. In so doing it will be impossible to confine the survey entirely to the buildings of the Franciscans who contributed but their share to the common artistic and architectural legacy of the mendicant orders generally, but wherever possible the principal characteristics of the friars' buildings will be illustrated from Franciscan examples.[1]

THE CHURCH

The earliest Franciscan churches like those of the early Cistercians appear to have been generally of a temporary nature. They were doubtless of wood and plaster and of the smallest size in accordance with the founder's injunctions. Eccleston records that under Agnellus of Pisa (d. 1235) the chapel at Cambridge " was built so very poor that a carpenter in one day made and put up fifteen pairs of rafters." [2] At Oxford the original chapel, in the quire of which Agnellus was buried, was also apparently of timber

---

[1] Throughout this chapter where a place is mentioned, the Franciscan house there is referred to unless otherwise stated.
[2] Eccleston, p. 28.

and was demolished when a more permanent building was erected about 1246.[1] When the nature of the site demanded it, however, special precautions were sometimes taken even in the earliest buildings to ensure their stability, and we find the Friars Minor of Winchester receiving a gift of piles of beech wood in 1239 " for the foundations of their church." [2] None of these primitive structures have survived, and it is therefore only with the earliest stone buildings which superseded them that our knowledge of the church architecture of the mendicant orders in this country may be said to begin.   There is no evidence, however, that the advent of stone brought about any general departure from the modest scale of the early buildings before the middle of the thirteenth century.   The excitement caused by the glass windows at Gloucester,[3] the ornate roof of the church in London and the elaborate chapel at Reading [4] clearly indicate that these were exceptions to the general rule of extreme simplicity which in many of the smaller houses in England persisted down to the Dissolution.

With the exception of the curious building at Lincoln none of the surviving English Franciscan churches date from before the last quarter of the thirteenth century, and one has therefore to turn to the few surviving examples of early churches of the other mendicant orders to find analogies with the Lincoln building and evidence for the plan of the earliest Franciscan churches in this country.   An almost exact parallel with the original arrangement at Lincoln is to be found in the approximately contemporary church of the Black Friars at Brecon in South Wales, which is still largely intact.[5]   This consisted originally of an unaisled quire (65 feet by 26 feet) and an unaisled nave ($95\frac{1}{4}$ feet by 26 feet) [6] without any structural division between them. The width of the building at Brecon is only slightly more than that at Lincoln and its greater length (163 feet as compared with 101 feet at Lincoln) may be accounted for by the change of plan apparent in the latter building having involved the abandonment of a fully developed nave. Another building approximating even more closely in size to that at Lincoln was the church of the Carmelites at Hulne, near Alnwick in Northumberland, of which the south

[1] Little, *The Grey Friars in Oxford*, p. 21.
[2] *C. Lib. R.*, vol. 1, p. 394.   [3] See p. 83.   [4] See p. 108.
[5] *Arch. Journal*, vol. 84 (1930), pp. 92–5.
[6] The north aisle was a fourteenth-century addition.

wall and portions of the north and west walls survive.[1]
In plan it formed an aisleless parallelogram 119 feet long
and 19 feet 6 inches wide, the nave and quire being apparently
separated by screen walls placed one bay apart and enclosing
a passage from which the quire was entered by a central
door in the eastern screen.

These buildings represent the earliest type of friars'
church in this country. The most noticeable feature is the
absence of a transept and of any structural division between
the nave and quire. The roof was generally continued
from end to end without a break and the belfry, if any,
seems to have been restricted to a small timber structure
above the central passage or over the western gable. It
is probable that the great majority of friars' churches in
this country prior to the middle of the thirteenth century
were of this type. In Ireland the simple rectangular plan
persisted until the end of the century and many examples
survive, though often with additions of a later date.

Before proceeding to a consideration of the later developments in the friars' churches, there is one type of structure
to which reference must be made. The alterations carried
out to the original church at Lincoln by which the church
was placed on the first floor over a vaulted undercroft,
though unique so far as surviving remains in this country
are concerned, was probably not entirely without parallel
in other early Franciscan churches. It had an obvious
advantage in a low-lying site which was' liable to floods
and was in any case only an extension of a practice common
in the domestic buildings of friars' houses. The arrangement may perhaps be compared with that adopted in the
Franciscan church at Lübeck in north Germany, where the
quire is raised on a vaulted undercroft, though in this case
it stands open to the rest of the church and is approached
by a stairway within the building.[2] Lübeck is in fact
merely an unusual instance of the normal monastic crypt
beneath the quire being constructed above ground instead
of below it, and the analogy with Lincoln is therefore somewhat slight. A closer parallel, however, may have existed
in the first church of the Grey Friars at Reading. This
building was apparently finished in 1239, and in the
following year a storey (stagium) was being constructed

---

[1] *Arch. Journal*, vol. 47, pp. 105–29. Cf. also the foundations of the
somewhat later Carmelite Church at Luffness in the parish of Aberlady
(East Lothian), which measures 95 × 20 feet.

[2] See plan in the *Ecclesiologist*, vol. 16 (1855), p. 31.

in it,[1] which seems to imply an arrangement similar to that at Lincoln. It is significant that this site was finally abandoned owing to its liability to flooding.

With the growing popularity of preaching the small aisleless nave soon proved inadequate, and it was undoubtedly this fact more than any other which was primarily responsible for the imposing dimensions which many of the friars' churches ultimately attained. The method of enlargement usually took the form of the addition of an aisle to the nave on the side opposite the cloister, and in churches built after the beginning of the fourteenth century the fully aisled nave seems to have been normal. Side by side with this development was another which appears to have found only limited favour in this country. This was the addition of a single and generally disproportionate transept opening directly out of the nave by one or more arches on the side opposite the cloister. These single transepts forming an annex to the nave and often equalling or even exceeding it in dimensions are extremely common in the Irish houses, where they sometimes have a chapel-aisle on the east side and occasionally an aisle on the west also. In this country they seem to have been comparatively rare, though there is evidence for their former existence at Llanfaes [2] and at the church of the Austin Friars at Warrington [3] and probably also at Chester [4] (Grey Friars) and Newport (Austin Friars).[5] The general absence of this type of plan in the eastern and southern parts of England points to a western origin, and the fact that Llanfaes, Chester and Newport were all directly open to Irish influence, while Warrington is within easy reach of Chester, suggests that it originated in Ireland, where it became a standard feature of the later friars' churches. It may be noted here that the symmetrical or two-armed transept is almost unknown in friars' churches both in England and Ireland, though there is some evidence for its presence in the Franciscan church at Coventry.[6]

Unlike the nave, the quire of the average friars' church underwent little alteration with the progress of time.

---

[1] *C. Lib. R.*, vol. 1, p. 404.   [2] See p. 175.
[3] *Lancashire and Cheshire Hist. Soc. Trans.*, vol. 41 (1890), pp. 175–94 ; *Antiquaries Journ.*, vol. 12, pp. 448–9.
[4] See p. 232.
[5] As late as 1800 " the dilapidated body of the church and a small but elegant north transept " appear to have survived (Cox, *Tour in Monmouthshire*, p. 56).
[6] See p. 77.

Elaboration of plan in the eastern portion of the church with the object of increasing the sites available for additional altars was generally uncalled for in a community where a minority only were priests, and accordingly, though sometimes rebuilt and occasionally lengthened eastward, the quire generally remained aisleless. With the possible exception of Bedford and Bridgwater, the great church in London is the only Franciscan church with an aisled quire recorded in this country.[1] The principal feature of the quire was generally the magnificent proportions of its windows, of which the great east windows at Chichester and in the Black Friars' church at Norwich are notable examples. Even in the Observant churches this seems to have been the case to judge from the description of the glass in what was presumably the east window of the church at Greenwich.[2] In plan the quire was almost invariably square ended. The only instance in this country of the apsidal termination usual on the continent is at Winchelsea, where the three-sided apse is employed. A Scottish example of much later date, but also of the three-sided form, survives in the remains of the Dominican church at St. Andrews, though here it belonged to a small chapel on the north side of the church and is consequently of smaller dimensions. At St. Andrews both the apse and the chapel itself were vaulted in stone, part of the vaulting over the latter being still preserved, but at Winchelsea there is no indication of vaulting, and it is uncertain how the apse was roofed. The use of the apsidal end in both these cases may safely be ascribed in French influence which was particularly strong in the Cinque Ports and in the Scottish coastal towns at this period.

In connection with the quire, the evidence for the existence of crypts in friars' churches may be considered. Such instances in England are extremely uncommon. A small square vaulted crypt appears to have existed beneath the eastern portion of the quire of the Franciscan church at Great Yarmouth and a very similar Irish example survives in the same position in the Franciscan church at Buttevant, Co. Cork.[3] In both these cases the object appears to have

---

[1] This feature seems to have been equally uncommon in churches of the other mendicant orders. Only in the church of the Austin Friars in London is it definitely known to have occurred, though the measurements given by William of Worcester of the church of the Austin Friars in Norwich suggests that this also may have had an aisled choir.

[2] See p. 238.

[3] See the 77th Annual Report of the Commissioners of Public Works in Ireland, 1908–9.

been to compensate for the slope of the ground eastward, a difficulty which at Walsingham was met by raising the floor of the quire on a solid foundation of rammed earth. Owing to the extent of the slope at Buttevant there is a lower chamber beneath the main crypt. Both at Buttevant and Yarmouth the vaulting of the crypt was supported on a single central column, and their small size and the absence of any adequate provision for lighting suggests that they were used solely as burial vaults.

The most distinctive feature of the average friars' church has yet to be mentioned. In spite of the express prohibition of bell towers in the Franciscan constitutions of 1260, the English tradition proved too strong to be resisted and the belfry became an almost invariable adjunct to the later Franciscan churches. The history of the Cistercian order in this country affords an earlier instance of the triumph of local tradition over attempts at foreign control in the matter of architecture,[1] but while the Cistercian tower differed only in lowness and lack of enrichment from other contemporary models, the friars evolved a type of structure which seems to have been peculiar to the English mendicants, for there is no evidence of it having been borrowed from the continent or copied from the older orders at home. In the earlier churches as we have seen the belfries, if they existed at all, were light timber structures supported on the roof of the building. At the early churches at Lincoln, Llanfaes and Brecon (Black Friars), there does not seem to have been any original provision for a tower or steeple, but at Denbigh in North Wales the somewhat later Carmelite church which was erected about 1290 is described in a Suppression survey as " a long house slated like a barn with a steeple of timber like a louvre of a hall, boarded, the top leaded." [2] This description, which gives a very good idea of the probable appearance of the average friars' church in the late thirteenth century, is of especial interest, as part of the building still survives, including the charred remains of seven curved principals which supported the steeple referred to above. As this is apparently the only surviving trace of a timber steeple in a friars' church in this country, it may be noted that the principals which remain on the north side only are carried below the main wall plate

---

[1] A Statute of the Cistercian General Chapter of 1169 prohibited the erection of bell towers.
[2] *L. and P. Hen. VIII*, vol. 13 (2), no. 129.

on to a lower wall plate supported in its turn by stone corbels. On the south side a recess in the wall indicates the former existence of a similar arrangement.

It was probably the increase in size of the steeple which led to the introduction at first of one and later of two cross walls of masonry between the nave and the quire to carry the additional weight. With the introduction of the masonry steeple the two cross walls became essential, and as its height increased the two arches in these walls tended to become narrower. The earliest phase can be seen at Chichester and Winchelsea, where the great width of the single arches indicate that the steeple itself was still generally of timber. In the earlier churches the nave and quire were separated by a space occupying usually one bay and enclosed by stone or timber screen walls with central doors opening into the nave and quire respectively. This space, which is referred to as " the walking place " in medieval documents, formed a passage right across the church and served as the chief means of access to the quire and also frequently to provide direct communication between the cloister and the outer world. It was the desire to preserve this arrangement, coupled with the fact that the friars' belfries were usually intended to accommodate a single great bell in place of the usual peal, that was responsible for the adoption of the characteristic features of the later towers. The introduction of the masonry steeple led to the early abandonment of the wide chancel arch and the substitution of solid masonry walls pierced only by narrow central arches in place of the screens which formerly served to enclose the central passage. Over this oblong space the steeple itself was usually supported on the north and south by arches springing from the cross walls and seldom carried to the ground. Towers of this character survive at King's Lynn and Coventry, and also at Atherstone (Austin Friars) in Warwickshire. In Scotland there is one at Dunbar (Trinitarian Friars), while in Ireland the examples are numerous. The tower at Richmond in Yorkshire and that forming part of the Carmelite church at South Queensferry in Scotland are square in plan and of the more ordinary type, though in the former case the passageway which existed between the nave and the quire was carefully preserved when the tower was inserted. The upper part of the typical friars' tower consisted of a light stone or brick lantern either hexagonal in form as at King's Lynn and

Norwich (Black Friars) [1] or octagonal as at Coventry and
Atherstone (Austin Friars), though in Irish Franciscan
houses they were invariably square. [2] Occasionally as at
Coventry and apparently also at Chester, [3] a slender stone
spire surmounted the tower, [4] but this seems to have more
usually terminated in an embattled parapet. The tower
itself was usually divided into two or sometimes three
storeys, the upper one containing the bell and the lower
one being used as the ringing chamber. At Queensferry
(Carmelite) and in some of the Irish houses the rooms in
the tower seem to have been used as living apartments,
but this was probably rarely the case in England.

Notwithstanding the fact that only three Franciscan
towers have survived in this country, it is clear from documentary sources that they were a typical if not almost
universal feature of the later friars' churches. In addition
to the surviving examples excavation has furnished evidence
for the existence of bell towers at Walsingham and Lichfield, while the Suppression inventories and other contemporary documents mention steeples in the Franciscan
churches at Bridgnorth, Canterbury, Cardiff, Carmarthen,
Chester, Chichester, Dorchester, Exeter, Hereford, Llanfaes,
London, Norwich, Oxford, Plymouth, Salisbury and
Southampton. Some of these may have been timber
structures of the earlier type, but the list is certainly not
exhaustive and there can be little doubt that by the end
of the fifteenth century a masonry steeple was as common
a feature of the average friars' church in this country as it
is to-day among the numerous surviving remains in Ireland.
The Irish examples almost invariably date from the fourteenth or fifteenth century and except in the houses of late
foundations are usually inserted within the walls of the
thirteenth-century church. The same practice seems to
have been followed in England, as the towers at King's

---

[1] The lantern of the belfry of the Dominican church at Norwich fell
in 1712, but illustrations of it exist.
[2] In Dominican houses in Ireland the tower was generally of the full
width of the quire and thus oblong in plan.
[3] See p. 232.
[4] The tower of the Carmelite church at Bristol is described by William
of Worcester as " Turris et spera sive le broche ecclesiae carmelitarum
de fratribus carmelitarum Bristoll, continet altitudo 200 pedes.   Latitudo
dictae turris continebat nisi 9 pedes ex omni parte. Densitudo murorum
turris continet nisi duas pedes " (Worcester, *Itin.*, p. 244).   It was apparently of the more ordinary square type though surmounted by a spire
as at Coventry.

Lynn, Coventry, and Atherstone are all of mid- or late fourteenth-century date, and with the exception of the latter [1] were apparently additions to earlier buildings. Although it is scarcely safe to generalize with so few surviving examples, it seems likely that the masonry towers in friars' churches did not come into general use in England before the middle of the fourteenth century, and that from that date it became an increasingly common practice, whenever funds were available, to provide one either in any general scheme of rebuilding or more frequently by inserting it bodily within the structure of the earlier church.

Although the primary purpose of these towers was of course to house the bell which formed an essential possession of every friary, there were also clocks in the Franciscan towers at Plymouth [2] and Carmarthen.[3] There was normally a single bell in each house, but two bells are mentioned at Bridgnorth, Carmarthen, Chichester, Hereford,[4] Plymouth and Salisbury. At Exeter and Richmond (Yorks) there were three bells and at Dorchester three bells " each more than the other," while at Babwell there were four bells " in the Cloycher " weighing together 30,000 lb., as well as twelve bells in the steeple.[5] This record is interesting not only on account of the unusual number and size of the bells, but for the apparent implication that there was here a detached bell-tower as well as the usual steeple over the church, an arrangement for which there seems to be no other parallel in an English friars' house.

The principal features of the average friars' church have now been dealt with. The later buildings in the more important towns were chiefly distinguished by their imposing size, as the type of plan when once established seems to have been seldom varied. Chapels, however, were added when occasion demanded without any fixed rule as to their position, and the irregularity of the Coventry plan (Fig. 3) can be paralleled from some Irish examples such as the Franciscan church at Moyne Abbey, Co. Mayo, where in addition to a south transept a large chapel (41 feet by 21 feet 2 inches) projects from the south side of the quire.

---

[1] The house at Atherstone was not founded until 1378.
[2] *L. and P. Hen. VIII*, vol. 13(2), no. 389.   [3] *Ibid.*, no. 229.
[4] At Hereford there was also a bell at the gate (*L. and P. Hen. VIII*, vol. 13(2), no. 184).
[5] *L. and P. Hen. VIII*, vol. 13(2), no. 1213. The former were sold to a merchant of Ipswich and the latter were exchanged with the town of Mildenhall (*ibid*).

The roofs of the later churches seem to have been of open timber and there is no evidence that vaulting in stone was ever employed over the main span or even in the aisles of a friars' church in this country though in Scotland a simple barrel-vault sometimes occurs. Generally the nave and aisles were roofed in a single span and the type of double plan at Gloucester, where these are of nearly equal width and are roofed in two spans, has no parallel in England.[1] The clearstorey occurs in the fifteenth-century nave of the Dominican church at Norwich, but was probably confined to the largest town churches and seems to have been a comparatively late feature. The long range of clearstorey windows which is shown in a seventeenth-century drawing of the Grey Friars' church in London (Plate opposite p. 190) extending throughout its whole length, was apparently added after the completion of the main structure.

Only a faint idea of the size and extent of the later friars' churches can be gathered from existing remains, and it is rarely possible to supplement this with information from documentary sources. William of Worcester, however, quotes the measurements of the Franciscan churches at Bridgwater, Bristol, Norwich and Walsingham, while suppression surveys have survived for those at Babwell[2] and Coventry. Of the building at Norwich, of which no trace now survives, Worcester's account is unusually detailed. He writes: "Longitudo chori ecclesiae fratrum Sancti Francisci Norwici continet 60 gressus. Longitudo insterticii companilae, id est spacii valvae chori et valvarum navis ecclesiae, continet 24 gressus. Longitudo navis ecclesiae ab occidentali usque ad valvas primas versus orientem continet . . . gressus, et quae continent 35 virgas id est 105 pedes. Latitudo dictae ecclesiae continet 32 gressus. Longitudo claustri ex parte de la chapiter-house continet 61 gressus. Sed predicta latitudo ecclesiae ab occidentali ad valvas primas ecclesiae continet 35 virgas id est 105 pedes per mensuram meam cum virga trium pedum longitudinis."[3]

---

[1] As Mr. Clapham has pointed out, some of the French Jacobin churches, such as those in Paris (now destroyed), Agen and Toulouse, exhibit this feature (*Trans. Bristol and Glouc. Arch. Soc.*, vol. 54, p. 124).

[2] See appendix III. The church was 167 feet long with an aisled nave 50 feet wide.

[3] Worcester, *Itin.*, p. 306. The exact equivalent of Worcester's "paces" is in some doubt, as there are discrepancies in own estimate. On p. 83 (*Itin., cit. sup.*) he notes that "24 steppys sive gressus mei faciunt 12 virgas" and on p. 282 "quaelibet virga 3 pedes," so that one of his steps would have equalled 1½ feet; but on p. 83 occurs "50 virgae

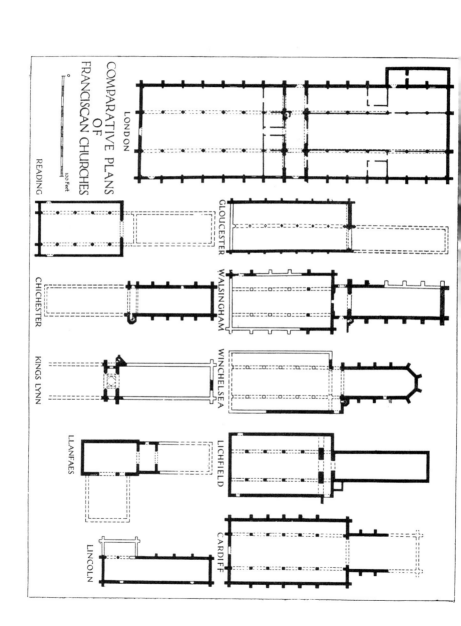

COMPARATIVE PLANS
OF
FRANCISCAN CHURCHES

LONDON

READING

GLOUCESTER

CHICHESTER

WALSINGHAM

KINGS LYNN

WINCHELSEA

LLANFAES

LICHFIELD

LINCOLN

CARDIFF

100 Feet

Later he adds : [1] " Longitudo ecclesiae navis fratrum Sancti Francisci Norwici ab occidentali fine chori ad fenestram orientalem (*sic*) [2] continet 82 gressus. Latitudo ejus continet quoad navem 32 gradus." This description implies an aisled nave measuring about 105 feet by 56 feet, and an apparently unaisled quire 105 feet in length with a belfry between them. [3] The total length therefore cannot have been far short of that of the great Dominican church at Norwich which is undoubtedly the most complete example of a friars' church now surviving in this country. [4] The church of the Austin Friars in the same city was apparently a structure of equally imposing dimensions. [5] Another building of the same class was the Franciscan church at Coventry, the length of which seems to have been identical with that of the Black Friars' church in Norwich. It was, however, in London where all the four orders were represented by churches of the first rank [6] that the efforts to produce the ideal congregational church with the maximum of light and spaciousness attained their most spectacular success in the great Franciscan church in Newgate. This magnificent building 300 feet in length and 90

faciunt 85 gradus sive steppys meos," and again " 34 virgas id est 60 steppys meos." There are numerous other references to show that his " gressus " varied somewhat in relation to the virga or yard, but though it was frequently rather more than 1½ feet, it was never apparently less than this figure. Generally it seems to have represented approximately 1¾ feet, and this figure has accordingly been adopted in calculating the measurements referred to in this book.

[1] Worcester, *Itin.*, p. 308.

[2] This appears to be a mistake for " occidentalem."

[3] Worcester's figure of 24 " gressus " (i.e. 42 feet) for the space under the belfry is somewhat difficult to understand as it seems too large for the width of the " walking place," and even if it refers to the length from north to south it would imply a quire of exceptional width. A figure of 23 " gressus " (i.e. 40 feet), however, appears in the same context in the description of the White Friars' church at Norwich, so that the first bay of the nave including the space before " the altars " may have been included in these figures.

[4] H. Harrod, *Castles and Convents of Norfolk* (1857), pp. 71–96. See also *Norfolk and Norwich Arch. Soc.*, vol. 22 (1926), pp. 86–108 and pp. 370–82. The building is about 254 feet long, the nave being 77 feet and the quire 38 feet wide.

[5] According to William of Worcester's measurements this church was 245 feet long and 66 feet wide. The Carmelite church in Norwich appears to have been somewhat smaller but was still a large building with a wide aisled nave. (Worcester, *Itin.*, pp. 306–7.)

[6] The following approximate measurements of the other friars' churches in London are given for comparison : Black Friars, length 220 feet, width of nave 66 feet, width of quire 35 feet ; White Friars, length 260 feet, width of nave 80 feet, width of quire 25 feet ; Austin Friars, length 285 feet, width 83 feet.

feet broad was with very little doubt the largest friars' church in England. With its slender columns and splendid series of lofty windows it represented the culmination of a new and original idea in church building which was to have a lasting effect on the subsequent development of that art in England.

The Franciscan revival of the fifteenth century reached this country too late to bring about any effective restraint on the architectural developments of the order generally,[1] though the attitude of the reformed Observants to the architectural products of the English conventual province seems to have been expressed in their own buildings. As one would expect in a movement favouring a return to the stricter observance of their founder's rule, the great aisled churches and lofty bell-towers were abandoned in favour of the smaller aisleless structures of the earlier period. At Greenwich the church is shown in Wyngaerdes' drawing as a comparatively simple building, though here as at Richmond the fact that it was annexed to a royal palace no doubt influenced its size. At Elgin in Scotland, however, the church of the Observant house founded in 1479 is still largely intact.[2] It is a long narrow structure (117 feet by 29 feet 2 inches) with large windows of four lights in the east and west walls and of perfectly plain construction. The Observant church at Aberdeen which was built between 1518–32 in place of an earlier and much smaller one erected in 1471 was of similar plan and almost identical dimensions,[3] and there can be little doubt that the normal type of Observant church in Scotland was a conscious copy of the earlier conventual churches.

Turning now from the structure to the internal arrangement and fittings of the later Franciscan churches, we find that almost the only source of information is the Suppression inventories and occasional references in contemporary wills. The arrangement by which the nave and the quire were separated by a passage enclosed by screens seems to have been adopted at a very early date, and although somewhat modified by the introduction of the masonry tower, the screens continued as a normal feature of the average friars' church down to the Suppression. A somewhat analogous

---

[1] In Ireland, where building continued to a much later date than in England, its influence was probably greater.
[2] It was restored in 1891.
[3] This building was only demolished in 1900.

arrangement existed of course in the ordinary monastic church where the rood screen and pulpitum were usually separated by the width of one or two bays. There, however, the quire stalls occupied two or three bays of the structural nave, while in friars' churches where all available space was required for the congregation the quire was kept within its structural limit and entirely shut off from the rest of the building. In the earlier churches the passage enclosed by the screens was probably ceiled over to form a loft or pulpitum, the normal monastic rood screen or pulpitum being thus blended into a single structure occupying usually the central bay of the church and completely separating the quire which was the private chapel of the friars from the public preaching nave. The insertion of the stone bell towers must generally have involved some interference with this arrangement, the screens thenceforth being separated by the cross walls of the tower, though at Sligo Abbey in Ireland (Dominican) where portions of the rood screen survive it is clear that the later tower was added within the west end of the quire, without materially disturbing the rood screen and loft against which it abutted.[1] In England no example of a rood screen or pulpitum in a friars' church has survived, though the detached fragments at Canterbury may have formed part of such a structure. The screen at Sligo consisted of three pointed arches carried on two octagonal columns 6 feet 4 inches apart and 6 feet 3 inches in height and surmounted by a gallery or loft 7 feet wide across the entire width of the church. There is some indication of a somewhat similar arrangement at Chichester. A stone screen of a later type seems to have formerly existed in the Grey Friars' church at Reading, as a drawing of it by J. C. Buckler is preserved in the British Museum.[2] It had a central doorway 4 feet 8 inches wide with single shafts 7 feet 10½ inches in height in the jambs. Unfortunately no trace of it has survived.

The Suppression inventories are of considerable interest, as they often throw light not only on the number of altars in the church but on many other details of the fittings. The quire being generally unaisled had normally a single altar dedicated to the patron saint, usually St. Francis.

[1] *Historical and Descriptive Notes of . . . Sligo Abbey*. Extract from the 82nd report of the Commissioners of Public Works in Ireland (1913–1914), p. 7.
[2] Add. MSS. 36433, no. 496. The drawing is dated 1860.

On it was frequently a table of alabaster apparently forming a reredos, the decoration of which is sometimes mentioned. Thus at Bridgwater the high altar had a table of
alabaster with nine images, while at Dorchester there was
a table " of imagery after the old fasion," and at Llanfaes
a fair table of alabaster. The nave when aisled had usually
two or three altars against the rood screen, but at Dorchester
and Stafford there were four alabaster tables in the nave
and at Cardiff and Carmarthen five each, while the nave
of the Black Friars' church at Salisbury had no less than
twelve altars including " one large altar with St. Barbara
in the midst." [1] Such cases as the last, however, were
exceptional. The altars themselves were separated and
protected in front by screens or parcloses, no doubt usually
of timber, though the Carmarthen inventory mentions " a
frame of iron through all the church before the altars for
taberys." This was apparently the screen in front of the
nave altars which divided the eastern bay of the nave from
the nave proper, an arrangement for which there is clear evidence in the London church, where the screen or the space
enclosed by it appears to have been known as the ' valens.' [2]

A curious variation in the spacing of the piers of the
nave arcades which is noticeable in some friars' churches
was probably connected with the arrangement of the altars.
At Walsingham the eastern bay of the nave was wider
than the other bays and the same characteristics occurred
in both the eastern and western bays at Cardiff. So far
as the eastern bay is concerned the reason was doubtless
to afford additional space before the nave altars, and the
Cardiff arrangement may indicate that there the western
bays of the aisles were also enclosed as chapels. Where, as
at Reading, the reverse arrangement occurs and the eastern
bay is narrower than those to the west, the object was
probably to counteract the thrust of the tower by reducing
the span of the easternmost arches of the nave arcade.

Apart from the altars the inventories frequently mention
statues in various parts of the church, either over the altars
or on brackets on the walls. Thus in the nave of the church

---

[1] St. Barbara appears to have been particularly venerated in Franciscan churches. There were chapels dedicated to her at Lewes, Winchelsea
and elsewhere.

[2] See wills of Margaret Yonge (1501) and Wm. Aleyn (1510) quoted
by Kingsford, *Coll. Franc.* (B.S.F.S.), 2 pp. 119, 126 ; cf. the Winchester
Supp. Inv. *L. and P. Hen. VIII*, vol. 13(1), no. 1108. At Coventry
the term appears to have had a somewhat different meaning (see p. 77).

at Dorchester were " three great images of alabaster, a new tabernacle for the image of St. Francis and divers images stolen." [1] Perhaps, however, the most interesting description of the interior of a Franciscan church is that of the Observant church at Southampton.[2] At the high altar in the quire was " a table of alabaster of the Passion and above that a fair table painted and gilt with a pageant of the Passion and curtains on bars to save the same ; in the midst of the altar a proper frame gilt for the sacrament and at the altars ends two small altars, a proper seat syleyd for the priest deacon and subdeacon." The quire was " double stalled and well and substantially graven " and had " a fair loft over the door with a good clock and a bell to warn the clock." In the nave were " 3 tables of alabaster at 3 altars, a sacry bell, a painted table, 12 close seats and other seats, two branches for tapers, a lamp and a basin." The seats in the nave evidently refer to pews. At Exeter there were " fair seats " in the quire in addition to the stalls, but the provision of seats in the nave apart from stone benches round the walls such as existed in the churches in London and Lichfield, appears to have been exceptional in friars' churches where the large congregations presumably stood. Another unusual feature is the mention of a clock in the loft overlooking the quire. The loft here must have been over the quire screen and was therefore probably distinct from the rood loft if the bell tower occupied its normal position between the nave and the quire. Placed in the quire loft would have been " the pair of organs " which are frequently referred to in the inventories.[3] Of the other fittings not much can be said. The stalls normally occupied the western half of the quire and were returned against the western screen. Holy water stoups in the quire are occasionally mentioned as also are lecterns which seem to have been invariably of timber. At Exeter two old timber lecterns in the quire were valued at £2, and the " fair stalls " at a like sum.[4] " Brass pillars in the quire " are mentioned at Babwell,[5] though it is doubtful to what this refers. At Worcester there was " a frame for the

---

[1] *L. and P. Hen. VIII*, vol. 13(2), no. 474.
[2] *Ibid.*, vol. 13(2), no. 545. On the suppression of the Observant Franciscans in 1534 Austin Friars had been put into possession, a fact which accounts for the inventory referring to this house as belonging to the Austin Friars.
[3] At Salisbury there were ' feyer stallys well sileid wt an orgayne lofte.'
[4] *Ibid.*, no. 354.   [5] *Ibid.*, no. 1213.

D

sepulchre in the quire," [1] which appears to be the only reference to an Easter sepulchre in a Franciscan house. With the vestments and draperies which form the bulk of the entries in these inventories we are not here concerned, but it is interesting to note that the church at Ipswich possessed in addition to a lenten veil " eighteen hangings in the quire " ; [2] and one would like to have known something more concerning the twenty banners which hung in the quire of the Black Friars' church at Hereford. [3]

As part of the fittings of the church mention may here be made of the tiles and a few tombs or tomb-slabs which have survived from Franciscan churches, and in many cases now form the only tangible remains of the building from which they came. The tiles seldom have any distinctive characteristics and are generally quite plain, though decorated examples with white slip inlay have survived from Chester, Reading, Lichfield, Bridgwater and elsewhere. A somewhat different type with the decoration in incised lines without any filling also occurs at Lichfield. Heraldic tiles are uncommon, though a number have been found on the site of the Bridgwater house. Some of the slabs of marble with which the great church in London was paved are still preserved in the floor of Christ Church, Newgate Street.

In view of the popularity of the Franciscan churches as places of burial, it is remarkable that so few tombs should have survived. Few places in England can have possessed such an extensive and representative series of monuments as the Franciscan church in London, and of these only one inscribed slab remains, while of the extensive series that existed at Coventry not a single example survives. Two tomb-slabs from Llanfaes and one from Lichfield and a decorated coffin lid from Bridgnorth, are described below, while Pishey Thompson mentions [4] a slab dug up on the site of the Franciscan house at Boston about 1796 on which was the effigy of a man with his feet resting on a dog and the inscription " Wisselus de Smalenburgh civis et mercator 1340." The two finest tombs from a Franciscan church in this country, however, are those of Edmund Tudor, Earl of Richmond, the father of Henry VII, and of Sir Rhys ap Thomas, both of which were formerly in the Franciscan church at Carmarthen.

---

[1] *L. and P. Hen. VIII*, vol. 13(1), no. 1513.
[2] *Ibid.*, no. 699.   [3] *Ibid.*, vol. 13(2), no. 184.
[4] *History of Boston* (1856), p. 112.

The Suppression inventory mentions a "pall of cloth of tussey on the earl of Richmonds tomb" and "a goodly tomb of Sir Rice ap Thomas with a grate of iron about him and a streamer and banner of his arms with his coat armour and helmet."[1] The former is now in St. David's Cathedral, where it was removed by the order of Henry VIII, while the magnificent monument of Sir Rhys ap Thomas and his wife is in St. Peter's church in Carmarthen. It is of early sixteenth-century date and, though extensively restored in 1865, the effigies appear to have been untouched.

THE DOMESTIC BUILDINGS

In the planning of the domestic buildings of a friary a marked disregard of the normal monastic arrangement is frequently noticeable. The principal buildings were arranged round the cloister without any well-defined rule, while the position of the cloister itself varied considerably in different houses and was no doubt determined by the general topography of the site. The church as we have seen generally abutted on a public thoroughfare and the cloister would naturally be placed on the opposite side in the more secluded part of the precinct. In England it generally adjoined the nave with the eastern range overlapping the quire so that the passage between the two gave direct access into the eastern walk of the cloister. Variations of this arrangement, however, were probably not uncommon and in the Irish houses the cloister is frequently so placed that half of it abuts on the nave and half on the quire. At Yarmouth and Chichester it apparently adjoined the quire, while at Lichfield there seems to have been a small cloister abutting on the quire as well as the great cloister on the south side of the nave.

In connection with the position of the cloister, a peculiarity common in houses of the mendicant orders but rarely found elsewhere [2] was the interposition of a small open court between the cloister walk and the wall of the church with a short covered corridor communicating between the cloister and the church. Such an arrangement existed at London and Walsingham and probably also at Reading as well as in the Black Friars at Norwich and the White

---

[1] *L. and P. Hen. VIII*, vol. 13(2), no. 229.
[2] The only existing example of this arrangement outside the friars' houses is the secular cathedral of Salisbury where a similar corridor connects the cloister and the church.

Friars in London. Its primary purpose was doubtless to afford light to the great windows of the nave, though it had the additional advantage of adding to the privacy of the cloister by separating it from the public preaching nave. At Chichester a similar yard seems to have intervened between the cloister and the quire, and no doubt served the same purpose.

The size of the Franciscan cloister naturally varied considerably in accordance with the importance of the house. In London it was no less than 135 feet square including the alleys, but 60 to 80 feet was probably a more normal dimension to judge from the somewhat scanty evidence available, and in many of the Irish houses it did not exceed 40 to 50 feet. In some houses such as London, Walsingham and Lichfield and the Dominican house at Bristol there was a second and smaller cloister around which were grouped some of the minor offices. In London this formed part of the infirmary block, and it is probable that this was its normal purpose. The position of the smaller cloister at Lichfield is unusual, though a similar arrangement of two cloisters adjoining the church may have existed at Chichester.

Turning now from the ground plan to the buildings themselves, the most noticeable feature is the general practice of placing the principal apartments on the first floor over one or more of the cloister walks which were thus incorporated in the structure of the flanking ranges. The object was no doubt primarily one of economy in building material,[1] though the arrangement served also to reduce the ground space required, an important point in the more congested towns. Instances of this arrangement exist at Ware, Walsingham and Dunwich, while there is evidence for it also at London, Bedford, and Yarmouth. The practice was not confined to the Franciscans and other examples may be seen in Dominican houses at Bristol, Hereford, Newcastle, and Norwich and in the Carmelite houses at Hulne and Aylesford.

The material used in these buildings varied naturally with the locality, but was generally rubble masonry with ashlar dressing to the quoins and windows. Brick was sparingly used in some of the later buildings at Walsingham,

[1] This is somewhat borne out by the fact that this method of building was also adopted by the Gilbertines, one of the most poorly endowed of the older orders.

and occurs also in the cloister of the Black Friars at Norwich. In many of the smaller houses the buildings were no doubt of timber or half-timber construction, but apart from the subsidiary building at Salisbury no examples of this type seem to have survived. Stone probably continued to be regarded as a luxury for the domestic buildings after it had begun to supersede timber in the construction of the church, and the occasional activities of the early ministers in suppressing its use suggests that wood was still the normal building material in the majority of houses towards the close of the thirteenth century. Thus at Shrewsbury, for instance, William of Nottingham, the third provincial Minister, had the stone walls of the dormitory removed and mud walls substituted, while Albert of Pisa had previously destroyed the stone cloister at Southampton, " though with great difficulty as the men of the town resisted." [1] In this case the cloister may have been vaulted in stone as was presumably the early cloister in London, the embossments of which were ordered to be removed by William of Nottingham. Vaulting in the cloister alleys, however, seems to have been unusual in friars' houses in England even in the fourteenth and fifteenth centuries. Generally where the cloister walk stood free of the adjoining building it had a sloping lean-to roof of wood covered with lead. The only example of a stone vaulted cloister in an English Franciscan house is at Yarmouth, but an elaborate stone vault of about the same dàte survives over the eastern walk of the Carmelite cloister at Coventry.

Some idea of the extent of the average Franciscan house can be gained from the Suppression inventories to which reference has already been made, and from the contemporary accounts of the collectors of the rents of the suppressed houses. Apart from the church and vestry the buildings most frequently mentioned are the frater with the buttery kitchen and brewhouse, and the dorter. The guest house and chapter house, though rarely referred to, were of course normal features, while there were no doubt usually separate apartments for the guardian and occasionally for the provincial minister when making his periodical visitations. Occasionally a school house or library is mentioned, and in several houses there is evidence for the existence of apartments set apart for the use of the king or other important persons.

[1] Eccleston, p. 99.

There were also in some houses buildings connected
with the farming activities of the community, while the
tailor's shop at Southampton and the barber's shop in the
London house indicate that the personal requirements of
the friars were not overlooked. It will be convenient to
refer to some of these buildings in greater detail.

THE FRATER

The frater in a friars' house was normally on the first
floor of one of the ranges of the principal cloister, generally
opposite the church but occasionally, as at the Black Friars,
Canterbury, in the western range. The latter is perhaps
the best preserved example of a frater in any English friary.
Among Franciscan houses the building at Denny alone
remains, apart from a gable end at Walsingham and the
undercrofts at Dunwich and Ware. At Denny the building
is one storey only, and therefore in no way a typical example.
At Bridgnorth the frater apparently survived until the
middle of last century ; at Cambridge it was converted
after the Suppression into the Chapel of Sidney Sussex
College and survived in a somewhat altered state until
1776. A description of this building by James Essex, the
architect of the new chapel, has been preserved, from which
a few extracts may be quoted. He describes it as " a room
69 feet 6 inches long and 23 feet 6 inches wide between the
walls and 25 feet high to the setting on of the roof which
formed a ceiling with arched principals and intermediate
spaces flat in the middle and sloped on the sides." [1] At
the point *b* on the plan (see Plate 2) were two holes in the
wall which Essex conjectured might have received the
timbers for the support of a pulpit. The building which
was apparently originally of one storey only was taken
down in August 1776 preparatory to the erection of the
new chapel, the axis of which differed slightly from that
of the earlier building.

A pulpit for the use of the reader during meals seems
to have been as usual a feature of the frater in a friars'
house as it was in those of the older orders. It was usually
constructed in a recess in the wall on the side opposite the
cloister and at some height above the floor and was frequently approached by steps built in the thickness of the
wall as at the Black Friars, Canterbury. Occasionally it

[1] B.M. Add. MSS. 6761, ff. 1–7.

Plate 2

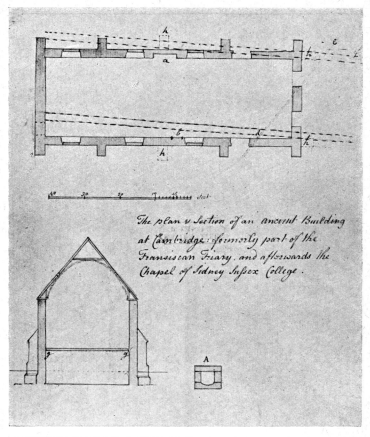

The plan & Section of an ancient Building
at Cambridge; formerly part of the
Fransiscan Friary. and afterwards the
Chapel of Sidney Sussex College.

CAMBRIDGE, PLAN AND SECTION OF CHAPEL OF SIDNEY SUSSEX COLLEGE,
DEMOLISHED 1776

(The dotted lines indicate the axis of the present chapel)

appears to have been a free standing stone structure within the building itself, as the base of a pulpit of this character is said to have been found in the frater of the Austin Friars at Ludlow [1] and possibly also at the Franciscan house at Bridgnorth.[2] That this was the earlier arrangement is suggested by an order made in 1244 for the construction of " a proper pulpit in the middle of the refectory " of the Friars Minor at Reading.[3] A small projection possibly for a pulpit formerly existed on the north side of the frater at Denny, and at Winchelsea early views indicate a similar recess which is said to have contained a stone seat and doubtless served the same purpose.

DORTER AND CHAPTER HOUSE

Of the dorter and chapter house which normally occupied the eastern range very little can be said, as no complete examples can be recognized with certainty. Buildings which may have served as the dorter survive in the Dominican houses at Gloucester and Bristol, the latter occupying a somewhat unusual position in the southern range and on the north side of the small cloister. At Walsingham the lower part of the walls of the chapter house remain and show that it was a rectangular building (46 feet by 25 feet) projecting from the east walk of the cloister. In London the chapter house measured 60 feet by 27 feet, and here as at Walsingham and elsewhere the dormitory probably extended over the western part of the chapter house as it did sometimes in houses of other orders. Occasionally as at Rhuddlan (Black Friars) there seems to have been a room above the chapter house.

INFIRMARY

Reference has already been made to the infirmary cloister at London and Walsingham. With the exception of the doubtful remains at Walsingham, however, no Franciscan infirmary has survived in this country. The best preserved building of this type in a friars' house is the small structure at Hulne near Alnwick (Carmelite), which although it has lost its original roof is otherwise almost intact. It consists of a small hall with a chapel at the east end placed

---

[1] *Journ. Brit. Arch. Assoc.*, vol. 24 (1868), p. 53 ; *Proc. Soc. Antiq.* (N.S.), vol 2, p. 78. See also *Archæologia*, vol 39 (1863), pp. 173–88.
[2] *Post*, p. 211.   [3] *C. Lib. R.*, vol. 2, p. 235.

close to the principal gatehouse of the precinct. Apart from this building the only friars' infirmaries that can with certainty be identified are at Clare in Suffolk (Austin Friars), and at Cardiff (Black Friars), where the foundations of an interesting infirmary block have been uncovered. It has, however, been suggested with some probability that the building forming the southern range of the little cloister at the Black Friars, Bristol, was the infirmary, and a detached group of buildings at Brecon (Black Friars) may have served as a combined infirmary and guest house.

THE GUEST HOUSE

It is probable that every Franciscan house had its guest house which was not infrequently situated in the western claustral range, like the surviving building at Walsingham. It was often of two storeys with a hall on the upper floor and would naturally be easily accessible from the principal gateway. Other examples of buildings possibly devoted to this purpose survive at Ware and Canterbury, and the Suppression inventories mention the guest hall (ostre) at Chichester and Hereford. In rare instances it may have had its own chapel, as occasionally also had the infirmary, but this would have been only in the larger and more important houses. In Scotland a fourteenth-century Franciscan guest house survives at Inverkeithing (Fifeshire). It has recently been carefully restored.

THE GUARDIAN'S LODGING

In the early period the guardian or warden of a Franciscan house probably slept in the common dorter with the other friars, but at a later date it became usual for a separate building to be set apart for his use. This would also have been normally used for the entertainment of the Provincial when he visited the convent on the occasion of a provincial chapter, though occasionally, as in the Black Friars in London, the Provincial had a separate chamber reserved for him elsewhere in the precinct. The warden's lodging was probably in many cases a typical small house of the period with a small hall, and living and sleeping apartments and a kitchen with the usual offices, though it doubtless varied considerably in size in accordance with the importance of the house. At Ipswich the Suppression survey mentions " the Warden's upper and nether chambers " in addition to " the chamber where the warden lies," and what is distinctly unusual, " the Vice-warden's chamber." At the Black Friars in London the prior had his own private chapel situated over the sacristy on the south side of the quire and communicating by a gallery with his lodging, and there is some evidence that the warden's house in the Grey Friars, London, was also furnished with a chapel. It is unlikely, however, that this was a normal feature in the smaller provincial houses. The position of the guardian's or warden's lodging varied considerably in different houses, though it seems not infrequently to have been in close proximity to the infirmary cloister and was naturally placed in the more secluded part of the site, having sometimes its own private gate in the precinct wall. The only surviving building in an English Franciscan house that can with reasonable probability be identified as having served this purpose is the picturesque structure at Canterbury described in a subsequent chapter, though the building at Salisbury may conceivably have been used by the warden of that house.

In some of the larger houses individual friars had also the privilege of private quarters occasionally confirmed to them by papal edict, but these cases were probably not numerous, though there are several instances as early as the fourteenth century of this practice in the London house where in one instance the grant was expressly made for the life of the friar in question.

LIBRARY

Buildings set apart for the storage of books were probably a comparatively late feature in Franciscan houses, although the great reputation of the English Franciscans for learning may be said to have begun as early as 1230, when Robert Grosseteste became reader to the Franciscans at Oxford.[1] In a register of English libraries drawn up by the Franciscans themselves and probably dating from about the middle of the thirteenth century no libraries of mendicant friaries appear, though a few, including those at Oxford and Babwell, were added later.[2] In the fifteenth century there were two libraries in the Franciscan convent at Oxford, one for the

---

[1] On his death in 1253 Grosseteste left all his books or writings to the Friars Minor of Oxford and this collection was augmented in 1258 by the collection of books of Adam Marsh.
[2] *Collectanea Franciscana* (B.S.F.S.), vol. 2, pp. 37–60.

use of the convent and the other the library of the student friars. At Cambridge there was also an important library. The Suppression inventories mention libraries at Chichester " with four and a half new stalls and divers old books and a new press with almers for books," at Gloucester with " many books of no value," and at the Observant house at Southampton " locked with two locks and many books in it chained." An account of the sale of the goods of the Grey Friars at Stafford mention " old books and a coffer in the library " there.[1]

In the London convent the library appears to have occupied the upper floor of the northern range of the great cloister possibly as early as the latter part of the thirteenth century. It was rebuilt by Richard Whittington in 1421 and survived until 1827. The identification of some twenty books from the Hereford convent, all except one of which retains its original press-mark, indicate that this house also had a library of some importance.[2] It was probably in the fourteenth century that the Franciscan libraries attained their greatest importance, and there is evidence that in the early sixteenth century many of them had become sadly neglected. When Leland visited Oxford shortly before the Dissolution he found " at the Franciscans house there are cobwebs 'in the library and bookworms ; more than this—whatever others may boast—nothing if you have regard to learned books. For I in spite of opposition of all the friars carefully examined all the bookcases of the library." [3]

THE SCHOOL HOUSE

From a very early date teaching found an important place in the activities of many Franciscan houses. The famous Franciscan schools at Oxford owed their origin to Agnellus himself, under whom according to Eccleston the first schoolhouse was erected. In 1246 the Franciscans of Gloucester were licensed to set up a school of theology in a tower of the town wall abutting on their precinct, and Stamford also before the end of the thirteenth century appears to have been a special place of study. At a later date there seems to have been a higher school of theology

[1] Wright's *Suppression*, p. 269.
[2] " The Library of the Grey Friars of Hereford," *Collect. Franc.* (B.S.F.S.), vol. 1, pp. 114–23.
[3] Leland, *Collectanea* (ed. Hearne, 1770), vol. 4, p. 60.

in each of the seven custodies with their headquarters in
the houses at London, York, Norwich, Newcastle, Stamford,
Coventry, and Exeter. Many other houses such as that at
Yarmouth probably had their own schools of divinity in
the fourteenth century and buildings set apart as a schoolhouse must have been fairly common in Franciscan houses
at this date. None that can be identified have survived,
though at Coventry it appears to have formed part of the
western range.

THE STUDIES

In several houses an apartment known as " the studies "
is mentioned. In London it probably formed part of the
ground floor of the eastern range. Generally it seems to
have been distinct from the library, but occasionally as at
Gloucester (Black Friars) the two may have been combined.
The building at Gloucester, which is of thirteenth-century
date, is very remarkable and apparently the only example
of its kind surviving.[1] It occupies the whole of the upper
floor of the south range of the cloister and has a series of
recesses in the north and south walls apparently designed
for purposes of private study.[2] There were originally
thirteen on either side, each lighted by a small square-
headed window. At the west end and possibly also at the
east there was a space without any recesses perhaps reserved
for book presses. At Richmond (Yorks) a room called
" the studies " was situated near the dormitory.

SECULAR LODGINGS

Well before the Suppression there are numerous instances
of private persons dwelling within the precinct of many of
the friars' houses. The rents of these lodgings no doubt
helped to augment the decreasing income from other sources,
but it is probable that the system was only an extension
of a practice that had been in force at a much earlier date.
The existence of a Bishop's lodging within the Grey Friars
at Lichfield may, as suggested below, have dated from the
foundation of that house, while there are other instances
at a comparatively early date of nobles and other privileged

[1] W. H. Knowles, F.S.A., " The Black Friars of Gloucester," *Trans.
Bristol and Glouc. Arch. Soc.*, vol. 54 (1932), pp. 167–201.
[2] They may be compared with the carrels frequently placed in the
cloister of Benedictine houses of which a good example survives in the
cloister of Gloucester Cathedral.

persons having lodgings assigned to them in a particular friary. Thus the Bishops of Lincoln when visiting Oxford made use of their own apartment in the Black Friars of that city, and in the fourteenth century the English Kings when in the north habitually lodged at the Grey Friars in York. The King's Chamber is mentioned in the Suppression inventories of the Grey Friars at Carmarthen and Dorchester, while " Sir Thomas Tyrrell's lodging " at Colchester, " Master Denhams Chamber " at Winchester, and " Lady Evynghern's chambre " at Coventry testify to the presence of less important lay persons within the precinct on the eve of the Suppression.

Occasionally this right of residence within the precinct appears to have been hereditary as in the case of the Black Friars at Exeter, where the Marquess of Exeter and his ancestors are stated to have had certain lodgings " of old time." Lord Wentworth may have had a similar privilege at Ipswich. The existence of royal and episcopal lodgings was of course a not uncommon feature in some of the larger Benedictine and Cluniac houses and the fact that the friars' houses shared this sometimes expensive privilege tends to emphasize the scale to which their buildings had attained even in the fourteenth century.

ANCHORITES CELLS

Another occasional resident within the precinct of a Franciscan house must be briefly mentioned. The existence of a male or female recluse was by no means uncommon in Dominican houses in the fifteenth and early sixteenth centuries, but they are rarely mentioned in connection with a Franciscan house. At Walsingham, however, there was an anchoress living in the precinct in the early sixteenth century and other instances of a similar practice could no doubt be found. The anchors house in the Black Friars in London stood in the cemetery not far from the principal gate, and this seems to have been its usual position.

FARM BUILDINGS

The site of most English friaries included a garden and orchard, but the number of houses that owned and cultivated land outside the precinct was probably small. There is evidence, however, in several Franciscan houses of farming activity on a more extensive scale than the mere cultivation of the friary gardens. Thus the Franciscans at Dorchester possessed a mill with two horses belonging to it, and at Preston there was a windmill, a watermill and a turbary called " le pete mosse." At Llanfaes the inventory mentions corn growing on the ground and sheep, while growing corn is also mentioned at Stafford. The house at Hereford had a horse and cart, and apparently grew corn and hay, and at Llanfaes and Ipswich there were barns or garners for the storage of farm produce. At Bedford the friars, who also owned a horse and cart, are said to have " long used husbandry " and here a large medieval barn survived until comparatively recently (see Plate 24B). At Babwell also the extent of the area occupied by the friars makes it clear that a large part of it must have been under cultivation.

Conduits

No account of Franciscan building would be complete without some reference to the provisions made for the supply of water to which the friars generally seem to have devoted so much attention. The conduits for the houses at Bridgnorth, Bristol, Chichester, Coventry, Lichfield, Lincoln, London and Richmond are referred to later, while others existed at Carmarthen, Exeter, Newcastle, Oxford, Scarborough, Southampton and elsewhere. In many cases these water systems were probably the first attempts to deal with the problem of water supply in their respective towns, and there is evidence that the towns themselves often profited directly from the enterprise of the friars. Thus at Southampton the friars' water supply which had been constructed in 1290 was transferred to the town in 1421, while the burgesses of Scarborough in 1283 gave a spring outside the town for the use of the Friars Minor on condition that the borough should have the joint use of the conduit when it was constructed. At the Suppression it was reported that the conduit of the Grey Friars at Coventry was " better than that of the town and has a better head," and that much of the city would lack water if they did not purchase it. At Bristol and Lincoln the water systems of the Friars Minor came into the possession of the town after the Suppression and continued in use until comparatively recent times.

It is probable that many of these conduits still in part survive, though their positions have long ago been lost sight of. The source of supply was usually situated some distance outside the town, and the water was brought to the precinct in leaden pipes. The arrangement in London, though possibly somewhat more elaborate, was no doubt typical of the majority of these water systems which were obviously planned with a considerable degree of technical skill. At Bristol the arrangements for the subterranean storage and outflow of water are said to be still in existence with leaden main pipes remaining in position.

The general features of the friars' buildings have now been noticed, but before proceeding to describe the existing remains of the Franciscan houses in relation to their documentary history, it is desirable to consider the question of the origin of the striking peculiarities observable in this remarkable group of buildings. It was in the design and construction of their churches that the originality of the friars was most in evidence, and with the history of the older orders as a precedent one would naturally look to a continental origin for some of their principal features. It is a curious fact, however, that although in certain areas of France, Italy and Germany, distinctive types of plan were adopted, there is apparently no instance where this bears any resemblance to the typical friars' church in the British Isles. It is true that the polygonal steeple is common in friars' houses in France, but it is generally more massive in form and invariably flanks the building on one side or the other, an arrangement unknown in England. In plan also the French buildings with their eastern apses and radiating chapels have little in common with the contemporary friars' churches in England, while the numerous Franciscan and Dominican churches of Central Italy [1] with their eastern transepts flanked by rows of chapels exhibit an even greater contrast to the typical English plan. One is forced therefore to the conclusion that the builders of the friars' churches in this country borrowed as little from the continent as they did from the older orders at home and that the buildings they erected were evolved independently within these islands.

[1] Kurt Biebrach, *Die holzgedeckten Franciskaner und Dominikaner-kirchen in Umbrien und Toskana* (1908).

CHAPTER II

HOUSES OF WHICH STRUCTURAL REMAINS SURVIVE

OF the sixty-one [1] Franciscan houses in England at the time of the Suppression only thirteen have left any substantial remains as evidence of their former existence. These will now be described in turn.

(1) CANTERBURY

HISTORY

The circumstances connected with the arrival of the Franciscans in Canterbury have already been touched upon. As the first house founded on English soil, the Canterbury foundation has an especial interest, and has consequently received greater attention at the hands of previous writers than have most of the other houses of the order. Its documentary history has been exhaustively dealt with elsewhere [2] and the account which follows is therefore confined to such records as help to throw light on the date and extent of the friars' buildings or the topography of their precinct. We have seen that the first temporary lodging of the friars was at the Poor Priests' Hospice on the banks of the Stour. The master of the Hospice at this time was Alexander of Gloucester, and he appears to have taken the friars under his care. Eccleston records that he " bestowed on them a site and built a chapel sufficiently dignified for the time. And because the brethren refused to take absolute possession of anything, it was made the property of the citizens, but lent to the brethren at their good pleasure. Very special help was afforded them by Sir Simon Langton, Archdeacon of Canterbury, by Sir Henry of Sandwich, and the noble countess, the anchoress at Hackington." [3]

[1] This figure does not include the nunneries.
[2] Charles Cotton, *The Grey Friars of Canterbury*, 1924 ; A. G. Little, in *V.C.H., Kent*, vol. 2, pp. 190–4, and *Arch. Cant.*, vol. 34 (1920), pp. 79–91.
[3] Eccleston, pp. 25–6.; *ibid.* (ed. Salter), p. 28. The anchoress was Loretta, widow of Robert de Beaumont, Earl of Leicester. See " Loretta Countess of Leicester " by F. M. Powicke in *Historical Essays in Honour of James Tait*, Manchester, 1933, pp. 247–72.

Some indication of the position of this first settlement is afforded by a fifteenth-century manuscript in the possession of the Dean and Chapter in which it is recorded that " in the year of our Lord's incarnation 1224 the Friars Minor arrived in England and were graciously received by King Henry, were lodged in Canterbury in Wyght and in London in Cornhill." [1] There can be little doubt that " Wyght " was the island usually called Binnewith which lies between the two main branches of the Stour and upon which the western part of the city is built. Between this main island and the Poor Priests' Hospice is a much smaller island formed by a channel of the Stour and probably regarded as part of Binnewith, which seems to have belonged to the Hospice and to have formed part of its garden. Here, in all probability, the first buildings of the friars were erected. The land was low-lying and liable to floods. The buildings of which nothing is definitely known were doubtless of the poorest kind, but they served the needs of the friars for close on fifty years. About 1268 a new and larger site on the main part of the island of Binnewith and divided from the old site by the branch stream already mentioned, was given to the friars by John Digge or Diggs, an alderman of the city, and a member of a wealthy local family. The fifteenth-century document quoted above records this event in the following terms : " In the year of our Lord's incarnation 1267 John Digge bought the island in Canterbury called Binnewyght and the place of the gate upon Stour street for the use of the Friars Minor and transferred them thither at a convenient time." [2] The new buildings were presumably begun at once, but there is a striking absence of reference to the work. Henry III appears to have done little for this house, though he lavished gifts upon the neighbouring Black Friars. [3] A gift of 10 marks " for maintenance " in 1239 [4] and a few subsequent orders for the supply of fuel [5] seem to have been the limit of his generosity, and in the following reign royal alms were few and no assistance from the King towards the new buildings is recorded. Consequently the progress seems to have been

[1] Canterbury Dean and Chapter MSS. Register O, fo. 407^v, printed in B.S.F.S. *Coll. Franc.*, vol. 2, p. 9.
[2] *Ibid.*
[3] A. R. Martin, " The Dominican Priory at Canterbury," *Arch. Journal*, vol. 86 (1930), pp. 152–77.
[4] *C. Lib. R.*, vol. 1, p. 370.
[5] *Ibid.*, vol. 2, p. 72 ; Close Roll 56 Hen. III, m. 7.

unusually slow, as it was not until 1325 that the new church and cemetery were consecrated by Archbishop Walter Reynolds.[1] In the meantime the old church may have continued to serve the needs of the friary, and it was possibly this building which is referred to in 1305, when Sir William of Gerberg, being indicted for murder, is stated to have taken sanctuary in the church of the Friars Minor in Canterbury and there remained for full half of year.[2]

The site was enlarged from time to time and gradually consolidated. In 1275 it was reported that the friars had appropriated a highway 10 perches in length and 11 feet wide " to the serious injury of the city and county," [3] but four years later they received a licence to enclose a road, which was probably the highway in question, forming the western boundary of their land.[4] Dr. Cotton has suggested [5] that this road was a south-westerly continuation of St. Peter's Grove, formerly known as Pocock Lane, and that the land to the west of this as far as Black Griffin Lane (formerly Mead Lane) [6] was not acquired until 1392–93, when the sacrist's accounts of Christ Church contain the following entry : " Item de iiij solidis de terra vocata Medland quia includitur per fratres minores." [7]

Previous to this in 1336 the friars had been licensed to acquire from the parson of St. Mildred's church and others a messuage and garden 10 perches square for the enlargement of their property [8] which, by the time of the suppression, comprised rather more than 18 acres. How far this area was enclosed by a wall is uncertain. The river doubtless formed the eastern boundary and on the west and south the boundary seems to have been marked by dykes. The principal entrance or North Gate was in St. Peter's Street almost opposite the gateway to the Black Friars, from where a passage now reduced to a narrow lane led southwards to the friars' church, and passing through " the walking place " between the nave and quire gave access to the cloister and domestic buildings on the south. The

[1] Lambeth MSS. Reg. Reynolds, fo. 186ᵛ.
[2] *Year Book of 33–35, Edw. I* (R.S.), p. 55.
[3] P.R.O., Inq. a.q.d. file 5, no. 1.
[4] *C.C.R. 1272–79*, p. 543 ; cf. *Hundred Rolls* (Rec. Com.), vol. 1, p. 203.
[5] *The Grey Friars of Canterbury, ut sup.*, p. 18.
[6] Dr. Cotton (*op. cit.*) states that at a still earlier date it was called Crinemelne Lane.
[7] Cotton, *op. cit.*, p. 18, from Ch. Ch. Cant. MSS. Sacrists Accounts, 1392–93.
[8] *C.P.R. 1334–38*, p. 238.

E

gate itself appears to have been demolished early in the seventeenth century, as a shop of that date now stands on the site. It is shown in Langdon's pictorial survey of the Black Friars' property in 1595 [1] as a structure very similar to the Black Friars' Gate with an opening or niche on either side of the central archway on the south front and an embattled parapet. A second and subsidiary gate stood to the east on the site of No. 6 Stour Street, formerly known as Lamb Lane. The original entrance from the east was probably the narrow passage to the north of the Poor Priests' Hospital, formerly known as the common washing-place. The passage to the north of this by which the site is approached at the present day was, however, in the possession of the friars before 1264, when they were licensed to build a bridge over the Stour between their house and their place called Brokmede.[2] The modern wooden bridge by which access to the site is now obtained must be on the site of the bridge erected at that time. Up to this period it is uncertain whether the friars' property had any frontage to the street on this side, but John Digges' gift in 1267 expressly mentions a piece of ground in Stour Street as the " place of a gate." Upon this site on the north side of the present entrance, the East Gate was erected,[3] but it was not apparently until 1309 that a more direct route across the main stream of the river was obtained. On 1 August in that year John de Burne was licensed to assign a roadway from the highway to the Stour to the friars who were at the same time licensed " to build a bridge across the Stour extending from the above roadway to their dwelling house for the benefit of persons wishing to attend service in their church ; the bridge to be so built as to allow a clear passage for boats underneath it." [4] This was probably the stone bridge leading from Lamb Lane to the Grey Friars which William Lovelace, who then owned the property, covenanted with the city to demolish in 1589. Part of the medieval structure, however, still survives, in the western arch of the existing brick bridge which now occupies the site.

The later history of the house so far as it concerns our present purpose is chiefly confined to requests for burial

[1] Reproduced in *Arch. Journal*, vol. 86, p. 156, from the engraving published in *Topographical Miscellanies* (1792).

[2] *C.P.R. 1258–66*, p. 342.

[3] No view of this building is known and it was probably demolished very soon after the suppression.

[4] *C.P.R. 1307–13*, p. 178.

within the precinct and other testamentary records. Bequests to the friars are numerous and occasionally of substantial amounts, while periodical gifts of money and in kind were made by the monastic houses in the city and by distinguished visitors and pilgrims. In 1360 for instance, King John of France, when passing through Canterbury on his return home from captivity, gave the Friars Minor 25 nobles (£8 6s. 8d.).[1] Some 113 wills mentioning the Canterbury Franciscans have been recorded by Dr. Cotton,[2] but of these comparatively few refer to the buildings of the house. The earliest direct reference to these is in the will of William Byllyngton, of All Saints, Canterbury, who, in 1444, left £10 to the minorites " to the building of le Dortour." [3] In 1450 William Woodland of Holy Cross in Canterbury left £5 for the repair of the church and 5 marks for the repair of the dormitory,[4] and in 1463 Thomas Somer of the Parish of Holy Cross in Canterbury desired to be buried in the churchyard of the Friars Minor and gave to them £10, of which 6s. 8d. was to be given to each friar and the remainder spent on " the beautifying of their church." [5] In 1488 Edmund Mynot, of the parish of St. Andrew, bequeathed 20 marks " to the reparation of the church and buildings of the Grey Friars," [6] and in 1492 Agnes Bochard, widow, left 6s. 8d. to the friars and 8d. to the guild of Corpus Christi in their church.[7]

As a place of burial this house seems to have been popular and some occasional light on the internal arrangement of the church can be gathered from this source. The earliest recorded request for burial within the friary is that of Thomas Somer already mentioned. In 1476 Thomas Barton of the parish of St. Mary Northgate desired to be buried in the church of the house of the Friars Minor in Canterbury, and directed that " a little square stone of marble be sett in the wall over the place where I shall be buried upon which there shall be graven the image of our Lady and the Four Evangelists and the figure of my father and mother, of me and my wife, my children, Richard Denys and Joan his wife with Margery her daughter and scripture upon the same to be made whereby the people

[1] *Gentleman's Mag.*, Sept. 1859, p. 277.
[2] *The Grey Friars of Canterbury* (1924), Appendix III, pp. 84–106.
[3] Lambeth MSS. Reg. Stafford, fo. 125ᵇ.
[4] Hasted, *History of Kent*, vol. IV, p. 447.
[5] Archd. Cant. Wills, vol. 1, fo. 8.   [6] *Ibid.*, vol. 5, fo. 4.
[7] Consist. Court Cant., vol. 3, fo. 366.

may remember my soul." [1] Margaret Cherche, of the
parish of St. Alphege, who died in 1486, desired to be buried
in the nave of the church of the Friars Minor before the
High Cross (i.e. the Rood) and she gave to the house 6s. 8d.
for her burial and a like sum to the warden and friars to
pray for her soul. [2] In the following year John Forde of
the parish of St. George in Canterbury directed that he
should be buried " within the church of the Friars Minor
in the north part of the church near the altar of St. Clement
there," and he left to the friars 6s. 8d. for his burial and
3s. 4d. for five masses after his death. [3]   Milo Denne, of
St. Mary Bredman parish, who died in 1491, desired to
be buried in the friars' church " where the Warden and
convent decide " and left " to the high altar of the Friars
church 20d.," and 5s. to the friars for a mass of Requiem. [4]
Hamo Bele of Elham, who was twice mayor of Canterbury
in the second half of the fifteenth century and died in 1492,
directed that he should be buried in the middle of the nave
of the friars' church and that a tomb 3 feet high should be
set over him and Elizabeth his wife, and he gave 40s. to the
reparation of the church. [5]   John Martin, the elder, who is
described in his will dated 1496 as " dwelling within the
house of the Friars Minor of Canterbury," desired to be
buried in their church, to the high altar of which he left
6s. 8d. and to the friars a like sum for his burial. [6]   Richard
Martin, who was probably a brother of John and describes
himself as bishop in the Universal Church, desired to be
buried in the church of the Grey Friars in Canterbury,
where he was also apparently living at the time of his
death, as he gave to the house " my great bed that standeth
in the chapel chamber with all the apparel thereto and
also all the hangings of the same chamber " together with
a standing cup of silver, ten books and " my crysmatory
of silver and parcel gilt thereof and the case thereto as it is,"
the latter in consideration of a daily dirige and mass of
Requiem.   He also gave to the Canterbury Franciscans
" half my wheat left in their place " and his altar cloths, a
vestment, chasuble, two candlesticks of laton and two cruets
" belonging to the chapel of St. Saviour in their church." [7]
The testator died in November 1498, though his will was

[1] Consist. Court Cant., vol. 2, fo. 355.   [2] *Ibid.*, vol. 3, fo. 99.
[3] *Ibid.*, vol. 3, fo. 160.   [4] Archd. Cant. Wills, vol. 5, fo. 14.
[5] *Ibid.*, vol 5, fo. 16.   [6] *Ibid.*, vol. 6, fo. 10.
[7] Consist. Court Cant., vol. 7, fo. 81.

not proved until March 1502–03. Finally, in 1524, Alexander Elyothe, priest of the parish of St. Mildred, desired to be buried " before Our Lady altar in the Observant Friars " and left 10s. for his funeral and 20s. for two trentals of masses for his soul.[1] Others who directed that they should be buried in the church without any indication of the position were Thomas Ketcham (1478), John Baker (1495), Henry Ramsey (1500), Sybilla, daughter of Sir John Lewknor and wife of Sir William Scott of Scott's Hall, Brabourne (1528), and George Chadworth, rector of St. Nicholas Ringwold (1530), while among those who mention the churchyard or cemetery or merely the house in connection with their burial, are Richard Annesley (1484), Thomas Colman of Harrietsham (1503), John Marys of St. George's parish, Canterbury (1507), Arnold Fromvar or Fromere of St. Andrew's parish (1514), Peter William of St. Mary Bredman parish (1517), Elizabeth Master (1522), Katherine Downe of All Saints parish (1531), Anne Culpeper (1532) and John Dibden of St. Mary Bredman parish (1538).[2]

This list can be supplemented by the names recorded by Weever, who, after referring to the foundation of the house, states that " herein were sometimes interred Bartholomew, Lord Badlesmere, steward of the household to King Edward the second, who . . . payed the due price of his disloyaltie upon the gallowes Ann. 1321. Sir Giles Badilsmere or Badlesmere, knight his sonne : Dame Elizabeth Lady of Chilham : Sir William Manston knight, Sir Roger Manston his brother : Sir Thomas Brockhall knight and Lady Joane his wife : Sir Thomas Brockhall knight sonne to the said Sir Thomas and Lady Editha his wife : Sir Falcon Playferer knight ; Sir Thomas Dayner knight, Lady Alice of Maryms : Lady Candlin : Sir Alan Pennington of . . . in the countie of Lancaster knight who comming from the warres beyond the seas died in this citie. Lady Ladrie of Valence : Sir William Trussell, Sir William Baloyle,[3] Sir Bartholomew Ashburnham knights, and Sir John Montenden knight ; and a Frier of this house ; lie all here interred." [4]

At the end of the fifteenth century the Canterbury house

[1] Archd. Cant. Wills, vol. 16, fo. 3.
[2] For extracts from these wills, see Cotton, *op. cit*, Appendix III.
[3] A deed dated 8 June 1312 between the Warden and Friars Minor and the Prior and Chapter of Christ Church relating to the burial of Sir William de Baliol is preserved in the muniments of the Dean and Chapter (Ch. ch. Cant. MSS. F. 152, printed in B.S.F.S., *Coll. Franc.*, vol. 2, p. 4.)
[4] Weever, *Anc. Funerall Monuments*, p. 238.

underwent a change of status and with the houses at New-castle and Southampton was transferred from the Con-ventuals to the Observants. The resolution authorizing this change which was largely brought about by the influence of the King was adopted at a provincial chapter held in London in 1498.[1] The history of the transfer is obscure, but it seems to have had little immediate effect on the friars, who for the most part probably remained on under the new conditions. With the suppression of the Observants in 1534, however, the fortunes of the Canterbury house began to decline. It was in that year that their Warden, Richard Risby, and a former Warden, Hugh Riche, were executed at Tyburn for complicity in the affair of the Holy Maid of Kent. Two other friars refused the oath of allegiance,[2] and were probably among those sent to the Tower in June of that year.[3] The house, however, continued under the rule of a conventual warden for four years, though little is recorded of its history during this period. It was surrendered to the Bishop of Dover in December 1538.[4] Neither the deed of surrender nor any inventory of the goods of the friary has survived, so that nothing is known of the inmates of the house or the extent of the buildings at that date.

The site was let to Thomas Spylman, a local receiver of the Court of Augmentations, in February 1539 at a rent of 40s. a year.[5] The reversion in fee was granted to him and his wife Isabella by letters patent dated 17 July 1539.[6] This grant expressly included " the whole church bell tower and cemetery." At the same time Spylman rendered an account of the property to the Exchequer, but this contains no further details concerning the buildings or lands.[7] In 1544 he sold the whole property to Thomas Rolf for £200 and the fine levied for effecting the transfer describes the property as " the site of the late house of Friars Minor with its appurtenances within the city of Canterbury and two

[1] " Grey Friars Chronicle," *Mon. Franc.* (R.S.), vol. 2, p. 182.
[2] *L. and P. Hen. VIII*, vol. 7, app. 27.
[3] *Ibid.*, no. 856.   [4] *Ibid.*, vol. 13(2), no. 1058.
[5] P.R.O. Augm. Off. Misc. Bks., vol. 211, fo. 40 ; *L. and P. Hen. VIII*, vol. 14(1), no. 1355 (p. 609).
[6] *L. and P. Hen. VIII*, vol. 14(1), no. 1354(40). The accommodation was apparently extensive, as in 1538 Archbishop Cranmer in a letter to Crom-weil had described it as " very commodious for my servant Thomas Cobham," for whom he desired a grant of the property (*L. and P. Hen. VIII*, vol. 13(2), no. 537), while John Bathurst, a wealthy clothier, who ultimately obtained the Black Friars for cloth-making, made every effort to obtain this property instead (*ibid.*, vol. 14(1), no. 423).
[7] P.R.O. Ministers Accounts, Hen. VIII, no. 1756, m. 72d.

messuages two orchards two gardens three acres of land
ten acres of meadow and four acres of pasture with their
appurtenances in the parishes of All Saints St. Peter St.
Mildred and St. Margaret in the said city."[1] Rolf sold
the property in February 1565–66 to William Lovelace and
others[2] and it remained in the possession of his family
until the death of his son in 1629. Its subsequent history
is given by Dr. Cotton.[3]

DESCRIPTION

The only surviving building is the beautiful thirteenth-
century structure spanning a branch of the Stour. It is
constructed of flint and stone with ashlar dressings and with
later repairs and additions carried out in red brick. The
longitudinal walls on either side of the stream are built on
solid foundations of calcareous tufa, which also occurs elsewhere in the retaining walls of the river banks. Each cross
wall is carried on two pointed arches springing from the
wall abutment on either side and supported on a central
circular shaft with moulded capital rising from the bed of
the stream. There is nothing to indicate the nature of
the bases of the shafts if these exist, as only the upper
parts are visible owing to the river bottom having risen
considerably since medieval times.

The building itself had suffered much alteration, particularly with regard to its internal arrangements, during its
use as a dwelling house, and·later as a prison, but in 1919
the then owner, Major H. G. James, had these additions
removed and the building carefully restored as nearly as
possible to its original condition.[4] In its present state it
consists of two storeys each divided into two rooms of
unequal size by an original timber framing. The ground
floor is entered from either bank by doorways which, though
not original, probably indicate the positions of the original
entrances. These doorways lead into a passage between

[1] Feet of Fines, Hen. VIII, Bundle 53, file 383, no. 18, quoted by
Miss Churchill, *Arch. Cant.*, vol. 34, p. 91.
[2] In the following year they assigned it to Rolf's widow for life in
compensation for her dower, and her marriage to Erasmus Finch accounts
for Hasted's statement that the latter acquired it from Spylman. (See
Arch. Cant., vol. 34, p. 91, n. 2.)
[3] *The Grey Friars of Canterbury*, pp. 64–5.
[4] The report of Mr. R. H. Goodsall, A.R.I.B.A., the architect responsible for this work, is printed in *The Grey Friars of Canterbury, ut sup.*,
pp. 66–75, and I am indebted to this for much of what is stated in connection with this building.

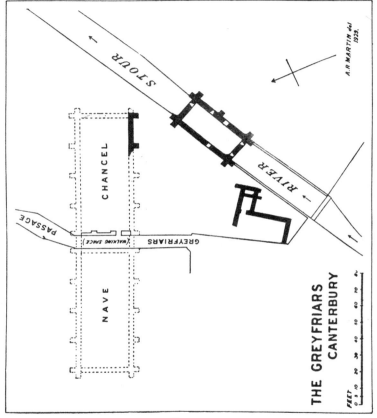

FIG. 1.

the original timber partition on the south-west and a wooden screen probably of eighteenth-century date on the north-east. The latter separates the passage from the principal room on the ground floor which was formerly lit by a large modern casement window in the south-east wall in addition

to the existing window in the gable end. The present single-light window of similar character to those on the upper floor was inserted in place of this casement in the restoration of 1919. The small room on the south-west of the passage is lit by two original single-light windows overlooking the river. This room was formerly used as a " lock-up " and in more recent times as a kitchen. It has now been restored and various modern fittings removed. In the floor is a trap-door of comparatively modern date which may have been used for fishing. The upper floor was presumably approached either by an outside staircase of which there is now no trace, or direct from the adjoining buildings which formerly abutted on both sides, as there is no indication of an original internal staircase. The existing wooden staircase was inserted in 1919 in place of a comparatively modern one of rough construction. The principal room on the upper floor is an apartment measuring 24 × 13 feet and is lit by a single lancet in the east gable end and on the south-east side by three narrow square-headed windows with the internal reveals splayed on the south-west side only, presumably for the purpose of obtaining the maximum of sunlight in the early morning. The two easternmost of these windows were opened out and partly reconstructed during the recent restoration when two casement windows of much later date were removed. During the course of this work it was discovered that the original sills of all the windows on this side had been about on a level with the existing floor and that these had been raised and the heads of the windows also raised, presumably when the present floor was inserted. The windows were accordingly restored to their former proportions and a small screen wall supporting a false sill built up in each window so as to obviate the somewhat awkward arrangement of having the sills on a level with the floor. The smaller room on the south-west is on a rather lower level and is approached by two steps. Its only light is from a narrow lancet in the gable end, the head of which is a reconstruction, as this had been destroyed by the insertion of a fireplace in the attic which formerly existed above. To the left of this window is an apparently original fireplace, one jamb of which breaks into the reveal of the adjoining lancet.

Prior to 1919 there was an attic storey over the entire building with two dormer windows on the south-east side. These have now been removed, the floors of the attics taken down and the plaster cleared away from the open timber roof. This work revealed that the roof was of two distinct periods, the line of division being marked by the original timber partition already referred to. The roof of the north-east part of the building was constructed of timbers of larger section than the presumably earlier work over the south-west room, and had apparently been re-used, as many of the mortice holes had not been cut for the present construction. Over the smaller room, on the other hand, the timbers were more decayed and had every appearance of being original. Externally, this portion of the roof is of a steeper pitch and springs from a lower wall plate. Below the wall plate of the later and larger section of the roof and also in the north-east gable end is a band of brickwork some 2 feet high, which suggests that at some period, probably not very long after the suppression, the walls of this portion of the building were raised and a new roof of old material added. The raising of the floor of the first floor and the consequent alteration in the windows may date from the same period.

The original purpose to which this building was devoted cannot be definitely stated. That it was the guest-house of the friary is not unlikely, though it may well have served at a somewhat later date as a lodging for the Warden. Its position to the east of the cloister and the presence of the contemporary fireplace in the smaller upper room perhaps support the latter use.

Of the other domestic buildings nothing now survives above ground. The foundations of a detached building with flint rubble walls and dressed stone quoins were found a short distance to the south-west of the existing structure a few years ago and these are indicated on the accompanying plan (Fig. 1). Early views show that there were formerly buildings on both banks of the stream abutting on the existing building, which thus served as a bridge connecting these two ranges. These were demolished in the early part of last century and it is uncertain how far they were of medieval date.

The church stood a short distance to the north of these buildings, but there is very little indication of its plan. About 27 feet of the south wall of the quire at the east end was uncovered about 1920. It was 2 feet 6 inches wide and had two buttresses with ashlar facings on its south side. The greater portion of the remainder of the foundations appear to have been entirely removed. There can be little doubt, however, that the existing lane which bounds the property on the west and is at this point about 9 feet wide, represents the original passage or " walking place " between the quire and the nave, and over which the steeple would

Plate 3

CANTERBURY, GREYFRIARS FROM THE NORTH-EAST

have stood.[1] Built into the eastern wall of this passage at the point where it crosses the site of the church are the jambs of a central doorway or arch, 10 feet in width with single attached shafts and moulded bases. The capitals have gone, but the original height of the jambs was about 5 feet, the bases being now some 2 feet below the present ground level. Immediately to the south of these is a modern gate in the wall flanked externally by jambs of similar character with single attached shafts, two of which retain their original caps and bases (Plate 8B). These are on a higher level, the bases being raised about a foot above the present surface of the ground. This difference in level, coupled with the fact that the bases in several cases rest on a brick foundation, suggest that these fragments have been largely reconstructed and are not all *in situ*, but there can be little doubt that they formed part of a stone screen enclosing the " walking place " similar to that which appears to have formerly existed in the Grey Friars' Church at Reading.

The extent of the church can only be approximately estimated. The buttress at the south-east corner of the quire was within about 10 feet of the river bank. From this buttress to the east wall of the passage referred to above the distance is 77 feet, which may thus be taken as the length of the quire. Its width, assuming the existing jambs of the arch at the west end were placed centrally in its western wall, was 27 feet. These dimensions correspond fairly closely with those of a normal aisleless quire of a late thirteenth- or early fourteenth-century friars' church. Of the plan of the nave, the site of which is now occupied by the orchard on the west side of Grey Friars Lane, nothing is known, though this might possibly be recovered by excavation. It probably had aisles, though in the absence of evidence on this point these have not been shown on the plan. On analogy with other similar buildings it would have been at least as long as the quire, so that, allowing for the width of the " walking place " which probably corresponded approximately with that of the existing lane, the total length of the church must have been about 180 feet.[2]

[1] A tower appears in Braun and Hogenberg's plan of Canterbury in 1572, but as the church is shown as a cruciform structure it is probable that this is a purely conventional representation.
[2] This was small in comparison with the larger Franciscan churches, but may be compared with the slightly later church of the same order at Walsingham which had a total length of 198 feet.

Of the positions of the various altars and chapels very little can be said. The altar of St. Clement mentioned in the will of John Forde in 1487 [1] is stated to be in the north part of the church and probably stood in the nave to the right of the entrance to the "walking place." There is nothing to suggest the position of the chapel of St. Saviour mentioned in the will of Richard Martin in 1498.[2] The cloister lay presumably to the south of the nave, as the position of the river makes it improbable that it abutted on the quire. To the north of the church was the cemetery extending towards St. Peter's Street.

(2) CHICHESTER

HISTORY

The exact date of the arrival of the Franciscans in Chichester is unknown, but it was probably shortly before 1242 when they received a grant of fuel from the King.[3] The site chosen was not that upon which the later buildings were erected, but was situated a little way to the south between St. Martin's Square and Little London, where St. Mary's Hospital now stands. This first site was soon enlarged by a gift of a close of land from Richard Earl of Cornwall and King of the Romans, who, like his brother Henry III, was a great patron of the Franciscans. This gift received the King's confirmation on 26 December 1252.[4] In the same year the house is mentioned in the will of Richard de la Wyche, Bishop of Chichester, who bequeathed his annotated book of psalms and 20s. to the friars. Whether the original site was found to be too restricted or what caused the friars to move is unknown, but at some date prior to October 1269 they received from their patron, the Earl of Cornwall, who was owner of the city and its liberties by virtue of a grant from Henry III, the site of the old castle (*vetus castellarium*) of Chichester in the north-east angle of the Roman town. The grant was confirmed by Henry III on 5 October 1269.[5] The old site passed into the hands of Henry de Chikehill, who, shortly before 1282, appears to have granted it to the Austin Friars of London. This was, however, disallowed on the ground that the establishment of a house of Austin Friars so near the Friars

---

[1] *Ante*, p. 46.   [2] *Ibid.*   [3] *C.C.R. 1242–47*, p. 424.
[4] *C.P.R. 1247–58*, p. 168.   [5] *C.P.R. 1266–72*, p. 369.

Minor would infringe the latters' privileges,[1] and accordingly the property was granted to the prior and brethren of the hospital of St. Mary, who were licensed to retain it on 4 November 1285.[2]

In the meantime, the new site which was already enclosed by the City Wall on the north and east had been adapted from its original purpose to that of the friary. The castle keep, a massive earthen mound, still in part surviving, was allowed to remain, and the new buildings were laid out in the eastern part of the area while the whole property was ultimately enclosed by a precinct wall on the south and west boundaries along the line of the present Priory Road, which itself probably indicates the limit of the outer bailey of the castle. The precinct then formed is now represented by the Priory park recreation ground and is approximately four acres in extent. There appears to be no record of any subsequent alteration or enlargement of the boundaries, which have remained practically unchanged to the present day.

References to the buildings themselves are few. The church was probably the first important building to be begun and the quire at least seems to have been substantially completed by 1282, for on Sunday, 25 May, in that year, Archbishop Peckham is recorded to have held an Ordination in the church of the Friars Minor at Chichester.[3] The church, according to Dugdale and Parkinson,[4] was dedicated to St. Peter, but this seems doubtful, as it is referred to as the church of St. Francis in the Obituary Roll of Richard Ebchester,[5] and in the will of John Hilly mentioned below. No record of the actual progress of the building seems to have survived and it is not until a much later date that some small light on its plan may be gained from the records of burials and contemporary wills. On 14 September 1314 Bishop Kellawe issued a letter of indulgence " pro anima dominae Johannae de Wyvonia cujus corpus in ecclesia Fratrum Minorum apud Cycestriam Cycestrensis diocesis requiescit humatum.'' [6] In 1457 John Hilly

---

[1] *Reg. Episc. Joh. Peckham* (R.S.), p. 365. It is interesting to note that the number of Friars Minor in Chichester dropped from 40 in 1285 and 1290 to 27 in 1297, possibly owing to the increasing counter-attraction of the Dominicans who had arrived in Chichester a few years before 1280.

[2] *C.P.R. 1281–92*, p. 197.

[3] *Reg. Epist. Joh. Peckham*, (R.S.), p. 1029.

[4] *Collectanea Anglo-Minoritica* (1726), Part II, p. 14.

[5] Surtees Soc., vol. 31, no. 543.

[6] *Regist. Palat. Dunelm* (R.S.), vol. I, p. 605.

desired to be buried in the chapel of St. Mary in the conventual church of St. Francis in Chichester and that a stone should be placed over his tomb, and he gave the friars 10s. on the day of his burial.[1] Again, in 1502, Richard Howyke of the parish of St. Peter-the-less, in Chichester, directed that he should be buried in the chapel of St. Katherine within the church and the Friars Minor, to whom he gave 6s. 8d.[2] In 1510 Richard Holte, Mercer of Chichester, desired to be buried near the entrance to the chancel of the church of the Friars Minor on the right-hand side of the said chancel,[3] while in 1512 Lady Maud Roos, widow of Sir Henry Roos, wished to be buried " in the quere " of the church of the Grey Friars to whom she forgave a debt of £7 6s. 8d.[4] In 1523 Agnes Wulgar desired to be buried " before Saint Fransys the space of X fote from him nye unto the wall of the north syde of ther wher my late hosband maister Thomas Wulgar lyth." [5] Finally, Richard Barnam directed that he should be buried " at the graye freres in Chichester " in 1525 without indicating the position.[6]

The house, together with that of the Dominicans in Chichester, was surrendered on 8 October 1538, the deed being signed by the warden and six friars. Almost the only evidence for the extent of the domestic buildings is contained in the detailed inventory which was prepared by the Crown Commissioners and is annexed to the deed of surrender.[7] This mentions the quire and two bells in the steeple, the cloister with " a fair laverys and a conduit coming to it," a vestry, and an ostre (guest house) " well syleyd," a parlour " well syleyd and benched," a brewhouse, a library with " four and a half new stalls with divers old books and a new press with almers for books " and a frater with 7 tables and 7 forms. The whole house was " new syleyd about the windows and all the windows well glazed." The mention of a library is unusual, though this is known to have existed in several Franciscan houses.[8]

The lead on the buildings was separately listed as fol-

---

[1] P.C.C. " Stokton," fo. 73b.   [2] P.C.C. " Blamyr," fo. 104.
[3] P.C.C. " Fetiplace," fo. 1.   [4] P.C.C. " Fetiplace," fo. 21.
[5] Chichester Consist. Court, vol. II, fo. 79b.
[6] P.C.C. " Bodfeld," fo. 38. These are the only testamentary references to the church or buildings of this house which have been noted. Others doubtless exist in the unprinted wills of the Chichester and Lewes Consistory Courts.
[7] Printed in full in *Sussex Arch. Coll.*, vol. 44, p. 71. See also *L. and P. Hen. VIII*, vol. 13(2), no. 562.
[8] e.g., London, Oxford and Hereford.

Plate 4

CHICHESTER, QUIRE OF GREY FRIARS' CHURCH FROM THE NORTH-EAST

lows : " The greyfreres in Chichester, a porch at the parler dore leade with divers gutters and a goodly conduyt leade." [1]

The property, " with orchards gardens cemetery and other waste lands containing 4 acres," was at first let at a yearly rent of 26s. 8d., but in 1541 the whole site with all the buildings was sold to the Mayor and citizens of Chichester, the furniture (utensilia) which had not apparently been removed being reserved to the Crown. [2] Its subsequent history has been fully dealt with elsewhere, [3] and it is only necessary to mention that the quire of the church, which is the only part of the structure now surviving, appears to have been immediately converted into the Guildhall of the city and it continued in use as an Assize Court and Sessions House until 1851, since when it has been unoccupied. The remainder of the site including the cloister and buildings were let by the corporation in 1544 to G. Gorringe, and subsequently a 999 years lease was granted to P. Williams. In 1790 this lease became vested in Admiral Frankland, who removed what then remained of the conventual buildings and erected a large house, known as the Priory Park Mansion, in their place. This house, in its turn, disappeared about 1820, when the property passed to the family of the Duke of Richmond, who presented it to the City in 1918.

DESCRIPTION

The only surviving portion of the friary buildings, apart from a detached fragment mentioned later, is the quire of the church which will now be described. It is a long unaisled apartment measuring internally 82 × 31 feet. The walls are of flint rubble with a certain amount of Pulborough and Midhurst stone and dressings of Caen and Binstead stone in the windows and buttresses. The building which has recently undergone a complete restoration is lighted on the north and south by five windows in each wall separated externally by stepped buttresses. [4] Each window is of two lights divided by a chamfered mullion with a plain quatrefoil in the head. Externally the jambs and mullions have a simple chamfer and internally the rear

[1] P.R.O., Treasury of Receipt Misc. Books, vol. 153, fo. 7.
[2] P.R.O., Ministers Accounts Hen. VIII, no. 3677, m. 15d.
[3] *Sussex Arch. Coll.*, vol. 51, pp. 30–6.
[4] These windows were until recently partially bricked up, but the filling was removed in 1934.

arches are deeply splayed and have hood moulds which are continued as a string-course throughout the length of the building. The great east window is of a slightly earlier type consisting of five slender lancet lights incorporated under a two-centred outer arch and divided internally by nearly detached circular shafts of bonded courses of stone with moulded capitals and bases. The two outer lancets have cinquefoil cusped heads of fifteenth-century date, which replaced the tops of the original lancets when an alteration in the angle of the roof necessitated a curtailment of their height. The effect of this alteration is clearly seen on the exterior. It appears to have also involved the removal of a parapet from the north and south walls, as one of the corbels of the corbel-table of this parapet still survives on the north side. The lower part of the east window was until recently bricked up and in Grose's view published in 1758 it is shown as completely blocked.

The present west wall together with the two adjoining buttresses are of post-suppression date and the two-light window and doorway therein were probably removed from the destroyed nave. The former is of similar character to those on the north and south sides, while the doorway has a two-centred outer arch with a segmental hollow-chamfered rear arch on plain chamfered jambs. The west wall blocks and partially obscures the chancel arch which spans the whole width of the chancel and is still intact beneath the later filling. It is of three chamfered orders supported on triple clustered shafts beneath a common abacus. The centre shaft which is partially visible from the inside has a broad fillet on its rectangular face and the side ones are circular. In general character as well as in its unusual span, which is approximately 24 feet, the chancel arch at Chichester bears an obvious similarity to that in the same position in the remains of the Grey Friars church at Winchelsea, with which it may be closely dated.

Of the plan and extent of the nave there is very little evidence. There can be little doubt, however, that the existing building extended several bays to the west,[1] and

---

[1] It is possible though perhaps improbable that the nave was never completed as was almost certainly the case at Lincoln. There is no mention of it in the suppression inventory which is otherwise unusually complete in its reference to the buildings, though this may merely indicate that there was nothing in the nave which the commissioners considered worthy of notice.

the fact that one jamb of a window on the north side still
survives in the fragment of wall to the west of the chancel
arch seems to imply that there was no aisle on this side.
A curious feature of this window is that its surviving jamb
is splayed outwards with its inner edge actually abutting
on the respond of the chancel arch. It is difficult to suggest a reason for this very unusual arrangement which
must have weakened the abutment of the chancel arch,
though it may perhaps be accounted for by a change of
plan during the progress of the building. That such a
change did in fact take place and that the existing chancel
arch was an afterthought is reasonably clear. Not only

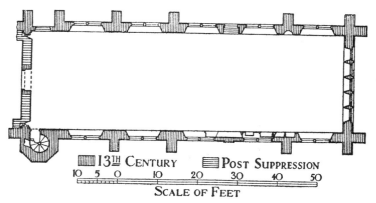

13TH CENTURY   POST SUPPRESSION

10   5   0   10   20   30   40   50

SCALE OF FEET

FIG. 2. Grey Friars, Chichester. Ground plan of quire.

is the hood moulding over the door to the stair turret on
the south side cut into by the responds of this arch, but
it is apparent that the massive buttress which supports
it on the north-west is an addition, as the moulded drip-
stone over the exterior of the north-west door is continued
behind the buttress and can be seen protruding on the
west side. That the chancel arch was inserted, however,
before the building was finished is implied by the fact that
the string course connecting the hood moulds of the side
windows forms a continuous moulding above the capitals
of the shafts of the chancel arch, while a second string
at a lower level is continued as bands round the shafts
themselves, thus proving them to have been substantially
of one build with the rest of the structure.

F

On analogy with other friars' churches, the steeple which is mentioned in the suppression inventory would have stood over the western bay of the chancel. It can scarcely have been more than a timber structure owing to the width of the chancel arch and the unusual narrowness of the western bay which must have been separated from the quire by a screen, against which the quire stalls were returned, as there is no indication of a masonry wall. From the passage thus formed access to the cloister on the north was obtained by means of a door which still survives, though now blocked up. Opposite this door in the south wall is another door with a two-centred hollow chamfered arch and plain chamfered jambs resting on moulded stops, which opens into a semi-octagonal stair turret projecting from the south wall. This turret which is approached from the interior only is constructed of flint rubble with quoins of Binstead stone and faced internally with Pulborough stone. It is lighted by two small rectangular slits, one above the other, in its southern face. At a height of 9 feet 4 inches from the original ground level a door 2 feet wide and 6 feet 2 inches high opens westward into a short length of passage constructed in the surviving fragment of the nave wall on this side, which is thickened to receive it by means of a corbelling out of the upper part on the exterior. This curious arrangement is difficult to explain but possibly represents what remains of an approach from the stair turret to a rood loft in front of the chancel arch. The upper part of the stair turret which is now roofed with Horsham slates is gone,[1] but it presumably originally gave access to the parapet referred to above as well as to the steeple and bells. Its position, which may be compared with the similar turret at Winchelsea, prevented the " walking-place " serving as a means of communication between the cloister and the outer world, as was usual in friars' churches of the following century.

The interior of the building is now cleared of modern obstructions and affords a remarkable example of the spaciousness of a Franciscan church even at this comparatively early date. The ground level, to judge from the position of the bases of the shafts of the chancel arch, is about 1 foot 8 inches above the original floor, though at the east end this was probably raised by means of steps to approximately its present level. The surviving fittings

---

[1] Twenty-nine steps survive above which the newel is broken off.

Plate 5

CHICHESTER, GREY FRIARS' CHURCH, INTERIOR

have been somewhat damaged during the various vicissi-
tudes through which the building has passed, but there
remain in the south wall triple sedilia [1] with trefoil-headed
canopies supported on nearly detached circular shafts of
late thirteenth-century date and to the west of these is an
aumbry with a two-centred head and attached shafts in
its jambs. Immediately to the west of the latter are the
somewhat mutilated remains of a handsome tomb recess [2]
with a wide moulded arch supported on short attached
shafts with moulded caps and bases and surmounted by the
remains of a gabled canopy pierced with a trefoil and terminating in a finely carved finial.[3] In the north wall is a
niche probably for a statue, and in the east wall beneath
the east window on the south side is a triple niche with
deep hollow chamfers on the arches and jambs which may
have served as a piscina (Plate 5).

With regard to the date of the structure, there seems no
reason to doubt the historical evidence which implies that
it was erected in the twelve years between 1269, when the
new site was acquired, and 1282, when the ordination service
took place within its walls. The fact that the east window
with its fully developed lancets and banded shafts is still
in the purely Early English style while the smaller windows suggest the beginnings of a transition to the Decorated
style can be explained sufficiently on the grounds that the
builders hesitated to employ the newer methods of construction in a window of the size of the former and need
not, as some writers have stated, imply any unusual delay
in the progress of the work.

It remains to consider the position of the cloister, a part
of which was incorporated in the house demolished in 1790
(Plate 6A). In the north wall of the quire between the second
and third windows from the east is a blocked doorway with
a segmental head and an external weathering which indicates the former abutment of a low gabled building or
porch. If this was the door into the eastern alley of the

---

[1] The base of the sedilia is 2 feet 2 inches and of the piscina 3 feet
from the present ground level. The former have a depth of 13½ inches and
a width of 3 feet 1 inch.

[2] A tradition that the Fitzalan monument in the north aisle of the
Cathedral church was removed from this recess does not seem to be supported by any evidence. This monument was almost certainly removed
from Lewes priory at the suppression.

[3] A modern door formerly existed in the back of this recess, but it has
been removed at the recent restoration and the external buttress at this
point replaced.

cloister as is usually stated, its position in relation to the
western cloister doorway implies a cloister measuring only
55 feet from east to west, unless this overlapped the nave,
an arrangement which, though common in Ireland, is seldom
found in England.   Moreover, the position of the remains
of the cloister which survived until 1790, although now
difficult to determine precisely, can scarcely be reconciled
with a cloister of this dimension on the north of the quire.
These remains consisted of three bays of the northern alley
of the cloister with three windows each of three lights
beneath four-centred main heads overlooking the cloister
garth (see Plate 6A).   The house in which they were incorporated stood to the north of the site of the nave of the
friars' church, and assuming the remains were *in situ* they
seem to imply a cloister in the more normal position abutting on the nave.   It is thus possible that the easternmost
of the two surviving doorways communicated with a vestry,
a not infrequent addition in the fourteenth and fifteenth
centuries, while on the other hand there may have been a
second and smaller cloister abutting on the quire as in the
recently discovered example at Lichfield.   In the latter case
the absence of any weather moulding on the north wall of
the quire coupled with the weatherings over the doorways
indicate that the cloister was separated from the quire
by an open court, as at London, Walsingham and elsewhere,
with covered passages communicating with the doorways,
an arrangement which is an almost necessary assumption
on account of the lowness of the sills of the windows of
the quire.
    The only fragment of the domestic buildings now sur-
viving is the north-east corner of a building standing about
180 feet to the north of the site of the nave.   The building
ran north and south and must have been about 25 feet wide.
Its length cannot be determined.   In the east wall is the
lower portion of a window, and to the east of this at a lower
level a doorway 2 feet 6 inches wide which must have given
access to an external staircase, as it is about 7 feet from the
ground.   That the building was divided into two storeys
is indicated by an offset in the surviving portion of the
east wall at a height of 6 feet 6 inches from the present
ground level.   The lower portion can have been little more
than cellars approached from the east by low and wide
arches, one of which survives in the east wall, though now
blocked up.   On the upper floor one jamb of a window

Plate 6

A. CHICHESTER, OLD HOUSE INCORPORATING PART OF THE GREY FRIARS'
CLOISTER, DEMOLISHED 1790

B. WINCHELSEA, QUIRE OF GREY FRIARS' CHURCH FROM THE SOUTH-EAST

on the east side remains. That this building was the hos-picium or guest-house is not improbable, as it clearly formed no part of the claustral range.

(3) COVENTRY

HISTORY

It seems probable that this house owed its foundation to Randulph de Blundevill, Earl of Chester, on whose Manor of Cheylesmore in the south-west part of the city the buildings were erected. It is not, however, until 1234, two years after Randulph's death, that the house is first mentioned. In that year Henry III granted the friars timber from Kenilworth woods for making shingles to cover their oratory or church.[1] The Cheylesmore property after Randulph's death passed to Hugh de Albini, Earl of Arundel, and subsequently to Roger de Montalt (or Mold) by virtue of his marriage with Cicely, daughter and co-heir of the Earl of Chester. Roger and Cicely when alienating part of their Coventry property about 1250 expressly excepted the dwelling-house of the Friars Minor by the park of Cheilesmore.[2] That the de Montalt family were closely associated with the friary in which several of their members were buried is shown by an early sixteenth-century list of the names of the founders of this house, in which Roger de Montalt is described as the third founder after the Earl of Chester and Hugh de Albini.[3] On 18 August 1289 Roger de Montalt, grandson of the first Roger, was licensed to assign to the friars certain tenements which he had acquired by exchange from the prior and convent of Coventry for the enlargement of their house,[4] and two days later the friars were authorized to close the way leading from Kenilworth to Coventry with the same object, on condition that they made another way of the same breadth on ground which belonged to the said Roger, and which he had given for the purpose.[5] The monks of Coventry priory, who appear to have regarded the friars with some jealousy, at first opposed this grant, but apparently gave way when, in a letter to the prior and chapter dated 30 June 1289, Arch-

[1] Dugdale, *Antiq. of Warwickshire* (1730) I, 182 ; *Monasticon* vi. p. 1533.
[2] P.R.O. Anc. Deeds A. 4464 (Cat., vol. 3, p. 70) : *Monasticon*, vol. 3, p. 181.
[3] B.M. Harl. MS. 6033. See Appendix I.
[4] *C.P.R. 1281–92*, p. 320.   [5] *Ibid.*

bishop Peckham supported the friars' cause.[1] During the reign of Edward III the Cheylesmore property passed into the hands of the King's mother, Isabella, ultimately becoming the property of successive Princes of Wales as part of the duchy of Cornwall. This was of importance to the friars, as the owners of the manor always appear to have regarded the friary as under their direct patronage.[2] Accordingly in December 1358 the friars received a grant of " as much stone in the Prince's (i.e. the Black Prince) park of Cheilesmore as they need for the works at their mansion with free ingress and egress for their workmen and the carriage of the stone and also of soil for the walls and plaster and that they might have a postern from their said house into the park for the recreation of the sick friars who were not to pass beyond the quarry." [3] This grant was inspected and confirmed by Richard II in November 1378.[4]

Later references to the house apart from those contained in wills are not numerous. Provincial chapters were held there in 1420,[5] 1472, 1489 and 1505, and on the latter occasion the friars went in procession to the Whitefriars and thence to the Benedictine priory where Dr. Standish, who was probably elected provincial minister at this chapter, preached a sermon.[6] Early in the fifteenth century William Norton, who is described [7] as " learned in philosophy and theology," was a friar here and at least one of his writings survives.[8] At a somewhat later date John Bredon, S.T.P., another friar of the Coventry house, came into some prominence and is frequently referred to in the *Coventry Leet Book*,[9] the City Annals,[10] as well as in the Public Records.[11]

[1] *Reg. Epist. Peckham* (R.S.), vol. III, pp. 962–3.
[2] A letter from Isabella to the city on behalf of the Coventry Franciscans is preserved. See T. Sharp, *History and Antiquities of the City of Coventry*, ed. W. G. Fretton (1871), p. 197.
[3] *C.P.R. 1377–81*, p. 286.   [4] *Ibid.*
[5] C. Davenport, *Hist. Minor.* (1665), vol. I, pp. 133–4 ; *Bullarium, Franciscanum*, vol. VII, no. 1466. (Robert Wellys was elected provincial at this chapter.)
[6] Coventry City Annals quoted in T. Sharp, *History of Coventry* (1871), *op. cit.*, p. 201. Standish was provincial in May 1506 : *Collectanea Top. et Geneal.* ed. Nichols, vol. I, p. 72.
[7] J. Pits, *De illustribus Angliae Scriptoribus* (1619) p. 557.
[8] Repertorium Liræ. MSS. Merton Coll. 12 ; Exeter Coll. 16 ; Lincoln Coll. 69.
[9] *Coventry Leet Book, 1420–1555*, ed. M. D. Harris (E.E.T.S.), Orig. Ser. Nos. 134–135, 138, 146.
[10] This seventeenth- and eighteenth-century collection of records of which several versions exist, although quoted occasionally below is of only secondary historical value for this period.
[11] *C.P.R. 1441*, p. 545 : *Early Chancery Proceedings*, vol. I, p. 185.

A number of documents concerning a dispute in 1446 in which he was involved are preserved in the British Museum, and in the Bodleian and elsewhere.[1]

Bequests to the friars are numerous as is to be expected in a town of the wealth of Coventry at this period, but they are for the most part of small sums and, with the few exceptions mentioned below, afford no information as to the plan or extent of the buildings. In 1369 Katherine, wife of Thomas Beauchamp, Earl of Warwick, bequeathed to the friars £10.[2] In 1493, Thomas Bradmedow, draper, left 40s. to the reparation of the church.[3] By his will dated 23 March 1518, John Haddon, draper, of Coventry, bequeathed to the Grey Friars 20s. for two trentals, and his will continues :

" Also I will the said Feliship of Drapers geve yerely to the gray freres in Coventre on saint Giles day vs. and the said gray freres to kepe a masse on the said day of saint Giles and the dirige on the evyn for me and my wyfe and all my frends soules And the kepers of the drapers for the yere beinge to be at the said masse and they to see a frere say daily masse for me and my wyfe in saint Anne's chapell for ever in the said freres as they be bounde for the reparacion made by me in the said freres church as it appereth by a pair of Indentures made betwene me and the Wardeyn and Convent of the said freres."[4]

Four years later Henry Pisford, of Coventry, grocer and merchant of the staple at Calais who was also a benefactor of Fords Hospital in the town, refers in his will to the friars' church. After desiring to be buried " in the gray freres church yarde before the Rode chapell," he directed that as soon as may be after his decease there be said for him five trentals in the worship of the five wounds of our Lord and that his executors should cause to be made five lights to be set before the picture of our Lord in the Grey Friars' church, and he bequeathed 100 marks to enlarge the Rood Chapel there " that people might have more room to see the devotion therein."[5] The reference to the Rood Chapel is of interest as the City Annals record in 1520, " This year was the Rode sett at the Grey Fryers

[1] B.M. Cotton MS. Cleopatra. E iii, fo. 90. (These are printed in full in Sharp's *History of Coventry, op. cit.,* pp. 206–7.) See also MSS. Bodley 692 (2508) ; Lincoln Cathedral, 108.
[2] *Test. Vet.,* p. 78. Dugdale *Warwickshire* (1730) I, 397.
[3] V. C. H., *Warwickshire,* II, p. 104. [4] *Ibid.*
[5] P.C.C. " Bodfelde," 37.

and the new Chappell made first in the churchyard." Further information regarding this chapel is contained in a deed preserved in the City records. This is dated 17 June 1532 and is made between William Wygston of Leicester and Thomas Whyttel of Shepey, the executors of Henry Pisford, and certain other persons of the one part and master William Wall, D.D., Master of the Grey Friars in Coventry, John Stafford, the Warden and the convent of the same of the other part, and recites that William Pisford the elder and Henry his son, merchants of Coventry, had in their lifetime given 400 marks and upwards for the building of a chapel in the churchyard of the said friars which is now called the Rood Chapel and had done many other charitable deeds to the said Convent. In consideration of these benefactions the friars covenanted that a priest of their house should daily say mass in the said chapel or else in the church of the Grey Friars if there should be any impediment to the saying of mass in the chapel, for the souls of William Pisford the elder, his two sons William and Henry and other named persons. The document also provides for an obit to be kept yearly about the 15th of May and contains detailed provisions regarding the saying of the mass before which a bell was to be rung " to stir the people to come to it." Finally the deed was to be read openly twice a year on the Vigil of Allhallows and " on the day of search when all the friars are bound to be afore the Chapter Provincial." Upon the execution of the deed Pisford's executors gave £10 for ornaments for the church.[1]

In addition to bequests in wills the friars received periodical support from the city guilds. The accounts of the Smiths' Company show that in 1449 and subsequent years the Company gave annually to the friars " Sawtfysch and stokefysh," the cost of which in 1449 was 9*d*.[2] Similarly 20*s*. was paid yearly by the Trinity Guild to the warden of the friars for wine and wax, and the accounts of the Corpus Christi Guild for 1521 and 1531 contain similar records of small money payments.[3]

It is in connection, however, with the records of burials that the principal information regarding the friars' church is to be derived. It would seem that among Franciscan churches in England, that at Coventry was second only to

---

[1] Original deed in the possession of the City Corporation, quoted in Sharp's *History of Coventry, op. cit.*
[2] T. Sharp, *History of Coventry, op. cit.*, p. 199.   [3] *Ibid.*, p. 200.

the great church in London in popularity as a place of burial for the wealthy, and although the records of these burials are by no means as complete as in the case of London, two documents have survived which throw an important light on the plan of the church. The first is an early sixteenth-century manuscript [1] obviously compiled for genealogical purposes which contains, among other material, lists of burials in the four houses of friars in London. Then follows " the names of the founders of the Friars Minor in Coventree " and the names of persons buried there. The Coventry list is divided into four sections according to the position of the tombs. In the first are the names of seven persons and their wives, who were regarded as founders, but it is not stated that they were all buried in the church. Roger de Montalt lay in the middle of the quire near the High Altar with his wife Cecily immediately on his left. Sir Thomas Hastings and Elizabeth his wife lay on the north side. In the next section are sixteen "names of other friends buried in the quire within the bottom step of the presbytery." Then follow the names of eleven persons buried in the chapel of the lords de Hastings and finally 127 names of other persons buried within the church, among whom were Henry de Vernoye, " founder of two places of friars in Ireland," Robert Fachaw or Fanchaw with Felice his wife " who gave the spring of Dodmanswell," John Warde, " the first mayor of Coventry," Henry Dodenhale who was Mayor in 1365 and Adam Botoner, who was several times Mayor in the last quarter of the fourteenth century and with his brother William built the great tower of St. Michael's Church close by. In all there were thus 158 persons whose names were presumably visible on the tombs in the church in the early part of the sixteenth century, apart from those " founders " who are not expressly stated to have been buried there. As no indication is given of the character or date of the tombs or monuments it is not possible to estimate their number with any certainty, but from the grouping of the names in the manuscript and on the assumption that a wife was buried with her husband and a child with its parents, the total number cannot have been far short of 100. That the list was not complete seems probable, as the names are for the most part of persons of some social importance, and it is therefore likely that the smaller memorials were overlooked by the compiler as of little genealogical interest.

[1] B.M. Harl. MS. 6033. See Appendix I.

One early burial of which there is no mention in the list is that of Sir Richard Mandeville, who in 1298 desired that his heart should be buried in the oratory of the Friars Minor in Coventry and left the residue of his property to be distributed by his executors between the friars and certain other persons.[1] In 1330 the body of Roger Mortimer, first Earl of March, who was hanged, drawn and quartered at Tyburn for complicity in the murder of Edward II, was apparently brought for burial to the Grey Friars at Coventry, for in November of the following year Joan, wife of Edmund Mortimer, the late Earl's second son, received a permit to take the body of the Earl from this church and convey it to Wigmore for reburial.[2] There are other instances of convicted traitors being buried at the Grey Friars. In 1487 the City Annals record that Thomas Harrington who claimed to be a son of the Duke of Clarence was captured at the battle of Newark and brought to Coventry, where he was beheaded " on the conditte by the bulle and was buried at the gray friers." Again in 1495 Sir Henry Mumford and Sir Robert Mallerie were beheaded for treason under Binley gallows, their heads being placed upon Bablake and the Grey Friars Gates and their bodies buried at the Grey Friars.[3] A few other references to the burial of persons not mentioned in the list are contained in contemporary wills. In 1512 Henry Smyth desired to be buried " in the churche of Saint Francis called the grey freres in coventre in or nygh unto the place before the high aulter and agenst or at the side of the toombe where my good father and mother with other my friends lye."[4] By his will dated 3 November 1519 John Hardwen of Coventry, draper, left £5 to the friars " to help them paye the dettes of the said howse and to every preest in the said freers 12*d*. and to every novys 6*d*.," and desired that he should be buried " within the gray freers of coventre in Saint Anneys Chappell " and that on the day of his burial the Abbott of Combe and four of his brethren should help to bear him, the abbott receiving for his labour " a coope of purpill velvet " and each of the four brethren 20*d*.[5] In August 1525 Peers Warter directed that he should be buried " in the churche of the freres mynor of coventre at the foot of Doctour

---

[1] Reg. Giffard Bishop of Worcester, fo. 445b.
[2] *C.P.R. 1330–34,* p. 213 ; *C.C.R. 1330–33,* p. 403.
[3] City Annals, quoted by Sharp, *op. cit.*
[4] P.C.C. " Holder," qu. 3.   [5] P.C.C. " Ayloffe," qu. 27.

Sandishe (*sic*) " and he gave 6*s.* 8*d.* for his burial, at which he desired that there be " 13 poor men to bere 13 tapers aboute my herse " and " oon frere to synge for my soule." [1]

The second document dealing with burials within the friars' church consists of a description of the Hastings chapel evidently written by someone who had seen it before the building was demolished. This manuscript, which is in French, was formerly in the collection of Sir Simon D'Ewes.[2] It was transcribed by Dugdale and first printed in his history of Warwickshire.[3] The Hastings family, who were descended through the female line from the Earls of Chester, had inherited part of the latter's extensive estates and appear to have been considerable benefactors of the Coventry Franciscans. The chapel contained two principal tombs, both of which appear to have borne recumbent effigies. On the first was that of Henry Hastings, the first baron, who died in 1268 with his wife Joanna, daughter of William 2nd Lord Cantelupe. The second bore the effigies of their son John, the 2nd Baron Hastings, who, according to the inscription thereon, died in 1312,[4] and his first wife, Isabella, daughter of William de Vallance and niece of Henry III, who died in 1305, together with their daughter Joanna, wife of William de Huntingfield. There appears to be no record of the building of this chapel, but unless the tomb of William Hastings was brought here from some other part of the church, its presence suggests that the building was erected about the middle of the thirteenth century. Its position in relation to the church seems to be fixed by the fact that it had a window on the north as well as two on the east side, which implies that it was on the north side of the quire. That it was in fact identical with the chapel of St. Nicholas mentioned below seems probable though it cannot be definitely proved.

The property of the friary was never extensive. In 1535 the royal commissioners recorded that " Friar John Stafford guardian of the house being examined on oath says that they have no lands nor tenements nor other

---

[1] P.C.C. " Bodfelde," qu. 37.

[2] The present whereabouts of this MS. is unknown to the writer.

[3] *The Antiquities of Warwickshire* (1656), p. 113 ; *ibid.*, 2nd edition (1730), vol. I. pp. 182–3. The translation printed in Appendix II below first appeared in Stevens' Supplement to the *Monasticon* (1722), vol. I, p. 138, and has been reprinted several times.

[4] He is stated to have been buried in the habit of the Friars Minor and was doubtless so represented on his tomb like the effigy of a man at Conington Hunts illustrated in R.C.H.M. (England), Hunts, pl. 115.

possessions nor revenues spiritual or temporal of any yearly value but only ' limitations ' in the country and uncertain charitable gifts of the people." [1]

The house was suppressed in October 1538. On 20 September the mayor and alderman wrote fo Cromwell that it was reported that the Grey Friars and White Friars in their town were to be suppressed. They pointed out that their churches could ill be spared, as in time of plague sick people resorted to them for divine service, that there were but two parish churches and if the sick went there the whole city would be infected ; they concluded by begging Cromwell to intercede with the King " that these two churches of friars remain, the religious persons thereof to be reformed at the King's pleasure." [2]   No notice was, however, taken of this request and the Greyfriars was surrendered to Doctor London on behalf of the King on 5 October 1538. The deed is signed by John Stafford, the guardian and ten others. [3] On 20 October the Mayor and aldermen wrote again to Cromwell complaining that, in spite of their previous request, the King's commissioner had defaced the church of the Grey Friars. [4] Two days later Dr. London himself informed Cromwell that, if he destroys the conduit of the late Grey Friars set almost a mile from the city which is better than that of the city and has a better head, much of the city shall lack water. [5] On 29 October he adds that he had " partly rased the Grey Friars because the poor people lay so sore upon it," but that he had done little to the White Friars. [6] In fact, the work of demolition appears to have been begun at once. In the City Chamberlain's accounts for 1539 occur several entries for expenses in carrying stone from the Grey Friars. [7] Early in the same year Dr. London notes : " It is expedient that I take down the lead of the Grey Friars church at Coventry and melt it in sows as also elsewhere for the poor people cut down the gutters and sheets of lead. I could sell the bells for 15s. a cwt. and so make ready money out of hand " ; and he adds, " At Coventry the grey friars church is covered with lead and the rest of the house is ruinous and covered with tile which would serve to repair the adjoining royal manor of Childesmore." [8]

[1] *Valor Ecclesiasticus* (*Rec. Com.*), vol. III, p. 57.
[2] *L. and P. Hen. VIII*, vol. 13(2), no. 394.   [3] *Ibid.*, no. 539.
[4] *Ibid.*, no. 650.   [5] *Ibid.*, no. 674.   [6] *Ibid.*, no. 719.
[7] T. Sharp, *History of Coventry, op. cit.*, p. 203.
[8] *L. and P. Hen. VIII*, vol. 14(1), no. 3.

There is no inventory of the possessions of this house appended to the Deed of Suppression, but its place is taken by a document of considerable interest, and of which no exact parallel exists for any other Franciscan house. It consists of a detailed survey of the church made with a view to ascertaining the amount of lead on its roof. The following is a transcript [1] :

" THE GREYE FRYERS CHURCHE OF COVENTRYE

The quere contaynythe in lengthe 36 yerdes and in bredthe 10 yerdes, all covered with ledde.
The lengithe of the roode chaple is 3 yerdes and the breddithe is 4½ yerdes, all covered with ledde.
The lengithe of saynt Nycholas chaple is 11¾ yerdes And the breddithe is 8 yerdes, all covered with ledde.
The lengithe of the northe valence is 11 yerdes and the bredithe is 7½ yerdes, all covered with ledde.
The lengithe of the sowthe valence is 9½ yerdes And the bredithe is 7¾ yerdes, all covered with ledde.
The lengithe of the bodye of the churche is 39½ yerdes and the bredithe is 10 yerdes, all covered with ledde.
The lengithe of the northe Ile is 31 yerdes and the bredithe is 5 yerdes all covered with ledde.
The lengithe of the sowthe Ile is 30¾ yerdes and the bredithe 4¾ yerdes all covered with ledde.
The hole churche ys newly covered all within thees 24 yeres, and all the hole howse besydes ys in moche ruyne, all covered thorowly with tile and nott worthe the stonding for any habitation. Adjoyning unto this fryery ys an old maner of the Kinges grace callyd Chyldesmore wher as they say of most noble memory Kinge Edwarde the 4th kept a parlyament. The hall is down butt many of the lodginges do stond and there ys a propre parke adjoynyng unto the same. Bycause the Kinges hignes hath as I here no convenyent lodging nye unto this cytie the tile of this olde fryery myght serve to repayer the sayd maner butt the tymbre of the howsyng is sterk nowgt. All the roff of the church ys very gudd tymbre.''

The evidence as to plan afforded by this document is considered below. Some indication of the extent of the domestic buildings of the friary at this time may be gathered from the accounts of John Foster, the local collector of the rents on behalf of the Crown.[2] The greater part of these

---

[1] P.R.O. Exch. Treasury of Receipt, Misc. Bks. 153, p. 72 ; cf. *L. and P. Hen. VIII*, vol. 13(2), no. 539.
[2] P.R.O. Ministers' Accounts, Hen. VIII, no. 7311. This account is printed in full in A. G. Little, *Studies in English Franciscan History* (1917), Appendix II, pp. 225–8. The accounts are continued annually until the sale of the property in 1542 (*ibid.*, nos. 7312–15).

had already been let before the suppression. All the buildings, houses, halls, parlours and chambers with their appurtenances within the precinct on the west of the cloister and stretching from the house or chamber called " le scolehouse " on the north to the chamber called " the lady Euyngherns chambre " on the south, with one garden and all lands lying between the said house and buildings and the stone wall of the city in breadth and length proceeding from the water conduit [1] at the west end to " les Garners " there, were held by Thomas Gregory, under a lease from the friars dated 10 August 1537, for a term of thirty years at a rent of 6s. 8d. A hall near Chellesmore within the precinct called " le Wardens chambre " and " le fryers orchard," with all fruit trees and ponds and a stable, were held by Thomas Downes for a term of fifty years under a lease granted by the friars in 1537 at a similar rent. When the first account was returned to the Court of Augmentations in 1539 the remainder of the property, consisting of the cemetery containing three roods with the cloister yard containing 20 perches, two gardens within the precinct, of which one lay southward to the east of the chancel of the church and contained 36 perches and the other lay to the south of the kitchen and contained 16 perches, and the rest of the site beyond the two gardens, cemetery and cloister, were also in the occupation of Thomas Downes under tenancies granted by George Gifford and Robert Burgoyne, the Crown officers into whose custody the property had been given at the dissolution. The total annual rent received from the property was 21s. 4d., from which was deducted 13s. 4d. handed to George Gifford, and 2s. each paid to the collector and his clerk, while 1s. 9d. was allowed to Gifford because the cemetery and garden was for a time unoccupied and a further 1s. 9d. towards his expenses before the dissolution of the house, leaving a net return of 6d. to be paid into the Exchequer. The cemetery, cloister yard and two gardens referred to above were granted to John Higford of Henwood, Warwickshire, on 10 February 1542 for a term of twenty-one years,[2] and on 29 July following the whole site, together with other properties, was sold for £1,378 10s. to the Mayor, bailiffs and commonalty of the city, subject, pre-

---

[1] The conduit apparently stood outside the city walls, as in 1578, the City Annals record that " the conduit without the Grey Friar Gate was brought within the gate and set over against the Red Lyon."

[2] P.R.O. Augm. Off. Misc. Bks. 214, fo. 17 ; *L. and P. Hen. VIII*, vol. 17, no. 1258.

sumably, to the various leases and tenancies then subsisting.[1]
The surviving buildings had apparently been separately
disposed of, for in the following April the Mayor and aldermen purchased on behalf of the city from William Neele,
" all tile tymber and stone and other stuff " on the buildings of the Greyfriars and on the churche and steple ther,"
excepting " the stone and other stuff of in and upon the
revestre and Chapter house ther," which Neele, who had
apparently purchased the buildings from the Crown surveyor,
expressly reserved.[2]

The demolition of the buildings proceeded slowly. In
1543 6s. 4d. was paid by the City for carrying 25 loads of
stone from the Grey Friars and similar payments occur in
1547 and 1562.[3] Eventually only the steeple of the church
remained. When, in April 1661, the Corporation sold to
Alderman Thomas Basnet the piece of ground called the
Grey Friars Churchyard and a barn standing thereon subject
to an annual fee farm rent of £5, they expressly reserved
" the steeple of stone and conduit called the Grey Friars
conduit with free liberty to repair and amend the same
and the Town wall." [4] The spire had been blown down
in 1551, and in 1607 certain repairs were undertaken by one
John Brookes. The subsequent history of the steeple can
be gathered from the city annals. In 1676 further repairs
were carried out and a gilt globe set on the top of the spire,
but in 1699 this was again blown down in a tempest. In
1739 considerable repairs were undertaken by Mr. Edward
Owen, a local attorney, at his own expense, " upwards of
eight yards " being rebuilt. The upper part of the spire
was again demolished in a storm in 1763 and was rebuilt
in 1771 and a gilt ball and vane placed on it. In 1830 the
present Christ Church was erected around the old steeple
which was presented by the Corporation for the purpose
and the new building was consecrated in July 1832.[5]

[1] *L. and P. Hen. VIII*, vol. 17, no. 556(21). The official " particulars "
for this grant (P.R.O. Partic. for Grants Hen. VIII, no. 321) are illegible.
[2] Original deed in possession of the City Corporation, printed in Sharp's
History of Coventry, op. cit., p. 203.
[3] Coventry City Chamberlain's accounts quoted in Sharp's *History
of Coventry, op. cit.*, p. 203.
[4] *History of Coventry, op. cit.*, p. 203.
[5] It may perhaps be mentioned here that the generally accepted
association of the Grey Friars of Coventry with the famous Corpus Christi
plays rests on very little authority. The fifteenth-century MS. of the
Ludus Coventriæ in the British Museum (Cotton MS. Vesp. D. VIII, edited
by Halliwell-Phillipps) was attributed by Dugdale and most later writers
to the Coventry Franciscans, but there is no real evidence for this and

DESCRIPTION

The precinct is now for the most part built over. The site was just within the city wall and a little to the east of the south gate of the city which, from its proximity to the friary, was known as the Grey Friars' Gate. It appears to have been bounded on the south-west by the city wall, on the north-west by Warwick Lane, which was then the principal entrance to the city from the south,[1] on the north-east by the lower part of Grey Friars' Lane, and on the south-east by a wall separating it from Cheylesmore Park. This area, which comprised about three acres, was cut in two by the construction of Union Street in 1820. In addition to the main site the friars owned an orchard outside the city wall where the Quadrant now is.

The sole remaining fragment of the buildings is the mid-fourteenth century steeple of the friars' church, which forms one of the three spires for which Coventry is famous. It is an octagonal structure of two stages, 96 feet in height excluding the spire and supported on parallel cross walls pierced by two main arches on the east and west which opened into the quire and nave in accordance with the normal arrangement in friars' churches, and surmounted by a lofty modern spire. The lower stage against which the line of the acutely pitched roofs of the nave and quire can still be seen on the exterior, is carried up from the rectangular substructure by means of corbelling supported on internal half-arches in each angle. This stage doubtless served as the ringing chamber as at present. It has solid walls pierced only by narrow slits on the north and south sides with wide internal splays. Above these slits on the interior is an open gallery encircling the Chamber in the thickness of the wall which must originally have communicated by doorways on the east and west with the space between the inner and outer roofs of the nave and quire. This gallery was lighted by four narrow loopholes now blocked up, and opens to the chamber by an arcade of twenty-four pointed arches—three in each wall—supported on slender shafts and each about 1 foot 3 inches wide.

still less for their ever having taken part in the plays themselves. The latter tradition, as has been pointed out by Dr. Craig (*Two Coventry Corpus Christi Plays*, E.E.T.S.), probably arose from the statement in some of the early annals that in 1493 the plays were acted " by the Greyfriars," where the intended meaning was on a site adjoining their house.

[1] Hertford Street is comparatively modern.

Plate 7

COVENTRY, GREYFRIARS' TOWER, *c.* 1800

The second stage was the bell chamber, the floor of which is supported by a corbel-table on a level with the string-course on the exterior. It is lit by four large Decorated windows, each of two lights, in the cardinal faces of the tower, while the solid alternate sides of the octagon are here decorated with blind arches representing windows of three lights with reticulated tracery in their heads. The circular stair turret on the north side of the tower is modern, but it appears to have replaced an earlier one in the same position, as the entrance to the ringing chamber in the east face of the tower is approached by an original passage in the thickness of the east wall from the top of the existing stair. The present parapet as well as the spire are entirely modern, the former having been apparently erected in the late eighteenth century in place of an earlier parapet of somewhat similar design, but with more slender finials at the angles (see Plate 8A).

The main arches which support the tower are 13 feet 6 inches wide and of four moulded orders each carried on attached shafts with bell-shaped capitals but no bases. The cross arches on the north and south are slightly higher and die into the main cross walls on either side. The area enclosed beneath the octagon now forms the chancel of the modern church, the eastern arch having been blocked, side walls erected outside the original lateral arches and the western arch partially masked by a stone screen of poor design.

During the excavations made in 1829–30 prior to the erection of the present church, a considerable portion of the walls of the friars' church seems to have been uncovered, but unfortunately no clear and accurate record of these discoveries has apparently been preserved.[1] A plan prepared from one made by William Reader in 1829 has been published,[2] but it seems probable that this was based rather on an attempted reconstruction from the measurements in the suppression survey than from measurements made on the spot.[3] There seems no justification therefore in

---

[1] William Reader's MSS. in the Coventry Public Library contain certain notes about the Grey Friars and the work carried out at this time (Reader MSS., vol. 14, ff. 90–138), but afford little assistance with regard to the plan.

[2] *Birmingham and Midland Institute Trans.*, vol. IX (1882), opp. p. 50. In spite of inquiries I have been unable to trace Reader's original plan.

[3] The survey, although then unpublished, was known to Reader, as he quotes from it in his MSS. (vol. 14, fo. 96).

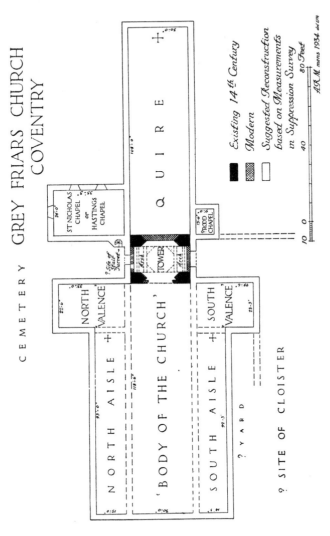

GREY FRIARS CHURCH
COVENTRY

CEMETERY

QUIRE

30'-0"

108'-0"

ST. NICHOLAS
CHAPEL
or
HASTINGS
CHAPEL

24'-0"

? Site of
Stair Turret

ROOD
CHAPEL

TOWER

NORTH
VALENCE

22'-0"

33'-0"

SOUTH
VALENCE

23'-3"

+

+

'BODY OF THE CHURCH'

NORTH AISLE

93'-0"

118'-9"

SOUTH AISLE

90'-3"

? YARD

? SITE OF CLOISTER

Existing 14ᵗʰ Century

Modern

*Suggested Reconstruction
based on Measurements
in Suppression Survey*

A.R.M. mens 1934 delin

0   10   40   80 Feet

FIG. 3.

placing too much reliance on this plan, especially as Reader's transcript of the survey does not appear to have been quite accurate, and in the preparation of the accompanying plan, the earlier plan has accordingly been ignored.

In any attempt to reconstruct the plan of the church the suppression survey is clearly of the utmost importance. Its measurements may be tabulated as follows :

				length.	breadth.
Quire	.	.	.	. 108 ft.	× 30 ft.
Nave	.	.	.	. 118 ft. 6 in.	× 30 ft.
North aisle	.	.	. 93 ft.	× 15 ft.
South aisle	.	.	. 92 ft. 3 in.	× 14 ft. 3 in.
North valence	.	.	. 33 ft.	× 22 ft. 6 in.
South valence	.	.	. 28 ft. 6 in.	× 23 ft. 3 in.
Rood chapel	.	.	. 9 ft.	× 13 ft. 6 in.
St. Nicholas' chapel	.	. 35 ft. 3 in.	× 24 ft.

It is at once apparent from these figures that the building consisted of an aisled nave and aisle-less quire with two chapels presumably on the north and south side of the quire respectively. The unusual features of the plan are the north and south " valences," which in view of their size were clearly important parts of the structure. The word " valence " is rarely met with as an architectural term and its exact significance is doubtful, but it appears, in friars' churches, to have normally denoted the space in front of the nave altars which would have been enclosed by a screen.[1] That this could not have been its meaning at Coventry is, however, apparent, not only from the size of the areas in question, but also from the fact that they had separate lead roofs. It is equally impossible to make the measurements suit the crossing or " walking-place " under the belfry which is not expressly referred to in the survey, presumably because it was not covered with lead. The inference therefore seems unavoidable that the term was used to denote the north and south arms of a transept whose average width was approximately 23 feet, and this is to some extent supported by the fact that the length of the nave is stated to exceed that of the aisles by approximately 25 feet, the assumption being that the former was measured from the western arch of the belfry and thus included the width of

[1] In 1519 William Aleyn desired to be buried at the Grey Friars in London " before the aulter of seynt Mighell within the valence of the same freers " (P.C.C. Bennett 32. See B.S.F.S. *Collectanea Franciscana*, vol. II, pp. 66, 119 and 126). The common altar, or altar of St. Michael, was the most southerly of the four altars in the eastern bay of the nave of the London church, which were screened off from the nave proper.

the transept. Some further corroboration of this and also
of the general accuracy of the measurements seems to be
afforded by the fact that the 9 inches by which the south
valence exceeded that on the north in width exactly corresponds with the difference between the length of the north
aisle and that on the south. The evidence, in fact, seems
to be sufficiently clear to justify the conclusion that the
church had a two-armed transept and was thus in this
respect, so far as surviving evidence can show, unique among
Franciscan churches in this country.[1]

Beyond this transept stood the belfry with the usual
passageway beneath and beyond this the quire, so that
the total length of the building must have been in the
neighbourhood of 248 feet, or rather more than that of
the neighbouring church of St. Michael, one of the largest
parish churches in England. The position of the nave is
to some extent fixed by Reader's statement that its north
wall, found during the excavations in 1829, was four feet
outside the present north wall of Christ Church.[2] Of the
position of the various chapels it is only possible to conjecture. In addition to the Hastings chapel which, for the
reason already stated, was apparently on the north side of
the quire, chapels of St. Anne and St. Nicholas are known
to have existed as well as the Rood chapel which was clearly
originally a detached building standing in the churchyard.
The suppression survey, however, seems to imply that the
latter was at that date a part of the church and it is therefore possible that a new chapel was built adjoining the
church shortly before the suppression, with the money left
by Henry Pisford for the enlargement of the old one. The
building, however, was small and its position on the accompanying plan is purely conjectural. St. Anne's chapel is
not mentioned in the survey and was therefore presumably
a screened area in the body of the church. At least two
altars probably existed at the east end of the nave on
either side of the entrance to the " walking-place " while
others would have stood against the east wall of the transept.
The chapel of St. Nicholas is only mentioned in the survey
and it seems probable that it is therefore identical with
the Hastings chapel as indicated on the plan.

[1] Cf. Reading, p. 114.
[2] Reader's MSS., vol. 14, fo. 120, where it is also stated that many
decorated tiles were found including ones bearing the arms of the Earl of
Chester and Earl Beauchamp.

Plate 8

B. CANTERBURY, ARCHITECTURAL FRAG-
MENTS FROM GREYFRIARS' CHURCH

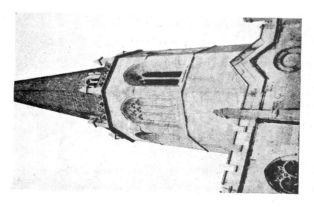

A. COVENTRY, GREYFRIARS' TOWER

Of the position of the domestic buildings even less can be stated with any certainty. The cloister seems to have been on the south side of the church, with its western range extending from the schoolhouse which was presumably near the west end of the church to the building known as Lady Euynghern's chamber on the south. The warden's chamber was apparently a detached building towards the south-east boundary. The cemetery containing three roods presumably occupied the land to the east and north of the church. During the recent erection of the large building abutting on the north side of the present church and facing the south side of Warwick Lane, evidence of burials was discovered as well as a short length of medieval wall. Unfortunately no record was made of this latter discovery, but it seems likely that it may have been a portion of the north transept of the friars' church.

(4) DUNWICH

HISTORY

WEEVER records that " the grey Friers of Dunwich was founded first by Richard FitzJohn and Alice his wife and after by King Henry the third : of which I have no further knowledge." [1] There is no definite record of this house, however, before 1277, when the friars received 13*s*. 4*d*. for two days' food, which at the usual daily rate of 4*d*. a head indicates that there were then about 20 friars. [2] As at Winchelsea, this first site had to be given up owing to incursions from the sea and in August 1290 the Commonalty of Dunwich received licence to alienate to the friars a plot of land containing 4 a. 2 r. 16 p. [3] At the same time the king granted them an adjoining dyke with licence to enclose their new site. [4] That the friars obtained part of their sustenance by sea fishing is suggested by an order in March 1305 to the mayor and bailiffs of the town to allow the friars minor there to have the King's galley in Dunwich with all its tackle and appurtenances in whosever hands they might be, as the King had given it to the friars. [5] The old site was not entirely abandoned and there is

[1] *Ancient Funeral Monuments* (1631), p. 721.
[2] P.R.O. Excheq. Accts. 350, no. 23, m. 2.
[3] *C.P.R. 1281–92*, p. 383 and Inq. a. q. d. file 13, no. 24.
[4] *Ibid.*   [5] *C.C.R. 1302–07*, p. 246.

evidence that, as in the case of the site of the first Franciscan settlement in Exeter, the friars continued to regard themselves as its guardians if not its actual owners.   In October 1328 they accordingly obtained a licence to enclose and hold the vacant plot in Dunwich, valued at 2s. yearly, which they used to inhabit and which was taken into the King's hands because they removed to another place in the town " as it would be indecent that a plot of ground for some time dedicated to divine worship where christian souls are buried should be converted to human uses." [1] This licence was inspected and confirmed by Henry IV in 1408.[2]   There is no record of actual building on the new site but it would seem that shortly before the Dissolution the reconstruction or repair of the friars' church was in contemplation, for by her will dated June 1514, Katharine Read bequeathed 3s. 4d. " to Friar Nicholas Wicet or to those that shall rebuild the church." [3]   There is no evidence that this work was ever carried out.

The deed of Surrender has not survived, but in December 1538 the Bishop of Dover informed Cromwell that since last he had been with him he had received this house among many others to the King's use.[4]   Before the close of the year the lead collected from the friars' houses in Norwich, Yarmouth, Dunwich and Oxford had been melted down and totalled 48 fodder, 3 quarters and this was near the water ready to be carried to London or elsewhere.   The lead on the churches which was regarded as safe from interference was still unmolten.[5]

In the following year when the first account was returned to the Exchequer, Ralph Onner and William Thurston, who were appointed collectors of the rents of the whole property were in occupation of the buildings with the gardens and orchards within the precinct at a yearly rent of 7s. 6d. There were also 2 acres of meadow in the tenure of George Moriss at a rent of 6s. 8d., two pieces of arable land contained 2 a. 3 r. 0 p. let to William Whichinghame at a rent of 5s., a piece of marshland containing one rood let to Thomas Wilson at a rent of 4d., a tenement in the occupation of John Procter at a rent of 10s. and a tenement with a curtilage in the tenure of Robert Grey at a rent of 8s. Apart from the main site and the two tenements, the friars

[1] *C.P.R. 1327-30*, p. 324.   [2] *C.P.R. 1408-13*, p. 26.
[3] T. Gardner, *History of Dunwich* (1754), p. 61.
[4] *L. and P. Hen. VIII*, vol. 13(2), no. 1021.   [5] *Ibid.*, no. 1023.

had thus held some 5 acres in the town and the total annual rent produced by their property was 37s. 6d. From this 18s. 2d. was deducted for various expenses during the period of the account, including 5s. 4d. " for the repair and stopping up of the stone walls around the site for the safe custody of the lead and buildings there."[1] A twenty-one years' lease of the site was granted on March 16 1542 to Edmund Rowce[2] and in February 1545 the reversion in fee was sold to John Eyre, a local receiver of Augmentations.[3] The official " particulars " for this grant describe the site as then in the occupation of Elizabeth Rabbett at an annual rent of 7s. 6d. but give no details as to the buildings.[4]

DESCRIPTION

The site of the buildings is a little to the south of the present village near the ruined church of All Saints and close to the edge of the cliff. It comprises about 7 acres and is surrounded by a precinct wall which is still largely intact. In this wall are the remains of two gateways in a fairly good state of preservation. There is said to have been a third gateway towards the east, but this has been demolished. Of the buildings themselves, only a part of the southern range of the cloister survives. (See Fig. 4.)

This is a building measuring externally about 66 feet by 24 feet with the cloister walk 6 feet wide incorporated within its structure. The upper floor was no doubt occupied by the frater. The cloister itself must have measured about 62 feet from east to west and was divided on this side into five bays by four buttresses projecting into the cloister garth, of which two remain. Four of the five windows over-looking the garth survive and two of these retain part of their original Perpendicular tracery. On the east side are acutely pointed openings which communicated originally with the eastern range, all trace of which has disappeared.

The church must have stood on the north side of the cloister but no remains of it survive above ground. In it, according to Weever, were buried Sir Robert Valence, the

---

[1] P.R.O. Ministers Accounts, Hen. VIII, no. 3440.
[2] P.R.O. Augm. Off. Misc. Bks. 213, fo. 21b ; *L. and P. Hen. VIII*, vol. 17, p. 699.
[3] *L. and P. Hen. VIII*, vol. 20(1), no. 282(37).
[4] P.R.O. Partic. for grants Hen. VIII, no. 422 ; D.K.R., vol. 9, app. 2, p. 207.

heart of Dame Hawise Ponyngs, Dame Iden of Ylketishal, Sir Peter Mellis and Dame Anne his wife, Dame Dunne his mother, John Francans and Margaret his wife, Dame Bert of Furnivall, . . . Austin of Cales and Jone his wife, John

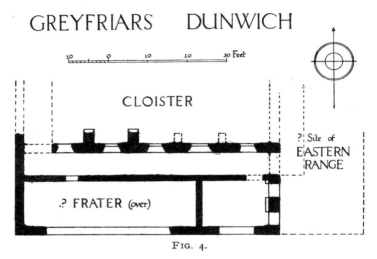

FIG. 4.

Falleys and Beatrix his wife and Augustine his son, . . . Walexnes, Sir Herbert Dernford, Katherine wife of William Phellip, Margaret wife of Richard Phellip and Peter Codum.[1]

(5) GLOUCESTER [2]

HISTORY

THIS house is first mentioned in March 1231 when the friars received a grant of trees from the forest of Dean, " ad se hospitandos," [3] which suggests that they had then but recently arrived. The founder was Thomas, Lord Berkeley, whose family remained connected with the foundation until the Dissolution. This may be inferred from Eccleston's statement [4] that the friars, by order of Agnellus

---

[1] *Ancient Funeral Monuments* (1631) p. 721. Quoted from the collections of William le Neve. The spelling of the names is Weevers.
[2] " The Grey Friars, Gloucester," by Vera M. Dallas (*Bristol and Glouc. Arch. Soc.*, vol. 54, pp. 117–27).
[3] *C.C.R. 1227–31*, p. 480.
[4] Eccleston, p. 56 ; *ibid.* (ed. Salter), p. 62.

of Pisa, relinquished a large piece of their original site but subsequently recovered it with great difficulty from Thomas de Berkeley through the wisdom and devotion of his wife. The latter event, which is recorded in the city archives,[1] took place probably in 1239, and Eccleston recounts how on this occasion Haymo of Faversham, who was then provincial minister, declared that he would rather the brethren had spacious grounds and cultivated them so that they might grow their own produce at home than that they should beg it of others.[2] This was, of course, a direct reversal of the policy of Agnellus and accounted for the enlargement of many Franciscan sites at this time.

In the meantime, though actual references to building are few,[3] we may infer that considerable progress had been made with the erection of the church, as Eccleston records that Agnellus, who died in 1235, took severe measures on account of its windows and deprived one of the friars of his hood for having painted the pulpitum or screen, and the guardian for having permitted it to be done.[4] The building was still unfinished however in January 1240 when the friars received a grant of 100s. for carrying their timber for the fabric of their church.[5] In August 1246, the King let to the friars, at an annual rent of 12s., a tower in the city wall and a way called Scadman, leading from their house to the tower for the purpose of holding a school of theology there.[6] In the same year Ralph of Maidstone, who was successively Archdeacon of Chester and Bishop of Hereford, and had entered the order about 1240, died and, according to an addition to Eccleston's chronicle in a fourteenth-century hand, was buried " in the Grey friars' quire at Gloucester in a certain arch in the north part of the presbytery." [7] In 1256 the custodian of the Forest of Dean was ordered to allow the friars to carry away six oaks which they had been given by John de Plesset, Earl of Warwick, from his wood in Lidney,[8] which may possibly indicate that further building was then in progress. In 1285 it was proposed to enlarge the site by the addition of a piece of land adjoining

---

[1] *Cal. of Records of Corporation of Gloucester*, edit. W. H. Stevenson, no. 319 ; cf. Eccleston, pp. 170–1.
[2] Eccleston, pp. 55–6.
[3] The numerous grants of timber recorded on the Close Rolls between 1231 and 1246 were for fuel.
[4] Eccleston, p. 47 ; *ibid.* (ed. Salter), p. 53.
[5] *C. Lib. R.* I, p. 441.   [6] *C.C.R.* 1242–47, p. 447.
[7] Eccleston, p. 107, n. 6 ; *Mon. Franc.* (R.S.), vol. I, p. 59, n. 1.
[8] *C.C.R.* 1254–6, p. 431.

the church, but beyond the holding of an inquisition *ad quod damnum*,[1] there is no record that the grant was ever made. In the same year a dispute arose with the Abbot and convent of Gloucester regarding burial rights in which Archbishop Peckham sided with the friars.[2] Another dispute regarding the right to take water from a spring at Breresclyft was settled in favour of the friars in 1357. The site was further enlarged between 1359 and 1364 by the addition of an acre and a half of land from Thomas de Berkeley and others.[3] The number of friars which was 24 in 1277 and 40 in 1284 and 1326,[4] had dropped to 31 by 1337.[5]

Early in the sixteenth century the church was rebuilt out of funds provided by the Berkeley family. William, Marquess of Berkeley, who died in 1492, had given £20 to the repair of the building [6] and in his will directed that a friar should sing perpetually in the Grey Friars at Gloucester for his soul and the souls of his father and mother and other members of his family.[7] His nephew, Maurice, Lord Berkeley, appears to have begun the rebuilding in 1519, for Smyth states that " in the tenth year of king Henry the 8th began this lord Maurice to allow 6 li. 13*s.* 4*d.* per annum ex eleemosyna sua (out of his alms and bounty), towards the repair of the church of the gray ffryars in Gloucester ; which liberality hee continued many years, yea, after his death till the same was finished ; of which place this family were founders." [8]   He died in 1523, and, in a codicil to his will, dated 1521, he refers to " the re-edifying and building of the church and chancel and stalls of the friars minor in Gloucester, whereof I am founder and where dame Isobel Berkeley, my grandame lieth buried,[9] which work I have now begun and in case I die then my executors substantially to finish the same." [10]   In 1528 Christopher Stoll desired to be buried in the church of the Friars Minor

<hr/>

[1] Inq. a. q. d. 13 Edw. I, file 8, no. 15 ; *Mon. Franc.* (R.S.), vol. II, p. 288.

[2] *Reg. Peckham* (R.S.), vol. III, pp. 905–6.

[3] *C.P.R. 1358–61*, p. 257 ; *1361–4*, p. 103 ; *1364–7*, p. 26.   Inq. a. q. d. file 354, no. 1 ; file 341, no. 2.

[4] A. G. Little, *The Grey Friars in Oxford*, p. 44, n. 1 ; Little, *Studies*, pp. 68 and 72.

[5] *Trans. Bristol and Glouc. Arch. Soc.*, vol. 13, p. 179.

[6] Smyth, *Lives of the Berkeleys* (ed. Maclean), vol. II, p. 134.

[7] *Test. Vet.* vol. 2, p. 408.

[8] Smyth, *op. cit.*, vol. 2, p. 203.

[9] She was buried in the chancel in 1452 (Smyth, *op. cit.* vol. 2, p. 81).

[10] P.C.C. " Bodfelde," qu. 14 ; Smyth, *op. cit.* vol. 2, p. 201.

Plate 9

GLOUCESTER, NORTH AISLE OF GREY FRIARS' CHURCH FROM THE NORTH-EAST

of Gloucester before the image of the Blessed Virgin Mary.[1]

The house was surrendered in July 1538 when the Bishop of Dover reported to Cromwell that " the Gray Friars is a goodly house much of it new builded specially the church, quire and dorter ; the rest small lodgings ; divers leases out for years of lodgings and gardens ; no lead but a conduit and small gutters." [2] The inventory [3] mentions the quire, vestry and library with " many books of no value " and 147½ oz. of plate. In April 1542 a 21-years lease of the site was granted to John Jennings [4] to whom the reversion was granted in the following year. In the official " particulars " [5] for this grant, the area of the precinct, which was valued at 20s. a year is stated to contain four acres and there was also in addition "one close of pasture with the appurtenances lying and extending from the walls of the city of Gloucester in length from the east side to the walls of the cemetery of the late house on the west and in width between the lane called Marelane on the north side and the church of the said late house on the south," let to Hugh Gethen by Indenture under the seal of the guardian and convent dated 27 April 1537, for a term of 20 years at an annual rent of 8s., and also a garden in Southgate street within the city situate " between the house in which Thomas Morgan lately dwelt and the walls of the late house," which was in the tenure of Thomas Morgan at an annual rent of 5s. The grant was made by letters patent dated 16 January 1544.[6]

DESCRIPTION

The sole surviving portion of the buildings is the nave and north aisle of the early sixteenth-century friars' church. This is a rectangular building, 108 feet long and 46 feet wide, internally and divided longitudinally by a central arcade of seven bays supported on lozenge-shaped

[1] P.C.C. " Porch," fo. 37 ; In his will dated 1403 John Banneburg of Gloucester directed that he should be buried in the friars church (P.C.C. " Marche," qu. 6, fo. 45b).

[2] Wright, *Suppression*, p. 199 ; *L. and P. Hen. VIII*, vol. 13(1) no. 1484. Enclosed with this letter is a list of five friars from this house for whom the visitor asks Cromwell's permission that they should change their habit.

[3] *L. and P. Hen. VIII*, vol. 13(1), no. 1109.

[4] *Ibid.*, vol. 17, no. 1258 (p. 704).

[5] P.R.O., Particulars for grants, Hen. VIII, no. 644.

[6] *L. and P. Hen. VIII*, vol. 19(1), no. 80(29).

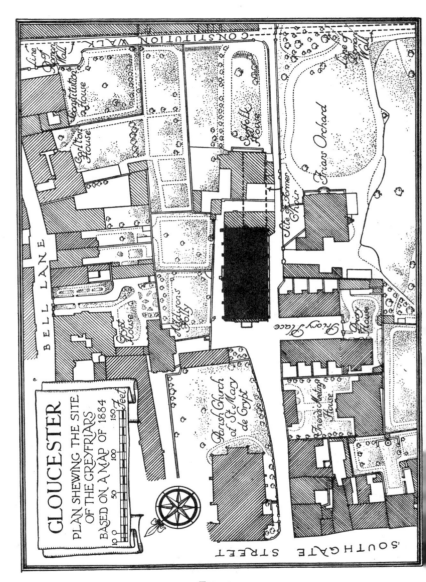

Fig. 5.

moulded piers with moulded caps and bases, of which only four and the eastern respond remain. The nave and aisle are thus of equal width, and are roofed in two spans, an arrangement for which there is no parallel among English houses of the mendicant orders. The building was lighted on the north and south by seven large windows, each of four lights, of which those on the north with one exception and four of those on the south are blocked, though their arches and in several cases portions of the tracery in their heads survive. The remaining three on the south retain their original tracery but have been boarded over externally. At the east end of the aisle is a six-light window also blocked, but of which the head, jambs and portions of the tracery remain. The chancel arch at the east end of the nave is blocked by a modern building to the east but its moulded arch and responds are visible from the interior. The west end was entirely rebuilt about 1800 and forms the front of a house occupying the two western bays of the building. The eastern portion, which has been in part restored, has suffered considerably from neglect, though much of the stone panelling with which the building appears to have been originally lined still remains. This portion of the building is now divided into two properties, the north aisle being occupied as a dwelling-house and the nave used as tenements. There is no indication of the position of the original doorways. The present entrance on the south may occupy the position of a doorway to the cloister while a west door may be assumed.

Of the quire nothing remains save the start of its north wall with the jamb of one of its windows, from the position of which it may be inferred that it was an aisleless building. In length, by analogy with other friars' churches, it would have been not far short of 100 feet so that the total length of the building may be estimated at approximately 200 feet. It seems probable that the usual masonry bell tower between the nave and the quire was not introduced into the Gloucester plan as the portion of the easternmost window on the north side of the quire, as indicated by the surviving jamb, would make anything but a timber belfry extremely unlikely.

From the Suppression documents quoted above it is clear that the cloister was on the south side of the church with the cemetery on the north. Nothing is now visible of the conventual buildings though it has been stated that

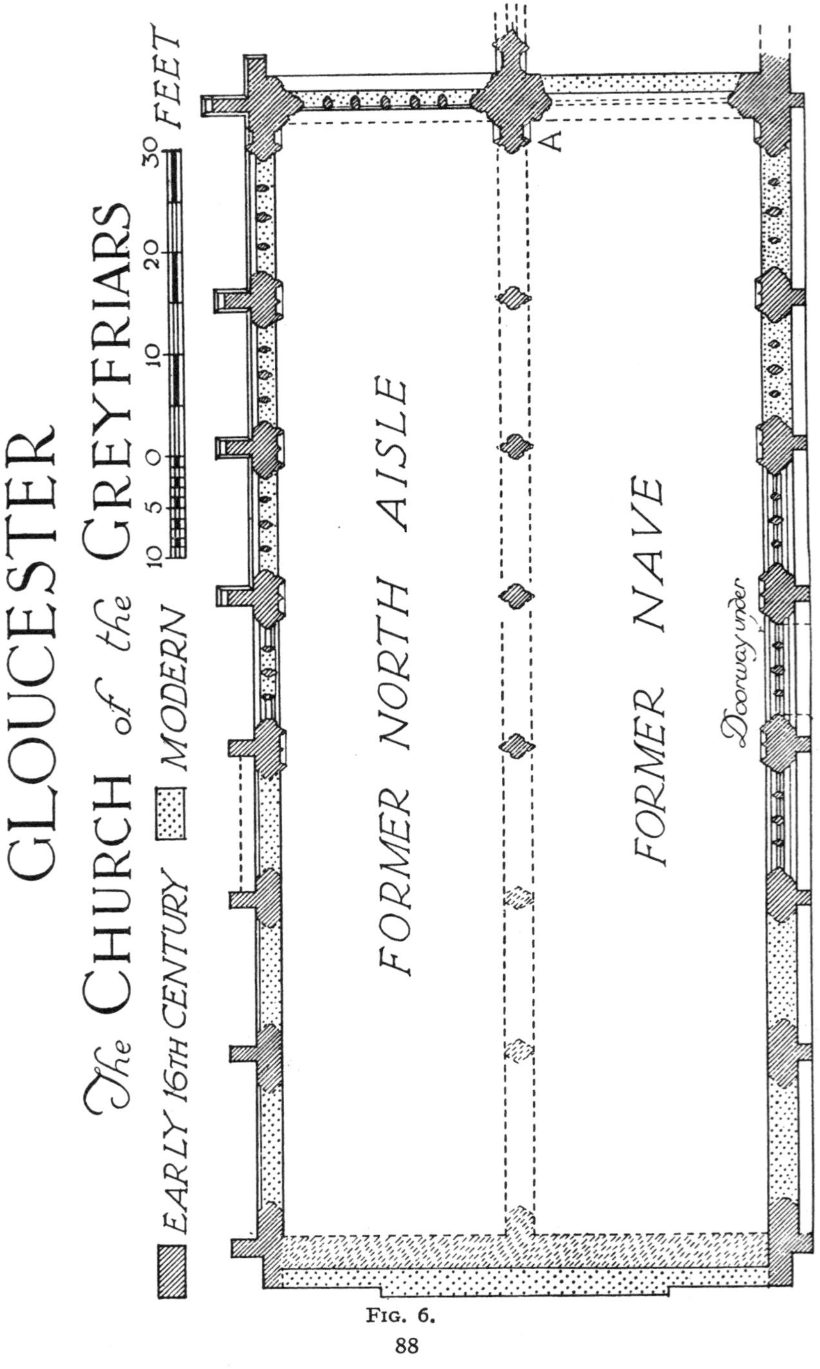

GLOUCESTER
The CHURCH of the GREYFRIARS

■ EARLY 16TH CENTURY ▦ MODERN

10 5 0 10 20 30 FEET

FORMER NORTH AISLE

FORMER NAVE

Doorway under

A

FIG. 6.

88

in the middle of last century parts of the prior's lodging and other buildings were still existing to the south of the church.[1]

Set in the exterior of the south wall of the nave over the present doorway, are two stone shields bearing the arms of Chandos (or, a pile gules) and Clifford of Frampton (checky, or and azure, on a bend gules, three lions argent). They possibly formed part of a tomb of Giles Brydges, who through his mother Alice, daughter of Thomas Berkeley of Cubberley, was heir to the Chandos barony, and his wife Katherine, daughter of James Clifford of Frampton, or one of their children, though there is no other record of any of this family having been buried in the friary.

(6) LINCOLN

HISTORY

THE exact date of the arrival of the Franciscans in Lincoln is unknown, but it was certainly as early as 1230, for, on 6 February 1231, the citizens with the consent of the King allocated a piece of land near their guildhall for the use of the friars and from the wording of this grant, it is evident that the friars were already in occupation of adjoining property which is stated to have been given them by William de Benningworth, a sub-dean of the cathedral church.[2]

The original area adjoining the old guildhall was extended on 5 October 1237 by the gift of the site of the guildhall itself which was assigned by the mayor and bailiffs to the friars at the personal request of Henry III.[3] The only subsequent addition to the friars' property appears to have been the gift of a messuage in 1350 by John de Pykering of Scopwich,[4] which from later documents seems to have brought the total area up to four acres. That the site was always small was no doubt partly due to its situation in the extreme south-east corner of the Roman city, the wall

---

[1] *Trans. Bristol and Glouc. Arch. Soc.* vol. 13, p. 186.

[2] *C.P.R. 1225–32*, pp. 422–3. There is considerable discrepancy in the earlier accounts of the foundation of this house. Speed mentions John Stainwike as founder, but Dugdale corrects this to John Pickering of Stampwick, who was merely a late benefactor. Leland on the other hand apparently confuses the house with that at Scarborough and states that Reginaldus Molendinarius, a merchant of Lincoln, was founder, adding that Henry Lacy, Earl of Lincoln, and one Nunny, his almoner, were great benefactors. (*Itin*, vol. I, p. 31).

[3] *C.P.R. 1234–37*, pp. 495 and 500.   [4] *Ibid., 1348–50*, p. 500.

of which, or its medieval successor, formed the precinct boundary on two sides and effectively barred any extension into the more open land of the suburbs.

In 1258 the friars were licensed to block up a postern in this wall and to enclose a lane which led thereto on the north side of their property.[1] The site thus consolidated was bounded by the present Silver Street on the north, by Free School Lane on the west, by the city wall to the west of Broadgate on the east and by its continuation along the south side of the present St. Swithin's Church on the south. Within this area the buildings were erected and there seems no reason to doubt that the surviving structure was begun soon after the acquisition of the final portion of the site in 1237. References to the actual progress of the work are unfortunately almost wholly absent. A gift of five oaks from the forest of Shirewood in 1258 is stated to be for the purpose of fuel,[2] but a later gift of 10 oaks from the same source in 1268 " for the fabric of their church "[3] indicates that building was then in hand. That the buildings were substantially completed some years before 1275 seems to be implied by the statements of the jurors in the Great Inquest of that year. It was then alleged that the friars had encroached upon the city wall for a length of 10 perches to the danger of the city fifteen years or more before ; that ten years or more before they had enclosed a certain lane and shut up a postern in the city wall ; that fifteen years or more before they had planted their houses and church on the wall itself for a length of 20 perches and to a depth of 14 perches, and finally that the encroachment extended " from the gable of a certain Robert Cotty on the north to the postern on the south." The statements of the different jurors vary somewhat in detail, but it is clear that the encroachments which included the church had occurred between ten and thirty years previously.[4] It is not, however, until 1280 that an order to Geoffrey de Nevill, justice of the forest beyond Trent, to furnish the friars with six oaks,[5] supplemented on 4 February 1284 by a similar order for six more oaks " fit for timber for the work of their church,"[6] suggests that some final work on the roof or interior was then being taken in hand.

[1] *C.P.R., 1247–58*, p. 652.   [2] *C.C.R., 1256–9*, p. 268.
[3] Close Roll, 52 Hen. III, m. 3.
[4] *Hundred Rolls* (Rec. Com.), vol. 1 (1812), pp. 311a, b, 318b, 319a, 325 and 398.
[5] *C.C.R. 1279–88*, p. 35.   [6] *Ibid.*, p. 251.

The confined nature of the site with which the friars as late arrivals had to contend, and which doubtless accounted for encroachment on the city walls, was probably a primary factor in the ultimate placing of the church on the upper floor over a vaulted undercroft. That these encroachments led to friction with the city authorities is perhaps not surprising. In 1321 the friars complained to the King that the mayor and bailiff had, for the better protection of the city, broken the enclosures of the friars which had previously adjoined the wall of the city and had broken and blocked up certain private chambers contiguous to the wall to the damage and danger of the friars. The King thereupon ordered that the enclosures should be restored and the chambers opened out provided that suitable gates be made in the enclosures whereby access might be had to the walls.[1] Three years later the guardian of the house had occasion to complain of a more private attack on his property when a number of persons broke his close and houses in Lincoln and carried away certain goods.[2]

In 1379 the Grey Friars' church is mentioned in connection with a claim to sanctuary,[3] but the remaining history of the house is confined for the most part to records of small pecuniary bequests in wills [4] and to some evidence of building activity on the eve of the suppression. Unlike many Franciscan churches, the Grey Friars' church at Lincoln never appears to have enjoyed any popularity as a place of burial and only four such burials have been noted. On 27 April 1286 an indulgence was granted by Bishop Kellawe of Durham for the soul of Alice de Ros who was buried in the friars' church.[5] Early in the fourteenth century Adam of Lincoln, D.D., the regent master of the Franciscans at Oxford, who succeeded as fifteenth Provincial Minister about 1304, is stated to have been buried at Lincoln presumably at the Grey Friars,[6] while on 30 January 1322–23, the King's almoner received 20s. 4d. for expenses " circa exequias corporis Vitalis de Gavenak (aliter Savynak) defuncti et in ecclesia fratrum minorum

---

[1] *C.C.R., 1318–23*, p. 487.   [2] *C.P.R. 1324–7*, p. 67.
[3] *Ibid., 1377–81*, p. 361.
[4] See C. W. Foster, *Lincolnshire Wills, 1271–1532*, 3 volumes (*Lincoln Record Society*) ; A. R. Maddison, *Lincolnshire Wills*, 1st series, 1500–1600 (1888), and A. Gibbons, *Early Lincoln Wills, 1280–1547* (abstracted from the Episcopal Registers) (1890).
[5] Dixon, *Fast. Ebor.*, vol. I, p. 335.
[6] A. G. Little, *Greyfriars in Oxford*, p. 160.   *Mon. Franc.* (R.S.), vol. 1, p. 537.

H

civitatis Lincoln' sepulti." [1] In 1509 Thomas Meryng of Lincoln, gentleman, by his will directed that he should be buried " in the church of the Friars minor of the said city," to whom he gave 6s. 8d. for his burial. [2]

There is some evidence that building was in progress or contemplated immediately prior to the suppression. On 12 September 1534 the Warden of the Grey Friars was authorized to have as much stone as he required from the churches of St. Augustine and Holy Trinity " at the Grece foot " which were ruined and falling down, " for the reparation of his house freely and of charity." [3] Again, on 12 July of the following year, he received a grant of the timber from the roof of " St. Bathe Church " for upholding and maintaining the house. [4] In the same year the friars' water system, which continued in use until comparatively modern times, was under construction. On 8 April the city records mention a licence granted to the Warden of the Grey Friars to lay his conduit in common ground of the city where he shall think most convenient. [5] The water was derived from a spring near Monks Abbey to the east of the city. After the suppression the conduit came into the possession of the town. [6] No trace of it now survives, but a writer in 1810 records that " the conduit for the supply of this part of the town is placed between the second and third buttress " of the existing building. [7]

On the first Sunday in Lent, 1539, the Bishop of Dover wrote to Cromwell, " I am now in Lincoln where that also I have received four poor houses nothing left but stones and poor glass but metely leaded. All lead and bells I leave to the King's use and as for plate also I save, the which is very little. If that I find 12 ounces in a house it is well ; for the more part 7 or 8 ounces is the most. In Lincoln in the Grey Friars is a goodly conduit for the which the Mayor and the Alderman was with me to make suit to have the conduit unto the city. I could not satisfy them till that I promised them to write in their behalf to your

[1] Wardrobe Accounts, 15–17 Edw. II (B. M. Stowe MS. 553, ff. 21ᵛ, 113).
[2] *Lincolnshire Wills*, vol. 1, *ut. sup.*, p. 39.
[3] *Hist. MSS. Com.* 14th Report, Appendix VIII, p. 33.
[4] *Ibid.*, p. 34. The church was possibly that of St. Peter ad fontem.
[5] *Hist. MSS. Com.*, 14th Report, Appendix VIII, p. 33.
[6] The White Friars in Lincoln also had an elaborate water system, the conduit head of which has been reconstructed in the churchyard of St. Mary-le-Wigford.
[7] A. Stark, *The History of Lincoln (1810)*, pp. 201–2. There is a small woodcut of the Greyfriars.

lordship for the same beseeching you to be good lord to them ; they ordered me very genteelly (jentylly) there." [1] The deed of Surrender has not survived, so that practically nothing is known of the inmates of the house at that date, though their number was certainly very small. No immediate purchaser for the property was found and the site was accordingly let to William Monson of Ingleby, near Lincoln, a member of a well-known local family, at a rent of 12s. a year.[2] Monson appears to have converted the buildings into a private residence and in 1540 he obtained a twenty-one years lease of the property at the same rent.[3] Five years later the reversion on this lease was sold to John Pope together with many other properties. The grant was made by Letters Patent dated 8 February 1545, and comprised " the whole site enclosure circuits, ambits and precincts of the late house of Friars minor in our city of Lincoln containing by estimation 4 acres in the tenure of William Monson."[4] The official " particulars " sent to the Court of Augmentations are dated two days after the grant itself and contain a note that there were growing about the site 42 ash trees of thirty or forty years growth whereof 32 were reserved for timber to repair the house standing upon the same and for stakes for hedgebotte to repair the hedges, and the residue valued at 6 pence a tree was to be included in the sale.[5]

Pope, who was merely a speculator in monastic property, sold the site of the Grey Friars almost at once to the tenant William Monson, whose son Robert ultimately succeeded to the property. On 8 May 1568 the city records contain the following entry : " Forasmuch as Robert Monson, Esq., is pleased to make a freeschool of his own charges in the late Grey·Friars, it is ordered that he shall have all the glass remaining in the freeschool (i.e. the old one) towards the glazing of the windows in the new school." [6] Six years

[1] Wright, *Suppression*, p. 192. *L. and P. Hen. VIII*, vol. 14(1), no. 348 and no. 413.
[2] P.R.O. Ministers' Accounts Hen. VIII, no. 2019.
[3] P.R.O. Exchequer, Augmentation Office, Misc. Bks. 212, fo. 38b. The great timber and woods and all such buildings within the precinct as the King should order to be pulled down were reserved.
[4] Pat. Roll 36 Hen. VIII, pt. 26, m. 30 and 33. *L. and P. Hen. VIII*, vol. 20(1), p. 1224, no. 282(19).
[5] P.R.O. Particulars for grants Hen. VIII, no. 874. An earlier application for a grant to John Bellow and Edward Bayliss in 1544/5 was not proceeded with and is deleted in the roll. (Partic. for grants, file 121, m. 24–5.)
[6] *Hist. MSS. Comm.*, 14th Report, Appendix VIII, p. 62.

later Monson conveyed the whole of the Grey Friars' property, subject to his own life interest therein, to the city for the purposes of the freeschool and in order that the city might "more quietly have and enjoy a conduit or water course lately in question." [1] On his death in 1583 the city came into complete possession of the property and have remained the owners ever since.

About this time some portions of the buildings appear to have been demolished, for in 1587 the city records mention a gift to two private individuals, of stones from the Grey Friars [2] and in the following year, "the fairest great free stones in the friars" were ordered to be piled up and laid up in the vaults under the school. [3] In 1602 more stones from the Friars were granted to a Mr. Ellis. [4]

The free school for a long time occupied the upper floor only of the existing building. The undercroft, according to the city records, was in use as a house of correction in 1612. [5] In 1624 it was let to Gregory Lawcock as a warehouse for wool, [6] and continued as a "Jersey School" for teaching knitting and spinning wool until about 1830. [7] From 1833 to 1862 it was the home of the mechanics' institute, after which date it was taken over as additional accommodation by the school above. [8] The school continued in occupation until about 1900. In 1903 it was decided to adapt the building as a museum for the city, and after extensive and careful restoration had been carried out by the architects, Messrs. W. Watkins & Son, [9] this was formally opened on 22 May 1907.

DESCRIPTION

The surviving building is a thirteenth-century structure of ragstone rubble with freestone dressings, 101 feet long and 21 feet 6 inches wide internally, divided into two storeys by a vaulted undercroft. That this vaulting is a later insertion and that the original structure was of one storey

[1] *Hist. M.S.S. Comm.*, 14th Report, Appendix VIII, p. 16.
[2] *Ibid.*, p. 72.   [3] *Ibid.*, p. 73.   [4] *Ibid.*, p. 77.
[5] *Ibid.*, p. 90.   [6] *Ibid.*, p. 97.
[7] For further details of the post-suppression history of the site see *The Greyfriary, Lincoln*, by A. M. Sympson. *Lincs. Notes & Queries*, vol. 7 (1903), pp. 193–202.
[8] In 1851, according to Padley, the undercroft was divided in five rooms by four modern partitions.
[9] See report of the Architects on the building, dated February 1903, and supplemental report dated October 22 1906. Printed in the *Catalogue of the Annual art and industrial Exhibition at the Greyfriars, 1906*.

Plate 10

LINCOLN, GREYFRIARS' BUILDING FROM SOUTH-EAST, WITH RUINS OF OLD ST. SWITHIN'S CHURCH ON LEFT. AUGUST, 1784

only is apparent from the fact that the sills of the original lancet windows on the north side and of the triple lancets in the east wall, which were revealed during the restoration of 1905, are some 4 feet below the level of the upper floor and can be partially seen in the undercroft below. Moreover, the responds of the vaulting piers are not bonded into the outer wall, while the blocked arcading between the main building and an aisle or chapel which originally existed on the north side, extends above the present vaulting and must have been blocked up when the latter was inserted. The building in its original form, therefore, consisted of a long and narrow apartment lit on the north side by tall lancets with wide internal splays arranged in pairs with their sills some 4 feet 6 inches from the present external ground level. On the south, owing to the abutment of the cloister walk, the lancets were shorter and did not extend below the present floor line, while their arrangement was varied by their being placed at regular intervals instead of in pairs. The original east window consisted of a triplet of lancet lights of similar character to those on the north, having plain chamfered rear arches without shafts or mouldings. Only the two outer lancets now survive to their full height, the head of the centre one having been removed when the present east window was inserted.

On the north side the upper portion of the jambs and rear arches of several of the lancets have been re-used when the later windows and the present modern doorway were inserted. The latter is placed in the head of the western-most lancet, the splay of which has been cut away to form the rebate for the door. On the south side, traces of three of the original lancets can be seen on the exterior. They probably extended along the whole length of the building, but the others have been obliterated by the insertion of later windows.

In the north wall of this building, towards the west end, there is a blocked arcade of two bays, supported on a central octagonal column with moulded cap and base which still survives embedded in the later filling. It is now partly exposed by a modern opening cut through the wall against its eastern face. The arches above are of three plain chamfered orders with a span of about 10 feet and rise to a height of some 16 feet from the present internal ground level. Of the aisle to which this arcade gave access nothing survives above ground, but some trial excavations carried

out about 1906 revealed a wall at this point, parallel to and
at a distance of 11 feet to the north of the main building,
which was doubtless the north wall of the aisle in question.
The absence of any extension of the arcading to the east,
coupled with the position of the westernmost of the lancet
windows on this side, indicates that the aisle cannot have
extended farther to the east than the position approximately
shown on the accompanying plan.

The only other original architectural feature in the
interior of the building is a small cap with the springers of
arches on either side set in the south wall at a point about
10 feet from the east end and at a height of about 9 feet.
From its position just below the present vaulting, by which
it is partly obscured, there can be little doubt that it formed
part of the fittings of the original quire before the vaulting
was inserted and it is not improbable that it is a fragment
of the sedilia. Its present height is accounted for partly by
the fact that the general floor level was lowered when the
vaulting was inserted and partly by the removal at the same
time of the steps upon which the altar was doubtless originally
raised.

The work of the second period included the division
of the building into two storeys. The first step undertaken
was the lowering of the ground level of the interior as stated
above to give the necessary additional height. This is
clearly shown by the position of the base of the column
of the arcade of the original north aisle, which is now some
2 feet above the present floor level, and the base of the
adjoining respond of the vaulting. The two existing bays
of the nave arcade were then blocked up and the vaulted
undercroft inserted throughout the entire length of the
building. It consists of nine bays divided longitudinally
by a central row of eight octagonal columns with moulded
caps and bases and semi-octagonal responds at the sides
and ends. The vaulting is quadripartite with two-centred
arches and plain chamfered ribs with small carved leaf
bosses at the intersections of the principal ribs.

The insertion of this vaulting, as already indicated,
involved the blocking up of the lancets on the north side
and at the east end. On the south side, owing to their
lesser height, they may have continued to light the upper
apartment, as all the existing upper windows on this side
appear to be modern insertions. Provision for lighting the
undercroft was made by the insertion of a row of plain

Plate II

LINCOLN, UNDERCROFT LOOKING EAST

pointed windows in the south wall overlooking the cloister
alley. These in part survive, though they have been extensively restored and much of the stonework renewed. They
have rear arches with hollow chamfered edges, dying into
the wall, and are without mullions, but there is some
evidence to suggest that they originally had a central
mullion divided at the head so as to form two simple lights.
The windows in the second bay from either end are entirely
modern and replace doorways which formerly existed in
these positions. The westernmost of these doors was used
as the entrance to the school and was replaced by the
existing window during the restoration of 1905. The other
door to the east had disappeared before 1851, but can be
seen in Grimm's drawing of 1784 (Plate 10), and there can be
little doubt that these doorways indicated the positions of,
if they were not in fact, the original doorways which gave
access to the cloister.

The upper floor, which is approached by a modern
external staircase on the north side, is now a single compartment, but was formerly divided into two rooms of unequal
size by a partition which was removed at the restoration of
1905. The east window which replaces the centre of the
original lancets is of three lights with intersecting tracery
in a two-centred head. Externally it has a moulded drip-
stone terminating in small carved heads, and over the window
in the apex of the gable is a small vesica-shaped opening,
probably of thirteenth-century date. In the west wall of
the upper apartment is a low window of three lights inserted
apparently in the nineteenth century within the jambs of a
larger window which was probably contemporary with that
at the east end. The remaining windows on this floor
are for the most part imitation Tudor work inserted in the
last century, but partly utilizing the rear arches and splays
of earlier openings.

There is no definite indication of the original entrance
to the upper chamber. In the north wall there is a small
blocked doorway at a distance of 4 feet from the east end,
and apparently constructed in the head of the easternmost
of the original lancets. It was presumably approached
by an external wooden staircase, but from its position can
hardly have been the principal entrance. Immediately
to the west of the present entrance, which is clearly a later
insertion, is the frame of a two-centred doorway with plain
chamfered jambs set against the outer face of the wall,

but it is doubtful whether this is in position and it may have been removed here in the restoration of 1905. Wherever the original entrance was it must have been approached by an external staircase, as the vaulting below is intact throughout the entire building.

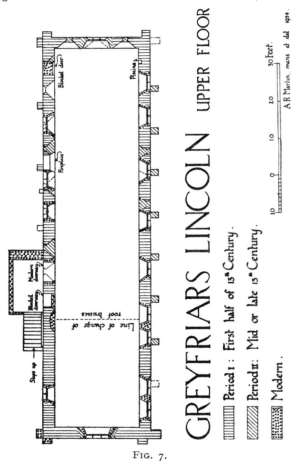

FIG. 7.

Of the fittings of the upper floor the most important is a double piscina of thirteenth-century date in the south wall at a distance of 4 feet from the east end and about 4 feet above the present floor level. The recess is 1 foot 10 inches in height with a chamfered edge and trefoil head, the

Plate 12

LINCOLN, GREYFRIARS' CHURCH LOOKING EAST

twin bowls being supported on slightly projecting moulded brackets. In the opposite wall a little farther to the west is a fireplace with a shouldered arch of apparently sixteenth-century date, which was probably inserted when the free school was established in the building. The projection for the chimney is supported externally on four large corbels.

The original open timber roof is still more or less intact over the whole length of the building, though its appearance has been considerably marred by the insertion of glass skylights in place of part of the tiling. Its construction is unusual and interesting and shows a change in design at a point 72 feet 6 inches from the east and 28 feet 6 inches from the west walls. The eastern portion consists of closely set oak rafters with semicircular trusses springing direct from the wall plate and without tie beams. In the western portion the trusses had been removed, but the mortice holes in the old rafters clearly indicated that these had been straight instead of semicircular and they were accordingly restored in this form in the restoration of 1905.

The fact that this change of design in the framing of the roof coincides with the position of the abutment of the easternmost arch of the nave arcade below and allows for a quire of normal length suggests that the roof is part of the original building before it was divided into two storeys and that, as in other early churches of the mendicant orders, no structural division between the nave and the quire was originally provided, its place, no doubt, being taken by a timber screen. Whether this arrangement was perpetuated when the church was removed to the upper floor it is impossible to say in the absence of any analogy, but it is not improbable that a portion of the west end would have been screened off to provide a return for the quire stalls and a sort of ante-chamber to what must have been in fact the private chapel of the friars.

Of the domestic buildings of the friary no trace survives. That they were fairly commodious may be inferred from the fact that Provincial Chapters were held here in 1288, 1293 and 1295,[1] while on three occasions in the fifteenth century Provincial Chapters of the Premonstratensian canons also met in the Lincoln friary.[2] The cloister lay to the south of

---

[1] *V.C.H. Lincoln*, vol. 2, p. 223.

[2] Gasquet, *Collectanea Anglo-Premonstratensia* (Camden Society), Third Ser., vol. I, pp. 136, 139, 160. The years of these chapters were 1459, 1476 and 1489.

the existing building where the modern church of St. Swithin now stands. That this was its position from the first is indicated by the fact that the sills of the original lancets on this side rest on the string-course which marks the abutment of the cloister roof. The positions of the two doorways referred to above suggest that the cloister was approximately 78 feet square.

It is of interest in conclusion to consider the reason for the complete change of plan evidenced in the structure of the existing building. There can be no doubt that this was originally planned as the friars' church and, as such, it is the earliest example of a Franciscan church now surviving in England. That the original plan contemplated a nave extending several bays farther to the west seems to be implied by the two surviving arches of the arcade of the north aisle and by the change in the construction of the roof timbers already noticed, as well as by analogy with other early churches of the mendicant orders. There is no evidence, however, that this portion of the building was ever completed, and such structural indications as exist seem to suggest that it was not. The present west wall appears to be substantially part of the original structure. There is no indication of any opening in it of a date prior to the division of the building into two storeys, while the two corner buttresses on the north-west corner though somewhat restored are apparently original. Moreover, the responds of the vaulting of the undercroft are built against the present west wall, and the inference is therefore strong that this was erected possibly as a temporary expedient when the original and more ambitious scheme of a fully developed nave was abandoned.

It is difficult to suggest a reason for this sudden change of plan apart from lack of funds, which affected in varying degrees most of the English friaries especially during the earlier period of their history. That this was a primary cause of the suspension of the work on the nave is probable, but one may suspect a further reason for so unusual and drastic an alteration as that subsequently adopted at Lincoln. Possibly some disaster of which we have now no record, such as the flooding of the site by the river Witham which flows within 80 yards of the precinct on the south side, may have been the determining factor, or the quarrels with the city over the encroachments on the city walls may have led to so great a restriction on available space as to necessitate a drastic remedy.. It seems probable, on historical as well as architectural grounds, that the quire of the original building was completed and in use for some years before the alteration was carried out. Not only does the early date of the main structure suggest this, but the presence of the remains of the sedilia, which clearly belong to the early building, discountenances a change of plan during the actual progress of the building. On the other hand, the general similarity of style between the work of the two periods—particularly in the columns of the nave arcade and those of the undercroft—indicates that the interval cannot have been a long one. The facts suggest that the building in its original form was erected in the first half of the thirteenth century and probably soon after acquisition of the final portion of the site in 1237 and that the insertion of the undercroft and the consequent alterations to the structure were carried out during the second half of the century and were probably completed well before its close.

(7) LYNN REGIS

HISTORY

THE history of this house is exceptionally scanty. According to Blomefield [1] it was founded by Thomas Feltham in the latter part of the reign of Henry III, but as Eccleston, whose chronicle appears to have been finished in 1258, mentions [2] by name two guardians of the house, who had subsequently been transferred elsewhere, and expressly states that one of these, Robert de Thornham, was for many years custodian at Cambridge after leaving Lynn and before finally setting out on a Crusade to the Holy Land, it is clear that the house had been in existence some time before this date. Dr. Little has shown [3] that Robert de Thornham's departure for the Holy Land took place in 1250, so that his association with Lynn can scarcely have been later than about 1240. That the house was in fact in existence at least five years before this date is implied by Eccleston's reference to Geoffrey of Salisbury when a friar at Lynn hearing the confession of Alexander of Bassingbourn as the latter died in 1235.

[1] *History of Norfolk*, vol. 8 (1808), p. 526.
[2] Eccleston, pp. 110, 111 ; translation (ed. Salter), pp. 107–8.
[3] *The Grey Friars in Oxford*, p. 139, note 8.

The original site was enlarged in 1287 by the gift from Bernard le Estree of a piece of land in St. James' Street, which he had purchased from William de Lindesey, and in the same year Richard Seful granted the friars an annual rent of 12*d.* issuing out of a plot of land to the west of the churchyard of St. James " for enlarging the area which the friars now inhabit." [1] In April 1301 Robert de Scales, Lord of Middleton, granted to the Friars Minor of Lynn a spring-head at Hardwick in his lordship of Runcton with the right to lead water thence to Lynn.[2] This was doubtless the well which the guardian and friars were licensed to retain in July 1314. It was then described as a well in North Runcton called " Bukenwelle " which had been acquired without the late King's licence after the publication of the Statute of Mortmain from Thomas Bardolf and Robert de Scales, and the licence expressly authorized the friars to lead the water from the well by an underground conduit to their house in Lynn.[3] In June 1364 the site was further enlarged by the gift of two messuages. The letters patent granted on this occasion recite that Queen Isabel, the King's late mother, had acquired in fee a messuage in Lynn and the Mayor and commonalty of the town had acquired another messuage there to be appropriated to the guardian and friars for the enlargement of their house, but that the Queen had died before she could accomplish her intention and that the property acquired by her had descended to the King by inheritance. Edward III, accordingly, " to save his mother's soul " gave this messuage to the friars and at the same time licensed the corporation to assign the other messuage to them.[4]

Testamentary bequests [5] which were occasionally of substantial amounts throw little light on the buildings of this house, nor does it seem to have been extensively used as a place of burial. The only person of importance who is recorded [6] to have been buried here is John of Stamford, the friend of Adam Marsh and custodian at Oxford, who became provincial minister about 1256. He is said to have died in

[1] Blomefield, *History of Norfolk*, p. 526.
[2] *Hist. MSS. Com.*, 11th Report, pt. III, p. 239.
[3] *C.P.R. 1313–17*, p. 128.
[4] *Ibid., 1361–64*, pp. 512–13.
[5] Some 20 bequests are recorded between 1310 and 1390 in the *Red Register of King's Lynn* (ed. H. Ingleby, 2 vols, 1919–22). See also *Hist. MSS. Com.*, 11th Report, pt. III, p. 231.
[6] Registrum Fratrum Minorum Londonie, ed Kingsford, *The Grey Friars of London*, p. 192.

Plate 13

KING'S LYNN, GREYFRIARS' TOWER FROM THE WEST

1264.[1] In 1369 John de Ennemethe, merchant, desired to be buried in the church of the Friars Minor at Lynn and left 2s. to the guardian and 1s. to each friar.[2] In 1423 Richard Peverel of Tylney desired to be buried in the church of the Friars Minor of Bishop's Lynn[3] and in 1524 John Tinmouth or Maynelyn, vicar of Boston and suffragan bishop of Sarum, who had been a member of this house, bequeathed to them £5.[4] In 1325 the number of friars was 38, in 1327, 36.[5]

The deed of Surrender[6] is dated 1 October 1538, and is signed by the warden, Edmund Brygat or Bricott,[7] and nine others. On 20 February 1545 the site, together with the sites of the Black Friars and Austin Friars in Lynn, and the Carmelites of South Lynn and many other properties in Norfolk, was sold to John Eyre, a local receiver of Augmentations.[8] The official " particulars " for this grant describe the site with the orchards and gardens within the precinct as then in the tenure of Humfrey Cavyle or Carvyll,[9] at an annual rent of 6s. 8d., but make no mention of the buildings.[10] The site ultimately became the property of the town of Lynn and the greater part of it is now laid out as a public garden.

DESCRIPTION

The site of the friary is in the older part of the town a little to the east of St. Margaret's Church. The precinct probably comprised the whole of the land between St. James' Street on the north, Tower Place on the west, London Road on the east and Greyfriars Road, which follows the course of the Mill Fleet stream, on the south.

The sole remaining fragment of the buildings is the

---

[1] Little, *Grey Friars in Oxford*, pp. 128–9, where it is pointed out that there is little authority for this date.

[2] *Red Register of King's Lynn*, *op. cit.*, vol. 2, p. 90.

[3] Blomfield, *ut. sup.* from Reg. Hurning, fo. 122.

[4] *Grey Friars in Oxford*, p. 271.

[5] P.R.O. Accts., etc. (E 101), 381/14, 383/14. The Friars Preachers in these years numbered 45 and 44.

[6] *L. and P. Hen. VIII*, vol. 13(2), no. 502 ; D.K.R. 8th, Appendix II, p. 30.

[7] For further particulars of him see *Grey Friars in Oxford*, p. 283.

[8] *L. and P. Hen. VIII*, vol. 20(1), no. 282(37).

[9] Humfrey Carvyll was in occupation of the property in 1539 when he was allowed 16s. 4d. for repairing the stone walls of the site. P.R.O. Ministers' Accounts, Hen. VIII, no. 2632.

[10] P.R.O. Particulars for grants Hen. VIII, no. 422, m. 14. The Ministers' Accounts, no. 2632, m. 51, give no more information.

graceful steeple of the church (Plates 1 and 13).   This is of
the typical friars' form, built over an oblong crossing and

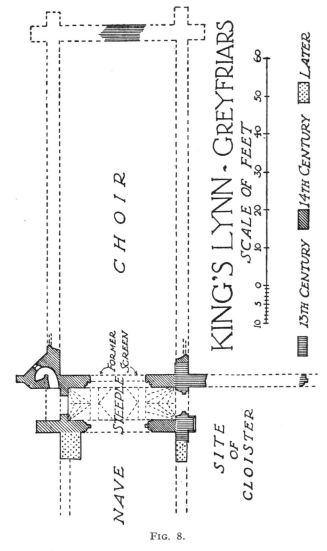

FIG. 8.

supported on cross arches, springing from the two parallel
walls of the crossing.   The tower, which is of late fourteenth-

century date, has been built within the original thirteenth-century church, and may therefore have replaced a timber belfry. The south door of the crossing is part of the original structure and a few feet of the south walls of the nave and quire of this building remain. On the north side the insertion of the belfry stair turret involved the removal of the whole of the thirteenth-century wall. The crossing is 8 feet 6 inches wide and its east and west walls are pierced by lofty two-centred arches which opened into the quire and nave respectively. The original ribbed vault within the crossing survives and above it rises a light hexagonal tower of two stages, with slender buttresses at the angles, and surmounted by a battlemented parapet decorated with blind arcading. The stair turret, which is approached by a door on the left of the north entrance to the crossing, rises to the full height of the tower with its summit projecting above the parapet and similarly decorated by a double row of blind arcading on the exterior. Both stages of the tower are lit by a lofty unglazed window of two lights divided horizontally by a single transom, in each of its disengaged walls. The tower is constructed of red brick, which contrasts well with the ashlar dressings of the quoins and windows.

The quire (88 ft. × 29 ft.) was without aisles, as the western jambs and the springing of the arches of the western-most windows on either side remain. Its length is deter-mined by a fragment of its east wall which is crossed by the present footpath. It appears to have been rebuilt in the fourteenth century to judge from the remains of the windows referred to. There is nothing to indicate the plan of the nave which extended into the site now occupied by the theatre, though it probably had at least one aisle. At a distance of some 30 feet to the south of the crossing is the base of the northern jamb of a doorway apparently *in situ*, which may have led into the chapter house.[1]

Immediately on the right of the south doorway of the crossing in a fragment of the cloister wall is a small recess which is probably the remains of a holy water stoup.

[1] It may be mentioned here that the arches standing to the S.E. of the tower are portions of a fourteenth-century house removed from the S.W. corner of the Tuesday Market Place and have no connection with the friary.

(8) READING

HISTORY

THE first Franciscan settlement at Reading was in the suburb to the north of the medieval town and close to Caversham Bridge. The site was provided by the neighbouring Benedictine Monastery and the deed setting out the terms of the grant is preserved in the cartulary of that house. It is dated 14 July 1233 and by it Abbot Adam de Lathbury and the convent of Reading granted the friars " a certain piece of waste land near the King's highway leading to Caversham Bridge containing 33 perches in length and 23 perches in breadth with permission to build and dwell there." [1] The grant was subject to stringent safeguards by which the friars bound themselves not to seek any other site on the land of the Abbey nor to extend the site given to them, and if they should at any time acquire any property of their own or should voluntarily relinquish the site then given, the monks should be entitled to resume possession of their property forthwith, together with any buildings thereon. [2] That the gift of the site was not entirely voluntary is clear from the following entry under this year in the contemporary Annals of Dunstable : " Eodem anno fratres minores volentes habitare in burgo Sancti Edmundi, item in burgo de Redingis, ad ipsum abbatem de Redingis literas tam Apostolicas quam regis impetrarunt ut liceret eis habitare in villa de Redingis. Impetraverunt etiam literas protectionis domini Papae ad episcopum Wintoniensem ut eos protegeret contra inimicos Christi. Et sic per instantiam multam impetraverunt locum ad inhabitandum ab invito abbate juxta pontem Redingis." [3]

The materials for the buildings seem to have been largely supplied by the King and the progress of the work can be

[1] B.M. Cotton MS. Vespasian. E, XXV, fo. 217. Charter Rolls, 17 Hen. III, m. 2d. The deed is printed in full in C. Coates' *History and Antiquities of Reading* (1802), Appendix II, and in Eccleston, pp. 171–72.

[2] A curious saving clause in this deed, providing that, if the monks should at any time wish to expel the friars for any cause other than those mentioned, the King might intervene on behalf of the friars who should thenceforth hold the property from him instead of from the monks, led to unforeseen difficulties, as Albert of Pisa is stated to have fervently resisted this clause and to have offered to remove the friars if the monks wished it on the ground that the quasi-legal right to the property thereby conferred was incompatible with the rule and spirit of the order. (Eccleston, pp. 99–100 ; Translation (ed. Salter), p. 96.)

[3] *Annales prioratus de Dunstaplia. Ann. Mon.* (R.S.), vol. 3, p. 134.

closely followed from these periodical grants. In May 1234 the friars were allowed to take timber from Windsor forest for their buildings which were in course of erection at Reading [1] and in the following June they received a gift of seventy oaks to make rafters (*cheverones*) for the work of their church.[2] The church was evidently substantially completed by August 1237, when the sheriff of Berkshire was ordered to cause the chapel of the Friars Minor to be wainscotted (*lambruscari*).[3] In the following April the friars received three oaks for the construction of the stalls in their quire,[4] and in August 1239 the sheriff was ordered to have these completed and to cause two altars to be made in the church.[5] A few days later a similar order was issued " for a dorter and chapter house to be built for the Friars Minor at the pond and to cause a board for the altar to be painted and starred with gold for their use." [6] The cost of the stalls and two altars amounted to 12 marks 9s. 2d.[7] In 1240 some alterations appear to have become necessary, as building material was provided for making a storey (*stagium*) in the chapel and dormitory.[8] In December 1241 fifty marks were spent on a privy chamber in two storeys (*ad stagium*) [9] and in May 1244 the Sheriff of Berkshire was ordered " to have the walls of the refectory raised and to make three large permanent windows in the roof beside the one already there and a proper pulpit in the middle of the refectory and to roof it well with shingles." [10]

Besides providing for their buildings the personal comforts of the friars were not forgotten, for in October 1239 the sheriff was ordered to purchase 52 ells of russet to make tunics for the use of the 13 Friars Minor at Reading, " to wit 11d. an ell at most," [11] while, in December 1241, 100s. was paid for clothing them during the year.[12] In 1244 brushwood to the value of 5 marks was ordered to be purchased for the friars in lieu of four logs which the King had granted them from Windsor forest,[13] and in 1247 three oaks were given for fuel.[14]

[1] *C.C.R. 1231–34*, p. 415.　　　　[2] *Ibid.*, p. 461.
[3] *C. Lib. R.*, vol. I, p. 290.
[4] *C.C.R. 1237–42*, p. 47 ; *C. Lib. R.*, vol. I, p. 328.
[5] *C. Lib. R.*, vol. I, p. 404.　[6] *Ibid.*, pp. 409–10.　[7] *Ibid.*, p. 450.
[8] *C. Lib. R.*, vol. I, p. 504 ; cf. Lincoln, p.
[9] *Ibid.*, vol. II, p. 93.　　　　[10] *Ibid.*, p. 235.
[11] *C. Lib. R.*, vol. I, p. 420 (*twelve* friars is a mistake ; the MS. has xiij).
[12] *Ibid.*, vol. II, p. 93.　　　　[13] *Ibid.*, p. 248.
[14] *C.C.R. 1242–47*, p. 520.

I

The chapel which had been furnished at the King's
expense was evidently unusually ornate for a Franciscan
church of this early date, and as such was regarded with
disfavour by Albert of Pisa, who had succeeded as second
provincial Minister in 1236, and who, according to Eccleston,
because he could not pull it down on account of the King
who had built it, hoped that heaven might destroy it.[1] As
it chanced misfortune from another source did ultimately
overtake the house and cause the entire site to be abandoned.
The property was low-lying and liable to floods, and there
is probably an early hint of difficulty met with on this
account in the alteration involving the insertion of an upper
storey in the church and dorter and the construction of
later buildings in two storeys.   In 1282 Archbishop Peckham, himself a Franciscan, wrote to the Abbot and Convent
of Reading on behalf of the friars, requesting that in spite
of the terms of the deed under which the site was held they
might be permitted to enlarge it, " as their buildings were
so often inundated with flood water in winter." [2]   At length
the friars were allowed to remove to a fresh site on higher
ground within the town.   The deed by which the Abbot
and convent gave their consent is dated 26 May 1285.[3]
The new site, which was smaller than the old one, measured
16 perches in breadth and 16½ perches in width and is
described as " a piece of ground between the house of Sir
Stephen the chaplain then rector of the church of Sulham
on the east and the sandy ditch on the west and extending
from the common way called New Street (Vicus Novus) to
the end of the piece of ground the use whereof the friars
have hitherto had and have and shall have henceforth of the
abbot and convent."   The wording of this grant suggests
that the old site which apparently extended up to the
boundary of the new property was not entirely abandoned,
though the buildings were presumably demolished when the
new ones were ready.[4]   The conditions of the grant were

[1] Eccleston, pp. 100, 173 ; Translation (ed. Salter), p. 96.
[2] *Reg. Epist. Peckham* (R.S.), vol. 2, pp. 414–16 ; Coates' *History of
Reading, op. cit.*, Appendix III.
[3] B.M. Cotton MS. Vespasian E, XXV, fo. 217, printed in full in
Coates, *op. cit.*, Appendix IV ; *C.C.R. 1279–88*, pp. 428–9.
[4] Peckham's second letter contains no hint that the two sites were
actually contiguous, and as the low-lying meadows adjoining Caversham
Bridge are some distance to the north of the second site the statement
may not have been strictly accurate.   Leland must have been in error
when he states that the site of the Grey Friars was on the north side of
Castle Street (*Itin.*, vol. I, p. 110), but his statement has led several later
writers to describe a second Franciscan house in this position.

even more stringent than before and included an additional
provision restraining the friars from burying in their
cemetery, church or any other place any person who was a
parishioner of any of the churches belonging to the Abbey in
Reading or elsewhere without special licence. In the same
year Archbishop Peckham wrote to the minister general of
the order asking him to confirm ·the change of site, and he
remarks that " the simplicity of the friars had caused them
to show more ignorance than prudence in the choice of a site
and in the erection of buildings to the inconvenience of
posterity. At Reading, compelled by the monks who owned
the town, they had accepted a marshy site so liable to
floods that at times they had to leave or be subject to much
danger and that their distance outside the town made it
inconvenient to procure necessaries." [1] The new site was
enlarged in 1288 by a bequest from Robert Fulco of certain
other void plots of ground in New Street adjoining the
land given by the Abbey.[2] The only references to the
erection of the new buildings appears to be the issue of an
order in 1302 to the constable of Windsor Castle to permit
the friars to fell and carry wherever they wished 56 oaks
fit for timber in the wood of Henry de Lacy, Earl of Lincoln,
at Ashridge which was within the bounds of Windsor Forest
as the Earl had given them to the friars,[3] and a bequest of 5s.
" to the works of the Friars Minor " from Alan de Banbury
in 1311.[4] There can be little doubt that the work then
in progress was the church, the nave of which still survives.

Later references to the house are equally scanty and it
seems to be but rarely mentioned in local wills in comparison
with many houses of the order. In 1501 Margaret Twynhoe
of Reading, widow, desired to be buried in the chapel of
Francis in the Grey Friars' church near the tomb of her
father and mother,[5] while in 1535 William Wattes of Reading left 6s. 8d. for the reparation of the friars' church.[6]
In April 1537 the Warden of the Grey Friars in Reading
was in correspondence with John Hussey regarding masses
to be said for the soul of the late Duke of Richmond.[7] The
house was surrendered to Dr. London on 13 September 1538,

[1] *Reg. Epist. Peckham* (R.S.), vol. II, pp. 211–12 ; Coates, *op. cit.*,
Appendix III.
[2] B.M. Cotton MS. Vespasian E, XXV, fo. 55.
[3] *C.C.R. 1302–07*, p. 3.
[4] B.M. Cotton MS. Vespasian E, XXV, fo. 189.
[5] Hutchins' *History of Dorset*, vol. 2, p. 171.
[6] P.C.C. " Hogen," fo. 28.
[7] *L. and P. Hen. VIII*, vol. 12(1), nos. 947 and 1068.

the deed being signed by Peter Schefford, the guardian,
Giles Coventry and ten others.[1] In August London had
written to Cromwell " a frynde of myne the warden of the
Grey Fryers in Reding hathe also desyred me to be an humble
sutar for hym and his brothern that they may with your
lordeschips favour also chaunge ther garmentes with ther
papisticall maner of lyvinges. The most partt of them be
very agede men and be nott of strength to go muche abrode
for ther lyvinges wherfor ther desyr ys that yt myght please
your lordeschippe to be a mediator unto the kinges grace
for them that they myght during ther lyves enjoy ther
chambres and orcharde." [2] On the day following the
surrender London again wrote to Cromwell informing him
that " in the house are three pretty lodgings, the warden
keeps one, Mr. Ogle the king's servant another and an old
lady called my lady Seynt Jone the third. None is out by
convent seal but they say they promised one to Mr. Ogle.
There is a goodly walk in their backside with trees ponds
and an orchard in all 20 acres. . . . What little plate and
jewels there is I will send up this week.[3] There is a great
trough of lead at their well and another in their kitchen
and the bell turret is covered with lead. . . . The inside
of the church and windows decked with Grey Friars I have
defaced and yet made some money of these things." [4] Three
days later he wrote again, " As soon as I hadde taken the
Fryers surrendre the multytude of the poverty of the town
resortyd thedyr and all thinge that myght be hadde stole
away insomyche that they hadde convayd the very clapers
of the bellys And saving that Mr. Fachell wiche made me
great chere at hys howse and the mayer dydde assist me they
wolde have made no litell spoyle " ; he then supports the
town in their plea for the grant of the friars' church, pointing out that their town hall was very small·and stood near
the river where was the common washing-place and on
session days there was such " betyng with batildores " that
one man could not hear another speak. " The body of the

---

[1] *L. and P. Hen. VIII*, vol. 13(2), no. 340, printed in full in Coates,
op. cit., pp. 303-4. The original has not survived, but there is a comparatively modern copy at Lambeth (MSS. 594, fo. 129).

[2] *L. and P. Hen. VIII*, vol. 13(2), no. 235 ; Wright, *Suppression*, p. 217.
In spite of this petition, Peter Lawrence, alias Schefford, late warden of
the Reading friars, and Giles Coventry appear in a list of prisoners in the
Tower in November 1539 (B.M. Cotton MS. Titus B 1, fo. 133).

[3] The plate consisted of 14 oz. gilt, $32\frac{1}{2}$ oz. parcel gilt, and 40 oz. white.
Monastic Treasures (Abbotsford Club), 1836, p. 14.

[4] *L. and P. Hen. VIII*, vol. 13(2), no. 346.

church of the Grey Fryers wiche ys selyd with lath and lyme wold be a very commodiose rowme for them. And now I have rydde all the fasschen of that church in parcleses, ymages, and awlters it wolde mak a gudly towne hall. . . . The wallys besyd the coyne stonys be butt chalk and flynt and the coveryng butt tile. And if it please the kinges grace to bestow that howse upon any of hys servantes, he may spare the body of the churche wiche stondith next the strete very well and yit have rowme sufficient for a great man." [1] The following day London reported that he had sent to Cromwell the deed of surrender " with ther plate such as yt ys," and he continues, " I have inwardly defacyd the churche and dorter ; the resydew of the howse I have left hole. . . . Thys ys a towne of moch power people and they fell to steling so fast in every corner of the howse that I have be fayne to tary a hole wek here to sett every thing in dew ordre and have and schall receyve to the kinges grace use I trust above xl li. the mansion holy re-servyd." [2] It appears that London was accused of exceed-ing his authority with regard to the destruction of the buildings at Reading, for on 29 October he protests to Crom-well, " I have not rased the houses so much as I perceive the king and your lordship are informed." He then re-hearses what has been done at the Grey Friars where he had " defaced the church the windows being full of friars and left the roof and walls whole to the king's use and had sold their ornaments, ' sellys ' in the dortoir and certain utensils which else had been stolen." [3]

In January 1540 the site was granted in fee to Robert Stanshawe, a groom of the King's chamber, in consideration of a sum of £30 and an annual rent of 6s. 8d.,[4] but the nave of the church was apparently excluded, as the petition of the town for this was granted in April 1544, when the body (i.e. the nave) and side aisles of the church were assigned to the Mayor and burgesses as a new guild hall at a yearly rent of ½d.[5]

<hr/>

[1] *L. and P. Hen. VIII*, no. 367 ; Wright, *Suppression*, pp. 222–23.
[2] *L. and P. Hen. VIII*, vol. 13(2), no. 377 ; Wright, p. 225.
[3] *L. and P. Hen. VIII*, vol. 13(2), no. 719 ; Ellis, *Original Letters*, 3rd ser., III, p. 130.
[4] *L. and P. Hen. VIII*, vol. 15, no. 282(12). There is no rental of his house among the post-dissolution ministers' accounts.
[5] In April 1545 the mayor was summoned by writ to appear and to do homage to the King " pro le body et le syde iles ecclesiæ domus dudum Fratrum minorum vulgariter nuncupatæ ley Grey Freres ac una com-petente et sufficiente via ad eandem quae præfati major et burgesses

The subsequent history of the building may be briefly stated. There is no evidence that it was ever used for the purpose for which it was granted, but it seems to have been adapted as a poor house for the town. In 1590 it was proposed to convert it into a " house of correction " or workhouse for poor people, but this does not seem to have been carried out until 1614.[1] At a later date it became the town bridewell or prison, the arcades being blocked up with brick and wooden partitions and the cells constructed in the aisles. The original roof is said to have been removed soon after 1786,[2] and from that date the nave proper remained open to the sky and served as an exercising yard for the prisoners. There is no definite record of the destruction of the chancel, although John Man, writing in 1816, states that this had taken place many years before.[3] Coates observes in 1802 that the existing arch at the east end of the nave had been stopped up many years before, the kitchen of Mr. Haycock's house having been built against it, on the east side.[4] This house was erected in 1728, and it was probably about this time that the quire was demolished, as in October of that year a tapered stone coffin without a lid was found at a depth of about 3 feet, " about a yard from the middle of the foundation of the east end of the Bridewell." [5] This coffin, which contained a quantity of bones, must have been that of a person buried in the centre of the space beneath the steeple at the entrance to the quire.

In 1862 a proposal was started to acquire the building which had ceased to be used as the bridewell, and to restore it as the church of a new parish. It was accordingly purchased with some adjoining property from the corporation and restored in 1863 under the direction of Mr. Woodman, the architect. The work then undertaken included the addition of the north and south transepts, the demolition and re-

nuper hauerunt ex dono domini Regis " (MS. Register of Acts of the Mayors of Reading, quoted in *Hist. MSS. Com.*, 11th Report, p. 181). There were subsequent proceedings in the Exchequer regarding the homage claimed for this property (J. M. Guilding, *Records of the Borough of Reading*, vol. I, pp. 195–98).
   [1] *Records of Reading, op. cit.*, vol. I, p. 403 ; vol. II, p. 59.
   [2] Coates, *op. cit.*, p. 308.   A tradition that it was re-erected over the nave of St. Mary's Church appears to have been due to a confusion arising out of an entry in the churchwardens' accounts of that parish recording the purchase in 1551 of a roof from Reading Abbey.
   [3] *History of Reading* (1816), p. 289.   [4] *Ibid.* (1802), p. 308.
   [5] Coates, *op. cit.*, p. 302.   Elsewhere he gives the distance as 2 yards. The present vicarage occupies part of the site of the quire.

building of the east end with the blocked arch into the
" walking-place," and the reconstruction of the two easternmost piers of the north and south arcades.[1]

DESCRIPTION

The site, which according to Dr. London's statement,
ultimately comprised some 20 acres, appears to have been
bounded on the south by the present Friars Road and on the
west by Caversham Road at the junction of which a gateway
is shown giving access to the precinct on Speed's map of
Reading in 1610.[2] The sole surviving building consists
of the early fourteenth-century nave of the friars' church,
much altered and restored, but retaining its very fine west
window and part of its arcading, more or less intact. The
walls are constructed of flint rubble with stone dressings
in the quoins and windows and are faced externally with
dressed flints laid in regular courses. In plan the building,
at the present day, consists of an aisled nave measuring
internally 79 feet by 54 feet with north and south transepts
added at the restoration of 1863. The aisles which are
9 feet 6 inches wide are separated from the nave by arcades
of five two-centred arches each of three orders, and supported
on square piers with a semicircular attached shaft on each
face. The shafts have bell capitals and double roll moulded
bases and stand on large plinths. On both sides of the
arcades are labels over the arches with small head stops at
their intersections, some of which are original. The easternmost arch on either side is of smaller span than the others,
and the piers supporting them, which appear to have been
entirely rebuilt, are of slightly different character and
consist of four clustered shafts without the solid core. The
western responds are half-piers of the same form as the
main piers, but at the east end the inner order of the arches
is carried on short shafts corbelled off and stopped by
foliage, the outer orders dying into the wall with small
head stops. This must, however, be largely a modern
reconstruction, as the whole of the east wall appears to have
been rebuilt, the original arch into the " walking-place "
having been reconstructed in the new wall with its blocking

[1] See circulars and appeals relative to the restoration reprinted for
private circulation 1874, and C. Hole, *The Life of the Rev. and Ven. W. W.
Phelps*, 2 vols., 1871–73 *passim*.
[2] The buildings shown on this plan appear to be purely conventional

retained. This arch is 17 feet wide and is of three moulded orders with responds consisting of triple shafts with moulded capitals and bases.[1] The aisle windows have segmental heads with an external label and are of three trefoiled ogee lights. There are no west windows to the aisles, but the splendid west window of the nave is a remarkably fine example of the period. It is of five lights with trefoiled ogee heads and has elaborate reticulated tracery within a two-centred arch with an external label. There is no west door, the principal entrance being on the south. This is of two recessed and deeply moulded orders which continue down the jambs and die away on the plinth. It has a segmental rear arch and an external label stopped with carved leaves. Opposite in the north wall is a small doorway with a two-centred external head of two chamfered orders which Coates describes in 1802 [2] as then blocked up, as were also the aisle windows on this side.

The transepts in their present form are entirely modern, but it has been stated that the south transept was rebuilt on its original foundations.[3] The absence of the transept, as already noticed, was a marked peculiarity of churches of the Franciscans and of the mendicant orders generally in England, and it is therefore perhaps worth while to consider somewhat closely the evidence for its existence at Reading. This appears to rest on Coates' statement in 1802 that galleries were erected in the south transept in 1625 and that : " here are now the solitary cells and adjoining is the keeper's kitchen in the chambers of which the arches of this transept are still remaining." [4] Elsewhere he notes that the two eastern arches of the arcades were equal to the width of the south transept. These statements seem to imply that a building corresponding in width to the present transept stood on the south side of the nave at that time, but it is curious that John Man, writing in 1816, makes no mention of a transept though he describes the church in some detail and gives its principal measurements. If it existed, therefore, all trace of it had presumably disappeared before 1816, as was almost certainly the case by 1846, when John Billings described the building.[5] His account is accompanied by a plan which contains no indication of a transept and shows

[1] Traces of painting are said to have been visible on either side of this arch before the restoration (Coates, *op. cit.* p. 308).
[2] *Coates, op. cit.,* p. 309.   [3] *V.C.H. Berks,* vol. 3, p. 374.
[4] *Coates, op. cit.,* p. 309.   [5] *Arch. Journal.,* vol. 3, pp. 141–48.

the aisle walls as continuous up to the east wall of the nave with an east window at the end of each aisle. One of these windows, the writer observes, was bricked up while the other was so completely covered with ivy that no trace of it was visible. If the section of the south wall corresponding to the width of the supposed south transept had been built since 1802 it is difficult to see how Billings, who was an architect, could have failed to notice it as his plan was carefully prepared, and the inference is therefore strong that the aisle walls were at that date either intact on both sides up to the east wall or that there was reasonable evidence for assuming that this was the original arrangement. On the other hand, Coates' reference to " the arches " of the transept as visible in the adjoining building is difficult to explain except on the assumption that he was here confusing the transept with the " walking-place," the existing arch into which was, as already stated, visible in the kitchen of the house erected in 1728. This, it must be admitted, is pure conjecture, but the evidence for the existence of an original south transept is in any case slender. One feature, however, of the existing building is of importance in this connection as, if it is original, it seems of necessity to imply that such a transept existed. This consists of a two-centred drop arch of two chamfered orders carrying the west wall of the existing transept across the south aisle to the second pier from the east of the nave arcade. The inner order of this arch is supported on the north side on the attached shaft of the pier and on the south side by a corbel on the aisle wall, while the outer order dies on to the aisle wall on one side and is roughly stopped against the outer order of the nave arcade on the other. A similar arch exists in a corresponding position across the north aisle, but as there is even less evidence for assuming the existence of an original north transept it seems probable that both these arches were inserted at the restoration of 1863 and have no bearing on the plan of the building.[1] Unfortunately no precise record of the work carried out at that time appears to have survived. That certain foundations were discovered during the building of the present south transept is probable, as Coates' statement clearly implies that a building of some kind had

[1] The evidence of the stone is not always a safe guide, as a quantity of old material seems to have been re-used at the restoration, but from a superficial examination of these arches, that on the south would appear to be a modern insertion, while that on the north has more the appearance of early work.

stood in this position, but there is very little evidence that it was of medieval date. The decision to include a south transept as part of the scheme of restoration was presumably made on the strength of Coates' statement, but during the progress of clearing the site evidence was found that was at the time considered to indicate the former existence of a north transept also, and the scheme was enlarged and further funds obtained for the addition of the present north transept, thus, as it was thought, restoring the plan of the original church. The foundations on the north side, however, can be sufficiently explained on the assumption that they were the western wall of the passage leading from the belfry into the cloister and part of the south wall of the cloister itself, as the latter must have been on the north side of the church and, from the position of the aisle windows, the sills of which are only 5 feet 6 inches from the ground, and the absence of any indication of the abutment of its roof on the existing wall of the church, was presumably separated from it by an open yard as in many friars' churches. With the possible exception of Coventry there is no known example of the presence of both arms of the cross in English Franciscan churches, and from what has been said it will be seen that the evidence for their existence at Reading is inadequate, while the evidence for a one-armed transept on the south side is scarcely more satisfactory.

Of the original fittings of the church nothing survives. In 1843 the moulded wall plate and two or three purlin braces and rafters of the original roof are said to have remained over the aisles. The present roofs are all modern. On the wall at the west end of the north aisle is a case containing a number of decorated fourteenth-century tiles found during the restoration of 1863. They are of red clay inlaid with white slip and glazed. The designs include a dog with a collar and bell upon a background of oak leaves and acorns ; a hare upon a background of trefoil foliage ; an antlered stag, a lion, and a geometrical design of four squares divided gyronwise. There are no heraldic shields depicted.

(9) RICHMOND (YORKSHIRE)

HISTORY

ACCORDING to Gale [1] and Clarkson,[2] this house was founded in 1257–58 by Ralph Fitz Randal, Lord of Middleham, who died in 1270. Clarkson adds that the founder was buried in the abbey church at Coverham, but that his heart, enclosed in a leaden urn, was placed in the quire of the church of the Richmond friars under an arched recess in the wall.[3] The date of the foundation is confirmed by the evidence produced in the celebrated law suit of Scrope *v.* Grosvenor in the latter part of the fourteenth century, when it was stated on the authority of a lost chronicle of the Richmond Franciscans that the house was founded in 1258, in the time of Peter of Savoy, Earl of Richmond. This Peter held the Honour of Richmond until 1266, and died two years later, and the fact that, according to the evidence of the same law suit, the friars were in possession of a cope which had been presented to them by him, is further proof that the house was in existence before the latter date. At a somewhat later period the Richmond friary, like that of the neighbouring Premonstratensian abbey of Easby, came under the patronage of the powerful family of Scrope, but a continued association with the founder's kin is evidenced by the fact that the Neville arms [4] appeared beside those of Scrope over the outer gate as well as on the seal of the house.[5]

The earliest contemporary reference to the house appears to be in 1304, when Arthur de Hartlepool, an apostate friar who had recently escaped from the Richmond friary, was arrested for theft at Whitehaven (Quitonthavene) and ordered to be handed over to the friars in Richmond for punishment.[6] In the same year John of Brittany, Earl of Richmond, left the friars of this house £5.[7] In 1314–15 the Archbishop of York sent special instructions to the warden of the Richmond house to preach against the Scots

[1] R. Gale, *Registrum Honoris de Richmond* (1722), p. 235.
[2] Christopher Clarkson, *The History and Antiquities of Richmond* (1821), p. 214.
[3] *Ibid.*, p. 216. Following Gale, *op. cit.*, p. 235.
[4] Robert Neville, 2nd lord Neville of Raby, who died in 1282, married Mary, daughter and heiress of Ralph Fitz Randal.
[5] See evidence in Scrope *v.* Grosvenor case, *post.*
[6] *C.C.R. 1302–07*, p. 174; *Prynne Records*, vol. III, p. 1042.
[7] Clarkson, *op. cit.*, p. 33.

and rouse the people to resist.[1]   In June 1364 the guardian
and friars were licensed to acquire five tofts containing
together four acres from Sir Richard le Scrope and William
de Huddeswell for the enlargement of their property.[2]
This gift is interesting as it is the first recorded association
of the Scropes with this house.   A further extension of
the site was effected in March 1383, when John de Neville,
5th Lord Neville of Raby, was licensed to alienate to the
friars 1½ acres of meadows adjoining their house.[3]

That the benefactions of Sir Richard le Scrope were
limited to the grant referred to above and to a gift of £10
to the friars by his will [4] is unlikely, as the evidence given in
the Scrope *v.* Grosvenor case suggests that he or his immediate ancestors had been largely responsible for the erection
of the friary buildings.   This evidence incidentally throws
considerable light on the arrangement and extent of the
buildings at the end of the fourteenth century and no
excuse therefore is needed for quoting in full the material
portion.   The case, which concerned the rival claims of
Richard le Scrope and Robert Grosvenor to the right to
bear the arms, *azure, a bend or,* was before the courts from
1385 to 1390 before being finally decided in favour of
Scrope.   At a hearing in the Whitehall of Westminster on
21 January 1386–87 there was exhibited on behalf of Scrope
a common seal of the Friars Minor of Richmond on one
side of which were the disputed arms.[5]   At a later hearing
an interesting document was put in by William Irby, official
of Richmond, also in favour of Scrope.   It consisted of a
list of places in the Archdeaconry of Richmond, where the
arms in question were visible.   The portion relating to the
friary is as follows :

Arma nobilis viri domini Ricardi le Scrope militis videlicet de azura
cum uno bende de auro continentur et sunt depicta sculpta et facta
in locis infrascriptis. . . .
Item in ecclesia Fratrum Minorum Richm' in quatuor fenestris
vitreis in vestibulo sunt dicta arma depicta in fenestris fact' centum
annis elapsis.
Item in quadam capa in eadem ecclesia existente de etate et tempore
cuius inicij memoria hominum non existit sunt dicta arma facta

---

[1] *Hist. Papers & Letters from Northern Registers* (R.S.), p. 239 n.
[2] *C.P.R. 1361–64*, p. 510.   [3] *Ibid. 1381–85*, p. 234.
[4] *Test. Ebor.*, vol. I, p. 274.
[5] *Scrope v. Grosvenor controversy*, ed. by Sir Harris Nicolas (1832),
vol. I, p. 43.

in duobus locis que quidem capa fuit donata per Petrum de Sabaudia quondam comitem Richm'.
Item in duabus fenestris vitreis ad utrumque finem dicte ecclesie etatis quinquaginta annorum.
Item in eadem ecclesia picta sunt dicta arma in quadam tabula antiqua et fuerunt a tempore cuius memoria hominum non existit.
Item in quadam alia tabula depicta sunt dicta arma de etate centum annorum.
Item in domo hospicii dictorum Fratrum sunt dicta arma de etate quinquaginta annorum. . . .
Item quia dictus dominus Ricardus est unus fundatorum Fratrum Minorum Richemondie dicti fratres fecerunt dicta arma solempniter fieri et poni supra portam eorundem exteriorem videlicet dicta ex una parte et arma domini de Nevyll ex alia parte. Que quidem arma ibidem fuerant et sunt a tempore fundacionis dicte domus. Que quidem domus fuerat fundata in tempore domini Petri de Sebaudia quondam comitis Richm' videlicet anno domini 1258 prout in cronicis dicte domus vidimus plenius contineri.
Item quia antecessores dicti domini Ricardi ac domini de Nevill fuerunt ut premittitur fundatores dicte domus dicti fratres in memoriam antecessorum dicti domini Ricardi fecerant dicta arma fieri sculpta in eorum sigillo communi ex parte una et arma domini de Nevill ex parte alia dicti sigilli.
Item dicta arma dicti domini Ricardi sunt facta in quadam fenestra vitrea dicte domus in quadam domo ubi fratres dicte domus communiter se lavant cum ad eandem domum venerint fessi sive lassi que quidem fenestra fuerat facta in prima fundacione dicte domus suprascripte.
Item in eadem domo in quadam domo vocata lez studies juxta dormitorium sunt dicta arma in verrura duarum fenestrarum factarum in prima fundacione domus supradicte.
Item in refectorio dicte domus continentur dicta arma in duobus locis facta statim post primam fundacionem domus supradicte.
Item in quadam domo dictorum fratrum vocata le parlour dicta arma continentur in verrura antiquiore omni verrura ut estimatur verisimiliter facta in dicta domo.
Item in ecclesia fratrum dictorum dicta arma sunt depicta in septem locis preter loca superius expressata aliqua facta centum et viginti quedam centum alia nonniginta et reliqua septuaginta annis elapsis.
Item in prefata ecclesia ac in singulis monasteriis ecclesiis parochialibus et locis aliis suprascriptis arma predicta cum uno label de argento modo pertinencia ad nobilem virum dominum Henricum le Scrop cognatum sive nepotem dicti domini Ricardi fuerunt et sunt depicta sculpta et facta aliqua de etate cuius inicij memoria hominum non existit, quedam de centum quedam de nonaginta quedam de lxxx^ta quedam de lxx^ta quedam de sexaginta quinquaginta quadraginta triginta et viginti annis elapsis.[1]

The importance of this evidence is not only in the light it throws on the extent of the Scrope connection with the house, but in the fact that it contains what is probably a

---

[1] *Scrope v. Grosvenor controversy*, ed. by Sir Harris Nicolas (1832), vol. I, pp. 222–26.

fairly complete list of the domestic buildings of the friary with some indication of their relative dates. Apart from the church the Scrope arms appeared in the guest house (then fifty years old), in a window dating from the foundation of the house in the lavatory which is described as " a certain apartment where the friars commonly wash themselves when they come to the house tired and weary," in two other windows of the same period in a room called " the studies " near the dormitory, in two positions in the refectory dating from immediately after the first foundation of the house, and in the parlour where the arms were confined to a glass window " more ancient as it is thought than all the other windows in the house." In the church itself the arms occurred in four windows in the vestibule (i.e. vestry) constructed about 100 years before, in two windows at either end of the church which were about 50 years old, on a certain ancient board dating from before the memory of men and on other boards about 100 years old, as well as in seven other places not specified, dating from 70 to 120 years before, and finally twice on a cope given to the friars by Peter of Savoy, formerly Earl of Richmond. The mention of the two windows about fifty years old at either end of the church possibly points to the addition of the south aisle of the nave about 1340, while one may perhaps infer that the guest house was added or rebuilt about the same time.

Clarkson states [1] that several of the Scropes, the Plessys and the Franks were buried in this house, but gives no evidence for the statement. Besides Sir Richard le Scrope, however, other members of the family mentioned the Richmond friars in their wills. In 1409 Sir Stephen le Scrope of Bentley left them 10 marks for an obit [2] and in 1418 Stephen Scrope, archdeacon of Richmond, left them 20s. [3] The wills of some 26 persons who refer to this house are mentioned in *Testamenta Eboracensia*, among whom may be mentioned Henry, Lord Percy, who in 1349 gave £7 to be divided between this and five other houses of the order, [4] Sir Alexander Neville, who in 1457 left the Richmond h̄use 13s. 4d., [5] Sir Ralph FitzRandal, presumably a descendant of the founder, who in the same year left 7 marks for one year's divine service in the friars' church, [6] and Dame Jane Strangways, who in 1500 left 10s. for a trental

[1] Clarkson, *op. cit.*, p. 216.   [2] *Test. Ebor.*, vol. 3, p. 39.
[3] *Ibid.*, vol. 1, p. 386.   [4] *Ibid.*, vol. 1, p. 58.
[5] *Ibid.*, vol. 2, p. 208.   [6] Surtees Soc., vol. 26, p. 4.

Plate 14

RICHMOND, GREYFRIARS' TOWER FROM THE NORTH-WEST

of masses and 10s. " unto the reparaciones of their place,"
as well as 40s. to " freire Fraunch of Richmount." [1]   In
May 1484 Richard III ordered Geoffrey Franke, receiver of
Middleham, " to content the friars of Richmond with
12½ marks for the saying of a thousand masses for king
Edward IV." [2]   Six years later William Billyngham, the
warden of the Grey Friars, was involved in a dispute with
the Abbot of Easby and the burgesses, concerning the
goods of Margaret Richmond, an anchoress in the parish
church, who had died after taking the habit of the friars.
The case was referred to arbitration and was only finally
settled by the warden being given the goods of the late
anchoress and the abbot the right to dispose of those of the
present anchoress. [3]   A curious reference to the house at
about this period is contained in the fifteenth-century comic
ballad entitled " The Felon Sow of Rokeby," which relates
how, when friar Theobald was warden, Ralph Rokeby of
Morton gave a savage sow to the Richmond friars " to
mend their fare," and the exciting adventures of friar
Middleton and his assistants in their attempts to capture
the beast, its final capture and the triumphal return to
Richmond. [4]

The house was surrendered on 19 January 1539, the deed
being signed by Dr. Robert Sanderson the warden, 13 priests
and one other. [5]   No inventory of the goods has survived,
but the lead on the church was estimated at 3 fother, the
three bells weighed 2,000 lb. and the plate 31 oz. [6]   The
custody was given to Ralph Gower and Richard Crosby and
on 26 May 1540 the site was granted on a twenty-one years'
lease to the former. [7]   The property comprised : the site
of the house with the edifices, and

One garden near the outer gates and one garden adjoining the
quire of the church worth 12d. yearly :
waste ground lying upon the east part of the site containing 1 acre
valued at 12d. yearly :
ground lying nere upon the west side of the site called " the
Orteyerd " containing 1 acre valued at 2s. :

[1] *Test. Ebor.*, vol. 4, p. 188.   [2] B.M. Harl. MSS. 433.
[3] *Test. Ebor.*, vol. 2, p. 114 n.
[4] Printed in Clarkson, *op. cit.*, Appendix 35, and in T. Whitaker's
Hist. of the Deanery of Craven, 3rd edit., 1878, pp. 568–70.
[5] *L. and P. Hen. VIII*, vol. 14, no. 96.   The deed is printed in Clarkson,
op. cit., Appendix 33, pp. cii-civ.   A good seal is attached to the original.
D.K.R. 8th Report, Appendix II, p. 38.
[6] B.M. Harl. MSS. 604, fo. 104.
[7] *L. and P. Hen. VIII*, vol. 15, no. 1032, p. 556.

a close called the friars close lying enclosed within a stone wall containing 7 acres valued at 21s. yearly.

A tenement lying in Richmond in Broadgate with edifices and rents valued at 6s. 8d. yearly.

Two cottages adjoining the friars' wall besides Pinfold (Punfald) green " now in decay for lak of reparacion " valued at nothing.[1]

The whole of this property, subject to Gower's lease, was sold on 20 June 1544 to John Banaster, the King's servant, and William Metcalfe of London,[2] from whom it was apparently subsequently acquired by Gower. Its later history is given by Clarkson.[3] The property was purchased in 1895 by the Marquess of Zetland.

DESCRIPTION

Leland states, " At the bakke of the Frenchgate is the Grey Freres, a little withowte the waullis. Their howse, medow orchard and a little wood is waullid yn. Men go from the market place to hit by a posterne gate. There is a conducte of water at the Grey Freres, els there is none in Richemount." [4] The site which was outside the walls on the north side of the town is shown in Thomas Bradley's plan of Richmond in 1817.[5] It then consisted of seven closes besides the meadow where the steeple is shown and the site of a modern house called " The Friary," and occupied the whole area between Quaker Lane on the north, a road called " Back of the Fryers," now Queen's Road on the east, a road to the north of the market-place, now Victoria Road on the south, and another road to the east of "Nun's close " on the west. It comprised, according to Whitaker, nearly 16 acres.[6]

The sole remaining portion of the buildings is the beautiful fifteenth-century bell tower (Plate 14), with some fragments of the walls of the church adjoining.[7] The tower was inserted within walls of the fourteenth-century quire and over the passage which previously divided the nave

---

[1] P.R.O. Ministers' Accounts, Hen. VIII, no. 197 (Yorks).
[2] *L. and P. Hen. VIII*, vol. 19(I), no. 812(74).
[3] Clarkson, *op. cit.*, pp. 220–23 : cf. *V.C.H., North Riding*, vol. I, pp. 21–22.
[4] Leland, *Itin.*, vol. 4, p. 25.
[5] Frontispiece to Clarkson, *op. cit.*
[6] *History of Richmondshire* (1823), vol. I, p. 99.
[7] Engravings of the tower appear in Dugdale's *Monasticon* (1846), vol. vi, p. 1544 ; Whitaker's *History of Richmondshire, ut sup.*, vol. I, p. 99 and Clarkson, *op. cit.*, p. 214.

from the quire (Fig. 9). The portions of the side walls of
the latter where they abut on the later tower still survive,
together with the original doorway with a two-centred
chamfered arch on the north side. A fragment of the north
wall and part of a buttress also remain, farther to the east,
from which it is apparent that the quire was unaisled. Its
width was approximately 22 feet, but there is little now to
indicate its length. Clarkson mentions [1] that scattered
foundations were occasionally visible in times of drought to
the east of the tower, and it was presumably on such evidence
that the writer in the *Victoria County History* estimated
its length at 52 feet, which, allowing for the space occupied
by the tower, would give a total length for the original

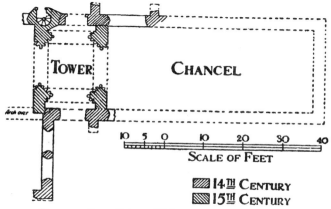

FIG. 9.—Grey Friars, Richmond. Ground plan

structural quire of 68 feet. The greater part of this area,
however, has now been excavated and the level lowered in
connection with the laying out of the site around the town's
War Memorial which was unveiled in 1921. Of the nave
nothing survives, but on the south side there was a chapel
or aisle, 17 feet 9 inches wide internally, the eastern wall of
which is still intact and contains two fourteenth-century
windows with heads and jambs complete, but devoid of
tracery. Externally there are traces of a diagonal buttress
at its south-east corner and the springing of the arcade
which divided it from the nave can be seen against the
abutment of the tower. The jamb of a window on the

[1] Clarkson, *op. cit.*, p. 216.

K

north side of the nave near the tower seems to imply that there was no aisle on this side.

Within this structure the tower was inserted, as stated, in the latter part of the fifteenth century possibly in place of a timber belfry. It is square in plan and of considerable height. The angles are supported by pairs of buttresses, which rest on the chancel walls on the north and south and are corbelled out on the east and west on either side of the slender lofty arches which gave access to the quire and nave respectively. These arches have two-centred heads with elaborate mouldings and the jambs consist of clustered shafts with moulded capitals and bases. On the north and south the openings are lower but of similar character and are constructed within the walls of the earlier quire so as to preserve the passage or walking-place which gave access into the cloister. The top stage of the tower is marked off by an offset and is lit on each side by a large perpendicular window of two trefoiled lights beneath a three-centred head with an external moulded hood terminated by flowers. Above is a parapet with pierced trefoiled battlements and in the middle of each side a projecting pinnacle supported on a corbel above the windows of the top storey and corresponding to the foliated finials of the buttresses at the angles. The middle storey of the tower is lit on the east and west by one and on the north and south by two small square-headed windows with cinqefoiled cusped lights and moulded and returned labels, while above the crown of the main arches on the east and west is a doorway a little to the north of the central line in each case. On the north side of the tower near its north-west angle is an external staircase, terminating just above the offset of the upper stage. The floors of the several stages of the tower have gone so that only the shell of the building remains.

¶(10) WALSINGHAM [1]

HISTORY

THE history of the Franciscan house at Walsingham is extremely scanty. On 1 February 1347 Elizabeth de Burgh, Countess of Clare and daughter of Gilbert the Red, 9th Earl of Clare, was licensed to found a house of Friars Minor in

[1] " The Grey Friars of Walsingham," by A. R. Martin, *Norfolk & Norwich Arch. Soc.*, vol. 25, pp. 227–71.

Walsingham.[1]   The licence was renewed in February of the following year, when the proposed site was stated to contain 4 acres 1 rood.[2]   The settlement of the friars was not carried out, however, without strenuous opposition from the Canons of the Augustinian Priory, who appear to have feared a diversion of offerings and bequests from their own house to that of the newcomers.   Their case is set forth at great length in a curiously naïve and somewhat unconvincing document which is still preserved in the cartulary of their house.[3]   It is in the form of a petition to the Lady Clare.   Among the arguments put forward were the prospective loss of tithes ; that the friars would draw the parishioners away from their parish churches and by celebrating mass and hearing confessions would deprive the parish priest of his effective cure of souls ; that the offerings at churchings of women and burials would, " through the enticements, blandishments and deceptions of the Friars," be lost to the church ; that many other parochial rights would be infringed ; that the gates of the priory were closed at night against thieves so that the pilgrim who arrived during the night made his offering on the following day, which he would probably no longer do if he lodged at the friary ; that the friars could not acquire a site without papal licence, and that, if they did, they would be excommunicated ; and finally, that no further house of friars was needed, as there were already houses of the Carmelite Order at Burnham, 4 miles from Walsingham in one direction, and at Sniterley (i.e. Blakeney), 5 miles in the other.   All opposition, however, was unavailing, as both Royal and Papal sanction were duly obtained ; and by July 1348 the friars were already in possession.   The licence of Pope Clement VI, which was granted at the request of Edward III and his Queen Philippa, is dated 28 September 1347, and is directed to the Provincial of the Friars Minor in England, authorizing him to acquire a site at Walsingham to accommodate 12 friars.[4]

[1] *C.P.R. 1345–48*, p. 255.   In 1314, on the death of her brother, the 10th Earl, she had inherited the extensive estates of the Earls of Clare, which included the Manor of Walsingham, and subsequently endowed University Hall, afterwards Clare College, Cambridge.   On her death, in 1360, she left the Friars of Walsingham 100s. (Nichols *Royal Wills*, 1780, p. 33).
[2] *C.P.R. 1348–50*, p. 7.
[3] B.M. Cotton MSS., Nero E, VII, ff. 152–53 (in pencil, ff. 160–1). Printed in *Norfolk & Norwich Arch. Soc.*, vol. 25, pp. 269–71.
[4] *C. Pap. L.*, vol. 3., p. 252.

The subsequent history of the house is chiefly confined to an occasional record of the acquisition of further land. The original site soon proved inadequate, for, on 7 July 1348, the guardian of the Friars Minor at Walsingham was licensed to acquire in mortmain a further 3 acres of land adjoining their dwelling-place for its enlargement.[1] Two years later, on 4 May 1351, a further licence was granted following an inquisition held by William de Midleton, the escheater for Norfolk, authorizing the friars, in consideration of half a mark paid into the King's hanaper, to enlarge their dwelling-place by enclosing " a way leading from North Barsham to the chapel of St. Mary in Little Walsingham beneath the said dwelling-place on condition that they make on their own soil there a way of the same length and breadth to wit 60 perches by 16 perches for public use." [2] The main road which now skirts the site on the east was probably constructed at this time, in place of an earlier route leading more directly to the market-place. This licence was confirmed by Richard II on 18 December 1384.[3]

Some time before his death in 1425 the friars obtained by gift from Edmund Mortimer, 5th Earl of March, a close of 3 acres on the south side of the mansion of the Priory. Owing to the absence of the necessary licence this property was forfeited to the Crown, but on 20 May 1441, at the request of Richard, Duke of York, who had inherited the Manor of Walsingham from his uncle, the Earl of March, and is described in the licence (presumably on account of his descent through his mother, Anne Mortimer, from Elizabeth de Clare) as founder of the house, Henry VI granted this property to John Hekelyng, the then warden, and the brethren in frankalmoign, and at the same time licensed the Duke of York to grant a cottage and another 3 acres and a garden containing a ¼ rood in Little Walsingham to the warden and brethren in frankalmoign.[4] This is the last recorded gift of land to the friars. If carried into effect it brought the total area of their property up to 13 acres 1 rood 10 perches.

Testamentary references to the house are comparatively few and throw no light on the arrangement of its buildings. In 1491 Robert Pigot desired to be buried within the Friary and gave 6s. 8d. for his burial, 6s. 8d. for prayers for his

---

[1] *C.P.R. 1348–50*, p. 122.   [2] *Ibid. 1350–54*, p. 71.
[3] *Ibid. 1381–85*, p. 490.   [4] *Ibid. 1436–41*, p. 544.

Plate 15

WALSINGHAM FRIARY, FROM THE SOUTH-WEST

soul and 6s. 8d. for a breakfast,[1] and in 1514 Robert Grey of Walsingham gave to the friars two pair of censers of silver valued at 10 marks each.[2] Early in the sixteenth century there was an anchoress living within the Friary. She is mentioned in the will of John Burdion of Little Walsingham, who, in 1507, left 10s. to the friars and 4d. to " the ankeres in the same frerys." [3] She was still there in 1526,[4] but there is no indication of the position of her cell, though in other houses this frequently stood in the cemetery or near the principal gateway.

There is no further mention of the house until the eve of the suppression, when *Valor Ecclesiaticus* of 1535 records that Giles Coventry was then guardian, and the annual value of three tenements is returned at 40s. and of the remainder of the property at 6s.[5] Three years later the house was surrendered to the Bishop of Dover. The deed of surrender has not survived, so that nothing is known of the inmates of the house at this date.

As soon as the surrender had been effected, Thomas Sydney, who was Master of the Hospital in Little Walsingham and grantee of the site of the Augustinian Priory, appears to have been appointed collector of the rents of the friars' property. It is probable that most of this property had already been let by the friars before the suppression. In 1541, when Sydney returned his first account to the Exchequer, part of the site " with divers buildings lately built " and a close and another piece of land were in the occupation of Sir Roger Townshend [6] and Anne, his wife, at a total yearly rent of 42s. ; two cottages with 2 acres of land had been let to Sydney himself for 3s. 4d. a year ; a tenement with a garden was in the tenure of William Reynolds at a yearly rent of 16s., another tenement was in the occupation of Thomas Jennynges at 20s., and another tenement or inn called the White Horse with two gardens and a parcel of land called " le Carre " containing

---

[1] Blomefield, *History of Norfolk*, vol. 9, p. 281.

[2] Ibid., *ut sup.*

[3] J. L'Estrange MSS. Norfolk Wills in Norwich Public Library, vol. 3, fo. 1600.

[4] Blomefield, *History of Norfolk*, vol. 9, p. 281.

[5] *Val. Eccles.* (R.C.), vol. 3, p. 388.

[6] This was apparently Sir Roger Townshend, the eldest son of Sir Roger Townshend, the judge, who died in 1493, and the ancestor of the Townshends of Rainham. He died at a great age in 1551, and in his will (Norwich Consistory Court) mentions his house in Little Walsingham called the Friary. (Norfolk Arch. Soc., *Visitation of Norfolk*, vol. I, p. 315.)

1 acre was held under a lease by Richard Grene at an annual rent of 26s. 8d., so that the total income from the friars' property in that year was 108s.[1] In the following year a further 2s. rent is included in respect of a ½ acre of land called " Aldercarre " with certain reeds (lez Redes) growing there in the tenure of Thomas Sydney.[2] This was either unlet or had been forgotten in the previous year, and brought the total income to 110s., at which figure it is returned in the accounts from 1543 to 1545.[3] On 20 February in the latter year the whole of this property was sold, subject to the leases to Townshend, Sydney and Grene and to the various tenancies, to John Eyre, a local receiver of Augmentations.[4] In the official " particulars " sent to the Court of Augmentations the description of the property is similar to that in Thomas Sydney's accounts for the preceding years.[5] The grant was made by letters patent dated 20 February 1545, but the purchase was as usual purely a matter of speculation, as the property soon passed into other hands. Its subsequent history is obscure.[6]

Of the fate of the buildings very little is known. At the very end of 1538, the Walsingham Friary appears in a list of houses that had not yet been defaced or razed " as Mr. Sydney is accomptant for the buildings and all things left by the visitor." [7] In the following year the accounts of the Guild of the Annunciation of the Blessed Mary at Walsingham record the laying out of 40s., " in part payment for the great bell of the late Friars Minor," [8] and it is probable that the church was demolished very shortly after this date. The buildings around the little cloister appear to have been subsequently converted into a dwelling-house, and the remainder were apparently allowed to fall into gradual ruin. The state of the buildings in the early part of the last century, with a small cottage on the site of the present house, is shown in an engraving published about 1800 (plate 17A).

[1] P.R.O., Ministers' Accounts, 31–32, Hen. VIII, Norfolk, no. 2632.
[2] Ibid., 32–33, Hen. VIII, no. 2633.
[3] Ibid., nos. 2634–36.
[4] *L. and P. Hen. VIII*, vol. 20(1), p. 1545, no. 282 (37) ; Pat. Roll, 36 Hen. VIII, p. 26, m. 12.
[5] P.R.O. Augmentation Office ; Partic. for grants, Hen. VIII, no. 422.
[6] See Blomefield, *History of Norfolk*, vol. 9 (1808), p. 281.
[7] *L. and P. Hen. VIII*, vol. 13(2), no. 1212.
[8] *Proceedings of the Archæological Institute, Norwich volume (1847)*, p. 151.   The original accounts are in the P.R.O.   See *L. and P. Hen. VIII*, vol. 20(1), p. 383, no. 757.

DESCRIPTION

The buildings stand in an enclosure on the southern outskirts of the town and on the west side of the road to Fakenham. The site is bounded on the north by cottages and gardens, on the west by an ancient lane called Back Lane, and on the south by an open pasture field, and is enclosed on all sides by a stone wall. It is now a little over $2\frac{1}{2}$ acres in extent, but the cottages and the Methodist Chapel on the north are clearly encroachments ; and it is probable that all the land northwards to the market-place was originally owned by the friars. The whole of this area is considerably less than the 4 acres acquired by the friars in 1347 ; and as they subsequently extended their holdings to some 13 acres, it is clear that several of the adjoining fields must have been in their occupation, and were doubtless a principal source of supply for their daily sustenance. Some slight indication of the extent and position of the friars' property about the time of the Dissolution can be gained from a survey of the lands in Walsingham belonging to the neighbouring Augustinian Priory. In this it is stated that " in the Friday Market beginning at the house of the Friars proceeding west by the market the Friars Minor hold their house there in pure and perpetual alms ; Also the messuage called the White Horse [1] ; Also six cottages." This was within the town. Outside in the twentieth furlong, which lay between the London Way on the west and the common ·watercourse on the east, the friars held " four messuages and nine curtilages in pure and perpetual alms : rent per annum 6s. 1d." and also " two acres by the gift of the Duke." [2] These entries show that the friars owned property not only in the Friday Market (or market-place, as it is now called), but also on the east side of the London or Fakenham road.

To what extent this property was encircled by a precinct wall is uncertain. The walls of the existing pasture field on the north and south are comparatively modern, but part of those on the frontage to the Fakenham road and the Back Lane may be original. No original entrance to the precinct remains. The main public approach seems to have been direct from the south-west corner of the market-

[1] This property was held by the friars at the suppression and was then in the occupation of Richard Grene.
[2] Harrod, *Castles and Convents of Norfolk*, pp. 192–93, from P.R.O., Augmentation Office Misc. Books, vol. 424.

place, where a *cul-de-sac* now extends in the direction of the friary. This is obviously an ancient way and here probably stood the main precinct gateway. A second or postern gate presumably existed on the east side at or close to the point where the present gate gives access from the road.

In plan the buildings comprised a great cloister with the church on the north, the dormitory and chapter house on the east, a guest-hall on the west, and the frater occupying the southern range, to the south of which was a second or little cloister surrounded by the kitchens and other subsidiary offices.

The church is described by William of Worcester, who visited Walsingham in the second half of the fifteenth century, when the building was, of course, standing and in use. His reference is brief but of considerable interest. It reads : " Longitudo ecclesiæ fratrum Walsyngham 54 gressus. Latitudo ejus 32 gressus. Interstitium spacii Campanilis 10 gressus. Longitudo chori continet 50 gressus. Latitudo chori continet 17 gressus." [1] Assuming Worcester's " pace " represented approximately 1¾ feet, the friars' church had a nave measuring 94 feet by 56 feet and a quire 87 feet by 30 feet, separated by the typical passage or " walking-place " beneath the bell-tower, to which Worcester's " interstitium spacii campanilis " clearly refers. These measurements imply an aisled nave and an aisleless quire, but apart from this the extent and general arrangement of the church, prior to the excavation of the site in 1932, were unknown. What was then discovered confirmed the plan deduced from William of Worcester's statement, and afforded a remarkable testimony to the general accuracy with which this medieval antiquary made and recorded his measurements.

The church, in fact, consisted of a broad aisled nave 94 feet 8 inches long and 50 feet 2 inches wide and a long aisleless quire 86 feet by 28 feet 3 inches separated by a " walking-place," 11 feet wide internally over which stood a steeple approached by a stair turret on the south side. The apparent discrepancy between the latter measurement and William of Worcester's 10 gressus (i.e. 17½ feet) is doubtless accounted for by the fact that he would have paced out the distance from the door into the nave to the screen across the entrance to the quire, thus including the thick-

---

[1] Worcester, *Itin.*, p. 335.

Plate 16

WALSINGHAM FRIARY, EASTERN RANGE OF THE LITTLE CLOISTER

ness of the walls. This measurement, as far as it could be obtained from the surviving foundations, almost exactly agreed with Worcester's figure.

The only substantial portion of the building which survives above ground is the lower part of the south and east walls of the chancel. This part of the site slopes abruptly to the east, and the ground within these walls has been artifically heightened to the level of the nave, so that it is now on a line with the top of the original work, which acts as a retaining wall and has been carried up to form a low modern boundary wall for the cottage garden within. The result of this curious and obviously artificial arrangement is that there is a drop varying from about 1 foot at the west end to some 12 feet at the extreme east end between the internal and external levels. This fact makes it somewhat difficult to visualize the precise arrangement of the interior when the church was built, in the absence of further excavation at the east end. There appears, however, to be no evidence that the chancel was raised on a crypt ; and presumably when the outer wall had been constructed the interior was filled up to the level required with soil brought from the west end and the floor laid on a solid foundation of rammed earth. This might perhaps account for the unusually massive buttresses on the exterior. On the exterior, which is the only part of the chancel walls now visible, very little of the original face survives. The position of the buttresses, however, is clearly indicated, and their original projection can be ascertained from the more complete ones. One at the south-east corner is practically entire, while a modern shed has been built against and obscures the remains of one of the north-east angle buttresses. In the exterior of the east wall are two roughly semicircular recesses which have apparently been constructed in later times and partially lined with brick, to form ornamental garden houses.

The only other fragment of the church standing above ground is the south-east corner buttress of the nave, with a part of the east wall of the south aisle adjoining. The buttress itself is of neatly faced flintwork with a moulded stone plinth, but the modern walls which have been built against it have left only a portion of the original work visible. The broad rubble foundations of the cross walls enclosing the " walking-place " on the east and west, together with the base of the doorway giving access from it

to the cloister on the south, were discovered in 1932.   In
the western of the two cross walls was an opening scarcely
3 feet 4 inches wide, which doubtless indicated the position
of an unusual narrow doorway, giving access into the nave.
On the east side the opening was wider and must have
been approximately 14 feet across, though the precise width
of the arch could not be ascertained, as the north side
had been destroyed practically to the lowest foundation.
Across it a screen would have served to shut off the quire.
That these walls served to support a masonry bell tower
is proved, not only by Worcester's statement, but by the
fact that the base of an unusually massive buttress with a
chamfered stone plinth was found on the north side while
the well-preserved remains of the stair turret which led up
to the tower survived on the south side.   The latter was
of flint with dressings of Barnack stone, and to judge
from fragments of moulded stone found in association with
it was of fifteenth-century date, a fact which makes it
likely that the whole tower was an insertion of this date,
built within the fourteenth-century walls of the quire, like
the surviving example at Richmond.

     To the south of the church and separated apparently
from it by an open yard or court lay the Great Cloister,
so called to distinguish it from the Little Cloister, of which
substantial remains survive.   It is now indicated by the
roughly square enclosure used as a kitchen garden, which
measures 108 feet from east to west and 99 feet 6 inches
from north to south, but was certainly less when the surrounding buildings were complete.   The late date of the
present guest-house implies that there must have been an
earlier western range, and it seems reasonable to conjecture
that this may have stood somewhat east of the present
building as has been provisionally shown on the plan, though
there is at present no structural evidence for this building.
There is no indication, however, of the abutment of a
cloister walk on the east face of the existing guest-house,
and it is therefore possible that when the earlier building
was demolished an open yard was left between the new
building and the cloister, into which the doorways in the
east wall of the present building opened.   If this is accepted,
the original cloister must have been approximately 60 feet
square.   The disposition of the various buildings around the
cloister appears to have followed a more normal arrangement than was often the case in friars' houses.   On the

Plate 17

SOUTH VIEW OF WALSINGHAM FRIERY.

A. WALSINGHAM FRIARY FROM THE SOUTH-WEST, *c.* 1800
[*From an engraving by J. Page after H. Repton.*

B. WALSINGHAM FRIARY. THE GUEST HOUSE FROM THE WEST

east side were the dormitory and chapter house, the former probably projecting on the upper floor over the cloister walk. The existing wall on this side is in part original, and seems to have served as the inner wall of the cloister alley.

The walls of the chapter house still stand to a height of about 9 feet, and, like those of the chancel, now serve as retaining walls, the ground within being on a level with their top. The building, which is in the normal position to the east of the great cloister, is rectangular, measuring 25 feet by 46 feet internally, and was entered apparently direct from the east cloister walk. The walls are of flint laid in fairly regular courses, and the present angle buttresses are modern. The whole of the west wall abutting on the site of the cloister seems to have been rebuilt. In it is a narrow brick doorway, possibly of eighteenth-century date. No trace of the original door survives.

The frater stood in the normal position to the south of the great cloister, and in accordance with the not uncommon practice in friars' houses already noticed, was placed on the upper floor projecting over the cloister walk. Here, however, the arrangement seems to have been carried a step farther owing to the proximity of the little cloister on the south, the north walk of which was apparently only separated from the south walk of the main cloister by a solid wall, which formed the central support of the frater above, which thus projected over the alleys of both cloisters. Only the west gable of this building, with a large window, now devoid of tracery, survives. The main entrance was probably at the east end, but a small door high up in the west wall apparently gave access to the stairs adjoining the guest-house, and thence to the upper floor of that building and the cloister below.

On the east side of the great cloister and to the south of the chapter house are the remains of a building of apparently late date, to judge from its inferior construction. It measures 46 feet 10 inches long and 13 feet wide internally, and the present ground level inside is considerably lower than that of the cloister and chapter house adjoining. It seems probable that this was the sub-vault of the dorter range. The upper portion of the building has entirely gone except for part of the south gable end; but unless the dormitory was unusually small it must have extended over the cloister walk and possibly across the western portion of the chapter house. The basement was approached from a passage from the little cloister by a flight of steps, some of which probably exist beneath the earth bank which marks their site. A small pointed window, about 9 inches wide, with a broad splay which served to light these stairs, still survives. The greater part of the eastern wall of this building has at some date been demolished and the gap filled in by a later and thinner wall. In the south end is a blocked doorway, 3 feet wide, which communicated with the exterior on the lower level, and over this are the jambs of a two-light window which lit the upper storey.

To the west of the great cloister is a large hall of five bays, measuring internally 77 feet by 24 feet 3 inches. It is now roofless, but the walls are fairly well preserved, those of the north and south ends standing complete to the top of the gable. They are constructed of flint with stone dressings and a single course of brick over the arches of the windows and doors. In the east and west walls, 19 feet from the north end and at a height of about 12 feet, are two carved stone corbels for the floor beam carrying one bay of the flooring, and in the north gable wall are corresponding joist holes. How the floor of the rest of the building was supported is uncertain, as there is no indication of further corbels, apart from a small one at the south end, and no joist holes in the south gable wall. That the whole building was on two storeys, however, seems clear from the indication of an upper series of windows on both sides and from the remains of the external staircase on the east side which must have given access direct to the first floor. The building has at some time been used for farm purposes, and several of the openings have been widened to admit farm carts ; but enough remains to show that on the ground floor on the west side there was a series of splayed windows with arches so depressed as to be almost flat. The openings on the east side, which are now blocked up, are somewhat similar, though wider, and appear to have been doorways rather than windows, as there is no indication of a sill, the openings being continued to the ground. In the centre of the south wall is a doorway of earlier date with moulded jambs and pointed arch which is still in use, and gives access to the kitchen apartments of the modern house. It has probably been rebuilt but may indicate an original opening. The upper floor was lit by a range of windows on either side, whose jambs survive though the arches have gone. These are worked in brick, the ends of which have not, however, been cut to the angle of the splay, leaving a rough and unfinished appearance. In the south gable is a large window of better construction, though none of its tracery remains. In the eastern continuation of this wall, which formed the enclosing wall of the external staircase, is a narrow blocked doorway, which apparently communicated possibly by means of a bridge with the frater on the upper floor of the southern range. On the west side, in place of one of the buttresses, is a massive projection of flint with stone quoins, which presumably provided thickness for a fireplace and chimney recess on the upper floor. The existence of this fireplace coupled with the general character of the work, the almost flat arches of the windows and the texture and size of the bricks used suggest a very late date for the building, and it seems probable that it was erected only a few years before the suppression of the house. As to its purpose, it is difficult to speak with certainty. Locally it is always referred to as the refectory, but it was more probably the guest-hall built to accommodate some of the numerous pilgrims who continued to be attracted by the fame of Walsingham until the eve of the Dissolution. These would have been accommodated on the upper floor, while the lower storey may have been used for stabling or storage and similar purposes. The possibility of an earlier guest-house or western claustral range having existed to the east of the building has already been mentioned.

The little cloister is the best-preserved part of the surviving buildings, the inner wall of the garth standing in one place almost to the top of the upper storey, which seems to have projected here on all sides over the cloister alleys. The garth itself is 50 feet square. The walls are of flint, with stone dressings for the windows and buttresses. The lower windows on the east and west are of three lights with square heads and moulded drip-stones, two on each side retaining their tracery intact. These were glazed only in the heads of the lights. On the east side, where the wall is considerably higher, one of the upper windows with the sill and jambs of a second survive. Like the lower series it has a square-headed frame, but with two cinquefoil cusped lights divided horizontally by a single transom. The upper part appears to have been rebuilt with the original stone. On the north side only the sills of the windows survive, but they seem to have been similar to those of the east and west. On the south side the three windows have slightly pointed arches worked in flint and brick. In the south-east corner a stair turret projects into the cloister garth. It is approached by a plain doorway with a four-centred arch from the site of the south walk of the cloister, and gave access to the upper floor of the southern range, all trace of which has disappeared.

A long narrow apartment on the west side of the little cloister was probably the conventual kitchen. It is constructed of substantial flint walls and measures internally 51 feet 6 inches by 20 feet 6 inches. The northern part has recently been enclosed and now forms the drawing-room of the modern house, a doorway having been cut through the original wall in the north-west corner. In the north wall are two original single-light windows, and a door with moulded jambs and pointed arch, all of which are now blocked up. There are also several blocked doors and windows in the unenclosed part of the building, and the whole bears evident traces of having been much altered. An original feature, however, is a recess in the exterior of the east wall with a pointed brick arch of good workmanship. It is 7 feet wide and 5 feet 6 inches high to the apex of the arch, and contains a timber frame within, which is also visible on the other side of the wall where it extends 2 feet 1 inch to the south. The rubble filling of the wooden frame is modern, but the frame itself is undoubtedly original and is almost certainly the buttery hatch opening into the western walk of the little cloister, from where the food must have been carried up to the frater. The extension of the wooden frame on the inner side was doubtless to allow for the sliding back of a shutter.

A large building of uncertain use stood on the eastern side of the little cloister, constructed, as were most of the buildings on this side, on the lower ground so that its upper storey was on a level with the adjoining cloister. Part of the south wall and gable of this building survives, and sufficient of the east wall to determine its size. On the west side, where it abutted on the cloister walk, the wall stands to a height of some 7 feet from the cloister level. In this wall are two narrow doorways of similar design, which retain the hinge pins for the doors. They are constructed of stone with four-centred arches, and must

LAY FOLKS CEMETERY

Q U I R E

Plinth

Plinth

STEEPLE

N A V E

CHAPTER HOUSE

DORTER (over)

Windows over

Niche

GREAT CLOISTER

FRATER (over)

LITTLE CLOISTER

Door over

Yard

Modern Shed

Modern House

Modern Drawing Room

Hatch

? Kitchen

Arch

GUEST HOUSE

Existing original work 14th or early 15th Century

Existing later work late 15th or early 16th Century or in some cases early post-suppression on line of older work

Existing Foundations

Modern

Dotted Lines = Conjectural Restoration

GREY FRIARS WALSINGHAM

Ground Plan

A.R.Martin. Mens et Del 1952

10   0   20   40   60 Feet

originally have opened direct into the upper floor of the building, as there is now a drop of about 8 feet to the ground on the east side. These doorways are apparently late insertions, as the upper part of the wall in which they are set seems to have been rebuilt. They are probably part of the apparently extensive work undertaken in the early part of the sixteenth century and may have given access to the rere-dorter, the position of which, owing to the absence of running water on the site, would have been fixed by the general lie of the ground in relation to the adjoining buildings.

The ground to the south of the little cloister is rough and uneven, and almost certainly conceals foundations of other buildings in this direction. This is borne out by a view of the site in the early part of last century, which indicates a fairly lofty fragment of a building standing in this area, which may have been the warden's lodging (Plate 17A). Among the objects discovered during the recent excavations were a number of tiles of dark brown, green and pale yellow glazes, but otherwise undecorated, and also a large quantity of fragments of painted glass, mostly of fifteenth-century date.

(11) WARE

History

THE Franciscan house in the little market town of Ware on the River Lea in Hertfordshire was one of the four houses of the order established in the fourteenth century after the first enthusiasm had to a great extent subsided and before its partial revival under the reformed Observants. Its founder was Thomas, 2nd Lord Wake of Liddel,[1] who married Blanche, daughter of Henry, Earl of Lancaster. On the 18 February 1338 he received licence to assign to the Friars Minor of Ware a messuage and seven acres of land in Ware on which to build an oratory, houses and other buildings.[2] It is doubtful, however, whether possession

---

[1] He is shown on the seal of the house in full armour holding a shield of his arms and kneeling before the Seraph of St. Francis' Vision on Mount Alverna. On the opposite side is a kneeling figure variously stated to be Lady Blanche Wake, or St. Francis himself. (B.M. Seal casts LXIV, 73, and original attached to Add. Ch. 36070).

[2] *C.P.R. 1338–40*, p. 14. Many of the earlier writers confuse this house with the small alien priory which arose out of the grant of lands in Ware to the Benedictine Abbey of St. Evroul in Normandy in the eleventh century and thus attribute its foundation to a much earlier date.

was immediately taken of this site and it is possible that the founder never lived to see the completion of his scheme, for he died in 1349, and it was not till September 1350 that the Pope confirmed the acceptance of the site by the Provincial Minister in England in pursuance of a general faculty to accept six new sites, three in Italy and three north of the Alps.[1] Subsequent references to the house are very few. In July 1372 Blanche, Lady Wake, was licensed to assign to the guardian and Friars Minor of Ware a further four acres of land with the buildings thereon valued at 2s. a year for the enlargement of their house.[2] A somewhat unusual instance of jealousy between neighbouring houses of the same order is afforded by the conflict which arose in 1395 between this house and the Franciscans of Cambridge, who alleged that the new arrivals had encroached on their area in collecting alms. This led to a papal order forbidding the friars of Ware from extending their bounds for begging within 5 miles of any place except Puckeridge, which before their house was founded had been within the district of the Cambridge friars.[3]

On the death of Thomas Holland, 3rd Earl of Kent, his Hertfordshire estates, which he had inherited from the Wakes, became forfeited to the crown and in February 1400 Henry IV granted the friars of Ware the underwood of an acre of wood, two cartloads of hay and the fishing in the water running along the length of their property.[4] The friary was flooded in September 1408.[5] The house is occasionally mentioned in wills, but these give no information concerning the buildings.[6] Among its benefactors was Elizabeth de Burgh, the founder of the house at Walsingham, who gave them 40s. on her death in 1360.[7] In 1524 John Hooke of Chichester desired to be buried " within the freres of the order of St. Francis in Ware."[8]

A curious agreement is preserved between Paul warden of the Grey Friars of Ware and the convent there and

---

[1] *C. Pap. L.*, vol. 3, p. 394 ; Wadding, vol. 8, p. 75.
[2] *C.P.R. 1370–74*, p. 185 ; Chan. Inq. a.q.d., file 378, no. 9.
[3] *C. Pap. L.*, vol. 4, p. 517.
[4] *C.P.R. 1399–1401*, p. 226. This grant probably continued an existing arrangement.
[5] *Eulog. Hist.* (R.S.), vol. 3, p. 413.
[6] For references to these wills see *Herts. Genealogist and Antiquary*, vol. I, pp. 47, 236, 316(2), 318 ; II, 91(2), 238 ; III, 274, and P.C.C. 21 Bodfelde and 22 Porch.
[7] Nichols *Royal Wills* (1780), pp. 23, 33.
[8] P.C.C. " Bodfelde," fo. 21.

Plate 18

A. WINCHELSEA, GREYFRIARS' CHURCH FROM THE SOUTH, 1784

B. WINCHELSEA, GREYFRIARS, INTERIOR OF QUIRE, 1784

Thomas Hyde establishing a perpetual obit "in the conventuall cherche of the freeres in Ware." [1] It is dated 3 October 1525, and by it the friars undertake that whoever shall sing the second mass before the common altar on Thursday in each week shall pray for the good estate and welfare of the said Thomas Hyde and Joan his wife, during their lives and for their souls after they be departed, and for the souls of the father and mother and two former wives of the said Thomas Hyde. The document further provides that the obit shall be kept once a year on the Sunday following Easter Day and that the deed itself shall be read twice a year to the whole convent in their chapter house to ensure its terms remaining in mind. Thirteen years later, however, the house was dissolved. Towards the close of 1538, the Bishop of Dover wrote to Cromwell that he had received the Grey Friars of Ware, Babwell and Walsingham among other houses. [2] The deed of surrender has not survived. In the following year the site with the orchards, gardens and ponds was in the occupation of Robert Birch at a rent of 20s.

The remainder of the friars' property, all of which was in the same occupation, comprised three roods of meadows adjoining the precinct let at 3s., the "osierhope" let at 20d., an orchard lying near the east side of the site let at 3s. 4d. and a garden near the entrance of the late house let at 20d. The total rent was 29s. 8d. [3]

The whole property was granted on 21 May 1544, in consideration of services, to Thomas Birch, Yeoman of the Crown, [4] who died, seized of the premises in 1550. [5]

DESCRIPTION

Weever, writing in 1631, states that " at the north end of this Towne was a Frierie whose ruines, not altogether beaten downe, are to be seene at this day . . . Here lieth Thomas Heton and Jone his wife, which Thomas died xix Aug. mccccix and Joyce, . . . Will. Litlebury and Elizabeth his wife ; he died xxii of July, mcccc." [6]

---

[1] B.M. Add. Charters 36070. Printed in full in *St. Albans and Herts. Archit. and Arch. Soc. Trans* (1925), p. 121.
[2] *L. and P. Hen. VIII*, vol. 13(2), no. 1021.
[3] P.R.O. Ministers' Accounts Hen. VIII, no. 1617.
[4] *L. and P. Hen. VIII*, vol. 19, no. 610(68).
[5] Chan. Inq. P.M. (Ser. 2), XC, 124. For the later history of the site see *V.C.H. Herts.*, vol. 3, p. 392.
[6] *Ancient Funeral Monuments* (1631), p. 544.

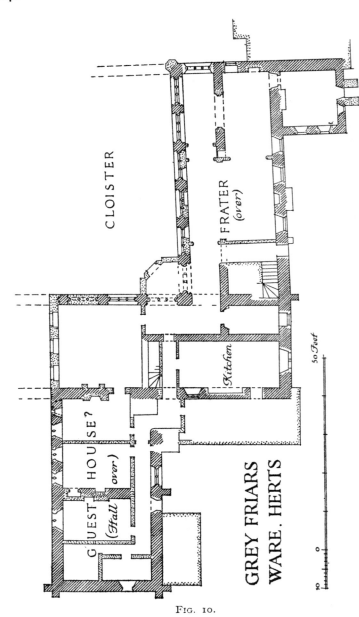

CLOISTER

FRATER
(over)

Kitchen

GUEST HOUSE?
(Hall over)

GREY FRIARS
WARE. HERTS

50 Feet

0

10

Fig. 10.

The site lies a short distance to the south of the parish church and is now the property of the town and used as a public garden. The house, which is occupied by the Council's Offices, incorporates a considerable portion of the friary buildings, though there is no work now visible of earlier date than the late fifteenth century. The church must have stood on the north side of the cloister and its foundations probably exist beneath the lawn in front of the house. The surviving buildings [1] consist of the greater part of the southern range, three bays of the western range and the Great Hall or Guest House projecting to the west of the latter. The walls are of plastered rubble with stone dressings and the post-suppression additions and alterations are for the most part of brick and plastered timber. The building throughout is of two storeys with an attic, the latter being a later insertion. Both the southern and western ranges have the cloister alley, which is here about 8 feet in width, incorporated within their structure in accordance with the common practice in mendicant houses, but most of the back wall of the alleys on both sides has been removed.

The southern range had originally a series of six windows each of three cinqefoil lights with hollow moulded jambs and four-centred main heads on the ground floor overlooking the cloister garth, but the westernmost of these, together with the first window of the west claustral walk, have been replaced by arches opening into the modern porch in the south-west corner of the garth. The remaining windows are much restored and partially blocked with plaster. The upper floor of this range was occupied by the frater and is now divided up into a number of rooms by modern partitions and lit on the north side by modern sash windows. To the south of this range at the east end is a small projecting wing of two storeys measuring 14 feet by 14 feet 6 inches which may possibly have been connected with the frater pulpit, though its dimensions suggest a more important use. The plain beams of the ceiling on the ground floor of this wing are probably original, as is also a small window on the south side.

The west range is approached from the south cloister alley by a three-centred arch of two chamfered orders on grotesque moulded corbels, which is apparently an addition. In the south-west corner is the modern kitchen, probably in its original position, and in its west wall is a blocked

[1] See *R.C.H.M. Herts.* (1910), p. 228 ; *V.C.H. Herts.*, vol. 3, p. 392.

window of two cinqefoiled lights under a square head with an external label now covered by a modern building on the west side. To the east of the kitchen at the south-west corner of the cloister is a small apartment approached by a fifteenth-century doorway with a pointed hollow chamfered head.

The hall wing is divided externally into four bays by thin ashlar buttresses of slight projection of which three remain on the south and one on the north. It consists of an undercroft, originally divided into at least two rooms by a cross wall in which is a pointed chamfered doorway, now blocked. The undercroft is now sub-divided into several other rooms and a corridor on its southern side which may be an original feature, as the moulded arch carried across it at the point where it passes the original cross wall is perhaps old, though now largely hidden by plaster. Above the undercroft is the hall measuring about 48 feet by 22 feet in four bays with an open timber roof now hidden by the attic above. Five of its original windows survive, two on the south and three on the north, and are similar in detail to those on the south side of the undercroft and that in the west wall of the kitchen. On the north side there is another original window on the ground floor at a height so that its head cuts into the upper floor in such a way as to suggest that it may have been the window of an internal staircase. Below this window in the undercroft is a small quatrefoil opening with an internal splay and a four-centred rear arch. In the north-east corner of the hall is a small niche with a pointed chamfered head about 4½ feet above the floor. The hall is now divided up into a number of rooms with ceilings inserted at the level of the tie beams to form an attic. Most of the roof of the hall is probably original,[1] but of the three roof trusses only one of the octagonal king posts with moulded cap and base is visible in the attic. That this building with its undercroft served as the guest-house is not improbable, but its interior arrangements have been so altered and obscured in post-suppression times, that its purpose can only be conjectured.

[1] See *The Builder*, vol. 7, p. 342 (21 July, 1849).

Plate 19

WINCHELSEA, QUIRE OF GREYFRIARS' CHURCH, INTERIOR

(12) WINCHELSEA

HISTORY

THE original Franciscan house at Winchelsea was in the old town which was finally destroyed by the sea in 1287. The date of this first settlement is not known, but it was certainly before 1242.[1]

The town was refounded by Edward I and laid out on a careful plan, the site being divided into 39 quarters. The barons stipulated that the King should allow no religious house to be erected within this area except a house of Friars Minor.[2] There can be little doubt that the transfer to the new site was effected almost at once. The position chosen was in the eastern part of the town, bounded on the south by the 27th quarter, on the west by the 23rd quarter and on the north by the 17th quarter. To-day the site is on the edge of the cliff overlooking the marshes which now stretch for about a mile to the present coastline.

There appears to be no record of the progress of the new buildings though work was probably begun without delay as help came from an unexpected source. As a result of a protracted law suit the Abbot of Westminster was fined 60 marks for infringing the privileges of the Friars Minor by housing an apostate of their order, and the money was ordered to be divided between the Franciscan houses at Winchelsea and Lichfield to relieve their necessities. This involuntary contribution towards the cost of the new buildings was paid by instalments in 1294–95.[3] Apart from this practically nothing is recorded regarding the house.[4] It is only occasionally referred to in wills, but Cooper mentions as its special benefactors Vincent Finch and Isabella his wife, for whom masses were offered in 1413.[5] In 1496 Adam Oxenbrigge of Rye bequeathed to the friars of this house a chalice which belonged to them but had been pledged to him

---

[1] *Rôles gascons*, ed. F. Michel (1885), vol. I, no. 1969.

[2] P.R.O. Parl. Proc., file 2, no. 6. In spite of this stipulation Edward II gave a site to the Black Friars in 1318 (*C.P.R. 1317–21*, p. 117).

[3] *Mon. Franc.* (R.S.), vol. 2, pp. 31–65.

[4] The names of five guardians have survived : William de Waleden, who died *c.* 1327 (*B.S.F.S. Collectanea*, vol. I, p. 148) and had been penitentiary at Southampton in 1318 (Sandale's Register, *Hants Record Society* 1897, p. 85) ; John Beere, who witnessed the will of Robert Bawdwen in 1509 (P.C.C. Bennett, fo. 26) ; Charles Lawrence (1521) ; Thomas Man (1526) and Robert Benyngton (1530).

[5] *The History of Winchelsea*, (1850), p. 146, from the Dering MSS.

for 30s.[1] Thomas Fysshe left to them in 1500 " a single goune of blak saten for to make a vestment or els to make curteyns for the awter endes which pleasith theym best." [2] The church, like the neighbouring church of the Friars Minor at Lewes, had a chapel dedicated to St. Barbara. This is mentioned in the will of James Marschall, who in 1521 desired a taper to be kept " before Saint Barbara in the Freers Mynors " for a year after his death,[3] and again by Gregory Wylgate, who in 1526 desired to be buried " within the churche of the Gray Freres in Wynchelse within the chapell of and before Saint Barbara,'' and whose will continues, " I will that frere Thomas Man wardeyn in the said Gray Freres doo synge for my soule and for my father and mother in the chapell of Saint Barbara the space of oon hole yere and to have for his labor vj *li.* xiij *s.* iiij *d.*" [4] Finally Sir Godard Oxenbryge of Brede left 20s. " to the reparacyons of the churche and house of the Gray Fryers of Wynchelsee " in 1530.[5]

The Deed of Surrender has not survived, but on 25 July 1538 the Bishop of Dover wrote to Cromwell : " The Greyfriars (at Winchelsea) are very poor and not able to continue," and he adds that he thinks the warden would have given it up if he had been at home.[6] Later he reported that " at Winchelsea according to your commandment I have sold the stuff : the house is at the King's commandment and yours." [7]

The site of the buildings with a garden, one close and an orchard contained 4 acres and was valued at 20s. per annum.[8] In addition the friars appear to have owned various properties including four houses in other parts of the town which were retained in the hands of the Crown until 1586, when they were sold to the Corporation.[9] The main site was let for a term of twenty-one years by a lease dated

---

[1] P.C.C. " Horne," fo. 17. [2] Ibid. " Moone," fo. 19.
[3] Ibid. " Maynwaryng," fo. 17. The will is witnessed by " Sir Charles Lawrence guardian of the Freers Mynors."
[4] Ibid. " Porch," fo. 8. The will which is witnessed by the warden Thomas Man to whom in addition is given " a gowne of the newe colour furred with fox," makes provision for the keeping of the testator's months mind and twelve months mind and a yearly obit with " dirige and masse of requiem by note " in the friars' church.
[5] Ibid. " Thower," fo. 8. The will is witnessed by Robert Benyngton, " wardeyn of the Graye Fryers in Winchelsey."
[6] *L. and P. Hen. VIII*, vol. 13, (1), no. 1456.
[7] Wright, *Suppression*, p. 200.
[8] P.R.O. Ministers' Accounts Hen. VIII, no. 3677, m. 15.
[9] W. D. Cooper, *History of Winchelsea, ut sup.*, p. 109.

Plate 20

GREYFRIARS, WINCHELSEA. BUCKS' VIEW, 1737

20 June 1542 to Philip Chowte, who was at that time captain of Camber Castle. On 12 February 1545 the reversion was granted to Michael Welbore and George Clifford.[1] The official " particulars " for the grant do not throw any light on the extent of the buildings, but there is a memorandum endorsed that all the bells and bell metal and lead upon the premises, which also included the property of the Blackfriars, were to be reserved.[2] The subsequent history of the site is given by Cooper,[3] and it is only necessary to add that the old mansion which apparently incorporated part of the friary buildings was demolished in 1819, when the present house was erected.

DESCRIPTION

The church which was dedicated to St. Francis [4] is the only part of the buildings of which any trace survives. The ruined quire (68¾ feet by 26¾ feet) is a fine example of early Decorated work and is remarkable as being the only instance of an apsidal termination to a church of the Mendicant Orders in this country. It is an unaisled structure of four bays with a three-sided apse at the east end. The walls, which are of lenticular rag with ashlar quoins, stand practically entire up to the wall plate and still retain on the interior traces of the plaster facing with which they were formerly covered. In each bay on the north and south is a tall window, formerly of two lights, though now devoid of tracery, except for a few ·fragments which indicate that the heads had pointed trefoils enclosing cusped quatrefoils. The rear arches have mouldings which die into the jambs. The windows of the apse were of similar character though the centre one was slightly larger and of three lights (Plate 19). As at Chichester, an internal hood moulding encloses the heads of each window and is returned and continued as a string-course on a level with the springing point of the rear arches of the windows though, unlike the Chichester example, it stops at the quire arch and is not continued as a necking to the shafts of the responds. A second stringcourse, portions of which still remain, ran along the sill level of the windows on the interior and was continued as a band

---

[1] Pat. 36 Hen. VIII, m. 15 ; *L. and P. Hen. VIII*, vol. 20, pt. 1, no. 465(55).
[2] P.R.O. Particulars for grants 36 Hen. VIII, no. 1193, m. 2.
[3] *History of Winchelsea, ut sup.*, pp. 147–49.
[4] *Obituary Roll*, Surtees Soc., vol. 31, no. 393.

round the responds of the quire arch. This arch, which spans the whole width of the quire as at Chichester, is of simple symmetrical section with a quarter round moulding on either face. On each side there is a broad hood-mould of ogee section separated from the arch by a simple chamfer and on the west side terminating in carved stops. The responds consist of triple clustered shafts with moulded caps and bases. The former have a single semi-circular upper mould of a quarter roll with a common abacus of scroll section. The bases consist of two rolls on a chamfered plinth. There is no indication of the screen which must have filled this arch and there can be little doubt, therefore, that it was of timber.

In the third bay from the west of the quire on each side there are small doorways, neither of which are central, with the windows above. That on the south has a segmental head and is probably original, though the stone dressings have for the most part gone. The north door is probably of comparatively modern date. It has a pointed arch and is of rougher construction with some re-used stones in its jambs.

At the south-west corner of the quire is a semi-octagonal stair turret very similar to that at Chichester. It stands practically entire with its stairway intact though the upper part appears to have been rebuilt. It is approached by a doorway on the west side, and also by another door at a higher level on the south, which apparently gave access to a passage in the thickness of the east wall of the " walking place." A third opening at the top overlooks the quire arch. The width of this arch and the absence of any indication of transom arches on its western face makes it reasonably certain that the belfry which it supported was of timber.

Of the nave practically nothing remains. To the west of the quire arch, which here formed the actual western limit of the quire and not as at Chichester merely its structural termination, one bay must have been screened off to serve as the " walking place." The low arch by which it was approached from the north survives though now robbed of its stone dressings, and to the east of this is a fragment of a wall running in a northerly direction. That this was the east wall of a north aisle and not merely a buttress seems clear from the engraving published by Grose.[1] A

[1] Published 2 June, 1772, Canot sculp.

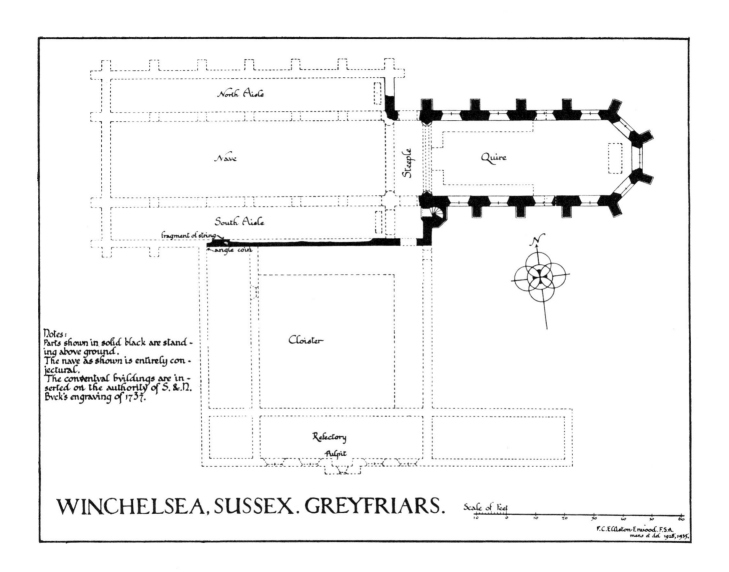

North Aisle

Nave

South Aisle

fragment of string

angle coin

Steeple

Quire

N

Notes:
Parts shown in solid black are stand-
ing above ground.
The nave as shown is entirely con-
jectural.
The conventual buildings are in-
serted on the authority of S. & N.
Buck's engraving of 1737.

Cloister

Refectory
Pulpit

WINCHELSEA, SUSSEX. GREYFRIARS.

Scale of Feet

10   0   10   20   30   40   50   60

F. C. Elliston-Erwood. F.S.A.
mens.t del. 1928, 1935.

corresponding aisle apparently existed on the south side where a length of wall, varying in height from about a foot to five or six feet, extends for a distance of some 75 feet westward from the stair turret. At its eastern end there are indications of the doorway which gave access into the cloister, the abutment of the roof of which was formerly marked by a row of corbels on its southern face (Plate 18A). Towards the west end on the inner face of this wall is a fragment of a moulded string-course (see Plan) which suggests that it formed the outer wall of a south aisle rather than that of a cloister separated from the church by an open court as was not infrequently the case in mendicant houses.[1]

The only indication of the roof of the building is a small section of weather moulding on the western face of the tower which shows that it was gabled and of fairly steep pitch. It was almost certainly of the open timber type as there is no evidence of vaulting in the quire or even in the eastern apse.

There are no remains of the domestic buildings, though a considerable part of them seems to have been standing in 1737 when the brothers Buck published their view (Plate 20). Part of the western walk of the cloister was incorporated in the mansion demolished in 1819 (Plate 18A) and the general layout indicated on the accompanying Plan is based on these sources. In the left foreground of Bucks' view there is shown what is almost certainly the remains of the pulpit recess in the frater, lit by a small trefoil-headed window in its south wall.[2]

(13) YARMOUTH

HISTORY

THE Grey Friars had arrived in Norwich in 1226 and it is not improbable that the house at Yarmouth was founded soon after this date. It is not, however, until 1271 that the earliest known mention of it occurs. On 10 April of that year the friars were licensed to enclose and build over a lane on the north side of their church which had been granted

---

[1] This point and the general plan of the nave could easily be ascertained by excavation. Its length as shown on the Plan is only conjecture.

[2] A drawing of the interior of this recess made by S. H. Grimm in 1784 shows a stone seat which may have been original (B.M. Add. MSS. 5670, fo. 25, no. 46).

to them by the town at the instance of the King, acting on
the advice of his son, Edward, who, the document states, had
lately observed " the narrowness of the place where the
Friars Minors of the town of Gernemuth are lodged." [1]
In the following February Peter of Aldeburg left two marks
for an obit to the Friars Minor of Yarmouth.[2] In June
1285 the friars received a further licence to hold a reugiate [3]
of land with the buildings thereon adjoining their precinct,
which had been granted to the King on behalf of the friars
by John, son of William Gereberge or Gerbrigge, for the
enlargement of their site.[4]   This licence was made expressly
subject to the lane between the reugiate in question and that
of Thomas Gerbrigge remaining open for the common use
of both properties and of other persons as theretofore.   It
is probably on the strength of this document that Speed [5]
and others have attributed the foundation of the house to
Sir William Gerbrigge of Wickhampton,[6] who was bailiff of
Yarmouth in 1271, but the evidence is inconclusive and it
seems probable that he was a later benefactor.   The site
was again enlarged in 1290, when John, son of Nicholas de
Bromholm of Great Yarmouth, transferred to the King and
his council, " ad opus fratrum minorum," his right in a plot
of land which had belonged to his father, " lying between the
dwelling-house of the said friars on the north side and the
common lane on the south side." [7] A reminder of the
exposed position of the precinct, which abutted on the wide
harbour formed by the mouth of the Yar, occurs in 1302,
when a commission was appointed to investigate a complaint
of the friars that certain malefactors " broke the pavement
near their wall whereby rainwater runs under it to the
destruction of the pavement and that some of the townsmen
with strangers threw down and broke to pieces their hedge
which they made for the defence of their dwelling-place against
the flow and violence of the sea by putting timber and other
heavy weights upon it." [8]
    Very little is known of the later history of the house.
On 6 May 1356 10s. was paid to the King by the guardian of

[1] *C.P.R. 1266–72*, p. 530.
[2] *Cat. Anc. Deeds*, vol. 5, p. 170 (A. 11569).
[3] A local measure of land.
[4] *C.P.R. 1281–92*, p. 169 : cf. p. 167.
[5] *Theatre of the Empire of Great Britain* (1611).
[6] His altar tomb in Wickhampton church survives.
[7] *C.P.R. 1281–92*, p. 358 ;   P.R.O. T.R. Misc. Books, vol. 274, fol.
265 ;   *Rot. Parl.*, vol. 1, p. 33.
[8] *C.P.R., 1301–07*, p. 86.

Plate 21

GREAT YARMOUTH, GREYFRIARS' CLOISTER LOOKING SOUTH

the Friars Minor of Great Yarmouth for a licence for alien-
ation in mortmain by Thomas de Drayton of three void
places in the town measuring 100 feet broad and 250 feet
long " on the north side of their dwelling-place between
which places and a quay opposite them on the port of the
sea towards the west a highway runs from south to north." [1]
Comparatively few burials in the house appear to be recorded,
but according to a " Register of the Friars Minor at Yarmouth," [2] mentioned by Palmer, many of the once powerful
family of Fastolfe were buried there. In 1349 Charles
Beneyt desired to be buried in the friars' church and left
6s. 8d. to the house.[3] It was in this year that the Black
Death attacked Yarmouth with particular severity, and this
fact makes it probable that the surviving building may be
attributed to the period shortly before rather than after
this event. That the community recovered rapidly from
its effects may perhaps be inferred from the fact that three
years later it had its own lecturer, who is mentioned in the
will of William atte Mawe and presumably presided over a
divinity school attached to the friary.[4] In 1492 the town
records mention that John Rokeby, a friar of this house,
weighed 24 stone.[5]

The house was suppressed in the autumn of 1538, but the
deed of surrender has not survived. The buildings were not
demolished, as it was reported that " the house was delivered
to Mr. Millesent servant to the lord Privy Seal by the visitor
of whom he bought most part of the things and his inventory
was not there." [6] In April 1540 the site was included with
other properties granted to Thomas Cromwell, Keeper of the
Privy Seal.[7] The property included the site with the
buildings and appurtenances which were in hand and valued
at 6s. 8d. yearly, a parcel of land adjoining on which was
built a house called " a mast howse," let to Robert Peres
at a like rent and another piece of land adjoining the said
site called " a yerde platte," let to Robert Tasborughe at a
yearly rent of 12d.[8] On Cromwell's attainder and execution

---

[1] *Ibid. 1354–58*, p. 372. There was a proviso that the friars should
be bound to repair and build the quay when necessary, for which they
should have an easement thereon to store, bring and take away victuals
and other necessaries.
[2] Manship's *Hist. of Great Yarmouth*, ed. Palmer, vol. 1, p. 420. I
have not been able to trace the existence of this " Register."
[3] Palmer, *op. cit.*, p. 420.   [4] *Ibid.*   [5] *Ibid.*
[6] *L. and P. Hen. VIII*, vol. 13(2), no. 1212.
[7] *Ibid.*, vol. 15, no. 611(8).
[8] P.R.O. Rentals and Surveys, Hen. VIII, 13/8.

a few months later this property reverted to the Crown and in March 1542 was granted by way of exchange to Cromwell's nephew, Sir Richard Williams, the grandfather of the Protector,[1] who sold it the same year to John Milsent and Alice his wife.[2] Its subsequent history is given by Palmer,[3] and it need only be stated that by 1569 it was already in the occupation of the corporation, who acquired the freehold in 1593. The town records contain several references to the periodical repairs of the buildings, but these throw little light on their extent.

DESCRIPTION

The site was bounded on the west by South Quay and the river Yar and on the east by Middlegate Street.[4] On the north the title deeds of properties appear to show that it extended as far as the row numbered 83. That row 96 formed its southern boundary is indicated by the portion of medieval wall still surviving on the north side of this row. The church and buildings were situated in the southern part of this enclosure in the neighbourhood of the present Queen Street. The latter was originally known as New Broad Row and is doubtless that referred to in January 1657, when the site was sold by the corporation to Mr. John Woodroffe on condition that he should within five years "cause a broad row and a narrow row[5] to be made on the premises according to a plan made thereof."[6]

The sole surviving portion of the buildings consists of the four southern bays of the western walk of the cloister with a projecting annex of two bays at the south-west corner (see Plan opp. p. 152). The sills and outer jambs of the cloister windows which were of three lights are largely intact, but the tracery has gone. The roof consists of an elaborate quadripartite vault with moulded ribs springing from responds of triple-attached shafts with moulded caps and bases. At the intersection of the ribs are a series of carved bosses in a fair state of preservation of which the

---

[1] *L. and P. Henry VIII*, vol. 17, no. 220(95).
[2] B.M. Add. Charter 39417.
[3] *History of Great Yarmouth, ut sup.*, vol. I, pp. 421–5.
[4] Palmer appears to have thought it might have extended to the east side of Middlegate street, but this seems to be unlikely as the latter was a medieval thoroughfare.
[5] i.e. row 92.
[6] *History of Great Yarmouth, ut sup.*, p. 424.

Plate 22

GREAT YARMOUTH, WEST WALK OF CLOISTER LOOKING NORTH

centre one in the second bay from the south represents the Lord's Supper. The other subjects are for the most part difficult to make out, though it has been suggested that the central bosses illustrated the life of our Lord. The super-structure above this vaulting has been entirely rebuilt with the exception of part of the wall facing the cloister and the supporting buttresses, but it is clear that the upper storey of the claustral range projected over the cloister walk in accordance with the common practice already noted elsewhere. The elaborate nature of the vaulting, however, was unusual in houses of the mendicant orders where a flat timber roof seems to have been usually employed.

In the west wall of the northern bay is a narrow door-way with a two-centred moulded arch, the mouldings of which die into the plain chamfered jambs. In the bay to the south of this in a similar position is a blocked arch with a two-centred head with hollow chamfered mouldings, and immediately to the north of this but on a higher level is another doorway of later date with a segmental head and moulded jambs. The buildings to which these openings must have given access have disappeared, but projecting from the west side of the southern bay of the cloister walk is a small apartment (11 feet 6 inches by 8 feet) with a groined vault of two bays, the ribs of which are carried on carved corbels.

The width of the cloister walk is 10 feet and, assuming that it was square in plan, it must have enclosed a garth about 50 feet square. There is, of course, no evidence that the remaining sides were of similar construction, and in this respect the conjectural restoration shown on the accompanying Plan must be regarded as only tentative. It seems probable that on the north side where the cloister abutted on the church and consequently stood free of buildings a sloping pent roof would have been used.

The church stood on the north side of the cloister and some traces of it were found during excavations for a new sewer in Queen Street in 1896. An account of these dis-coveries has been published by Dr. John Bately [1] and it is only necessary to summarize them here. The positions of the various walls recorded are indicated on the accom-panying Plan. Across the western end of the street on a line with the front of the houses in South Quay was a rubble

[1] " Recent discoveries on the site of Grey Friars, Great Yarmouth," *Norfolk Arch. Soc.*, vol. 13 (1896), pp. 21–8.

wall faced in flint and 3 feet in width. Both sides of the
wall were similarly finished, and as it appeared to have no
relation to any building there can be little doubt that
it was the western wall of the precinct. At a distance of
39 feet to the east of this wall was a second wall running
at right angles to the line of the street. It was 3 feet
6 inches wide and about 9 feet 6 inches high beneath the
ground level and was constructed of rubble rendered smooth
with pointing on the east side and faced with dressed flints
on the west side. About 3 feet below the surface on its
west face was a freestone plinth in good preservation. Later
discoveries made it reasonably certain that this was the
west wall of the church. From this point for a distance
of 152 feet 6 inches there was no further evidence of
buildings, but a considerable number of human interments
were found spread over the centre part of this area. At a
point 122 feet 6 inches east of the last-mentioned wall the
nature of the soil changed. No further burials were found
beyond this point and for a distance of about 30 feet the
ground appeared to have been disturbed and contained much
loose building material and moulded stones. It seems
probable that this was the site of the western portion of the
quire which had doubtless been demolished at the time of the
suppression. To the east of this area were found the remains
of a vaulted chamber or crypt measuring 25 feet from east
to west and enclosed on the west by a rubble wall
2 feet 3 inches in width and on the east by a wall,
3 feet 6 inches in width, corresponding to that at the west
end of the church. The precise width of this crypt could
not be ascertained as its side walls extended beyond the
area excavated, but Dr. Bately considered that it was
square in plan and conjectured with some probability that
the front walls of the houses on either side of the street
stand in part at least on the foundations of the church walls.
The depth of the crypt was not ascertained as the excavation,
which was carried to a depth of 9 feet, failed to reveal either
the floor or the base of the walls. Evidence of its groined
vault was, however, clear as the inner face of its east and
west walls had attached shafts with the springer stones of
the groining arches still in position. The span of the main
arches which must have been supported by a central column
appears to have been about 12 feet.

The discovery of this crypt is of unusual interest as it is
the only known instance of such an arrangement in an

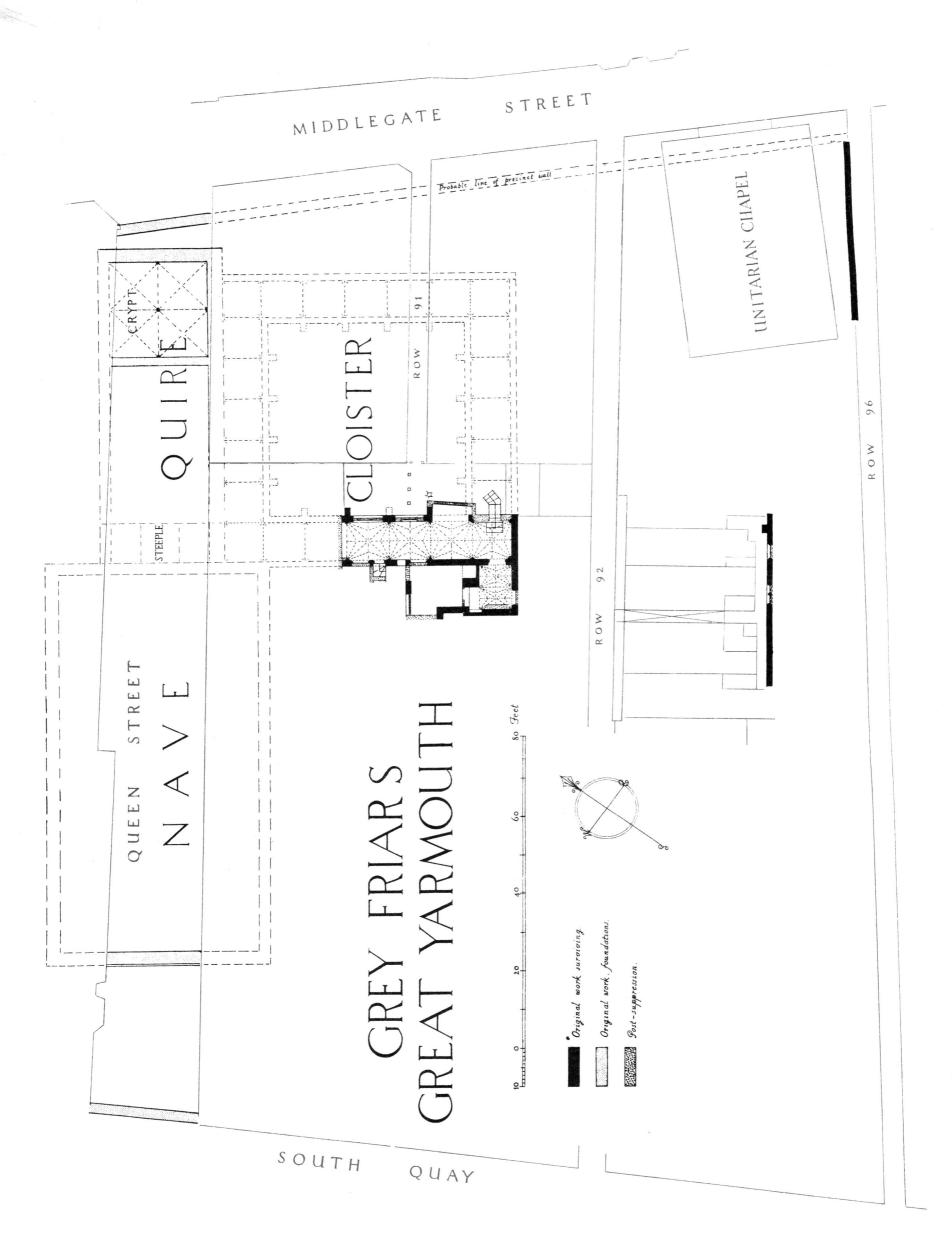

MIDDLEGATE STREET

Probable line of precinct wall

UNITARIAN CHAPEL

ROW 96

ROW 92

ROW 91

CRYPT

QUIRE

STEEPLE

CLOISTER

NAVE

Queen Street

GREY FRIARS
GREAT YARMOUTH

Original work surviving.
Original work foundations.
Post-suppression.

80 Feet
60
40
20
0
10

SOUTH QUAY

English Franciscan church.[1]   That its purpose was primarily to compensate for a fall in the natural ground level is probable, though it may also have served as a means of preserving the quire from the danger of flooding.   At a distance of only 3 feet from and at a slightly different axis to the east wall of the crypt was another wall 2 feet 6 inches in width which was presumably the eastern boundary of the precinct.   This is clearly shown passing close to the east wall of the church in a curious map of the town in the time of Queen Elizabeth.[2]   The total internal length of the church indicated by these excavations was about 177 feet.   The position of the crypt and of the cloister abutting on the quire suggests that the latter was aisleless.   That the nave had aisles is probable, though there is no evidence of this or of the existence of the steeple, which has been tentatively shown on the Plan.

Apart from the remains already noticed there is a short section of medieval wall now partly rendered in cement which, however, retains a blocked two-light window probably of fifteenth-century date at the back of some cottages on the south side of row 92 in the position indicated on the Plan. This possibly formed part of the warden's lodging, but the remains are too slight to determine the extent of the building.

In addition to many fragments of worked stone found during the excavation on the site of the church portions of three small statues were discovered and are now preserved in the cloister.   They are finely carved and when found retained traces of colour and gilding.   One of the figures has his hands resting apparently on a heart and may therefore form part of a monument over a heart burial.[3]

---

[1] Cf. the Franciscan church at Walsingham where, owing to the slope of the ground, the quire was raised on a solid foundation of rammed chalk.

[2] Reproduced in Manship's *History of Great Yarmouth, ut sup.*, vol. I, at p. 287.

[3] Illustration in *Norfolk Arch. Soc.*, vol. 13, p. 23.

CHAPTER III

HOUSES FOR WHICH EVIDENCE OF PLAN SURVIVES

We have hitherto confined our attention to houses which are represented by some substantial remains. In a few cases, however, though little or nothing has survived above ground, the ground plan of destroyed buildings has been preserved or recovered by excavation and in one instance is capable of reconstruction from documentary sources. It is with these houses that it is proposed to deal in this chapter.

(1) BEDFORD

The Franciscans were established in Bedford before 1238, as, in that year, they received a grant from the King of ten oak stumps for fuel.[1] Leland, quoting John Rous, claims this as their first house in England, but this was certainly not so.[2] No record of the original gift of the site appears to have survived, though according to the inscription on a tomb slab which Leland found in the friars' church at Bedford, the founder was Lady Mabel Pateshull, a member of a well-known Bedfordshire family.[3]

The friars were buying timber in 1242 presumably for building purposes,[4] but there is no mention of the church until 3 November 1295, when Oliver Sutton, Bishop of Lincoln, granted indulgences to those who should visit it on the day of its dedication.[5] This probably indicates a rebuilding in stone of the original timber structure. In 1310 the site was enlarged by the acquisition of "divers small plots of land" from three Bedford citizens and the prioress and convent of the Augustinian nunnery of Harrold.[6] A further 3½ acres of land was added in 1353[7]

---

[1] *C.C.R. 1237–42*, p. 62 ; *C. Lib. R. 1226–40*, p. 338.
[2] Leland, *Itin.*, vol. II, p. 165.   [3] *Ibid.*, vol. IV, p. 23.
[4] *C. Lib. R. 1240–45*, p. 115.
[5] Linc. Episc. Reg. Memo. Sutton, fo. 127.
[6] *C.P.R. 1307–13*, p. 276.   [7] *Ibid. 1350–54*, p. 487.

Plate 23

GREY FRIARS, BEDFORD, IN 1730

(THE LETTERPRESS ON THE PLATE IS INCORRECT)

and in 1460 the friars were granted a tenement in Bedford called Boyomesplace with a croft called curreiscrofte containing about 3½ acres and a dovecote built thereon adjoining their house.[1] The acknowledgment of the Royal supremacy was signed on 14 May 1534,[2] and in the following year the Valor Ecclesiasticus sets out the extent of the property belonging to the house. This comprised rather over twenty acres of pasture of an annual value of 100s., from which was deducted rent of 28s. 10d. paid to the holder of a Bedford prebend for two closes and 3s. paid to the priory of Caldwell for another close, leaving a clear annual value of £3 13s. 2d.[3] The deed of surrender is dated 3 October 1538 and is signed by the warden, whose name is illegible, Thomas Roberts, the vice-warden and eleven others.[4] On the same day, Dr. John London wrote to Cromwell, " Now I have taken the surrender of the Grey Friars in Bedford. I kept Mr. Geffreys to help me till I got Mr. Gostwick with whom according to your pleasure after I have dispatched them I will leave the house. . . . This is a pretty house of plate jewels and other necessaries and they have long used husbandry. They intended to make away all and sold their cart and horses within these 14 days. When I came I found six threshers in one end of a barn and two in another and ' if moo myzt have stonde ther moo shulde have be ther.' With Mr. Gostwikkes help I trust to make them all secular priests for such friars I never met with. ' To declare what persons many of them be before time at the very wardens hands I chanced upon this bill enclosed.' He had it in his sleeve and delivered it me instead of his inventory. It will move you to mirth. I trust to make a better inventory to the Kings use than this bill and then to repair to the other places in this commission." [5]

It appears that the warden, foreseeing the impending doom of his house, had attempted to dispose of the whole property a few days before the arrival of the commissioners, for on the day of Dr. London's letter, John Gostwyk also wrote to Cromwell informing him that " Dr. London and

---

[1] *Ibid. 1452–61*, p. 581.
[2] *L. and P. Hen. VIII*, vol. 7, No. 665.
[3] *Valor Eccles.* (Rec. Com.), vol. IV, p. 190. Sir John St. John is incorrectly described in the Valor as founder of the house.
[4] *L. and P. Hen. VIII*, vol. 13(2), no. 525 ; Rymer, *Fœdera*, vol. XIV, p. 610.
[5] *Ibid.*, no. 526.

I met at the Grey Friars in Bedford for the dissolution of the same. The warden had sold his house the Sunday before for £40 to Sir John Seynt John who I am assured has since surrendered it to the King. I desire a gift of it to me and my heirs (annual value 5 marks) and will give you £40. The King will have a great profit there in lead and other things. Mr. Seynt John intends shortly to be at London about this." [1]

On 29 October Dr. London informed Cromwell that he had sold the church ornaments and certain utensils and had saved all the rest with some utensils to have with Mr. Gostwike, [2] and at a later date he notes that the whole of the church and other places were leaded. [3]

The site was eventually sold with many other properties to John Gostwyk who is described as of Willington and Joan his wife for a total sum of £1404 5s. 10d. The grant is dated 3 March 1540 and included the house and site of the late Friars Minor with the church steeple and churchyard thereof, a meadow called Hanchurche meade in the tenure of John Scott, a close called " Busshoppes close " in the tenure of William Clerke lying on the west side of a lane called " le commen lane," land called " le Freers Grove " in the tenure of Thomas Smith, and two closes called " Dovehouse " and " Spicers cloase " and a pigeon house in the tenure of William Borne. [4] Gostwyk appears to have sold the entire property a month later to this William Borne and Elizabeth his wife, who presumably converted the buildings into a dwelling-house. [5] It was probably about this time that Leland visited Bedford and his account of the friary is of sufficient interest to quote in full :

" Thinges notable in the Gray Freres of Bedford. The very original founderes of the Grey Freres of Bedford was Mabil Pateshull Lady of Blettesho, [6] wher now Syr John S John dwellith, and of Stoke, as sum say, in Lincolnshire a 4 miles a this side Granteham in Lincolnshir, and this Stoke longith now to Master S John.

[1] *L. and P. Hen. VIII*, vol. 13(2), no. 527.
[2] *Ibid.*, no. 719 ; Ellis, *Original Letters*, 3rd Ser., vol. III, p. 130.
[3] *Ibid.*, vol. 14(1), no. 3.
[4] *Ibid.*, vol. 15, no. 436(9) ; Pat. Roll 31 Hen. VIII, pt. 2, m. 30. P.R.O. partic. for grants Hen. VIII, no. 502, fo. 3.
[5] *Ibid.*, vol. 15, no. 613(14).
[6] This may have been Mabel, niece of Otho de Grandison, and wife of Sir John de Pateshull, who died in 1349. Their daughter was Maud, wife of Walter de Fauconberg, who inherited the Pattishall property. Bletsoe is about 6 miles north of Bedford.

Plate 24

A. GREY FRIARS, BEDFORD, WEST RANGE OF CLOISTER FROM THE NORTH-EAST
(DEMOLISHED 1899)

B. GREY FRIARS, BEDFORD, BARN
(DEMOLISHED 1899)

" This Mabil was byried at the south side of the high altare under an arche. Epitaph : *Hic jacet Dᵃ Mabilla Pateshulle, Dnā de Blettesho, iᵃ fundatrix hujus loci.* She was biried under a flat stone. ˬTher was also buried on the northe side of the high altare under a plain stone, one of the Lord Mowbrays.[1] And one Quene Elenor was buried right afore the high altare undèr a flat stone of marble with an image of plaine plate of brasse encrounid.[2] Richard Hastinges, an esquier, chaumberlayn to Edward the 3, was buried on the north side of the quier in a low tumbe.

" Syr Richard Irencester [3] was biried in the midle of the body of the chirch and this Irencester, as it is said, made the body of the chirch of the Graye Freres. Blake S John of late tyme was buried of (off) the quier by Hastinges. The Freres stand flat in the north end of the towne." [4]

The site of the Grey Friars ultimately became the property of the Earl of Ashburnham.

The principal buildings stood on the west side of Priory Street to the south of Beauchamp Row and in the north-west part of the town. No trace of these now survive, but considerable remains existed until April 1899, when they were demolished by the Bedford Corporation who had purchased the property three years previously. The site is now laid out as a public recreation ground. The most important building consisted of the western range and two bays of the southern range of the cloister which appears to have measured approximately 60 feet from north to south. The building was of two storeys with the original cloister alleys incorporated within the main wall. The western range was divided into five bays by slender but-tresses reaching almost to the eave and in each bay was a wide blocked ·arch with segmental head in the filling of which had been inserted modern windows and a doorway (Plate 24A).

These arches had contained square headed windows of four lights filling the whole width of the arch when the brothers Buck made their drawing in 1730 (Plate 23) and

---

[1] John de Mowbray, 9th baron, who died of the plague at York in 1361·

[2] Leland is apparently in error here as Eleanor of Provence, who died in 1291, was buried at Amesbury and her heart in the Grey Friars in London and Eleanor of Castile, who died in 1290, was buried at West-minster and her heart in the Black Friars in London.

[3] Richard of Irchester held the eighth part of a knight's fee in Irchester, co. Northants, of the Earl of Ferrers in 1242–43. *Liber Feodorum* (R.S.), pt. II, pp. 933, 945. See also *C.P.R. 1266–72*, p. 521.

[4] Leland, *Itin.*, vol. IV, p. 23.

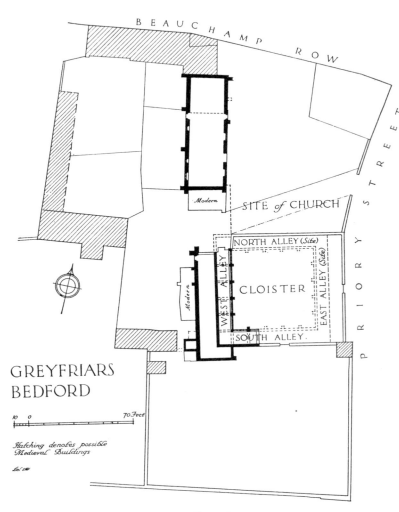

GREYFRIARS
BEDFORD

10   0   70 Feet

Hatching denotes possible
Medieval Buildings

Fig. 11.

above in each bay was a two-light window of similar character. About 30 feet to the north of this range was another
large building about 100 feet in length and 30 feet wide
with massive stepped buttresses and windows set high in
the wall (Plate 24B). The heads of the windows had been
cut off by the lowering of the side walls of the building for
the greater part of its length so that the roof of the northern
portion was at a different pitch to that of the rest of the
structure. This building was locally known as the refectory,
but its position and character suggest that it was either
the guest-house or more probably the friars' barn, which
on Dr. London's testimony was clearly a large building.
Farther to the west were various other subsidiary buildings
which are indicated on the Plan and which may have in
part dated from before the suppression.

There appears to be no definite evidence for the site
of the church, but it stood presumably on the north side of
the cloister. It had a bell-tower [1] and Leland's reference to
the tomb of Blake St. John as " off the quier " near the
tomb of Hastings which stood on the north side of the quire
seems to imply that the latter was aisled. Beyond this
nothing is known of its plan.

(2) CARDIFF

HISTORY

The date of the arrival of the Franciscans in Cardiff
is uncertain, but Rice Merrick, writing in 1578 after referring
to the foundation of the Black Friars by Richard de Clare
in 1256, observes, " Sir Gilbert de Clare his son after the
death of his father was Earl of Gloucester and Lord of
Glamorgan who founded the Graye fryers in the east part
of the Castle of Cardiff." [2] Merrick assigns the date 1280
to this event, and as Gilbert the Red, ninth Earl of Clare,
who succeeded to the earldom in 1262 and died in 1295,
was at that time holder of the lordship of Glamorgan with
its centre at Cardiff Castle, there seems to be no reason
to doubt the tradition as to the founder, while the date itself
is not unlikely.

Very little is recorded regarding the house. The earliest

[1] See *ante*, p. 156.
[2] *A Book of Glamorganshire Antiquities*, 1578 (ed. Sir T. Phillipps,
1825), pp. 31, 54 ; *ibid.* (ed. J. A. Corbett), 1887, pp. 57, 94.

contemporary record is a grant by Edward I in 1284, when
the friars seem to have numbered eighteen.[1]   Another early
reference to it appears to be the inclusion of the names of
two friars of this house in an obituary roll read at a provincial chapter at Cambridge in 1304.[2]   Two further names
of members of the house occur in a similar list drawn up for
the Lincoln provincial chapter in August 1327.[3]   When
Owen Glyndwr captured the town in 1404 and burnt the
Black Friars' house, he spared the property of the Grey
Friars on account of his well-known favour for the Franciscan
order.   It was in the same year that the Provincial, John
Zouche, who had probably been a friar of this house and
subsequently became Bishop of Llandaff, was deposed, an
event which produced a temporary schism in the order.[4]
He died in 1423 and is said to have been buried at the
Cardiff   friary.[5]   Another   provincial   minister,   John
David, D.D., who was probably a native of the town and
died about 1427, was also buried there.[6]   Early in the
previous century the Welsh chieftain, Llewellyn Brenn, and
his English opponent, Sir William Fleming, were put to
death at Cardiff and appear to have been buried at the
Grey Friars, as Merrick mentions their tombs, the former
of wood and the latter of " a fair stone," as having been
defaced at the suppression.[7]   In connection with these
burials it is of interest to note that during the excavation
of 1925 five mural vaults were found in the south wall
of the church in one of which was a female skeleton on
which was placed an embalmed heart.

The declaration of supremacy was signed on 2 July 1534
in the presence of the visitor, Dr. John Hilsey,[8] and in
the same year John Robynson, a friar of this house, wrote
to Cromwell asking for permission to become a secular
priest.[9]   The Bishop of Dover began his visitation of South
Wales for the purpose of receiving the surrender of the
friaries on 27 August 1538, and on 6 September he reached

[1] P.R.O. Chancery Misc., 4/2, fo. 16.
[2] B.M. Cotton Charter XXX, 40, printed in *Collectanea Franciscana*,
(B.S.F.S.), vol. I, p. 152.   The date, 1304, is, however, uncertain and as
Dr. Little points out, may be a mistake for 1334.
[3] *Ibid.*, pp. 148, 152.
[4] Little, *Grey Friars in Oxford*, p. 70.
[5] Kingsford, *Grey Friars of London*, p. 194.   [6] *Ibid.*
[7] *A Book of Glamorganshire Antiquities, ut sup.*, (1825) p. 42, (1887)
p. 78.
[8] *L. and P. Hen. VIII*, vol. 7, no. 1020.
[9] *Ibid.*, no. 1196.

Cardiff. The Deed of Surrender of the Grey Friary is dated on that day and is signed by the guardian, Thomas Gwyn, and eight others.[1] The custody of the property was placed in the hands of the deputy bailiff, John Loveday, who prepared an inventory of the friars' goods.[2] This mentions the quire in which was a " fayer tabull of allebastre," and a pair of organs, the church (i.e. the nave) with five tables of alabaster, one bell in the steeple, the vestry, the kitchen, the hall, and the new chamber. Among the items allowed to the warden for the visitor's expenses was " A grate of yeren yt stode in ye Quere," while the visitor had taken with him some of the plate including " a crosse with Mary and John," weighing 25 oz. The total weight of the plate and jewels, some of which had been pledged, was 154 oz. There was also a box containing deeds relating to the Grey Friars as well as 5 deeds belonging to the Black Friars, a fact which suggests that the two houses were on friendly terms.

The site, which comprised a garden, three chambers, a kitchen, a stable with other houses, a barn, a meadow of two acres, a close called Cow close and another called, " grette fryers close "[3] was leased in 1542 to John White, one of the bailiffs of the town, for a term of 21 years, at a yearly rental of 53s. 4d.[4] From some proceedings before the Court of Augmentations it appears that John Norrys claimed to be entitled to an old ruinous house which formerly belonged to the friars and. had been purchased by one Dafydd ap Jevan from the King's commissioners at the time of the Dissolution, and that he and others had begun to demolish the building. His title was disputed by White though with what success does not appear.[5] The property was granted early in 1546 to James Gunter and Henry Wescott, who in the same year were licensed to sell the site of the Grey Friars to Sir George Herbert of Swansea.[6] His grandson constructed a mansion out of the ruins. Merrick, in 1578, refers to the Grey Friars where " Sir William Herbert Kt hath builded a splendid house of late." This house continued to be occupied by the Herberts until

[1] *Ibid.*, vol. 13(2), no. 295.
[2] *Arch. Camb. Orig. Documents*, p. xxxviii.
[3] P.R.O. Ministers' Accounts, Hen. VIII, no. 5595.
[4] *L. and P. Hen. VIII*, vol. 17, p. 697 ; *Cardiff Records*, vol. III, p. 34.
[5] *Cardiff Records*, vol. III, p. 38.
[6] *L. and P. Hen. VIII*, vol. 21(2), no. 772(4).

about 1730, when it was allowed to fall into decay.[1]   It
soon became a ruin and only a few fragments of it survive
to-day.

DESCRIPTION

The site was in the suburb of Crockerton to the north-
east of the medieval town and a little to the east of the
castle.   Leland notes that " the biggest suburbe of the town
is caullid Crokerton and there was a house of Gray Freres." [2]
To judge from Speed's map of 1610 the precinct did not
actually abut on Crockerton Street which is now known as
Queen Street, but was a roughly rectangular enclosure a
short distance to the north with its south-west corner
abutting on the north gate of the town.

Although fragments of Herbert's mansion survive as
stated no part of the friary buildings remain above ground.
The site was, however, excavated in 1896 by the late
Marquess of Bute,[3] and the rubble walls which were then
exposed have been brought to a general level in brick and
the floor spaces of the church repaved so that the plan of
the latter can still be seen.   Further excavations were
carried out in 1925 by Mr. J. P. Grant, F.S.A., and the
accompanying Plan, which is based on that of Mr. Grant,
incorporates some modifications of the earlier plans suggested by the later investigations.   There is little to indicate
the date of the various structures, but the extensive remains
of the nave arcades of the church discovered during the
excavations show that they were erected about 1300.   A
curious feature of the plan of the church is the extra width of
both the east and west bays of the nave, which Mr. Clapham
has suggested [4] may be in some sort a legacy from an earlier
building which occupied the site.   A similar feature, however, occurred in the eastern bay of the nave at Walsingham,
and there can be little doubt that it served as a means of
providing additional space for the chapels at the ends of the
aisles.   The western bay, on the other hand, is normally of

---

[1] This mansion, which was originally called " The Greyfriars," and
later " The Friars," became known as " White Friars " in the latter
part of the seventeenth century, a fact which has led to a certain amount
of confusion with some local writers.   There was no house of Carmelites
in Cardiff.
[2] Leland, *Itin.*, vol. 3, p. 35.
[3] C. B. Fowler, *Excavations on the Site of the Grey Friars Monastery,
Cardiff*, 1896.
[4] " Architectural Remains of the Mendicant Orders in Wales," by
A. W. Clapham, *Arch. J.*, vol. 84 (1927), pp. 88–104.

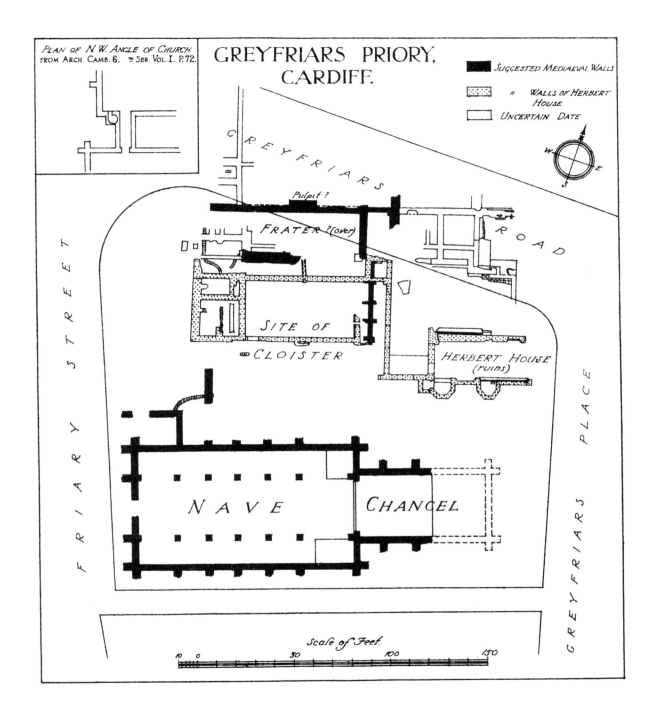

PLAN OF N.W. ANGLE OF CHURCH.
FROM ARCH. CAMB. 6. TH SER. VOL. I. P. 72.

GREYFRIARS PRIORY,
CARDIFF.

SUGGESTED MEDIAEVAL WALLS

" WALLS OF HERBERT HOUSE

UNCERTAIN DATE

W

S

E

GREYFRIARS ROAD

Pulpit?

FRATER ?(over)

SITE OF

CLOISTER

HERBERT HOUSE
(ruins)

FRIARY STREET

NAVE

CHANCEL

GREYFRIARS PLACE

Scale of Feet.

10 0   30   100   150

the same width as the remaining bays of the arcade and in this respect the arrangement at Cardiff is unusual.

Of the chancel only the foundations of the western portion were found, while the absence of any indication of the usual bell tower is a feature shared with the neighbouring Black Friars' house. As a steeple is mentioned in the suppression inventory, it is probable that this was of timber.

The remains of the domestic buildings on the north side of the church were so involved with the later mansion of the Herbert family that the identification of the various parts of the medieval structure is peculiarly difficult, and the indications of date shown on the Plan must therefore be considered only tentative. In the earlier plans an open yard is shown intervening between the nave and the cloister in accordance with the not uncommon arrangement already noticed, but its existence in this instance does not seem to have been substantiated by the latest excavations, and it has accordingly been omitted. Of the claustral buildings only the northern range, the upper part of which was presumably occupied by the frater, was definitely recognizable and a projection in the centre of its north wall may possibly indicate the position of the pulpit. The cloister would seem to have been rather over 90 feet square.

(3) LICHFIELD

HISTORY

The house at Lichfield appears to have been established in or shortly before 1237, for in October of that year the friars received from the King a gift of 30 oaks, of which 10 were to be furnished from each of the three forests of Alrewas, Hopwas and Benetl' (? Bednall), " for the construction of their house and chapel." [1] They subsequently reported that there was no timber at Hopwas suitable for the fabric of the church, and John Byset was accordingly ordered in the following September to allow the friars to have these ten oaks from Alrewas instead. [2]

There seems to be no contemporary record of the acquisition of the site, but Alexander de Stavensby, who was Bishop of Coventry and Lichfield from 1224 to 1238, has

[1] *C.C.R. 1234–37*, p. 502. [2] *Ibid. 1237–42*, p. 106.

been accredited with having been instrumental in this, probably owing to Leland's statement that he "gave first certaine free burgages in the towne for to sett this house on and was the first founder of it." [1] The King continued to support the house with liberal gifts of money. In March 1239 the friars received 10 marks [2] and in the following August 100s.[3] In September 1241 the Sheriff of Staffordshire was ordered to provide them with clothing [4] and in December 1244 the keeper of the bishopric of Chester was ordered to furnish them with 100s. to pay their debts.[5] In April 1286 the King presented the friars with a further eight oaks from the forest of Cannock, which may indicate the completion of the buildings.[6] Five years later these were burnt down together with the greater part of the town. The contemporary Annals of Dunstable record "Anno gratiæ MCCXCI per infortunium combusta est fere tota villa de Lycheffeld et habitatio Fratrum Minorum." [7] Harwood states that the church survived presumably by inference from the use of the word "habitation" and there is certainly no record of a rededication. The rebuilding was probably begun at once, as help came from an unexpected source. A fine of 60 marks, imposed on the Abbot and Convent of Westminster for housing an apostate friar, was ordered to be divided between this house and the Franciscans of Winchelsea whose buildings had been destroyed by the sea, to relieve their special necessities.[8] The sum was paid by instalments in 1294 and 1295. No reference to the work of reconstruction, however, has survived, and, apart from a licence granted in November 1329 to Ralph Basset of Drayton to assign to the friars two acres of land adjoining their house for its enlargement,[9] a lawsuit and some bequests,[10] there appears to be no further mention of the house until the Dissolution. The quire of the church was rebuilt shortly before the suppression if we may judge from an entry in the list of debts appended

[1] Leland, *Itin.*, vol. 2, p. 100. [2] *C. Lib. R.*, vol. 1, p. 373.
[3] *Ibid.*, vol. 1, p. 407. [4] *Ibid.*, vol. 2, p. 71.
[5] *Ibid.*, vol. 2, p. 283. [6] *C.C.R. 1279–88*, p. 390.
[7] *Annales Prioratus de Dunstaplia. Ann. Mon.* (R.S.), vol. 3, p. 365 ; cf. H. Wharton, *Anglia Sacra* (1691), vol. 1, p. 447.
[8] *Mon. Franc.* (R.S.), vol. 2, pp. 31–65.
[9] *C.P.R. 1327–30*, p. 465.
[10] Worc. Epis. Reg., Wulstan de Bransford, vol. I, fo. 7ᵛ (1339) ; *Sede Vacante Wills*, ed. C. E. Woodruff, p. 119 ; *Test. Vet.*, p. 54 ; Cotton, *Grey Friars of Canterbury*, p. 96, and Brit. Mus. MS. Royal 3D, I, gifts of books.

to the suppression inventory which included 30s. borrowed
" for bylding the quere." [1]

In August 1538 the Bishop of Dover wrote to Cromwell
informing him that he was then in Lichfield, and that the
Grey Friars were loath to give up though in debt.[2] The
house was, however, surrendered to the visitor on 7 August,
and the custody handed over to Richard Wetwode, master
of the local guild, and the two constables of the town.[3]
On the following day Ingworth informed Cromwell that the
friars had given up their house and adds : " The warden is
sore diseased in his face, whether of a canker or a pocke
or a fistula I know not. He has been little at home this
half year yet now he came home and was loth to give up his
house though it be more in debt than all the stuff that
belongs to it would pay, chalice, bells and all, by 20 nobles." [4]

Four days later Thomas Legh wrote to Cromwell on
behalf of the custodian Richard Wetwode, asking that he
should have the preferment of the house.[5] The buildings
and contents were, however, sold on 4 October 1538 and a
detailed account of this sale prepared by John Scudamore
has survived.[6] As this throws considerable light on the
extent and arrangement of the buildings the items referring
to these are set out below :

Item, the paving tyle in both the cloysters, sold to Mr.
   Strete   xls.
Item, the tymber, tyle and stone of the old hostery
   and the ffermery sold to Rychard Rawson   iiij*li*.
Item, the tyle and tymber of the lytle cloyster sold
   to Johan ap Glim̄   xiijs. iiij*d*.
Item, ij worte leddes in the bruehouse sold to Johan
   Sandelond   vis. viij*d*.
Item, sold to Thomas Fanne, the bryck wall at the
   churche ende   ijs.
Item, sold to the Master of the Ile a fate in the bruehouse   iiij*d*.
Item, sold to Johan Genynges the tymber tyle and
   stone of the stable buttyng upon the churche
   ende   iiij*li*.
Item, sold to John Mylward the tymber tyle and
   stone of the iij houses joyning together in the
   court called the Tenys Court   xls.
Item, sold to Rychard Ballard, the lytle house over
   the ovyn   iijs. iiij*d*.

---

[1] *L. and P. Hen. VIII*, vol. 13(2), no. 44.
[2] *Ibid.*, vol. 13(2), no. 49.   [3] *Ibid.*, vol. 13(2), no. 44.
[4] *Ibid.*, vol. 13(2), no. 50.   [5] *Ibid.*, vol. 13(2), no. 79.
[6] B.M. Add. MSS. 11041, fo. 86. Printed in full in Wright's *Suppression*
(Camden Soc.), pp. 274-7 ; *L. and P. Hen. VIII*, vol. 13(2), no. 666.

Item, the tymber tyle and stone of the kechyn and the bruehouse sold to Edward Spratte   liijs. iiijd.

Item, sold to Johan Laughton, a cofere and a hutche in the buttery   xijd.

Item, the cesterne of ledd and the stone that hyt standythe in, in the kechyn sold to John Genynges   xiijs. iiijd.

Item, the glasse that ys lewse in the newe loggyng sold to William Colman   iijs.

Item, a presse in the vestrye sold to the Warden of the gyld   xvjd.

Item, the stone wall betwene the old ostery and the frater sold to Johan Sadeler   vs.

Item, the pavement of the quyere sold to Mr. Stretes   xiijs. iiijd.

Item, the fryers setes in the quyere sold to Johan Laughton   vjs. viijd.

Item, the cundyt of ledd in the cloyster sold to the Master of the gyld and his brethren   xxxs.

Item, a halywaterstocke sold to Johan Howlat   xxd.

Item, the lytle cundyt standyng at the revestrye dore sold to George Stonyng   vs.

Item, the cesterne of ledd standyng in the porche at the Tenys Court ende sold to Mr. Lytleton   xxs.

Item, a lytle porche standyng by the dwellyng house sold to Mr. Lytylton   xs.

Item, the frater and the chambers stretchyng to the kechyn with all the quadrant of the inner cloyster joynyng to the church and steple and the church and quyer and the long newe house on the est syde of the same cloyster except and reservyd ledd belles pavement and gravestones within all the seyd buyldynges save only the pavement of the seyd churche whyche ys parcelle of the seyd bargayne sold to different persons (names set out) and hath day (sic) to deface the steple cloyster and quyer forth wyth the churche unles they obteyne lycens otherwyse of the kyng and hys councell athyssyde the feast of the Purification of our Lady next commyng and for all the residewe of the buyldynges iij yeres day to pull down and carye away and to have egresse and regresse for the same   xlijli. xiijs. iiijd.

The money received from this sale was paid into the Court of Augmentations in September 1539.[1] The lead on the buildings was reserved for the King, and the following entry occurs in an inventory of the lead from various friars' houses : " The grey ffreres of Lichfield, the church and the quere ij yles and one pane of the cloyster with divers gutters

---

[1] *L. and P. Hen. VIII*, vol. 14(2), no. 236, p. 72.

leade." [1] The site was let out to various tenants at a total rent of 28s. 4d. [2] and on 14 May 1544 the whole property was sold to Richard Crimibilheme or Crumbilhome of Dutton in Lancashire. The more important buildings had apparently not then been demolished as the church, dorter, frater, cloister, chapter-house and all lead bells, glass and iron were expressly excepted save only the leaden gutters upon the buildings. [3] Crumbilhome appears to have disposed of the property almost at once, for on 22 May 1544 he was licensed to assign it to Gregory Stonyng and Alice his wife, who were already in occupation. This licence mentions in addition to the site itself a water-course within the said site descending from a place called Polefurlonge to a place called the Crucifixe [in Lychefeld Street] in the tenure of John Weston, an inn [or messuage] called the Bisshoppe's Lodging or le Great Chamber within the precinct of the said friars and a garden there and little feedings and pastures called le Bareplecke, le Colyers Plek and the orchard within the precinct in the tenure of the said Gregory and also le Churche Yarde in tenure of John Strynger all which belonged to the said Grey Friars." [4]

The water-course referred to doubtless served the conduit head in the cloister which was purchased by the master and brethren of the guild and also the little conduit at the revestry door. In 1301 one Henry, a bellfounder, son of Michael of Lichfield, bellfounder, granted " for the use and solace of the Friars Minor in Lichfield " his fountains or springs in Fowlewell near Alreshawe, with provision for the erection of a conduit head of stone and the bringing of the water in pipes to the friary on condition that the friars should give no vessel (*vasum*) of the water to anyone else without the grantor's consent. [5] This water system is also mentioned by Leland, who visited Lichfield shortly

[1] P.R.O. Exch. Treasury of Receipt Misc. Bks., vol. 153, fo. 7.

[2] *Ibid.* Ministers' Accounts Hen. VIII, nos. 7428, 7430, 7444.

[3] *L. and P. Hen. VIII*, vol. 18(1), no. 623(79), and vol. 19(1), no. 610(63).

[4] *Ibid.*, vol. 19(1), no. 610(116). Stonyng had been Master of the guild in 1536 and was the first bailiff on the incorporation of the city by Charter in 1548. On 11 July 1552 he was licensed to assign this property to Francis Sandebache and Humphrey Ilseley upon trust for himself and his wife Elizabeth (*C.P.R. Edward VI*, vol. 4, p. 430). The description of the property in this licence is very similar to that in the former licence, the words in square brackets in the text having been inserted from the later document.

[5] *Lichfield Magnum Registrum Album*, ed. Savage (Wm. Salt, Arch. Soc., 1924), no. 528 ; T. Harwood, *History and Antiquities of Lichfield* (1806), p. 488.

after the suppression. He says : " There was a howse of
Gray Friers in Lichfield in the southe west parte of the
towne . . . There comithe a conduite of water out of an
hill browght in lead to the towne and hathe 2 castelets in
the towne one in the est waule of this fryers close on the
strete syd, another about the Market place."[1]

DESCRIPTION

The site of the friary is in the southern part of the town
on the south-west side of Bird Street and St. John Street,
formerly known as Lichfield Street.   The house called " The
Friars," which has recently been incorporated in the new
building of the Lichfield High School for girls, was probably
built by Gregory Stoning shortly after the suppression and
in part dates from that period.   It was erected on the site
of the building referred to in the dissolution documents ·as
the Great Chamber or Bishop's lodging, and portions of the
latter building may have to some extent survived in its
structure.   The friars' church and main claustral buildings
lay to the north-west of the house in what was until recently
the private gardens of the Friary School.   In 1925
the ground on the north-west side of " The Friars " was
acquired by the City Council in connection with the construction of a new by-pass road, which was laid out between
1925 and 1928 and is now known as Friary Road.   During
the progress of this work, which involved the demolition
of a portion of the house, traces of early walls were discovered as well as several burials.   Unfortunately no record
of these discoveries appears to have been kept, but in 1933
the excavation of the land on the north-west side of the new
road was undertaken by the Council and this work was
continued in 1934, with the result that the greater part of
the ground plan of the friary buildings has been recovered [2]
(see Plan opposite p. 172).

The church consisted of an aisled nave measuring
approximately 95 feet by 58 feet with an aisleless quire, 86 feet
long and 25 feet wide internally.   The nave was apparently
of five bays with its arcades supported on octagonal piers

[1] Leland, *Itin.*, vol. 2, p. 100.   For later documents relating to this
water system see T. Harwood, *ut sup.*, pp. 488–95.
[2] This work was undertaken at the instance of the present Mayor,
Councillor Thomas Moseley, and the writer's thanks are due to him and
to Mr. C. T. Read, the city surveyor, for kindly furnishing information
as to the work carried out and for permission to reproduce the accompanying Plan.

3 feet in diameter. The easternmost of these piers on either side were of more massive construction and doubtless served to support a belfry, the lower part of which separated the nave from the quire in accordance with the normal arrangement. A portion of the north wall of the nave, 3 feet 2 inches in width, still stands to a height of 2 or 3 feet, and against its internal face are the remains of a stone seat which apparently extended the whole length of the nave. In this wall towards the west end is a doorway, approximately 4 feet 6 inches wide with moulded external jambs and approached by 3 steps on the outside leading down to the church from the higher ground to the north. The eastern jamb of this door is well preserved to a height of some 3 feet and is constructed of the local red sandstone which is the normal building stone of the district.

The projection shown on the Plan at the west end of the church may not be part of the original structure, as a post-suppression building seems to have stood on this part of the site and it was often difficult to distinguish the medieval foundations with absolute certainty.

The arrangement of the domestic buildings is shown on the Plan. That their extent was considerable is clear from the dissolution documents and they probably covered the whole of the ground between the present house and the church. The little or inner cloister is described in John Scudamore's accounts [1] as adjoining the church and steeple. It was found on the south side of the quire and measured with its alleys about 60 feet square. The base of the doorway into the quire on the east was preserved and in the north-west corner was a large block of masonry which may have been the base of a stair turret giving access to the belfry. A larger cloister appears to have occupied the space to the south of the nave and extended under the present roadway. In this stood the friars' conduit connected with the town conduit, just outside the friars' wall in St. John Street, by a water-course along the line of the new road. Of the disposition of the remaining buildings it is only possible to conjecture with the aid of a plan of the site made by John Hill in 1638 [2] (Plate 27B). The " tennis court " may have been the area immediately within the principal gateway which stood opposite the west end

[1] See *ante*, p. 166.
[2] Reproduced in T. Harwood's *History and Antiquities of Lichfield* (1806), opp. p. 483.

of Bore Street. Scudamore mentions the old hostery or guest-house, which implies that there was also a newer building devoted to the same purpose, and these were probably in the vicinity of the gateway. The "frater and chambers stretching to the kitchen " were sold with the inner cloister and presumably therefore formed its western or southern range. Between the frater and the old guest-house was a stone wall, while the "new loggyng " may have been the Great Chamber or Bishop's lodging already mentioned which is not otherwise referred to by Scudamore. The existence of a special building set apart for the Bishop within the friary is unusual, as houses of the mendicant orders were exempt from episcopal visitation, while the Bishop of the Diocese had his own palace in the Cathedral close as well as houses at Beaudesert, Pipe and Haywood in the immediate neighbourhood and the castle of Eccleshall to the north-west. A parallel, however, existed in the Bishops' lodging in the Black Friars at Oxford which was used by the bishops of Lincoln when visiting Oxford.[1] A long range of buildings appears to have connected the existing house with the west end of the church, and part of its foundations have been recovered. A building in this position was standing in 1638 and was then described as a barn.[2]

The extent of the friars' property is clearly shown in the map of 1638. It extended from Bird Street and St. John Street on the north-east to approximately the fork in the new Friary road on the south-west. The north-western boundary was the friars' alley which seems to have been formed within the precinct wall, while on the south-east a ditch and wall divided the property from land belonging to the hospital of St. John the Baptist. Outside the precinct wall on the north-east facing Bird Street was a house belonging to the friars and immediately on the left of the friars' gateway as one entered stood the crucifix, where one of the town's conduit heads was still standing in 1806.[3]

----

[1] *V.C.H. Oxfordshire*, vol. 2, p. 110 ; at Lichfield the reservation of a building for the Bishop may have dated from the foundation and is some confirmation of the tradition that the original site was provided by Bishop Stavensby ; cf. Chester, p. 233. On the other hand, the Bishops' lodging may have been apartments assigned to some suffragan bishop belonging to the Order, like those occupied by Bishop Richard Martin at Canterbury ; Cotton, *Grey Friars of Canterbury*, pp. 25, 96–8.

[2] See references to Hill's plan in Harwood, *op. cit.*

[3] T. Harwood, *ut sup.*, p. 488. In 1553 there is mention of a piece of waste ground " betwixt the gate called the ffrere gate and the howsse

The friars' cemetery was probably to the east and north of the quire, as several burials have been discovered here.[1] Four burials were also found during the recent excavations in the north aisle of the nave. Built into the wall of the existing house is a stone coffin lid 6 feet 8 inches long and 2 feet 6 inches wide at the top, slightly tapering to 2 feet 3 inches at the bottom on which is carved in low relief a foliated cross and an inscription in Gothic letters round the edge which reads :

> " RICARD': MERCATOR: VICT': MORT': NOVCA:
> Q': CESSAT: M̄CARI: PAVSAT: Ī: HAC:
> IERIARCA: EXTVLIT: EPHEB': PAVCIS:
> VI VINDO: DIEB': ECCLĪAM: REB': SIC:
> ET: VARIIS: SPECIEB': VIVAT: ET: Ī:
> CELIS: NV̄C: M̄CATOR: MICAELIS: ✠ "

(which when extended forms the following rather curious verse) :

> " Ricardus Mercator victus morte noverca
> Qui cessat mercari pausat in hac ierarca :
> Extulit ephebus paucis vivendo diebus
> Ecclesiam rebus sic et variis speciebus
> Vivat et in celis nunc Mercator Micaelis."

This stone is apparently of late thirteenth-century date and was found during the removal of an old wall in 1746 about 6 feet below the surface.[2] Dugdale mentions [3] another stone showing a male figure in a surcoat of arms, kneeling before the figures of Christ and St. Francis, with an inscription over his head which read : " Orate pro animabus mgri Rogeri Jllari et dominæ Mar . . ." but this seems to have disappeared. Harwood states that the following epitaph formerly existed in the friary : " Hac iij die Julii et anno Dom̄. millmo ccccmo lx mo iiijto obiit Johēs Harpur armig. ac Dom. de Ruyssheale int' horam septimam et octavam post nonam cujus anime propicietur Deus. Amen." [4]

Robert of Leicester, at one time a Franciscan lecturer

wherein one Richard Fawken nowe dwellithe upon which wast ground standithe a howse comonly called the Crucifix " (T. Harwood, *ut sup.*, p. 496).

[1] T. Harwood, *ut sup.*, p. 488.

[2] *Gentleman's Magazine*, 1746, vol. 16 (1746), p. 646. See also *ibid.*, pp. 465, 545 ; T. Harwood, *ut sup.*, p. 487.

[3] *Visitation of Staffs.* (1663–4), c. 36, p. 41. Quoted in Shaw's *Hist. of Staffs.*, vol. 1 (1798), p. 321.

[4] T. Harwood, *ut sup.*, p. 482, note 90.

at Oxford, was buried at the friary, according to Harwood in the cloister.[1]   He is said to have died in 1348, but Wood adds, " I suppose 'twas sooner." [2]   Another to be buried here was Richard Leke or Leech, D.D., who became 36th Provincial Minister between 1430 and 1438 and was guardian of the house in 1451.[3]

A good many examples of pavement tiles were discovered during the progress of the recent excavations on the site of the Friary.   Some of them were of the usual kind with an impressed pattern filled with white clay and covered with a yellow glaze ; the majority, however, were of another type with the patterns formed of sunk lines with no filling and covered with both green and yellow glaze. Perhaps the most interesting were those of this latter type forming part of what had been apparently the pavement on the south side of the quire.   These were found *in situ*. Each part of the pattern consists of a circular tile round which are six others so shaped as to form a slightly cusped circle ; on the central tile is the impressed design of a triangle interlacing with a trefoil with points *flory*.   The surrounding tiles are each decorated with a six-pointed star within a crescent.   Each group thus formed is placed, honey-comb fashion, a short distance apart, the space between being filled with a narrow band made up of Y-shaped tiles having on them a series of impressed rosettes, alternately large and small.   In the angle of the Y there is a small plain triangular tile.   Another pattern consists of a series of interlacing circles impressed on each square tile.   This is also found in Coventry and elsewhere in Warwickshire, sometimes with the lines filled with white clay.   Two of the ordinary type of tile with white clay filling from Lichfield are also found in the remaining part of the old church of Ullenhall, Warwickshire and also in Coventry.[4]

---

[1] T. Harwood, *ut sup.*, p. 482. Harwood confuses him with Ralph of Leicester, who was a canon of the cathedral church and Prebendary of Stotford (*ibid.*, p. 247).

[2] A. G. Little, *Grey Friars in Oxford*, p. 269.

[3] *Ibid.*, p. 359 ; T. Harwood, *ut sup.*, pp. 275 and 482.

[4] I am indebted to Mr. P. B. Chatwin, F.S.A., for this description of the Lichfield tiles.

GREYFRIARS LICHFIELD

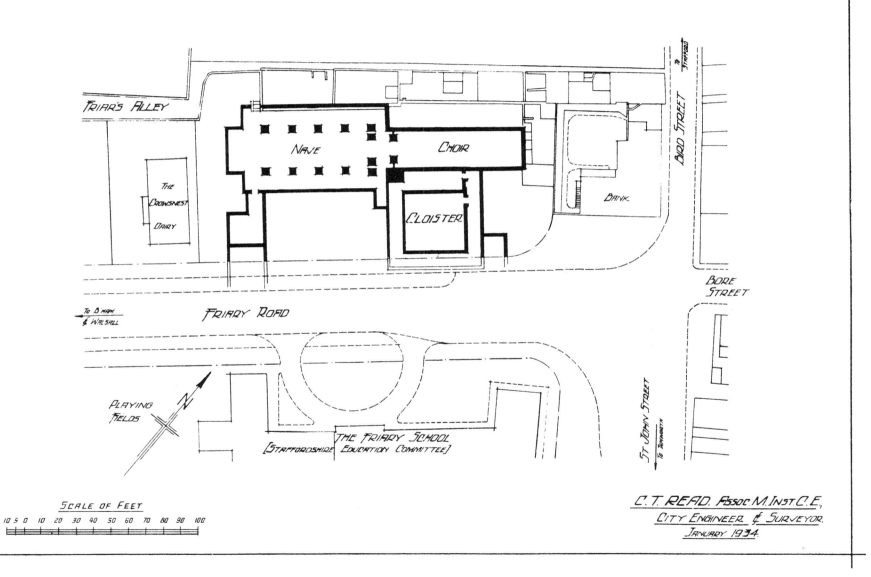

FRIAR'S ALLEY

THE CROWSNEST DAIRY

NAVE

CHOIR

CLOISTER

BANK

BIRD STREET

To Stafford

BORE STREET

FRIARY ROAD

To B'HAM & WALSALL

PLAYING FIELDS

N

THE FRIARY SCHOOL
[STAFFORDSHIRE EDUCATION COMMITTEE]

ST JOHN STREET

To Tamworth

SCALE OF FEET

10 5 0 10 20 30 40 50 60 70 80 90 100

C.T. READ. ASSOC. M. INST. C.E.,
CITY ENGINEER & SURVEYOR.
JANUARY 1934.

(4) LLANFAES

History

At Llanfaes, in Anglesey, was established the earliest Franciscan settlement in Wales. Its foundation in 1237 by Llewelyn ap Iorwerth in memory of his wife Joan, daughter of King John, is mentioned in the *Brut y Tywysogion*.[1] At that time Llanfaes was a small town with a parish church and a port of its own. Very little is known with regard to the early history of the house, but after the battle of Menai in November 1282 many of the knights and gentlemen among the slain are stated to have been buried in the friars' cemetery.[2] The erection of Beaumaris Castle in 1296 after the suppression of the Welsh revolt under Madoc ap Llewelyn led to the foundation of a new borough at Beaumaris, and the gradual transfer of the population there, with the result that by 1319, when the remaining parishioners were removed to the new town,[3] the friary was left isolated, a fact which explains the present deserted situation of the site. The friars, however, remained in occupation of their property and from the extent of their land at the Dissolution appear to have been engaged largely in farming. In 1316 the site was enlarged.[4] In the rising of Owen Glyndwr in 1400 the friary was attacked by the English troops and the friars dispersed as rebels, but at the instigation of the provincial Minister Henry IV ultimately undertook some reparation of the buildings to which they returned.[5]

That the house was regarded as a royal foundation is apparent from a charter of Henry V, which provided that there should be always eight friars, of whom two at least were' to be Welsh, in this house " of the foundation of the King's progenitors."[6] In 1534 the property of the friary was valued at 34s. 4d. a year.[7] The house was surrendered on 19 August 1538, the deed being signed by four friars.[8]

[1] *Brut* (R.S.), pp. 325–6 ; *Ann. Camb.* (R.S.), p. 82 ; Powell, *Cambria*, p. 210. Henry III granted protection to the friary in 1245 : *C.P.R. 1232–47*, p. 460.
[2] *C.P.R. 1413–16*, p. 234 ; Rymer, *Fœdera*, vol. IX, p. 147 ; see list in *Ann Cest.* (Lanc. and Ches. Soc.), p. 111, and Camden, *Britannia*, vol. 2, p. 60.
[3] *C.C.R. 1318–23*, p. 71.   [4] *C.P.R. 1313–17*, p. 388.
[5] *Ibid. 1399–1401*, p. 418.   [6] *Ibid. 1413–16*, pp. 28–9.
[7] *Valor Ecclesiasticus* (Rec. Com.), vol. iv, p. 431. The visitor in 1538 valued their land at " 4 marks by year and better."
[8] *L. and P. Hen. VIII*, vol. 13(2), no. 138.

The inventory [1] mentions the quire, with a fair table of alabaster over the high altar, four tables of alabaster in the church (i.e. the nave), the vestry, brewhouse, kitchen, hall and storehouse and one bell in the steeple. The other items included a pack saddle, growing corn and about 20 sheep. That the friars farmed on a fairly extensive scale is apparent from the fact that at the suppression they appear to have had about 30 acres of arable and pasture land, [2] a figure greatly in excess of the normal holding of a Franciscan house.

On 22 November Sir Richard Bulkeley wrote to Cromwell to renew his request for a grant of the property and offered him 100 marks for his pains in the matter. [3]

DESCRIPTION

There are now no structural remains of the buildings above ground, but the modern house called " The Friars,"

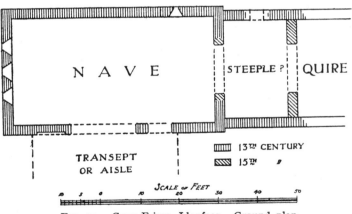

FIG. 12.—Grey Friars, Llanfaes. Ground plan

a short distance to the east of Beaumaris town, may contain some re-used material. The last surviving structure was destroyed in the third quarter of the last century, but its plan had fortunately been published, [4] and it has been

[1] *L. and P. Hen. VIII*, vol 13(2), no. 138. Printed in *Arch. Camb.*, *Original Documents* (1870), p. xliii.
[2] P.R.O. Ministers' Accounts, Hen. VIII, no. 5566.
[3] *L. and P. Hen. VIII*, vol. 13(2), no. 892.
[4] *Arch. Camb.*, 3rd ser., vol. i, p. 76.

described by Mr. A. W. Clapham, F.S.A.[1] The building (Fig. 12) consisted of the western part of the church and comprised the nave (51 feet by 28 feet) with a triplet of lancet lights in the west wall and a compartment (21 feet by 26 feet) to the east, opening to the east and west by segmental arches which are said to have been of " Perpendicular character." There can be little doubt that this was the " walking-place " between the quire and the nave and above it would have been the steeple. Nothing remained of the quire, but marks in the turf in 1855 indicated a destroyed building extending 18 feet farther east. Assuming that the space occupied by the steeple, which appears to have been a fifteenth century addition, was originally part of the quire, this would allow for a total length of 41½ feet for the original thirteenth quire. The latter was doubtless lengthened towards the east when the steeple was added. The most interesting feature of the plan, however, was the existence of a large arch, 17¾ feet wide with a door to the east of it, in the south wall of the nave. This must have opened into a large transept at least as wide as the nave. This arrangement which, as we have seen, is closely akin to the plans of many Irish friaries, seems to have been of rare occurrence in this country. It is significant that four altars are mentioned in the suppression inventory as being in the church which must here be taken to include not only the nave but the transept in which at least two altars would have probably stood. In the transept to the west of the large arch was a recess in the nave wall, probably for a tomb.

The cloister, no doubt, stood on the north side of the church opposite the transept, but no trace of it is recorded. In the grounds of Barons Hill, Beaumaris, is preserved an unusually fine tomb slab of apparently thirteenth-century date. It bears the half effigy of a lady and elaborate foliage and has been ascribed to Joan, daughter of King John and wife of the founder of the house. With it is another slab bearing a cross and interlaced knotwork.[2]

[1] *Arch. Journal*, vol. 84 (1927), pp. 100–1. The above account is based on Mr. Clapham's paper.
[2] The two stones are described and illustrated in *Arch. Camb.*, 3rd Ser., vol. I, (1855), p. 80.

(5) LONDON [1]

HISTORY

The circumstances connected with the arrival of the Franciscans in London are well known from the account given by Thomas of Eccleston.[2] After a sojourn of two days in Canterbury four of the party of nine Friars Minor, who had landed at Dover, went on to London. They were kindly received by the Friars Preachers, who entertained them for fifteen days. They then hired a house in Cornhill where they dwelt until the following summer. The first gift towards a permanent home was made by John Iwyn, a wealthy mercer of London, in the summer of 1225. He purchased for the use of the friars some land with houses thereon in the parish of St. Nicholas Shambles within Newgate.[3] There is no indication of the precise position or extent of this property, but from later documents it appears to have been situated on the west side of St. Nicholas or Stinking Lane [4] and Mr. Kingsford has conjectured [5] that it formed the site on which All Hallows chapel and the Vestry were subsequently built. This area was extended in 1227–28 by the gift from Joce Fitz Piers of all his land in Stinking Lane which is stated to have extended up to the city wall on the north.[6] In 1238–39 the city purchased for the use of the friars a piece of land in St. Ewens parish at a cost of 6 marks. Four years later the corporation paid 50 marks for two further plots in St. Sepulchre's parish, both of which extended to the city wall on the north. These, to

[1] The principal modern authorities for the history of this house are : G. H. Birch, " Greyfriars," *St. Pauls Eccles. Soc. Trans.*, vol. 3 (1892), pp. 101–4 ; E. B. S. Shepherd, " The Church of the Friars Minors in London," *Arch. Journ.*, vol. 59 (1902), pp. 238–87 ; E. H. Pearce, *Annals of Christ's Hospital* (1908) ; M. Reddan, article in *V.C.H. London*, vol. 1 (1909), pp. 502–7 ; C. L. Kingsford, *The Grey Friars of London*, B.S.F.S., vol. 6 (1915) ; C. L. Kingsford, " Additional material for the history of the Grey Friars London " (B.S.F.S. *Coll. Franc.*, vol. 2, 1922, pp. 61–149), and M. B. Honeybourne, " The Precinct of the Grey Friars," *London Topographical Record*, vol. 16 (1932), pp. 9–51. See also Appendix V.

[2] Eccleston, pp. 11–12 ; *ibid.*, ed. Salter, pp. 10, 14.

[3] Ibid., p. 26 ; *ibid.*, ed. Salter, p. 29.

[4] St. Nicholas or Stinking Lane is frequently referred to in early documents. It was later known as Fowle Lane (1617), Chicken Lane and Butcher Hall Lane (Ogilby, 1677), and is represented by the present King Edward Street, so named in 1843.

[5] *The Grey Friars of London, ut sup.*, p. 28.

[6] This and later grants of land where no other authority is mentioned are recorded in the " Register " of the house now preserved in the B.M. (Cotton MS. Vitellius F, XII) and printed in full in *The Grey Friars of London, ut sup.*

judge from the price paid, were of considerable extent, and as no land is mentioned as having been subsequently acquired in St. Sepulchre's parish they presumably formed the whole of the north-west portion of the later precinct and included the site of the little cloister and Boltons garden (see Plan).

On the site thus acquired the original buildings were erected. These were probably confined to the eastern part of the area where it fronted on Stinking Lane. Of the buildings themselves practically nothing is known. In 1229 the friars received an oak from Windsor forest for the building of their house [1] and the " Register " of the London house records that the chapel, which was erected about 1240, and ultimately became part of the great quire, was built by William Joyner who gave £200 towards the cost of the other buildings.[2] These were doubtless of a modest kind but they served the needs of the community for some forty years. It would seem that the precinct was at this time unenclosed as Eccleston records how William of Nottingham when Provincial Minister (i.e. 1240–54) was accused of not enclosing the London house, to which he replied, " I did not enter the Order to build walls." It is also related that in his dislike of elaborate buildings he had the roof of the church in London taken off and ordered the embossments on the cloister to be removed.[3]

The first great building period was between 1279 and 1290, when considerable additions were made to the site. In the interval several small properties had been acquired, most of which appear to have abutted on Stinking Lane. These included a gift in 1261 from the Countess of Warwick of her land with the house thereon adjoining Stinking Lane which she supplemented by a further gift in 1281–82. Between 1278 and 1292 seven gifts of property are recorded in the Register, six of which are described as either in Stinking Lane or in St. Nicholas Lane, while the other was stated to be in St. Nicholas parish and therefore also in the eastern portion of the area.

On this extended site the new domestic buildings were first erected. The " Register " supplies the names of some of the prominent citizens who provided the cost and incidentally enables the date of the erection of the various buildings to be fixed fairly closely. Thus we are told that

---

[1] *C.C.R. 1227–31*, p. 169.
[2] Kingsford, *op. cit.*, p. 157 ; Joyner was Mayor in 1238–9.
[3] Eccleston, p. 57 ; *ibid.*, ed. Salter, p. 63.

Walter Potter, an alderman who died in 1289, built the
chapter-house, that the Vestry was built out of the common
goods and alms and lengthened by friar Thomas Feltham
who furnished it richly with cupboards and brought thither
a supply of water from the cistern of the common lavatory,
that Gregory de Rokesley, who was several times Mayor
between 1274 and 1285 and died in 1291, built the dormitory
with the beds and necessary chambers, that Bartholomew de
Castro, who was alderman of Cripplegate from about 1260
to 1272, built the refectory and that Peter de Helyland, who
died before 1258, left £100 for the building of the infirmary,
while the Studies were for the most part built by one Bonde
who is described as " king of the Heralds." [1]

In the meantime Walter Joyner's chapel was still serving
the needs of the enlarged community,[2] though the statement in the Register that the nave of the church was built
at great cost by Sir Henry de Waleys, Mayor of London, who
also gave the timber for the altars, seems to imply that it
had been considerably enlarged.   Here a difficulty presents
itself.   Sir Henry le Waleys was five times Mayor of London
between 1274 and 1299 and died in 1302, so that the work
for which he was responsible was presumably completed
by the close of the thirteenth century.   Mr. Kingsford
assumes [3] that the nave built and in part furnished by
him was the nave of the great church which was left unfinished at Queen Margaret's death in 1318, and that her
share in the work was therefore confined to the quire.
This, however, is not only contrary to the statement in the
Register that she began to build the quire *and the church*,
but also implies that the lay-out and extent of the largest
Franciscan church in England had been planned before the
house came under the patronage of the Queen, which is itself
improbable.   Moreover, the names of those who contributed
to the nave of the great church are separately entered in the
Register, while the recorded features of this part of the later
structure make it unlikely that it was substantially a
thirteenth-century building or appreciably earlier than the
quire.   The account of the glazing of the windows in the
great church, as contained in the Register, also suggests that
the windows in the quire were somewhat earlier than those

[1] Kingsford, *op. cit.*, p. 158.
[2] The numbers of friars in the house, according to the evidence of royal
pittances, fluctuated from about 60 to 90 between the years 1243 to 1337.
In 1460 it had dropped to 34, and at the Dissolution to 26.
[3] *Op. cit.*, p. 36.

in the nave, and the fact that Henry le Waley's work is mentioned in the Register under the heading " first foundation of the church of the friars minor of London " while later benefactions, including that of the Queen, appear under the heading " Founders of the new church " seems to imply with reasonable certainty that the building conceived and planned by Queen Margaret was an independent structure on a far larger scale than anything hitherto contemplated. That this building incorporated Joyner's original chapel is expressly stated in the Register [1] and its builders may well have made use also of portions of Henry le Waley's nave, though of this there is no direct evidence.

Of the building of the great church and its internal arrangements a considerable amount of information is available. The Register records that " in the year of our Lord 1306, the most illustrious lady, Lady Margaret, Queen of England and second wife of Edward the first, began to build the quire and the church, to the building of which she gave in her lifetime two thousand marks. She was buried before the high altar in the same quire." To enable this work to be begun certain additional properties had to be acquired. Accordingly, as early as 1301–02, we find Queen Margaret acquiring land and houses in St. Nicholas parish for 60 marks. In the same year Dionisia or Denise de Munchensey, who eight years before had established the house of poor Clares at Waterbeach,[2] gave some further property in St. Nicholas parish for the enlargement of the precinct, and in 1303 and 1305–06 two further gifts for the same purpose were received. The site was now practically complete as only two further additions are recorded in 1313–14 and 1352–53 respectively. The foundation stone of the new church was laid in 1306 by Sir William Walden on behalf of the Queen. The Register elsewhere adds that " the work was completed in twenty-one years, for it was begun in 1327." The latter date however is clearly wrong unless, as Mr. Kingsford has suggested with some probability, the writer meant to write " finished " instead of " begun." In that case he can only have referred to the work upon which Margaret had spent 2,000 marks during her life and left unfinished at her death in 1318, as the whole building was certainly not completed until a much later date. Queen Margaret's benefactions were augmented by the gift of a hundred marks in her will.[3] The fact that she

[1] *Ibid.*, p. 157.   [2] See p. 257.   [3] Kingsford, *op. cit.*, p. 163.

was buried before the high altar in her new church implies that the quire at least was by this date far advanced. That work was simultaneously proceeding on the nave is probable. An account of expenses " about the chapel of St. Louis at the friars minor London " has been preserved, and although undated must belong to the beginning of the reign of Edward II.[1] By a process of elimination it is possible to show that this chapel was in all probability at the east end of the south aisle of the nave so that if the date attributed to the document is correct the latter must have been begun at least as early as the quire.[2]

The Register furnishes the names of the principal donors who supplied the funds out of which the nave was built. Among the earliest of these were John of Brittany, Earl of Richmond, who died in 1305[3] and gave £300 towards the work, and Gilbert de Clare, Earl of Gloucester, who supplied " twenty great beams from his forest of Tonbridge of the price of £20 and as much or more in money."[4] Margaret, Countess of Gloucester, gave £26 13s. 4d., for the construction of an altar and Lady Eleanor le Spencer, who died in 1337, £15 for another altar, while lord Robert Lisle, who died in 1342–43, and had after the death of his wife entered the order gave no less than £300 " and wrought many other benefits for the friars." In the meantime the death of Queen Margaret, probably caused a temporary check on the work on the quire, and it was apparently not until the accession of Edward III that the King's mother, Isabella de Valois, " finding the church which Queen Margaret her aunt began not yet finished spent about seven hundred pounds and more."[5] Queen Philippa also contributed to the work and particularly to the roofing, which was thus clearly still unfinished at the close of 1327 when she arrived in England for her marriage to Edward III. Work on the interior of the building certainly continued for another twenty years

[1] P.R.O. Exchequer (K.R.), accounts 507/5. Printed by Kingsford, *op. cit.*, pp. 202–3. From another contemporary version of the account in Brit. Mus. MS. Add. 7966A, fo. 28ᵛ, it appears that the money was disbursed by John de Sandale : he was treasurer 1308–11, and on some subsequent dates.

[2] The account clearly relates to alterations to an existing building as mention is made of the lengthening of a window, so that it is possible that some part of Henry le Walys nave was involved.

[3] This gift is merely stated to have been made " in aid of the friars " and does not necessarily imply, as Mr. Kingsford. apparently thought, that building had then been begun.

[4] He died in 1314.

[5] " Register " Kingsford, *op. cit.*, p. 165.

at least, and as late as January 1346 the friars were obtaining stone and wood for the fabric of their church and cloister and the repair of their house.[1] The glazing of the windows is minutely described in the register, but although the names of the donors are of value in showing that the glass was inserted at various dates between about 1314 and 1350, it is obvious that as an indication of the progress of the building these dates must be accepted with caution. The fact that most of the earlier gifts for glazing were confined to the quire is however significant, while as Mr. Shepherd has pointed out,[2] the presence of the earliest windows on the north side of the quire may indicate that this portion of the building incorporated what remained of the earlier church. It is however in the clue they provide to the reconstruction of the general ground plan of the church that these records of the glazing of the windows are chiefly of interest, and this evidence will be considered below. By about 1350 the church must have been substantially complete with all its fittings, and apart from the addition of a porch on the south side of the nave about 1398 there is no evidence of any subsequent addition to the structure. Even work of repair is rarely mentioned, though the great central window of the west front was restored by Edward III after it had been blown in by a storm on St. Maurice's day 1363, and about 1380 the countess of Norfolk provided new stalls for the quire at a cost of about 350 marks. In 1420 the ceiling of the quire was renewed at a cost of 200 marks and painted at a further cost of 50 marks. Some further work on the building may be inferred in 1486 by the grant of four oaks for the church of the Friars Minor in London, while as late as 1512 William Maryner left £10 " for the reparacion and paving of the said conventuall church." This work was carried out and the marble paving renewed four years later.

The completion of the building left a narrow strip of land with a considerable frontage to Newgate Street on the south side of the church, which was of no particular value to the friars. This property was accordingly granted in two portions to the city on perpetual leases for the support of London Bridge, and as these documents throw some further light on the position and extent of the friar's church it is convenient to consider them here. The first lease is dated

[1] *C.P.R. 1345–48*, p. 27.
[2] *Arch. Journ.*, vol. 59, p. 246.

1 March 1368 [1] and comprised 212 feet of land extending
from the house of Walter Attehyde on the east to the
buttress of the south door of the church on the west. In
breadth it was 33 feet 2 inches at the east end but narrowed
down to less than half that on the west, where it abutted
on the south wall of the church. The lease provides for the
erection of houses subject to elaborate provisions for the
protection of the friars and the safeguarding of the light
coming to their church. Thus at the east end, where the
measurements indicate that the friars must have retained a
piece of land between the church wall and the land let, the
houses might be 33 feet high and of three storeys, while at
the west end, where they would approach close to the church,
they were to be only two storeys and 17 feet in height.
Moreover, the privacy of the friars was also considered ; if
the corporation desired to open windows at the back of the
houses towards the friars' cemetery they were to be at least
6 feet above the floor of each room so that no one could
look out, and must be glazed, not made to open and carefully barred with iron. The most interesting provision,
however, is the reservation by the friars of a right of way
through the buildings to be erected for the passage of loaded
carts and victuals and other necessaries at any time, the
Mayor and aldermen undertaking to make a good and
convenient approach opposite the door of the church.
(" Une porte [2] bone et covenable faite encontre le huys de
lour eglise.") There can be very little doubt that the door
referred to was a door at the south end of the ambulatory or
walking place between the nave and the quire and that the
present Grey Friars' passage,[3] on the north side of Newgate
Street, preserves to this day the position of the approach
or passage constructed in pursuance of this lease.[4]

[1] The French original of this deed is recited in the patent rolls for
42 Edward III, whence Mr. Shepherd printed it in *Arch. Journ.*, vol. 59,
pp. 262–3. An English transcript appears in the " Register " (Kingsford,
op. cit., pp. 171–7).
    [2] There appears to be no necessity to translate this here as " gate."
    [3] Formerly Christ church passage.
    [4] Miss Honeybourne has recently contended (*London Top. Record*,
vol. 16, p. 13) that this passage, which is shown as " ye waie out of ye
street into church " in the St. Bartholomew's plan of 1617, and the
church door to which it led were sixteenth-century alterations made
after the suppression for the purpose of opening up the cloister, and she
accordingly excludes them from her plan of the precinct. Apart however
from the fact that the absence of a door in this position with the necessary
means of approach to it, would be a distinctly unusual feature in a friars'
church of this period, the reservation of a right of way to the south door

Nearly thirty years after the disposal of the first piece of land the friars parted with a further strip to the west, comprising the remaining portion of their frontage to Newgate street. This lease is dated 1 March 1398.[1] It is a repetition of an earlier deed dated 2 July 1397 [2] and may have been necessitated by the death in the interval of the guardian John Bruyll. It comprised a piece of land 95 feet 2 inches in length, stretching from the south-west corner of the church to the new gate of the friars which stood in Newgate Street opposite St. Ewen's church and the end of the present Warwick Lane. The width of this strip is given as 8 feet 4 inches at the south-west buttress of the church and 7 feet 9 inches at the west buttress beside the friars' gate. The extreme narrowness appears to have necessitated an encroachment on the roadway on the south in order to provide room for the erection of houses, the top floor of which were also to be allowed to project in the rear 6 feet 6 inches over the friars' cemetery to the west of their church. A similar encroachment on the roadway to the extent of 6 feet had been expressly mentioned in the earlier deed of 1368 and the new houses were to align with the old ones. The result of this arrangement was that vacant spaces were left in front of the friars' gateway and the south door of the nave, the latter of which became enclosed on either side by the projecting houses. These spaces were accordingly granted by the City in the same deed to the friars for the erection or rather extension of the existing gatehouse and the construction of a porch respectively. That the latter was duly erected is suggested by the plan of 1617, which marks a gate or porch in this position.

One further point of interest in connection with these deeds may be noted. Both of them contain provisions for the reservation of a passage round the church. In the earlier lease the back wall of the houses at the west end came right up to the wall of the church and accordingly a door was to be made at the west end of the wall behind the

---

of the nave, with which Miss Honeybourne identifies the door referred to, would have been meaningless, as the lease itself makes it clear that the land included therein extended up to and not in front of the nave door, while the latter at the date in question abutted on the public thoroughfare.

[1] A Latin abstract of this deed is contained in the Patent Rolls of Richard II and is printed in *Arch. Journal*, vol. 59, pp. 264–6 ; the English text appears in the " Register " (Kingsford, *op. cit.*, pp. 173–6).

[2] The deed is entered in Letter Book H at the Guildhall, and the French text is printed by Kingsford, *op. cit.*, pp. 204–7.

buttress so that the friars could have access to the south side of their church for purposes of repair. In the second lease an alley 2 feet wide with a door was reserved, extending from the west front of the church to the porch. The object of this was presumably to provide access direct to the west front of the church from the street when the friars erected their new porch. A passage of similar width must also have been left on its east side as a means of access to the door referred to in the deed of 1368. Mr. Shepherd thought that it was this latter strip, measuring 2 feet by 6 feet, which was sold by the friars to the City corporation as trustees of the Bridge House rents in 1529, but Mr. Kingsford has thrown some doubt on this.[1]

Before attempting to describe the ground plan of the convent it is desirable to refer briefly to the later history of the domestic building. These had been erected, as we have seen, at the cost of the citizens and were probably completed by 1290. Subsequent references to them are comparatively few, and it was not until the new church had been completed that any important work on the conventual buildings seems to have been again taken in hand. One of the earliest of such works was the addition of a storeroom to the guest-house, " with rooms towards the infirmary," which friar Knotte is stated to have procured from William Allon, probably in the first half of the fourteenth century.[2] The greatest period of activity however in the rebuilding of the claustral buildings appears to have been between 1370 and 1420. In the former year the Register records that a school with studies and other necessary buildings were constructed out of the common funds.[3] The London house possessed one of the chief conventual schools in the English province, and the great increase in the number of students at this time no doubt necessitated the replacement of the original studies which had been provided by Bonde " king of the heralds." At the close of the fourteenth century the principal gatehouse facing Newgate Street was apparently rebuilt or considerably altered as a result of the sale of the frontage land to the city. The most important addition to the domestic build-

[1] *The Grey Friars of London*, pp. 33–4 ; Mr. Kingsford has however misread Mr. Shepherd, who does not refer here to the passage reserved in the lease of 1398, but to the narrow strip of land left on the east side of the porch when the latter was constructed.

[2] " Register " (Kingsford, *op. cit.*, p. 161).

[3] *Ibid.*

ings, however, was the erection of the new Library which occupied the whole of the north side of the great cloister and was the gift of Sir Richard Whittington, mayor of London, in 1421. The foundation stone of this building was laid on 21 October in that year by Whittington himself, and the building was completed and the books installed within three years at a total cost of £456 16s. 8d., of which £400 was provided by Whittington and the rest by friar Thomas Winchelsea and his friends.[1] The latter was again a benefactor to the house in 1423, when he provided the money for making a new wall with a door and windows in the lavatory near the vestry and for raising the ground there.[2] In the same year £4 5s. 8d. was spent on work on the windows of the barber's shop and in the walk of the cloister adjoining the room of the master of the studies.[3] Finally £13 17s. 1d. was spent about the same time in covering the cloister walk beneath the refectory with tiles similar to those of the rest of the roof so as to protect the lead from the rain which had caused great damage to the wall and building.[4] Later references to the domestic build-ings are few. In 1501 Margaret Yonge left various articles to the Ostrye,[5] which apart from the reference to Friar Knotte's work appears to be the only specific mention of the guest house, and in 1537 Nicholas Newton left 10s. " to the reparacion of the library as in glasynge in the gray fryers." [6]

It remains to mention one other evidence of building activity in connection with this house. Like many of the provincial houses of the order that in London had an elaborate water system. Eccleston records that " the aqueduct was chiefly provided by the joint gifts of Sir Henry de Frowik and that right godly youth Salekin de Basings ; howbeit the king's bounty most generously assisted." [7] This statement fixes the date of the work as before 1258, which is confirmed by the fact that in 1255–56 Henry III granted 14½ marks to the friars for their aqueduct.[8] We have already seen that the vestry of the first church was supplied with water from the cistern of the common lavatory. The Register supplies some further details regarding this water system. The passage in question reads as follows :

[1] *Ibid.*, p. 170.   [2] *Ibid.*, p. 170.   [3] *Ibid.*, p. 171.   [4] *Ibid.*
[5] P.C.C. " Moone," fo. 20.   [6] Ibid. " Dyngeley," fo. 2.
[7] Eccleston, p. 27 ; *ibid.*, ed. Salter, p. 29.
[8] Lib. roll 40 Hen. III, m. 13.

Those whose names appear below constructed the aqueduct.

First William, tailor to our Lord king Henry the third after the conquest, gave the head of the aqueduct at the instance of brother William de Basynges who procured the means for making (procuravit) all the aqueduct and fully completed it. But the charges and expenses were supplied by our Lord Henry, King of England, of happy memory above named, by that right talented youth Salekin de Basynge, by Sir Henry de Frowyke and by Sir Henry de Basynges knights. These were the chief co-operators and coadjutors. And afterwards brother Geoffrey of the Chamber built the new house at the second head and improved the old one and examined and repaired all the notable defects and procured and did many other good things for the same ; whose chief assistants were Alan Gille, citizen of London, with his wife (and) Sir Henry Darcy who gave 100 shillings for the cistern from the goods of John Tryple ; these and others co-operating together, finished the work.[1]

The fact that Darcy was executor of the will of John Triple, who died in 1325,[2] enables one with certainty to assign the work of repair and the construction of the second conduit head to the early years of the fourteenth century. The course of this conduit with the position of its heads, which is minutely described in the Register, is referred to below. Its interest lies not only in the fact that it is the one example of which any detailed description has survived of a feature which appears to have been an almost universal adjunct to friars' houses in the more important towns, but also in the fact that the London conduit continued in use until well into the eighteenth century while the two sources of supply have been rediscovered in comparatively recent years.

The absence of mention of the buildings of the London house during the early years of the sixteenth century is unfortunate, as more is known of its general history during this period than at any other period of its existence. The reason is doubtless that little beyond minor repairs was undertaken. In 1508 a custom was established under which the mayor and aldermen as patrons and founders paid a yearly visit to the Greyfriars church on 4 October, being the Feast of St. Francis. On 17 April 1534, Thomas Cudnor joined with the priors of the other houses of friars in London in acknowledging the King's Supremacy.[3] The

---

[1] Kingsford, *op. cit.*, pp. 158–9.

[2] See will in Sharpe's *Cal. Wills proved in the Hustings Court*, vol. 1, p. 311. He and his wife presented the glass for the fifth and sixth windows from east on the south side of the quire.

[3] *L. and P. Hen. VIII*, vol. 7, no. 665.

deed of Surrender was signed on 12 November 1538 [1] by
Thomas Chapman, who had succeeded Cudnor as guardian
and appears to have been a willing instrument in Cromwell's hands.[2] Twenty-five friars joined in signing the deed.
After the surrender various tenements within the precinct
were granted for use as private dwellings.[3] Fourteen of
these grants are recorded and they help to throw some
additional light on the condition of the precinct at this date.

The fate of the buildings can only be briefly referred
to. Stow records that the church itself was closed and
used as a storehouse for goods taken in prizes from the
French.[4] However, on 17 January 1547, the King granted
the greater part of the site subject to the various leases and
interests mentioned above to the City of London for his new
foundation of Christ's Hospital. The Letters patent for
this grant describes the property in some detail.[5] It comprised the church, the frater, library dormitory and chapter
house and all the ground called "le Great Cloyster" and
"le Little Cloyster," as well as the goods and chattels which
then remained in the buildings. These included a lavatory
or washing-place of copper, lined with lead, 28 desks, 28
"double settylles de Waynscote" and all books remaining
in the desks, the partitions and screens both in the nave
and chancel of the church as well as the altars, tables and
images, and the pulpit and all monuments and grave-stones
there and the candlesticks, organs and desks. The church
was to be called Christ's church and to become the church
of a new parish. It was accordingly re-opened on
30 January 1547, and in the following September all the
tombs were destroyed and the stalls and fittings of the quire
removed and sold. The conventual buildings were subsequently adapted for the use of the new foundation and the
first children were admitted in 1552. The passage beneath
the belfry of the great church remained the principal means

[1] *Ibid.*, vol. 13(2), no. 808 ; printed in full in Kingsford, *op. cit.*, pp.
219–22.

[2] He writes to Cromwell of his obedience and " the longing of all his
brethren to change their papistical slanderous apparel " (B.M. Cotton
MS. Cleopatra E, IV, fo. 115, printed in Kingsford, *op. cit.*, pp. 216–17).

[3] It is clear that to a limited extent the precinct had been opened to
lay tenants prior to the suppression. As early as 1440 the friars had
granted a lease of the house over their gateway in Newgate Street to
private persons (*Cat. Anc. Deeds*, vol. 1, p. 533, printed in Kingsford,
op. cit., pp. 207–8).

[4] *Survey of London*, ed. Kingsford, vol. 1, p. 318.

[5] Printed in full in Trollope's *History of Christ's Hospital*, Appendix,
pp. xiii–xxix ; see also Kingsford, *op. cit.*, pp. 229–31.

of access to the cloister, and from this time the quire and nave appear to have been regarded as two distinct buildings, as the east and west or upper and lower churches are frequently referred to in the early minutes of the hospital. The parochial rights were probably confined to the former and the nave appears to have been put to various uses, including possibly the housing at one time of the printing press of Richard Grafton, the King's printer.[1] In this state the building continued until the Great Fire of 1666, when in common with the adjoining buildings it was seriously damaged. The hospital minutes contain the entry " this hospitall of Christs was almost consumed with the two great churches [2] adjoining excepting the 4 cloysters to which ye fire hath done no hurt and aboute 3 wards towards the sickward and severall other roomes there, as also the wardrobe of this hospitall over the south cloyster, the glazed windows of the church on that side being very little damnified."[3] That the church was not entirely destroyed is, however, apparent, as the vestry minutes in 1670 refer to the clearing of stones from the upper and lower churches and other works in connection therewith. It is probable that the outer walls survived more or less intact although the roof and belfry appear to have been consumed. Within the shell of the ruined quire a temporary wooden church, known as " the tabernacle," was constructed to serve the needs of the parish until the building of the present Christ Church was begun by Sir Christopher Wren in 1687. Prior to this in 1676 the vestry minutes record an order " that forthwith workmen shall be set at work to clear the foundations of all the pillars in the upper church and the four great pillars in the passage of this hospital."[4] This clearly refers to the clearing of the site of the quire and ambulatory, preparatory to the erection of the new church. It is probable that the lower portion of the outer walls was incorporated as a core to the walls of the new building, but apart from this the last remains of the friars' church disappeared with the completion of Wren's building.

In the meantime the gradual reconstruction of the conventual buildings took place. The great hall which had been the refectory on the west side of the cloister was

---

[1] *The Library*, 4th ser., vol. 11 (1930), p. 124. See also J. A. Kingdon, *Richard Grafton* (1901), pp. 10, 12.
[2] This presumably refers to the nave and quire respectively.
[3] E. H. Pearce, *Annals of Christ's Hospital* (1908), p. 208.
[4] Quoted by Mr. Shepherd in *Arch. Journal*, vol. 59, p. 252.

rebuilt about 1680 and the eastern range or dormitory about 1705. The Whittington library on the north side of the cloister appears to have been untouched by the Great Fire and survived more or less intact until about 1827 when it was demolished. On the south side, over the medieval cloister, Sir Christopher Wren erected in 1682 a building known as the Latin school. The cloister walk beneath, which in modern times was known as the " Giffs," survived as the sole remaining fragment of the medieval buildings until the general demolition of the school buildings in 1902, when Christ's Hospital was removed into Surrey. The whole of the precinct of the Grey Friars, with the exception of the site of their church, has now been absorbed into the General Post Office, whose buildings cover the greater part of the area.

DESCRIPTION

In spite of the absence of remains the material for the reconstruction of the ground plan is unusually abundant and has consequently received considerable attention. Not only can the site of the church be precisely fixed, but it has been possible to restore its plan and internal arrangement with considerable accuracy,[1] while the extent of the precinct and the position of the principal buildings within it can also be plotted with reasonable certainty. It is thus possible solely from documentary sources to produce what is possibly the most complete plan available of any of the English Franciscan houses. The primary source of information concerning the buildings is the Register itself and particularly the section containing the list of burials. This is supplemented by the wills of persons desiring to be buried in the friary and also by the well-known and important plan dated 1617 in the possession of the Governors of St. Bartholomew's Hospital (see Plate opposite p. 190). The latter, which is entitled " Ye Plat of ye Graye Friers," combines architectural detail and ground plan in a manner common to many early maps. It depicts Newgate Street from Newgate to the Shambles, opposite to the end of the present King Edward Street, with the whole of the land to the north enclosed by the city wall. It thus includes the greater part of the Grey Friars precinct within which the great church and other conventual buildings are shown, as well as various private

[1] The following account is largely based on Mr. Shepherd's paper, *ut sup.*, and on Mr. Kingsford's works referred to above.

houses and gardens of post-suppression date. The period represented by this plan has been the subject of some discussion. Mr. Kingsford observed [1] that it appeared to be based on material gathered seventy years earlier within a decade of the dissolution of the convent. Miss Honeybourne has pointed out, however,[2] that neither of the churches of St. Nicholas Shambles or St. Ewen, which were still standing in 1547, is shown, while there is evidence of an attempt to bring the earlier description up to date as in the case of the garden to the west of the precinct which is shown as " Boltons garden now Mallowes." The inference seems to be that the draughtsman had before him a sixteenth-century plan possibly prepared at the time of the grant of the property to Christ's Hospital in 1547, but attempted to bring this up to date in the more obvious details. The plan has therefore to be treated with some caution but yet forms an invaluable supplement to the evidence obtained from the other sources referred to above.

Before proceeding to describe the buildings themselves it is desirable to consider the extent of the precinct. On the north and south its boundaries were well defined, being the city wall on the north and the backs of the houses erected on the strips of land granted to the Bridge House Trustees in 1368 and 1398 on the south. The later strip terminated on the west at the Great Gate which formed the principal entrance to the precinct. It is shown as the Stone Gate in the St. Bartholomew's plan where its width to Newgate Street is given as 33 feet. It stood nearly opposite Warwick Lane and continued to be used as the gate of Christ's Hospital until 1825, when it was demolished, and its place taken by much wider gates occupying the whole of the present Post Office frontage to this part of Newgate Street. To the west of this gate the St. Bartholomew's plan shows a brewhouse and bakehouse, then apparently divided into a number of tenements, and to the rear of the latter a Mill house. That these had formed part of the domestic buildings of the friary there can be no reasonable doubt, and one must therefore assume that for a distance of 82 feet [3] to the west of the gatehouse the precinct boundary abutted on the highway. Beyond this are two tenements shown on the St. Bartholomew's plan as " ye

[1] *The Grey Friars of London*, p. 52.
[2] *London Topographical Record*, vol. 16, p. 11.
[3] According to the scale on the St. Bartholomew's plan.

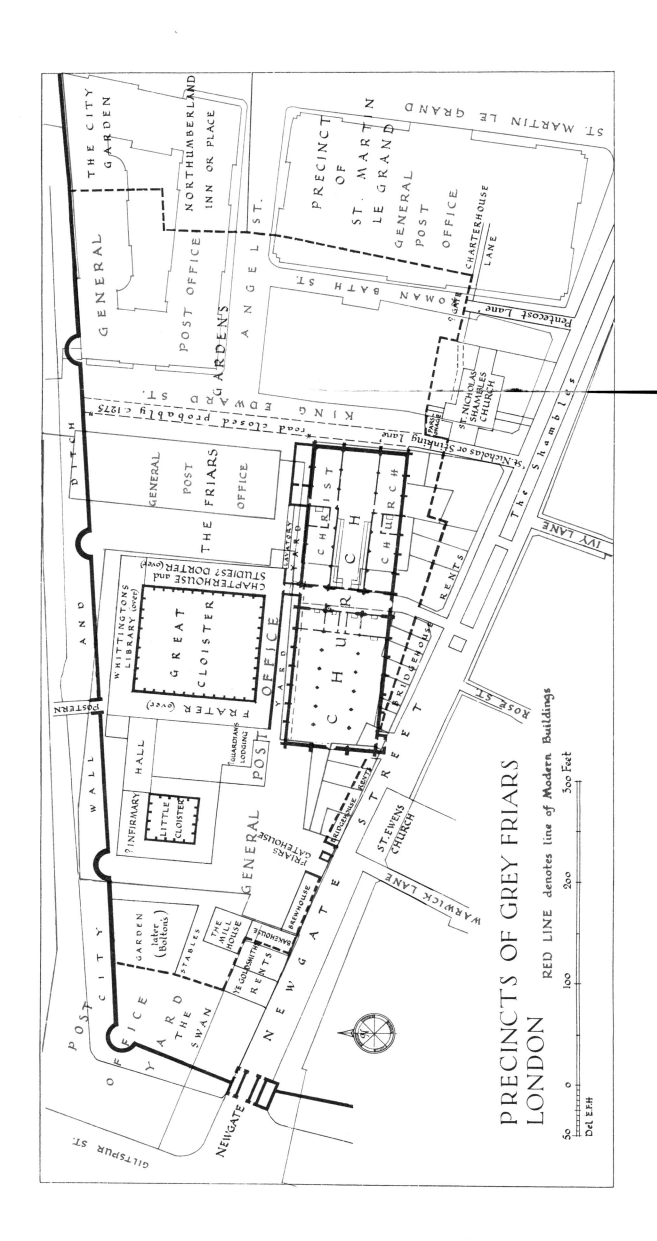

PRECINCTS OF GREY FRIARS
LONDON

RED LINE denotes line of Modern Buildings

50   0   100   200   300 Feet

Del E.H

GILTSPUR ST.

POST OFFICE YARD

CITY

THE SWAN

GARDEN
(later Boltons)

STABLES

YE GOLDSMITH RENTS

NEWGATE

THE MILL HOUSE

BAKEHOUSE

BREWHOUSE

FRIARS GATEHOUSE

LITTLE CLOISTER

?INFIRMARY HALL

?GUARDIANS LODGING

GENERAL POST OFFICE YARD

WALL

AND

DITCH

POSTERN

WHITTINGTONS LIBRARY (over)

CHAPTERHOUSE and STUDIES? DORTER (over)

GREAT CLOISTER

FRATER (over)

THE FRIARS

GENERAL POST OFFICE

LAVATORY YARD

CHURCH

CHRIST CHURCH

road closed probably c1275

KING EDWARD ST.

ARGYLL ST.

THE CITY GARDEN

GENERAL POST OFFICE

NORTHUMBERLAND INN OR PLACE

GARDENS

ANGEL ST.

ROMAN BATH ST.

PRECINCT OF ST. MARTIN LE GRAND GENERAL POST OFFICE

ST. MARTIN LE GRAND

CHARTERHOUSE LANE

Pentecost Lane

S GATE

ST. NICHOLAS SHAMBLES CHURCH

PARSONAGE

'St. Nicholas or Stinking Lane'

The Shambles

IVY LANE

ROSE ST.

RENTS

BRIDGEHOUSE

STREET

BRIDGEHOUSE RENTS

ST. EWENS CHURCH

WARWICK LANE

Goldesmeths rents." These were in private ownership as early as 1512 when they belonged to the owner of the adjoining property on the west known as The Swan, so that if they ever belonged to the friars they must have been disposed of before the Dissolution. The Swan itself was an ancient hostelry adjoining Newgate and occupied the whole of the land immediately within the city wall on the north (see Plan opposite p. 204) which never seems to have formed part of the precinct. The boundary therefore turned northwards between the bakehouse and the goldsmiths rents, then westward to include the mill house and its adjoining yard and again northward to meet the city wall on the west side of Bolton's garden.[1]

The eastern boundary is less certain, as the St. Bartholomew's map no longer helps us. Miss Honeybourne has shown [2] that the precinct extended considerably farther east than hitherto supposed and that the present King Edward Street, except at its extreme southern end opposite the church of St. Nicholas Shambles, could not have existed as a public thoroughfare in the later period of the friars occupation. Indeed, there can be little doubt that a complaint made in 1275 that the friars had obstructed Stinking Lane [3] fixes the date when the northern portion of this lane, which had probably previously continued up to the city wall, was enclosed. This enclosure was doubtless necessitated by the acquisition of lands on the eastern side of the lane, a fact which would thus explain the difficulty as to the r_ nber of gifts described as situated in this comparatively short thoroughfare. Some light on the extent of the land belonging to the friars to the east of King Edward Street is afforded by a grant of a part of the precinct in 1543 to Sir Edward North.[4] The description of the land included therein is somewhat obscure, but it apparently comprised the site of the great cloister with all the land to the north and east of the church. The significance of this document in which the boundaries of the site are set out in detail has been considered elsewhere,[5] and it is only necessary

[1] William Bolton was paying rent for property within the precinct shortly after the Dissolution (P.R.O. Rentals and Surveys 11/17).
[2] *London Topographical Record*, vol. 16, pp. 18–28.
[3] *Hundred Rolls* (R.C.), vol. 1, pp. 404, 429.
[4] *L. and P. Hen. VIII*, vol. 18, p. 132 ; printed in *The Grey Friars of London*, pp. 224–5.
[5] *The Grey Friars of London*, pp. 222–4 ; *London Topographical Record*, vol. 16, pp. 18–19.

here to state that it proves beyond reasonable doubt that
Christ's Hospital did not occupy the whole of the Grey
Friars precinct as was commonly supposed, but that the
latter extended eastward as far as the inn of the Earl of
Northumberland and the precinct of St. Martin-le-Grand,
from which it was separated by a wall.[1] At a distance
of about 100 feet to the north of Newgate Street
the boundary turned westward and after passing the upper
end of a narrow alley called Pentecost Lane, at a point
about half-way up its modern successor, Roman Bath Street,
it skirted the northern side of the churchyard of St. Nicholas
Shambles from where it crossed the present King Edward
Street and continued along the back of the Bridgehouse
Rents as already noted.

To turn now to the buildings.

THE CHURCH

The great fourteenth-century church was naturally the
most important building in the precinct. The Register
records that

" the church contains in length three hundred feet of the feet of
St. Paul. In breadth it contains 89 feet of the feet of St Paul.
In height from the floor to the roof 64 feet of the feet of St Paul,
and as is evident all the columns are of marble and all the pavement
is of marble." [2]

From the east wall of the present Christ Church to the west
wall of the churchyard there are 296 feet while the width
between the existing walls is approximately 83 feet, so
that the general accuracy of the measurements in the
Register is confirmed. The next step in the reconstruction
of the ground plan is the evidence afforded by the account
of the glazing of the windows. The description in the
Register begins as follows :

" Firstly beginning from the east in front, that is to say three
windows, the first towards the north was glazed by the most illustrious lady Isabella, Queen, mother of Edward the Third. The
middle window, the great one over the high altar, was glazed at
their common expense by the clothworkers or drapers of the city
of London. The third was glazed at the cost of the worshipful
Sir John Cobham kt." [3]

---

[1] Strype quotes a document of Henry VIII's reign in which part of
the western wall of St. Martin's is described as being also " the back
wall of the Grey Friars " from which it is clear that a single wall here
formed the boundary of both precincts (*Survey of London*, vol. 1(3), p. 108).

[2] Kingsford, *op. cit.*, pp. 169–70. [3] *Ibid.*, p. 165.

Then follows references to the fifteen windows on the south side, the eighth or middle one being stated to be "under the bell tower," while the ninth was "near the common altar." The three windows at the west end are next described and finally the fifteen windows on the north side, of which the seventh, corresponding to the ninth on the opposite side,[1] had under it an old altar which was repaired and painted when the window was glazed. The mention of the three windows at either end proves that both nave and quire were aisled. The whole building was clearly of fifteen bays, which when divided into the total length gives an approximate span of 18 feet for each bay. Definite confirmation of this was afforded many years ago when some excavations at the back of No. 20 King Edward Street, on the south side of Christ Church, brought to light the bases of three of the buttresses of the medieval church.[2] These buttresses were found to be exactly opposite the pillars in the existing building, which must thus occupy the site of the six eastern bays of the original quire. The present tower stands in the position of the seventh bay, while the eighth corresponds with Greyfriars passage. This fact, coupled with reference to the eighth window on the south side as being under the bell tower (" sub campanili ") is sufficient proof even in the absence of other evidence that the eighth or centre bay formed the " ambulatorium inter chorum et altaria " through which access was obtained to the cloister and over which, jn accordance with the normal practice, the bell tower was erected. Further confirmation of this is afforded by the entry already referred to in the churchwardens books of Christ Church in 1676, where it is ordered that " the four great pillars in the passage to the hospital " should be cleared away, as there can be little doubt that these were the piers which had supported the bell tower. To the west of the ambulatory extended the nave of seven bays occupying the whole of the area of the present churchyard.

The principal source of information concerning the interior of this building and the position of its various chapels is the list of burials already mentioned. No less than 765 interments [3] are recorded in the Register repre-

---

[1] The numbering is from east to west on the south and from west to east on the north.

[2] *London and Middlesex Arch. Soc.*, vol. 5 (1881), p. 421.

[3] In addition to the names on the Register many others can be supplied from contemporary wills. It is probable that many of the earlier stones

sented by some 550 monuments and gravestones in the
church alone apart from those in the cloister and chapter-
house. These are grouped in the Register according to
their situation in the church, while within each division
the exact position of every monument is described with
minute care, a fact which enabled Mr. Shepherd to plot
the entire series in his plan of the church.[1] The list is
divided under the following heads : The quire, the chapel of
All Hallows, the chapel of St. Mary, the chapel of the
Apostles on the south side of the quire, the chapel of St.
Francis, the passage between the quire and the altars
(" in ambulatorio inter chorum et altaria "), before the
altars (" coram altaribus ") and the nave and its aisles as
well as the four walks of the cloister and the chapter-house.
It is possible to fix the positions of these chapels with
absolute certainty from the details in the Register itself
supplemented with references in contemporary wills.   Mr.
Kingsford has collected extracts from some 219 wills of
persons desiring to be buried within the precinct of the Grey
Friars in London, of whom nearly one-half do not appear
in the Register.[2] The combined evidence from these
sources can only be briefly summarized here.   On the north
of the quire the three eastern bays formed the chapel of
All Hallows, which is referred to as the vestry chapel in the
will of Richard Lord Willoughby in 1513,[3] doubtless because
it gave access to the vestry on the north.   The chapel of
St. Mary occupied the four western bays of the north quire
aisle.   It contained an image of St. Bernardine, which no
doubt accounts for its being called the chapel of S. Bar-
nardyne in the will of Roger Spencer in 1492.   To the
south of the quire were the chapels of the Apostles and St.
Francis occupying corresponding positions to those on the
north.   The quire itself was enclosed by solid stone walls
against which the stalls were erected.   These were returned
against a screen wall on the west in the centre of which a
door gave access into the ambulatory beneath the bell

had been destroyed to make room for later ones before the Register was
compiled.   In other cases the person may not have been buried in accordance with the directions in the will, while in some cases the Register is
probably incomplete.

[1] *Arch. Journal*, vol. 59, opp. p. 248.

[2] *Coll. Franc.*, II, B.S.F.S., vol. 10, pp. 79–142.   This list takes no
account of the very numerous wills in which legacies are given to the
house.

[3] This and subsequent references to Wills are quoted from Mr. Kingsford's list, where the reference to the original will be found.

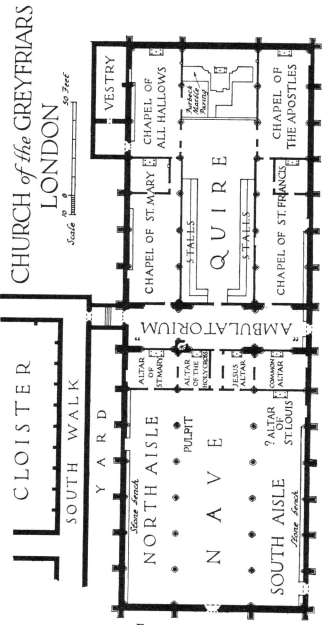

CHURCH *of the* GREYFRIARS
LONDON

Scale

FIG. 13.

tower. The eastern bay of the nave was screened off from
the rest of the nave and divided into four chapels with a
central doorway opening into the ambulatory and another
in the western screen giving access into the nave proper.
Of these four chapels which were probably separated by
screens, that on the north contained the altar of St. Mary
which was repaired and repainted by the countess of Pembroke when she provided the glass for the adjoining window.
It is referred to in 1524 as the morrow-mass altar and
appears to have been the same as the altar of St. Clement
which is mentioned in several fifteenth-century wills and
was associated with the fraternity of St. Clement of the
Craft of Bakers.[1] To the south of this was the altar of the
Holy Cross, then came the door into the ambulatory over
which was the rood, and then the Jesus altar, and finally
on the south the Common altar which is mentioned in
connection with the glazing of the eighth window on this
side. The remaining six bays to the west formed the nave
proper. Here was at least one more altar being probably
that dedicated to St. Louis to which reference has already
been made. It stood at the east end of the south aisle
against the screen in front of " the altars." The principal
entrance to the nave was by a doorway in the centre of the
west front, but there was another door in the westernmost
bay on the south side of the nave in front of which the
porch built in 1398 was erected. The site of this door and
porch is now marked by No. 101 Newgate Street.[2] Round
the walls of the nave on the interior extended a low
stone bench. The position of the pulpit can be fixed from
two wills as being against the easternmost pillar of the nave
proper on the north side. The organ, which is mentioned
in the will of Nicholas Pembyrton (1519) apparently stood
at the west end of the chapel of St. Mary.

Some light is also thrown on the disposition of the
various images throughout the church. There must have
been at least five images of the Virgin. One of these was
in the north aisle of the nave and is referred to in 1447 and
1485. On the right hand of the entry to the altar of St.
Mary stood the image of Our Lady of Pity, which was
probably that erected by John Arnold, who died in 1492 and

[1] This appears to be the only fraternity connected with the Grey
Friars church, of which there is record.
[2] Nos. 94 to 101 Newgate Street extending from Grey Friars passage
to the site of the south porch are now (1936) in course of demolition.

was buried close by. The position of the others cannot be identified with certainty, except one which stood in the chapel of St. Mary on the north side of the quire. Near the High altar was an image of St. Francis, while another image of this saint is referred to in 1406 as in the cemetery. This doubtless stood over or near to the west door. The image of St. Christopher is mentioned in 1406 and 1473 without any indication of its position. It may have stood, however, near the window of St. Christopher, which is referred to in the will of Richard Hallam in 1419 and apparently occupied the second bay from the west in the north aisle of the nave. Other images mentioned were those of St. James in the north aisle of the nave (1447), St. Mary Magdalen in St. Francis chapel (1530) and St. Erasmus (1474). The latter is probably again referred to in 1533 when Thomas Hewitt desired to be buried in the nave where there was " a tablet of S. Erasmus on the north side as you come out of the west door." [1]

Of the position of the tombs to which reference has already been made little can be said here. The quire was reserved for the interment of royal or other important persons and prominent benefactors. In front of the high altar, in the second bay from the east, was the tomb of Queen Margaret, the foundress, while in the middle of the quire stood the alabaster table tomb of Queen Isabella, beside whom was also placed the heart of her husband, Edward II. On her right lay the countess of Bedford, a daughter of Edward III, and immediately to the west was the tomb of Joan de la Tour, the wife of David Bruce, King of Scotland. A few of the burials must have been removed from the earlier church. Of these the most notable was the heart of Archbishop Peckham, which was placed " retro magnum altare in archu partis australis in sacrario " which, Mr. Shepherd conceived, meant that his monument was worked in with the decoration of the piscina and that the altar must therefore have stood somewhat in advance of the eastern wall. Another early monument removed from the old church was that of Beatrice, Duchess of Brittany and daughter of Henry III, which stood beneath one of the arches on the north side of the presbytery, while a little to the west of this monument was buried in a niche in the wall the heart of her mother, Eleanor of Provence,

---

[1] This was presumably an alabaster tablet representing the martyrdom of St. Erasmus, a subject not uncommon in fourteenth century alabasters.

whose body was buried at Amesbury in 1291. Next to the quire the most honourable places were the chapels on either side, the walking-place and " the Altars." The nave and its aisles were crowded with the monuments of less important people, and here it is noticeable that the burials were generally of later date than those in the eastern portion of the church.[1] The tombs in the cloister were mostly those of friars, the majority being undated.

Of this magnificent series of monuments only one survives and that by the irony of fate is not recorded in the Register. It is a late thirteenth- or early fourteenth-century incised slab measuring 6 feet 7¾ inches in length and 2 feet 3 inches in breadth at the top, tapering to 1 foot 5¼ inches at the bottom. It bears a shield containing a leg couped at the thigh within a border and round the edge in Lombardic lettering, now partly defaced, is the legend " Bernart de Jambe gist icy Dieu de sa alme eit merci. Amen. Pater Noster." [2] With one exception [3] all the then existing monuments in the Grey Friars' church were destroyed early in the reign of Edward VI. Stow records that they were " wholly defaced ; for there were nine tombs of alabaster and marble environed with spikes of iron in the quire, and one tomb in the body of the church also coped with iron all pulled down besides seven score grave stones of marble all sold for fifty pounds or thereabouts by Sir Martin Bowes goldsmith and alderman of London." [4]

Of the architecture of the church as distinct from its ground plan and fittings not much can be said. A clearstorey is shown in the St. Bartholomew's Hospital drawing, but as no clearstorey windows are referred to in the Register, this may have been an addition of comparatively late date. On analogy with other friars' churches the roofs were almost certainly of timber, and it is unlikely that even the aisles were vaulted. The belfry is omitted from the St. Bartholomew's plan, probably owing to the difficulty of showing it in a perpendicular view of this character, as it must almost certainly have been standing at the time the plan was made.

[1] The earlier tombs in the nave being of persons of minor importance had probably, as Mr. Kingsford suggests, been destroyed to make room for the later ones.

[2] *St. Paul's Ecclesiological Soc.*, vol. 7, p. 34 ; the stone is now fixed to the east wall of the south aisle of Christ Church.

[3] The tomb of Dr. Henry Standish is said to have survived until the Great Fire of 1666.

[4] *Survey*, ed. Kingsford, vol. 1, p. 322.

The reference to the destruction of the four great pillars in 1676 already quoted seems to imply that it was a fairly substantial structure possibly analogous to the somewhat later example at Richmond or to some of the surviving Franciscan towers in Ireland.[1] One notable feature of the interior must have been the splendour of the material used. The account in the Register states that all the columns and pavement were of marble. That this was true as regards the pavement is proved by the survival of a quantity of square slabs of brown reddish and green marble which almost certainly formed part of the pavement of the friars' church and are now set diagonally in the floor near the high altar in the present Christ Church.

THE GREAT CLOISTER

The cloister, as already stated, was little damaged by the Great Fire. It formed a quadrangle measuring approximately 120 feet from north to south and 105 feet from east to west. The chapter-house which measured 60 feet by 27 feet [2] was almost certainly in the eastern range [3] with the dormitory on the upper floor extending apparently throughout its entire length. The Studies may have occupied part of the ground floor on this side, and Mr. Kingsford has suggested that the barbers' shop, referred to in 1423, would have been close to the lavatory which is stated to have adjoined the vestibule. The latter was presumably the passage and steps connecting the " walking-place " with the cloister, and the lavatory was probably therefore the low building shown on the St. Bartholomew plan to the north of the open yard on the north side of the quire. The western range contained the frater which became the great hall of the hospital. In 1546 the " Repertory Book " of St. Bartholomew's Hospital mentions " the Fratrie above the west side of the cloister 140 feet long all paved and containing settles and nine tables of wainscot," from which it is clear that the frater like the dormitory was on the upper floor and projected probably over the cloister walk. To its north in the north-west angle of the cloister was a two-storied building occupied in the time of the Hospital

---

[1] In the maps of Ralph Agas (*c.* 1561) and William Faithorne (1658) the steeple is shown as a light pointed structure.

[2] Repertory Book of St. Bartholomew's Hospital.

[3] The grant to Sir John Williams and Sir Edward North in 1543 implies that the chapter-house was in the western range, but this is almost certainly incorrect.

and before its replacement by Wren's Writing School as the kitchen and buttery. There seems no reason to doubt that it served a similar purpose in the time of the friars.

The original northern range must have been demolished when Whittington's library was built in 1421. Several views of this building, which survived until 1827, exist. The library was on the upper floor and projected over the cloister walk. It is said to have been 129 feet long and 31 feet broad, and like the cloister below was divided into ten bays.

On the south side where the cloister abutted on the church there were probably originally no buildings, the east and west walks being merely connected by a covered alley set some distance away from the wall of the church so as not to encroach on the great windows of the nave. At a later date there is some evidence that an upper storey of small dimensions was added, although it was not until 1680, when Wren built the new Latin school on the site, that the intervening yard was finally built over. The cloister alley below survived until 1902. It was apparently of fifteenth-century date with wide two-centred arches which had been partly filled up with brick and was divided into ten bays by a stepped buttress facing the cloister garth.[1]

THE LITTLE CLOISTER

The little cloister lay to the west of the main cloister on what later became known as the Hall playground. According to the St. Bartholomew's plan it cannot have measured more than about 50 feet from north to south, and 45 feet from east to west. Mr. Kingsford conjectured with some probability that the infirmary occupied its northern range, a suggestion which finds some support in the fact that the hospital infirmary occupied the same position. Between the north-east corner of the little cloister and the western range of the great cloister was another building which the St. Bartholomew's Repertory Book refers to as " one great hall 72 feet long and 24 feet wide with a chimney." Its proximity to the kitchens suggests that it may have been the infirmary frater. Beneath it was a covered passage, connecting the two cloisters, which continued in use in the time of the Hospital when it was known

---

[1] When this part of the site was being excavated preparatory to the erection of the Post Office buildings a number of chalk foundation arches were discovered.

as " The Creek." Of the remaining buildings of the little cloister nothing is known, though, as the guest-house which was built by William Albon was stated to be near the infirmary, this may have formed part of one of its ranges. Trollope mentions [1] the discovery in this area in 1732, when the new infirmary was being built, of arched vaults forming three sides of a quadrangle, which presumably formed the foundations of the buildings around the little cloister.

GUARDIAN'S LODGING

In 1544 a tenement in the precinct called Dr. Vaughan's Lodging lately held by Lady Rose Wallope was granted to Hugh Willoughby. This grant resulted in a lawsuit before the Court of Augmentations [2] in which the building and an adjoining property, of which it originally formed part, are described in some detail. It was situated " between the church of the east part and the King's highway there leading from the great gate to the second cloister of the said house on the west part and the second cloister on the north part." Mr. Kingsford conjectured from the description of the building which contained " a parlar with the aulter there " and a study that it was the guardians' lodging. Its position is approximately indicated on the Plan.

Of the remaining buildings within the precinct shown on the St. Bartholomew's plan some are probably of pre-suppression date, but others undoubtedly represent the building activity which followed the departure of the friars. In this category is the elaborate battlemented gateway in the city wall at the north-west corner of the great cloister which took the place of a small postern constructed by the friars on the site of one of the bastions of the city wall.

THE WATER SYSTEM

Reference has already been made to the elaborate and carefully planned water system of the friary. It may be permitted in conclusion to refer to the buildings connected with it. The direction of the pipe from Newgate to the source of the supply in the fields to the north of the present Theobalds road is minutely described in the Register. From the precinct wall it ran along the north side of Newgate Street through Newgate, then following the old line of Snow Hill, it continued along Holborn to the corner of Leather Lane,

[1] *History of Christ's Hospital*, p. 351.
[2] See Kingsford, *op. cit.*, pp. 226–8.

where it turned northward along Leather Lane [1] to its junction with what is now Clerkenwell Road. From this point
it followed a straight line in a north-westerly direction
across what was then open country to a point in the north-
west corner of Queen's Square. The nearest water-head
which is described as "hidden four feet underground"
furnished the greater part of the supply. "From that
place," continues the survey, "(the pipe) extends to the
remoter Head towards the west the little stone house
whereof is seen from a distance." The early records of
Christ's Hospital contain many references to this water
supply which supplement the statements in the Register.
The two conduit heads were then known as the White
Conduit and the Chimney or Devils conduit, the latter
being stated to be in Red Lion Fields. That the Chimney
conduit was identical with the "remoter head" mentioned
in the Grey Friars' "Register" is apparent from these
entries, and a plan in the possession of Christ's Hospital,[2]
showing the water system as it existed in 1676, further assists
in the identification of its site. The actual building of the
Chimney Conduit was discovered by Dr. Philip Norman in
1893 in the garden at the back of No. 20 Queen's Square,
Bloomsbury.[3] The medieval portion of the structure consisted of an underground reservoir about 10 feet 6 inches
square constructed of large blocks of neatly jointed ashlar
with a floor about 18 feet below the existing ground level
consisting of large red tiles surrounded by a stone border.
The roof was a barrel vault of the same material as the
walls, and at its south-east end,[4] near the entrance arch, the
base of the chimney which must originally have risen above
the ground level and given the conduit its name, was still
intact.[5] The building was approached by a passage containing a flight of steps and spanned by three arches in
addition to that opening into the tank itself. The masonry
of the passage was similar to that of the tank and the

[1] This route was diverted to one continuing along Holborn and up
Gray's Inn Road about 1671.
[2] Reproduced in *Archæologia*, vol. 61, opp. p. 353.
[3] P. Norman, "On an ancient Conduit Head in Queen Square, Bloomsbury," *Archæologia*, vol. 56 (1899), pp. 251–66 (plan) ; P. Norman, "Demolition of the Conduit-head in Queen Square," *ibid.*, vol. 67 (1915–16),
pp. 18–26 (plan and illustrations).
[4] The building was not due north and south, the vault being N.W. and
and S.E.
[5] Part of the upper courses which had been rebuilt in brick also survived.

whole was clearly of one date. The highest arch at the top of the steps retained the iron hinge-pins for a door.[1] It must have stood well above the original ground level and with the upper part of the adjoining passage no doubt formed " the little stone house seen from afar." The building which had every indication of being the actual structure erected by Geoffrey of the Chamber in the early part of the fourteenth century was entirely demolished in 1911 and the site has now been built over. The stones, however, were carefully numbered and the building has recently been set up in the grounds of the Metropolitan Water Board in Rosebery Avenue.

In August 1907 Dr. Norman also succeeded in identifying the original conduit head known as the White Conduit.[2] This is situated below the floor of a workshop in the rear of No. 13 Chapel Street, a short thoroughfare leading out of Lamb's Conduit Street, Bloomsbury.[3] The reservoir, which is now approached by a perpendicular brick shaft at its southern end, is 9 feet long and 6 feet wide. Its walls are of stone which according to Dr. Norman has the appearance of roughly dressed blue Portland, while the roof is arched with closely jointed blocks of white limestone, a fact which may conceivably account for the name White Conduit, as the upper part of the building appears to have been originally above ground. In the south wall is a doorway rebated for a door and retaining one of its iron hinge-pins. The floor is now of earth and in the south-west corner is a shallow tank formed of slabs of hard stone 2½ inches thick, which Dr. Norman suggested may have been a settling tank for clearing the water before it was passed on to the supply pipe. This interesting building formed the original and principal source of the water supply of the Greyfriars and there seems no reason to doubt that it is the actual " head of the aqueduct " which William le Tailour gave to the convent about 1250. It is thus the only visible remains connected with the London Greyfriars which now survives *in situ*.

From these conduit heads the water was carried in

---

[1] From this doorway an eighteenth-century passage with several more steps gave access to the present ground level by a trap-door close to Queen's Square place.

[2] P. Norman, " On the White Conduit, Chapel Street, Bloomsbury, and its connection with the Grey Friars' water system," *Archæologia*, vol. 61 (1909), pp. 347–56.

[3] Lamb's Conduit was of much later date and had no connection with the Grey Friars' system.

leaden pipes along the route referred to above to the friary buildings. The distance from the Queen's Square conduit to the Greyfriars is about a mile and a quarter, and the fall in that distance seems to have been only 24 feet, which doubtless accounts for the frequent complaints that the water " did not come well home," entered in the Hospital records. The pipe entered the precinct at the Stone Gate in Newgate Street and passed across the site of the little cloister to " the conduit yard " which in the time of the Hospital was placed against the city wall to the north-west of the Great Cloister.

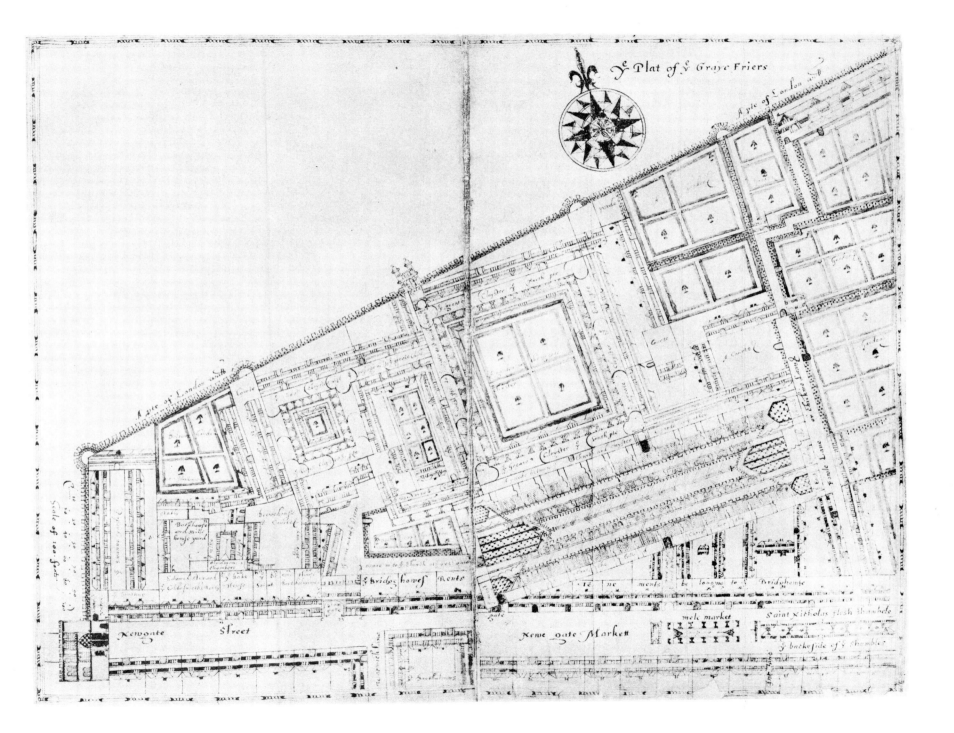

Y^e Plat of y^e Graye Friers

A gte of London Stroet

A gte of London Strete

Newgate   Street

Newe gate Markett

Saint Nicholas flesh shambels

CHAPTER IV

HOUSES WITH MINOR REMAINS OR SLIGHT EVIDENCE OF PLAN

OUR Survey of the more important Franciscan buildings in this county of which any record has survived is now complete. It remains, however, to consider certain houses where buildings of minor importance only exist or of which some slight architectural record has been preserved. In some instances such as Bodmin, Bridgnorth and Worcester where important buildings have been demolished in comparatively modern times drawings or plans may conceivably exist which would throw considerable light on their general ground plan but until these are forthcoming the brief descriptions which follow must suffice.

(1) BODMIN

The origin of this house is somewhat obscure, but there seems to be no reason to doubt the date quoted by William of Worcester apparently from a register or Martyrology belonging to the Bodmin friars. Worcester's account, however, is in part contradictory. Under date 1239 he states, " Ecclesia fratrum ordinis Sancti Francisci villae de Bodman fundatur per Edmundum primum comitem Cornubiae 13 kalend julii, (19 June)," [1] but a little later, among the obits, he notes, " Johannes filius Radulphi domini de Kayryshays primus fundator ecclesiæ fratrum obiit 3 die junii." [2] Again, in a subsequent passage we read " 1239. Ecclesiam fratrum Sancti Francisci de Bodman Ricardus comes Cornubiae filius fratris Henrici tercii fundavit, et anno 1352 dedicata est ecclesia per Johannem de Grandissono Exoniensem episcopum." [3]

A later tradition is preserved by Leland, who notes, " Ther was a place of Gray Freres by south on the market place of Bodmyn. One John of London a marchaunt began it. Edmunde Erle of Cornwaulle after was a great bene-

[1] Worcester, *Itin.*, p. 99.   [2] *Ibid.*, p. 100.
[3] *Ibid.*, p. 111.

factor to it. There lay Sir Hugh Peverelle and Sir Thomas
Peverelle benefactors to the house."[1]
Of John of London nothing is known, but the traditional
association with the Earls of Cornwall is probable enough.
The first Earl, however, was not Edmund, as stated by
Worcester, but his father, Richard, King of the Romans,
and as the house was certainly in existence before 1260,[2]
while Edmund, the second Earl, was not born until 1250,
there can be little doubt that it was the first Earl to whom
Worcester's statements refer. In this there is nothing
improbable, as Richard, Earl of Cornwall, is known to have
followed in the footsteps of his brother, Henry III, as a
patron of the Franciscans.[3] If William of Worcester is
correct in stating that the church was dedicated in 1352 by
John Grandison, who was Bishop of Exeter from 1327 to
1369, this must indicate a re-building at this date, but there
is no record of the dedication in the Episcopal registers.
This date is interesting, however, as it implies a rapid recovery
from the disastrous effects of the Black Death, which a few
years before had visited Bodmin with particular severity,
according to an entry in the Register quoted by Worcester.[4]
Further confirmation of this recovery is afforded by the
fact that in 1350 Thomas le Goldsmith of Bodmin applied
for a licence to give two messuages and two acres of land
in Bodmin to the friars : there is, however, no evidence
that this licence was granted, though the jurors declared it
would be to the advantage of the whole community of the
town.[5] There is some evidence that the house was a seat
of learning at about this period.[6]

[1] Leland, *Itin.*, vol. 1, p. 184.
[2] *Exeter Epis. Reg.*, *Bronescombe*, p. 30; Sir J. Maclean, *History of*
. . . *Trigg Minor*, vol. I, p. 188, states that Robert Clapethoyr, a noted
robber, took sanctuary in the church in 1253, referring to Assize Roll 11,
Edw. I, m. 8d : 1253 is a misprint for 1283.
[3] He subsequently provided a new site for the Franciscans of Chichester
(see p. 54), and his heart was buried in the Grey Friary in Oxford in 1272.
[4] Worcester, *Itin.*, p. 112.
[5] P.R.O. Inq. a.q.d. 299/10. A somewhat unusual degree of co-opera-
tion between the town and friary of Bodmin is illustrated by the choice
of the feast of St. Francis (4 Oct.) as the day for the election of the Mayor,
while Franciscan influence further afield is shown by the building and
maintenance of a chapel in honour of St. Francis at Metsole or Mitchell
from the end of the fourteenth century onwards. (*Exeter Epis. Reg*
Stafford, p. 257 ; *Lacy*, pt. II, p. 456.) Knowledge of the Cornish lan-
guage is mentioned as one of the qualifications of the Bodmin friars licensed
to hear confessions (*Ibid.*, *Grandisson*, pt. II, pp. 632, 1146).
[6] *Exeter Epis. Reg.*, *Grandisson*, pt. I, pp. 420–1. In the latter part
of the century the famous astronomer Fr. John Somer of Bridgwater was
warden of Bodmin (B.M. Add. MS. 10628, fo. 10).

Worcester mentions 31 persons whose names appeared in the obituary calendar of the Bodmin Franciscans, some of whom were, no doubt, buried in their church.[1] Among these are Walter Bronescombe, Bishop of Exeter, who is described as a principal benefactor, and several members of the Peverell family. It was doubtless a later member of this family who is referred to in a curious deed mentioned by Sir John Maclean.[2] It is an acquittance, dated 1442, for 22 marks by William Ford, who was evidently the contractor, for certain work done in the church of the Friars Minor of Bodmin ' about the tomb of the late Thomas Peverell Esquire according to an example portrayed on a certain parchment, with French stone in a goodly chapel.' As the Peverells are stated by Leland to have been benefactors it is not improbable that this chapel was of their foundation.

The house was surrendered on 20 September 1538, the deed being signed by Walter Rodd, the warden, and nine others.[3] The inventory [4] contains the following references to the buildings :

The quere. at the hey auter a fayer tabull of allebaster
a frame of olde organes wtout pypys.
3 olde lect'neys tymber
fayer stalles well syleyd.
In ye chyrche four auters allebaster
In ye stipull 2 belles
The Vestre, The Chambers, In ye gret Chamber 2 tabulls new wt syleyd ben heys. The frayters with 7 tabulls syleyd at ye backes, ye ketchyn and brewe howse, ye buttery, and also " a cheste with certain evydens belonging to divers gentilmen."

It is noted elsewhere that the upper parts of the cloister and part of the steeple were covered with lead.[5]

The site, which comprised $2\frac{1}{2}$ acres,[6] together with the house called " the gatehouse," was granted on 30 January 1546 to William Abbot Esquire, the King's servant,[7] who

[1] Worcester, *Itin.*, p. 111.
[2] *The Parochial and Family History of the Deanery of Trigg Minor*, vol. 1 (1868), p. 188. The friars were in receipt of annual rent charges amounting to £7 10s. from various properties including " Penelles londes " (i.e. Peverell's lands) : P.R.O. Ministers' Accounts Hen. VIII, no. 7300.
[3] *L. and P. Hen. VIII*, vol. 13(2), no. 396 ; the deed is printed in *Royal Inst. of Cornwall Trans.*, vol. 8 (1886), pp. 26–7.
[4] Printed in full in *Royal Inst. of Cornwall Trans.*, vol. 8 (1886), pp. 24–6.
[5] P.R.O. E. 36/153, p. 8.
[6] P.R.O. Ministers' Accounts 7300.
[7] *L. and P. Hen. VIII*, vol. 21(1), no. 149 (37).

in the following year conveyed it to William Vyvian and others, who sold it in 1566 to the corporation of Bodmin.[1] Practically nothing now remains of the friary buildings, but until about the middle of last century a substantial building 150 feet in length and 60 feet high was still standing to the south of Fore Street on the site now occupied by the present assize courts and the public rooms to the west. It apparently dated from the fourteenth century as it is said to have contained a magnificent east window " of second pointed work," [2] and Stockdale, writing in 1824, refers to the removal of two beautiful Gothic windows.[3] Although assumed by most contemporary authorities to have been the refectory, there can be little doubt that it was in fact the friary church, as, when the structure was demolished to make way for the present assize courts, a skeleton is stated to have been found enclosed in a tomb in the masonry of the wall together with many vaults and graves beneath the floor. It is greatly to be regretted that no detailed record of these discoveries or of the building itself appears to have been made. In 1868 the western end of the building which was then used as the cornmarket still survived, together with a buttress and a small piece of adjoining wall in which was part of a spiral staircase. To-day these fragments, so far as they still exist, are incorporated in the structure of some of the shops in Fore Street, and are consequently difficult to examine. Several pillars apparently removed from the church on its demolition were set up in various parts of the town. One of these was erected by a former vicar in the parish churchyard. It consists of an octagonal shaft with moulded cap and base and is apparently of fourteenth-century date.[4]

The only other portion of the buildings of which any record exists is the gatehouse mentioned in the grant of the site at the Dissolution. This stood in Fore Street and was at one time used as a house of correction, but in 1868 it had been converted into a dwelling-house and shop. The front had been stuccoed and modern windows inserted, but

[1] Sir J. Maclean, *History of the Deanery of Trigg Minor, op. cit.*, vol 1, p. 191.   [2] *Ibid.*
[3] F. W. L. Stockdale, *Excursions through Cornwall* (1824), p. 158, where it is stated that the building had been fitted up as an Assize Hall in the early eighteenth century and that the two ends were then occupied for the Courts of Assize, the centre portion being used as the Cornmarket, with the Grand Jury room and a ball-room on the first floor.
[4] It bears the modern inscription " From the friary church consecrated A.D. 1352."

beneath the plaster there was a large blocked archway springing from clustered shafts with a small window or niche above. The ancient carved wooden roof and a large stone arch within the house are stated to have been much altered or demolished about 1854, when several sculptured stones and some fragments of painted glass from the windows were also removed.[1] Nothing now survives of this building. The cemetery apparently lay to the north of the church on the space known as Mount Folly, as human remains and several stone coffin lids have been found from time to time in this area.

(2) BRIDGNORTH [2]

This house was established before 1244 when Henry III gave 40s. to the Friars Minor of Bruges " ad fabricam ecclesiæ sue."[3] There seems to be no definite record of the founder. Dugdale, following Tanner and Speed, states that it was founded by John Talbot who was Earl of Shrewsbury in the reign of Henry VI.[4] This date is of course impossible and Eyton [5] accordingly suggested that the Earl merely claimed to be hereditary founder by virtue of his descent from Ralph le Strange, whom the friars regarded as their founder, though the latter's title to the honour appears to be equally unsubstantiated. It was probably on a somewhat similar claim that Sir Thomas Lucy of Charlecote in 1525 left 66s. 8d. to the Grey Friars of Bridgnorth, " whereof I am founder."[6]

In 1247 the friars were licensed to enclose a road without the ditch on the western [7] side of the town and to remake the same within the ditch for the enlargement of their house.[8] This implies that the site was outside the medieval town. An escaped prisoner took sanctuary in the church in 1272.[9] There is no record of the erection of buildings apart from a

[1] *History of the Deanery of Trigg Minor, ut sup.*, pp. 190–3.
[2] W. G. Clark-Maxwell, F.S.A., " The Grey Friars of Bridgnorth," *Shropshire Arch. Soc. Trans.*, 4th series, vol. 11 (1927), pp. 49–66.
[3] *C. Lib. R. Hen. III*, vol. 2, p. 253.
[4] *Monasticon*, vol. 6, p. 1531.
[5] *Antiquities of Shropshire*, vol. 1, p. 350.
[6] *L. and P. Hen. VIII*, vol. 4, pp. 2626, 3093, and app. no. 52.
[7] This is apparently a mistake, as the present site is to the east of the medieval town and there is nothing to suggest that the site was ever changed.
[8] *C.C.R. 1242–47*, p. 517.
[9] Eyton, vol. 1, pp. 350–2.

grant in 1282 of six oaks fit for timber from the King's forest of Shirlot.[1]

The house was surrendered on 5 August 1538,[2] when the Bishop of Dover describes it as the poorest house he has seen with " all the houses at fallying downe." [3] The inventory [4] mentions the quire, a holy water stoup of latten, 2 bells in the steeple—" a great and a small "—a pair of organs, 5 tables in the frater, the kitchen and brewhouse and " a conduit coming from the high cross which was not seen many years." It is perhaps significant of the general decay of the house that the conduit which had doubtless been first brought into the town by the friars, as in so many other instances, had ceased to function so that its very existence had been lost sight of. The receiver appointed for the property was one Nicholas Holt, whose accounts show that in 1538–39 £11 0s. 5d. was received for the superfluous buildings, while the lead on the ridges (i.e. of the roofs) was sold to Thomas Holt for £1 6s. One of the bells, estimated to weigh 2 cwt. 3 qrs., was sold to Thomas Hall for £2 12s. The site and the remaining buildings were let at an annual rent of 15s. 6d. and a piece of land called " le conyagre " containing about ½ acre which had been given the friars by Thomas Horde [5] and another parcel called Actons Copie, were let at 16d. and 20s. respectively.[6] The property was leased to Nicholas Holt, the receiver, on 21 August 1540,[7] and on the 18 July 1544 the reversion was granted in fee to John Beaumont, but this grant contains no further particulars concerning the buildings.[8]

The site is on the west bank of the Severn between it and the present Friar Street. It is now and has for many years been occupied by Messrs. Southwell's carpet factory, and nothing now survives of the friary buildings. As recently as 1856, however, the Rev. G. Bellett describes its great hall or refectory as still standing. " Its oak panelled ceiling and stone fireplace," he writes, " have not yielded to

[1] *C.C.R. 1279–88*, p. 157.
[2] The Deed has not survived, but a certificate of the surrender was signed by the bailiffs to whom the custody was handed. *L. and P. Hen. VIII*, vol. 13(2), no. 41.
[3] *Ibid.*, vol. 13(2), no. 49 ; Ellis, 3rd ser., vol. 3, p. 189.
[4] Printed in full in *Shropshire Arch. Soc. Trans.*, 3rd ser., vol. 5, pp. 378–9.
[5] A Thomas Horde left the friars 20s. in 1498, but his will makes no mention of this gift of land.
[6] P.R.O. Ministers' Accounts, Hen. VIII, no. 7444, m. 27.
[7] *L. and P. Hen. VIII*, vol. 15, p. 557.
[8] *Ibid.*, vol. 19(1), no. 1035 (128).

the wear of time, but after the lapse of 600 years are still in good preservation." [1]

This building which had been converted into an alehouse was demolished in the 'sixties of last century for the extension of the carpet factory. That it was, in fact, the frater is borne out by a statement of one of the workmen engaged in its demolition, that it contained a stone pulpit. [2] It occupied the north part of the site and the church and cemetery were apparently to the south, as a considerable number of skeletons, together with a coffin lid bearing a partially obliterated floriated cross [3] and two stone coffins, have been dug up in this direction from time to time. At least one of the skeletons had buried with it a chalice and paten of base metal, which is now in the Stackhouse library attached to St. Leonard's Church.

(3) BRIDGWATER

Leland describes this house as " a goodly howse wher sumtyme a college was of gray freres. Wylliam Bruer, sunne to Willyam Bruer the first, buildid this house. One of the Lordes Botreaux and his wife were especial benefactors to this house. Thereapon his hert and his wifes body were buryed there. The accustomer of Bridgwater hath translatid this place to a right goodly and pleasaunt dwelling-house." [4] There is no reason to doubt the accuracy of the tradition current in Leland's day as to the founder. William Bruer, the father, had founded the hospital of St. John the Baptist in the town and the family were extensive landowners in the district. The original site, however, does not seem to have been held for long, for Thomas of Eccleston records that while William of Nottingham was provincial Minister the houses at York, Bristol and Bridgwater were moved. [5] The transfer was in fact carried out in 1245, for on 30 October in that year William de Cantęlupe, the constable of Bridgwater, was ordered to assign to the friars the place in Bridgwater which the King had given them for the erection of their church and

---

[1] *The Antiquities of Bridgnorth* (1856), p. 88 ; see also Cox, *Magna Brit.* (1720–31), pp. 693–4.
[2] Clark-Maxwell, *op. cit.*, p. 63.
[3] See illustration, *ibid.*, fig. 5.
[4] Leland, *Itin.*, vol. i, pp. 162–3.
[5] Eccleston, p. 56. *Ibid.*, trans. Salter, p. 62.

necessary buildings.¹ The assignment was duly ratified
on 21 January 1246.² Building was in progress in 1250,
when the keeper of the King's Park at Newton was ordered
to send to Bridgwater six oaks " fit for timber with their
branches for the work of the Friars Minor there." ³ The
church was presumably the first building erected and work
on the domestic buildings was still in hand in 1278, when the
friars were presented with five oaks from Petherton forest
for making their dormitory.⁴ A further gift of six good
oaks for timber is recorded in 1284.⁵ The friars had license
21 August 1349 to acquire six acres in Bridgwater for the
enlargement of their house provided that inquisitions *ad
quod damnum* be made. No record of an inquisition, however, remains. It may be noted that Bridgwater was one
of the earliest places in England to be attacked by the
Black Death and it suffered very severely.⁶

Very little is known of the subsequent history of this
house, though it is associated with several men who were
famous in their day. Robert Cross or Crouche, who became
provincial minister soon after 1280, was buried at Bridgwater and had probably been a friar of the house.⁷ He
wrote various philosophical and theological studies, though
none of his works are extant. In the latter part of the
fourteenth century, John Somer was a friar here. He
enjoyed a considerable reputation as a mathematician and
astronomer, and is referred to by Chaucer. Several of his
writings survive.⁸ He died, according to William of
Worcester, in 1419 or 1420, and gave to the fabric of the
church of Bridgwater (presumably that of the friary) 200
marks and for books 40 marks.⁹ This information was
extracted by Worcester from a Martyrology of the Franciscans of Bridgwater which he saw on his visit to the friary.¹⁰
Among others whose deaths were recorded therein, and
who were probably buried in or otherwise associated with the
friars' church, were Sir John Trivet who died on 3 June 1394,

¹ *C.C.R. 1242–47*, p. 367.
² *C.P.R. 1232–47*, p. 470.
³ *C.C.R. 1247–51*, p. 312 : Lib. R. 34 Hen. III, m. 4.
⁴ *Ibid. 1272–79*, p. 451.
⁵ *C.C.R. 1279–88*, p. 309.
⁶ *C.P.R. 1348–50*, p. 361 ; Gasquet, *The Great Pestilence 1348–49*
(1893), pp. 84, 168. A few years before—in 1335—the friars had complained of injuries done to them. Worc. Episc. Reg. Simon de Monte
Acuto II, fo. 10ᵛ.
⁷ Little, *Grey Friars in Oxford*, pp. 156–7.
⁸ *Ibid.*, pp. 244–6.
⁹ Worcester, *Itin.*, p. 137 ; cf. p. 92.   ¹⁰ *Ibid.*, p. 137.

the blessed Thomas, Duke of Lancaster,[1] Sir John Kemys, Lord Richard Typetot (Tiptoft), brother Geoffrey Pollard who was a contemporary of John Somer and died on 31 May, 1440,[2] Matthew Gornay,[3] Lord William de Cantelupe,[4] the blessed William de Bytton, Bishop of Bath, Alice, daughter of the Earl of Warwick and wife of Sir Matthew Gornay, who died about 1406 and was buried in the middle of the quire, and Roger de Mortuo-Mari. Another friar who was warden of the Bridgwater house in the late fourteenth century was William Auger or Anger, who, according to Leland, had studied in the Franciscan convent at Oxford. He died in 1404 and was buried at Bridgwater.[5]

The church was rebuilt in the fifteenth century. On 19 January 1445 Thomas Bekynton, Bishop of Bath and Wells, authorized his suffragan to dedicate, consecrate and bless the conventual church built by the Friars Minor of Bruggewater and the ground set apart for the churchyard thereof.[6]

A provincial chapter of the order was held at Bridgwater in 1514, when Dr. Henry Standish, the famous court preacher, who was provincial minister 1506–18, presided.[7] The house was surrendered on 13 September 1538, the deed being signed by John Harris, the warden and seven others.[8] The inventory taken at this time mentions among other items a table of alabaster with nine images and two goodly candlesticks, a pair of organs and an iron grate about a tomb in the quire ; three cloths before the altar in the church (i.e. the nave) ; a chapel with a frame barred with iron ; a sextry, the " rde " (? rood) house, chambers, frater, kitchen and buttery. The jewels and plate weighed 358 ounces.[9] In the following year when

---

[1] This was Thomas, Earl of Lancaster, who was beheaded in 1322 and subsequently regarded as a saint and martyr.

[2] Worcester, though apparently with some doubt, states that Pollard wrote the martyrology.

[3] Probably Sir Matthew Gourney, who died in 1406 (see *D.N.B.*).

[4] He is described as founder of the church and was no doubt the constable of Bridgwater in 1245.

[5] Little, *Grey Friars in Oxford*, p. 254 ; Somerset Record Soc., vol. 9, p. 737 (licensed to hear confessions, 1353).

[6] *Register of Thomas Bekynton*, Somerset Record Soc., vol. 49 (1934), no. 90. Sir Alexander Lutrel and his family had a confessor from the Bridgwater Friary in 1328 (*Reg. J. de Drokensford*, p. 282) and benefactors to whom the guardian issued letters of fraternity were William Dyst (1409), John and William Kendale and Marmaduke Lumley " ord. S. Joh. Bapt." (all in 1479) *Archæologia*, vol. 79 (1929), pp. 190, 211.

[7] *L. and P. Hen. VIII*, vol. 2, p. 1465.

[8] *Ibid.*, vol. 13(2), no. 341.   [9] *Ibid.*

Sir Thomas Arundel, a local receiver of Augmentations, returned his first account to the Exchequer, John Persone was in occupation of the site with the orchards and gardens containing six acres at a yearly rent of 20s. The property was charged with the sums of £12 10s. for the price of five casks (*dolia*) of lead, at the rate of 50s. a cask, £10 for the price of certain elms growing about the site and £10 for the superfluous buildings which had been sold to divers persons.[1] The lead on the buildings was entered as follows : " The Grey freres in bridgwater one pane of the cloyster, two grete gutters between the church and the batilment, divers grete, spowtes on bothe sides of the church w^t an oryall in a chamber all leaded." [2]

On 10 March 1544 the site was granted with many other properties to Emmanuel Lucar, a citizen and merchant of London.[3] It lies in the south-east part of the town just within the line of the town ditch, which doubtless formed the precinct boundary on two sides. A house known as " The Friars " on the south side of Friarn Street has long marked the position of the friary of which there are no remains surviving above ground.[4] The land to the west of this house has, however, recently been acquired by the corporation and laid out as a building estate, and during the progress of this work certain discoveries have been made including the foundations of buildings shown on the accompanying Plan [5] (Fig. 14).

William of Worcester visited the friars' church in the second half of the fifteenth century and his description though brief is of considerable importance. The building is mentioned twice and the two entries are at first sight a little difficult to reconcile. The first reads " Longitudo ecclesiæ fratrum minorum de Bryggewater 120 steppys et ejus latitudo 30 steppys et latitudo navis ecclesiæ 14 steppys. Guardianus ecclesiæ monasterii Bryggewater vocatur frater

[1] P.R.O. Ministers' Accounts Henry VIII, no. 3151.
[2] P.R.O. Exchequer (Treasury of Receipt) Misc. Bks., vol. 153 ; *L. and P. Hen. VIII*, vol. 13(2), no. 489.
[3] *L. and P. Hen. VIII*, vol. 19(1), no. 278(41).
[4] There is a stone gateway on the west side of Silver Street which is sometimes said to have belonged to the Friary, but this seems doubtful as the precinct does not appear to have extended to the north of Friarn Street.
[5] I am indebted to Mr. E. J. Highley of the Borough Surveyor's Department of the Bridgwater Town Council for kindly furnishing the information from which the accompanying Plan and the account which follows of the recent discoveries have been prepared.

Blackborow. Et frater Pollard est legista fratrum." [1] On a later page occurs " longitudo navis ecclesiæ hujus Sancti Francisci Brygewater 62 steppys mei. Longitudo vero 20 steppys mei." [2] The length of the whole church was thus 120 of Worcester's paces or approximately 210 feet, the width (i.e. with the aisles) about 52 feet and of the nave itself 24 feet, which implies two aisles each about 14 feet wide. That the quire as well as the nave was aisled may perhaps be inferred from the fact that the measurements of the former are not given separately and the width of 30 steps is clearly intended to apply to the whole church as distinct from the nave, which is separately mentioned. The second entry gives the length of the nave as 62 steps or about 103 feet, leaving 107 feet for the length of the quire and the space beneath the belfry which may have existed here, though it is not expressly mentioned.[3] The final statement in the second entry that " the length in fact is 20 of my steps " (i.e. about 35 feet) is difficult to under- stand. Strictly, it would apply to the nave which has just been mentioned, but it would then be in direct conflict with the previous statement. On the whole, it seems probable that there is some mis-reading of the text here, as 35 feet does not fit in with any of the measurements previously given for any portion of the building. Apart from this, Worcester's figures seem to indicate a building with nave and quire of approximately equal length each with north and south aisles and probably divided by " a walking-place " in accordance with the normal arrangement in friars' churches of the later period. That this building was not earlier than the fourteenth century seems definitely implied by its size and plan, and there can be no doubt it was in fact the new church consecrated, as mentioned above, in 1445.

While excavating for a sewer in connection with the Corporation housing estate a series of six masonry piers measuring about 6 feet 6 inches by 5 feet 6 inches were found in a line approximately north-west and south-east. Lying on one of these piers was a portion of a moulded column of Ham Hill stone, presumably part of the arcade which the pier had formerly supported. This stone was

---

[1] Worcester, *Itin.*, p. 92.
[2] *Ibid.*, p. 137. For the basis of calculation of Worcester's paces or steps, see p. 22, n.3.
[3] No steeple is mentioned in the dissolution inventory.

square in section with three-quarter round shafts at the angles and bore traces of limewash.[1] At a distance of about 8 feet to the north-east of these piers was a wall running parallel to them, and apparently forming the outer wall of an aisled building. An effort was made to trace a corresponding row of piers to the south, but without result, and, unfortunately, the circumstances did not permit

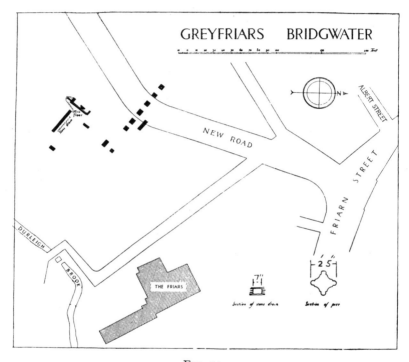

GREYFRIARS   BRIDGWATER

NEW ROAD

ALBERT STREET

STREET

FRIARN

DURLEIGH BROOK

THE FRIARS

Section of stone drain

Section of pier

FIG. 14.

of any thorough examination of the area. The extent of the building was not therefore ascertained, but its lack of orientation and its position at some distance from the medieval thoroughfare suggests that it may have been a domestic building—possibly the infirmary hall, rather than the church of the friary.

To the south of the foundations referred to, substantial

[1] A very similar section of a pillar was found by an allotment holder some years ago and is now in the grounds of " The Friars."

remains of another building were uncovered. These consisted of a wall, 20 feet long and about 15 inches thick with a well-preserved plinth of Ham Hill stone on its western face, and a central buttress of unusual shape round which the plinth was continued. Immediately to the east of this wall were indications of an original tiled floor. To the east of this, and running approximately at right angles to the first wall, was another substantial wall of limestone rubble, 3 feet in width and about 28 feet long. Its ends were not traced as it stopped abruptly towards the east with an uneven face, indicating that its continuation had been removed. Close to the north side of this wall and for some distance parallel to it, but ultimately passing beneath it and curving round the narrower wall to the west, was a well-built stone drain with a bottom formed of stone slabs and the top covered at intervals in a similar way. That this drain eventually discharged into the Durleigh brook on the east, there can be no doubt, though the actual outlet could not be traced.

These discoveries are at present insufficient to permit of any satisfactory reconstruction of the plan of the buildings, but as more may at any time come to light in the course of the further development of the site, it seems desirable to put them on record. No tiles or other evidence of a floor were found within the area of the aisled building, though numerous fragments of slate over this and other parts of the site indicated the nature of the roof covering. Many traces of charred timbers and woodwork over the site generally suggested that some portion of the buildings may have been destroyed by fire. Several boundary walls in the neighbourhood contain fragments of window mullions and other moulded stones doubtless derived from the destroyed buildings.[1]

Numerous fragments of decorated tiles were recovered from the vicinity of the covered drain, and from these it has been possible to restore several complete specimens. They are of the normal inlaid technique and vary in size from about $7\frac{1}{2}$ inches to $5\frac{1}{2}$ inches square.

The designs are largely heraldic in character, but floral and semi-floral motifs also occur. The latter are of a somewhat formal type which suggests a fourteenth- rather

[1] A piece of window tracery which is erected in the Blake Gardens in the town and is said to have been part of the former east window of the parish church may have come from the friary.

than a thirteenth-century date, and in some cases are clearly part of a composite pattern.

The identification of the heraldry is not easy, but among the shields is one with the leopards of England. Another is a plain checky coat and another bears three chevrons apparently within an orle. A fourth specimen shows a lion rampant within a border of roundles or bezants, while another, which has no shield, depicts an heraldic eagle displayed with two heads. These tiles are now in the possession of the Bridgwater Corporation.

(4) BRISTOL [1]

Eccleston [2] says that the visitor, who was the first to bring Gregory IX's exposition of the Rule to England, held visitations of the friars at London, Leicester and Bristol. As the exposition was issued on 28 September 1230, we may infer that the Bristol house was founded not later than that year. Apart from royal grants of wood for fuel in 1234 and 1237 [3] and for timber in 1236,[4] nothing is known of this first settlement, but Weare conjectures that it was within the city walls. About 1250 the friars moved to a new site, for Eccleston records that while William of Nottingham was provincial minister (i.e. 1240–54) " the places at York, Bristol and Bridgwater were changed." [5] The new site which was retained until the Dissolution was in Lewins Mead to the west of the Benedictine Priory of St. James and in the suburbs of the medieval city. It was enlarged in 1386 when five Bristol citizens were licensed to assign to the friars a toft with its appurtenances in the suburb of Bristol " in a certain place there called Lewynes-mede," and near to the house of the Friars Minor for its enlargement,[6] but apart from this there is no record of further gifts of land or of the erection of the new buildings. In February 1269 Walter Giffard, Archbishop of York,

---

[1] For a full account of this house see G. E. Weare, *A Collectanea relating to the Bristol Friars Minors and their convent* (1893).

[2] Eccleston, p. 47.

[3] *C.C.R. 1234–37*, p. 4 ; *C. Lib. R.*, vol. I, p. 251.

[4] *C.C.R. 1234–37*, p. 282.

[5] Eccleston, p. 56.

[6] *C.P.R. 1385–89*, p. 37. Walter Frompton or Frampton, one of the donors, who was sometime Mayor of Bristol, had in 1353 asked for a licence to grant ½ acre of land to the Friars Minor, but although the jurors reported favourably, there is no record of the grant on the Patent Rolls (P.R.O. Inq.a.q.d. 311/13).

granted an indulgence to those who visited the church of the Friars Minor of Bristol, and in 1279 the church is mentioned in connection with a penance imposed by the Bishop of Worcester.[1] Later references to the church occur in 1334 and 1336, when orders were celebrated there by Simon de Monte Acuto, Bishop of Worcester,[2] and on 10 July 1427, when John Carpenter, Bishop of Worcester, licensed the consecration of an altar which had been newly erected in the friars' church.[3]

The friars possessed a spring and conduit head on the north side of Upper Maudlin Street which appears to have been given them by Joan, wife of John de Lidiard, who was Mayor of Bristol in 1277. Some doubt as to the validity of the friars' title to this property seems to have arisen and they accordingly petitioned Edward III for a confirmation,[4] which was granted on 14 August 1374.[5] This document recites the gift by Joan de Lidiard to the King's grandfather, Edward I, for the use of the friars of one rood of land in the suburbs of Bristol together with the spring of fresh water and the conduit thereon. It is probably to this conduit to which William of Worcester refers when he mentions a lane going to the church of St. Michael and so continuing directly eastward up to the high cross of stone built of " frestone " with a well enclosed with " frestone." According to Weare [6] the subterranean passages and arrangements for the storage and outflow of water belonging to it are still in existence and extend under Upper Maudlin Street and beneath a house belonging to the Moravian chapel, while the leaden main pipes still in their original position pass under the burial ground of the Moravian chapel which occupies part of the friars' precinct and continue via Lewins Mead, St. John Bridge, Christmas Street, Broad Street and Corn Street to the tap in All Saints' Lane adjoining All Saints' Church.

Minor benefactions to this house in wills are very numerous, but these give little or no information concerning the buildings.[7] It is of interest, however, to note that according

---

[1] *Reg. of Walter Giffard* (Surtees Soc.), p. 217 : *Worc. Epis. Reg. Godf. Giffard* (ed. W. Bund), p. 112. Weare, *op. cit.*, p. 22.
[2] Worc. Epis. Reg. Monte Acuto, vol. 1, ff. 38ᵛ, 47.
[3] Ibid., Carpenter, vol. 2, fo. 30.
[4] P.R.O. Ancient Petitions, 11300.
[5] *C.P.R. 1370–74*, p. 471.
[6] Weare, *op. cit.*, pp. 32, 36.
[7] A fairly expensive though not complete list of these is given by Weare, *op. cit.*, pp. 55–66.

to a deed dated 1465 quoted by Barrett,[1] the famous Bristol citizen William Canynges was one of the benefactors to the house, the guardian undertaking to have his name and that of his wife Joanna inscribed in the gift book of the convent and to celebrate their obit yearly in the church. A curious gift occurs in the will of Lodowic Mors or.Morse in 1464, where he directs that of certain " pipes of woad in certain ships returning, by the grace of God, from parts beyond the seas " three should be given for the reparation of the house of the Friars Minor in Bristol.[2]

Occasional records of burials add but little to one's knowledge of the buildings. In 1385 Robert Gradely or Grately desired to be buried in the church of the Friars Minor of Bristol where the bodies of his wives were interred.[3] By his will dated 10 September 1403 William Godewyn of Bristol directed that he should be buried in the chapter-house of the Friars Minor in Bristol before the image of the blessed Mary.[4]	John Roper (1390),[5] Adam Frensch (1396)[6] and Agnes Spelly (1405)[7] each desired to be buried in the church but without mentioning the position. A later will is that of John Williams, merchant of Bristol, who in 1525 directed that he should be buried " at the Grey freres of Bristowe before the image of Jesus orells where that it please almighty Jesu " and gave the friars 16s. and a further 3s. 4d. for a trental for his soul.[8]

The deed of surrender is undated,[9] but was probably signed on the 10 September 1538—the date of the surrender of the Black Friars and the Austin Friars—as on that day the Mayor reported to Cromwell that the Grey Friars " which is of the foundation and purchasing of the town built by ancient burgesses at their cost " had surrendered, and begged for a grant of the house for the repair of buildings in the town.[10]	The deed is signed by six friars but not by the Warden, Robert Sanderson, who was probably at Richmond in Yorkshire, of which house he was also Warden.[11]	The inventory [12] mentions the quire and vestry, the

[1] W. Barrett, *History and Antiquities of the City of Bristol* (1789), p. 571.
[2] T. P. Wadley, *Bristol Wills*, pp. 138–9.	[3] *Ibid.*, p. 10.
[4] P.C.C. " Marche," qu. 4, fo. 30b.
[5] *Bristol Wills, ut sup.*, p. 31.	[6] *Ibid.*, p. 49.
[7] P.C.C. " Marche," qu. 9, fo. 67.
[8] P.C.C. " Bodfelde," qu. 38.
[9] *L. and P. Hen. VIII*, vol. 13(2), no. 321.	[10] *Ibid.*, no. 322.
[11] He signed the surrender there in the following January.
[12] Printed in full in Weare, *op. cit.*, pp. 88–90 ; *L. and P. Hen. VIII*, vol. 13(2), no. 321(2).

hall, the parlour " seyleid wt. Bowdley borde," the buttery, the chambers and the kitchen. The accounts of Jeremy Green, the receiver of the rents in 1539,[1] show that in addition to the site which was valued at 4s. 8d. a year there was a piece of land called the lower orchard with a little garden which had been leased by the friars in 1536 for a term of sixty years to William Jaye, a Bristol merchant, at a yearly rent of 6s. 8d., and " the cemetery on the west side of the church of the said house abutting on a street called Lewens Mede," let to Thomas White at an annual rent of 2s. and a garden with two lime kilns and a " slippe " and a little

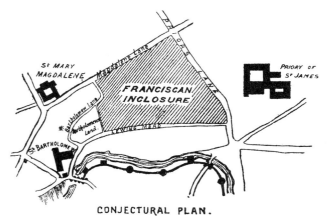

CONJECTURAL PLAN.

John à Ball Lane otherwise Johnny Ball Lane.

FIG. 15.

house built thereon situate in Lewens Mead, let by the friars in 1533 for a term of fourteen years to Thomas Haynes at a yearly rent of 20s. as well as an annual rent of 20s. paid by the receiver for a prisage of fish, a moiety of which had formerly been held by the Grey Friars.[2] On 16 March 1540 Jeremy Green obtained a twenty-one years' lease of the greater part of this property [3] and on 2 May 1541 the site which is described as enclosed with stone walls, with the water conduit and

---

[1] P.R.O. Ministers' Accounts Hen. VIII, no. 7407, printed in Weare, *op. cit.*, pp. 92–3.

[2] This valuable franchise which was shared with the Bristol Dominicans had been enjoyed by the friars from the reign of Edward I. *C.P.R, 1281–92*, p. 201.

[3] P.R.O. Exch. Augmentation Misc. Bks., vol. 112, fo. 110b, printed in Weare, *op. cit.*, pp. 91–2 ; see also *L. and P. Hen. VIII*, vol. 15, p. 566.

the piece of land called the lime kilns, together with the site of the White Friars, was sold to Corporation of Bristol subject to the existing leases.[1]

The extent of the precinct can be determined with some certainty. The northern boundary followed the line of Upper Maudlin Street, formerly Magdalene Lane, from Johnny Ball Lane, formerly known as Bartholomew Lane, to the corner of Lower Maudlin Street. From here the boundary turned southwards along the west side of Lower Maudlin Street. This street divided the land of the friars from that of the Priory of St. James, as William of Worcester describes it as " a great lane called the lane of the Prior of St. James which at the stile in the angle of the corner of Lewinsmead up to the outermost straight wall upon Montague hill in going by the wall of the friars of St. Francis on the one side and the walls of the monks on the east contains as far as the return to the hill of St. Michael in a straight line 360 paces." [2] The southern boundary, near which most of the buildings appear to have been situated, continued along Lewins Mead, up to a point some distance to the east of the present Lewins Mead Chapel. On the west the boundary is less certain, but it seems clear that it did not extend as far as the southern end of Johnny Ball Lane, as the land on which Lewins Mead Chapel is built formerly belonged to the Hospital of St. Bartholomew. The western boundary of the precinct would therefore appear to have been approximately a line drawn from the top end of Johnny Ball Lane to Lewins Mead at right angles to the latter. (See Fig. 15.) Of the position of the gateways there is no evidence except that Weare mentions [3] that beneath a modern house at the corner of Lower Maudlin Street and Lewins Mead, which was demolished shortly before 1893, and partly incorporated in its foundations, there was an ancient archway wide and high enough to admit of the passage of carts beneath it. This he considered to have been part of the eastern gateway into the friary.

Of the church itself more can be said. William of Worcester, who was a native of Bristol, must have known this building well. He mentions it on three occasions in his itinerary, but his measurements are at first sight a little difficult to reconcile. The earliest reference is very brief.

[1] P.R.O. Partic. for grants Hen. VIII, no. 173, printed in Weare, *op. cit.*, pp. 95-6 ; *L. and P. Hen. VIII*, vol. 16, no. 878 (10).
[2] Worcester, *Itin.*, p. 189.   [3] Weare, *op. cit.*, p. 28.

" Longitudo ecclesiæ fratrum minorum Bristolliæ continet 54 steppys. Latitudo continet 52 steppys." [1] A later entry is more explicit :

" Ecclesia et conventus fratrum Sancti Francisci Bristoll in parochia Sancti Jacobi in vico Lewenysmede videlicet chorus ecclesiæ continet in longitudine 28 virgas sive 50 gressus. Latitudo chori continet 9 virgas sive 18 gressus. Longitudo navis dictæ ecclesiæ cum duabus magnis alis continet 28 virgas sive 50 gressus. Latitudo dictæ navis cum duabus alis continet 27 virgas sive 52 gressus. Latitudo campanilis turris quadratæ continet 4 virgas sive 7 gressus. Archus 4 sunt in boriali navis ecclesiæ et tot in meridionali." [2]

Finally he adds :

" Longitudo ecclesiæ fratrum Sancti Francisci Bristolliæ cum 54 gressibus longitudinis chori et 64 gressibus longitudinis navis dictæ ecclesiæ continet in toto 118 gressus. Latitudo navis dictæ ecclesiæ continet 55 gressus." [3]

Several points of interest can be deduced from these statements. In the first place the church must have consisted of an aisled nave which seems to have been approximately square in plan owing to the width of its aisles, and a long unaisled quire with a square bell tower presumably between them. The exact equivalent of Worcester's " paces " has already been considered [4] and it is apparent from the above references that this varied slightly on different occasions as is perhaps only to be expected. In the case of Bristol, however, the measurements are also given in yards, which serves as a check on the general accuracy of the figures, and tallies fairly well with the standard " gressus " already suggested of $1\frac{3}{4}$ feet. Based on this figure the quire and nave which were of equal length were each between 84 and 87 feet long. The quire was between 27 and 31 feet wide, while the nave including " the two great aisles " had a width of no less than 80–90 feet. There is some discrepancy in the latter measurement, but even on the lowest estimate which is the most probable the aisles must have been each about 27 feet wide or equal to the width of the nave proper which presumably corresponded to that of the quire. This width, which must have been accentuated by the comparative shortness of the nave, was doubtless an extreme instance of the desire of the friars to obtain the maximum space for preaching, and may have been necessitated by the existence of the cemetery, which

[1] Worcester, *Itin.*, p. 116.   [2] *Ibid.*, pp. 237–8.
[3] *Ibid.*, p. 284.   [4] *Ante*, p. 22, n.3.

is known to have been to the west of the church, having prevented an extension in that direction. The unusual proportions of the nave led Weare [1] and some earlier writers to suggest that Worcester's earlier estimate of its length was inaccurate and that his later figure of 64 " gressus " represented a correction. This figure, however, is probably to be accounted for by the inclusion of the space under the belfry which is not otherwise referred to in the total length of the building.[2] That the nave was, in fact, unusually short is definitely implied by the statement that the north and south arcades each had only four arches, each of which must thus have had a span of at least 18–20 feet, even on

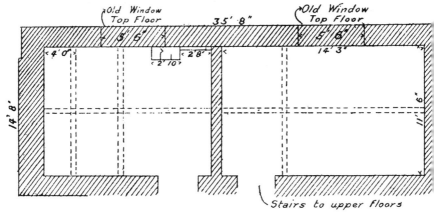

FIG. 16.—Bristol, plan of a building belonging to the Grey Friars

the most conservative estimate of the length of the nave. The total length of the church based on Worcester's earlier figures was between 180 and 187 feet. The later entry of 118 " gressus " is equivalent to 206 feet, but for the reasons stated above the earlier estimate is probably to be preferred.

Of the position of the church in relation to the other buildings and the surrounding streets it is difficult to speak with any certainty. The friars' cemetery appears to have

[1] Weare, *op. cit.*, p. 22 ; Stevens, *Continuation of Dugdale's Monasticon*, vol. 1, p. 158.
[2] It is, however, significant that the other measurements in Worcester's final entry are slightly increased, although to a less extent, and this feature has been noticed in the measurements of other buildings which are mentioned twice It is probable that Worcester in his later years took somewhat shorter steps.

occupied part of the site of the large warehouse in Lewins Mead belonging to Messrs. Gardner Thomas & Co., as a quantity of human bones and the remains of oak coffins were dug up here in 1851, when the warehouse was built, and similar discoveries were made during some excavations at the rear of the warehouse in 1878. That the building itself formerly incorporated a fragment of an earlier structure is suggested by the statement in 1851 that there was found in it " a part of the upper portion of a beautiful square-headed perpendicular English window." [1] As the church was to the east of the cemetery it must have stood parallel with Lewins Mead and approximately between the two lanes now called " Blackfriars " and " Whitefriars." [2]

Weare mentions that a wall forming part of some houses on the west side of the lane called " Whitefriars " was believed to be the east wall of part of the conventual buildings. Apart from this the only other building of medieval date which survived until comparatively recently stood at the foot of the steps leading from the Board School to Lewins Mead. It is described [3] as standing north and south and measuring 31 feet 6 inches by 11 feet 6 inches and 29 feet high to the apex of the roof, and to have been much altered by the addition of floors, partitions and windows (see Fig. 16). It was apparently of late fourteenth-century date and was originally divided into two storeys, the upper apartment being lit by two pointed windows with Decorated tracery and moulded rear arches in the west wall. The roof which was hidden by a modern ceiling appears to have been original and of the open waggon-head type with moulded oak cornice and ribs. The lower floor which was divided into two rooms contained the remains of a two-light window within a square head and part of an original stone chimney. The building which has now been demolished was possibly the little house in Lewins Mead which had been let by the friars to Thomas Haynes in 1533. [4] In 1926 during the

[1] Pryce's *History of Bristol* (1851), p. 53.
[2] The existence of these modern names within the precinct of the Grey Friars adds to the confusion already caused by the site of the Black Friars being called " Quaker Friars."
[3] Weare, *op. cit*, pp. 33–5.
[4] About 1858 Mr. E. W. Godwin described a structure of very similar proportions to this one, which he considered to be the friars' dormitory, but as certain of its details seem to have differed and the building is described as standing directly on Lewins Mead, there is some reason to think that this may have been a distinct building which had been demolished before 1893.

demol'tion of an old building at the back of Messrs. Henry Matthews & Co.'s warehouse in Lewins Mead, what is described as a wide and spacious corridor, 20 feet from wall to wall, was discovered. Its arched roof had a 20-foot span and its height from floor to roof was 39 feet.[1] Its limits were not ascertained, nor was any entrance apparently found, but that it was the sub-vault of one of the domestic buildings of the friary is not improbable. In another part of the site a small passage was uncovered which was probably connected with the water system already referred to.

(5) CHESTER [2]

Eccleston states that Albert of Pisa established brethren at Chester and Winchester, "but with great difficulty."[3] The opposition in the case of Chester appears to have come, curiously enough, from the Bishop of Coventry and Lichfield, Alexander de Stavensby, who was as we have seen largely instrumental in establishing the Franciscans in his own cathedral town of Lichfield.[4] The reason for his hostility to the Chester foundation is not apparent, though it has been suggested that it was instigated by the Dominicans who were already settled in the town. The Franciscans, found a powerful friend in Bishop Grosseteste of Lincoln, who wrote a strongly worded letter on their behalf to the Bishop of Coventry.[5] Since Albert of Pisa was not appointed provincial minister until 1236 while Alexander de Stavensby died in 1238, the initial steps connected with the foundation at Chester can be definitely assigned within these years. It was not, however, until February 1240 that the Sheriff of Chester was ordered to assist the Friars Minor in building a house of their order in the town,[6] and in the following year the King contributed £10 towards the construction of the buildings.[7] These were still in progress in September 1245, when a licence was granted for the friars to take as much stone from the fosse of the King's castle at Chester as they required for the construction of their

---

[1] *Brit. Arch. Assoc.*, New Ser., vol. 32, pp. 139–40.
[2] J. H. E. Bennett, *The Grey Friars of Chester*, 1921. Reprint from *Chester Arch. Soc. Journal*, vol. 24.
[3] Eccleston, p. 100.   [4] See *ante*, p. 163.
[5] *Letters of Robert Grosseteste, Bishop of Lincoln* (R.S.), p. 120.
[6] *C.C.R. 1237–42*, p. 171.
[7] *C. Lib. R.*, vol. 2, p. 68.

buildings.[1] At the same time they received permission to enclose a certain lane within their precinct provided it caused no injury to the city.[2] The site was within the walls of the Roman town, and in the spring of 1246 the friars were licensed to make a gate in the town wall for bringing in stone and wood for the construction of their church and houses.[3] After this date the records are silent as to the buildings until the eve of the suppression, and the later history is largely confined to an occasional mention of an addition to the friars' property. Thus, in October 1332, William de Brikhull, who had apparently been Mayor of Chester in the previous year, and Cicely, his wife, were licensed to assign a plot of land to the Prioress and Nuns of Chester in exchange for another plot adjoining the dwelling-house of the Friars Minor and measuring 102 feet by 32 feet, and to transfer the latter plot to the friars for the enlargement of their house.[4] In July 1360 the Mayor of Chester was commissioned to inquire concerning damage to the Crown if Robert de Huxelee, parson of Tatenhale, were licensed to grant a messuage with its appurtenances to the friars for the enlargement of their property,[5] but there appears to be no record of this grant having been made. In July 1403, as a result of a petition from the Warden and friars of Chester, Henry IV granted his licence for William Tewkesbury, chaplain, to assign to the Mayor of Chester for the use of the friars a rent of 10s., issuing out of three messuages which had formerly belonged to John le Chamberlein, citizen of Chester, for the foundation of perpetual obits in the friars' church for the souls of the said John and Agnes, his wife.[6] The situation of these properties, two of which were in " Baxterrowe in Estgatestrete " and the other in " Bruggestrete," are described in detail in the friars' petition, but they clearly formed no part of the precinct.

An interesting and early instance of burial in the friars' church was that of Robert Grosvenor of Hulme, who died about 1286. He was an ancestor of the defendant in the celebrated case of Scrope *v.* Grosvenor, to which reference has already been made, and among the depositions taken on that occasion were those of several witnesses who testified

---

[1] *C.C.R. 1242–47*, p. 339.   [2] *Ibid.*   [3] *Ibid.*, p. 408.
[4] *C.P.R. 1330–34*, p. 360 ; P.R.O. Inq. ad. quod damnum 223, no. 1.
[5] P.R.O. Augmentation Office Misc. Bks., vol. 279.
[6] P.R.O. Cheshire Recog. Roll. 2/76.

to having seen the disputed arms—azure, a bend or—on his tomb in the church of the Friars Minor at Chester.[1] One of these, Sir Laurence de Dutton, stated that he had seen the arms in an ancient painting on an altar in the church, while other witnesses added that the arms appeared on an old panel below (or above) an altar where the ancestor of the said Robert Grosvenor was buried a hundred years before.

In 1520, Margaret Hawarden of Chester left 6s. 8d. " to the reparation of the church of the Grey Friars," [2] but as this is about the only bequest for repairs hitherto noted in local wills, it cannot be taken as an indication that work was actually then in progress. Eight years later the warden and friars took the very unusual step of granting to the merchants and sailors of Chester " the nave of our church which they have built together with three aisles of the same church " for the stowage of sails and other necessaries connected with the fitting and repairing of their ships " as often as may be necessary as they have hitherto been accustomed," on condition that the grantees carried out the repairs to the said church and its aisles at their own cost.[3] This document, which bears an impression of the seal of the house and is dated 13 July 1528, is of considerable interest, as it not only implies that the nave of the church had been erected at the cost of the guild of merchant sailors, but also that the latter had reserved, or at any rate for some time past had exercised, the right to use the building on occasions for their own secular purposes. It is also probably significant of the general poverty of the community at this time that the nave of their church, with its facilities for preaching, should have been abandoned and the services presumably confined to the quire ten years before the ultimate surrender of the house. In 1530, Thomas Croughton of Chester bequeathed " to Sanct' Francis within ye gray freis a taper of wax." [4] In 1536 William Wall, the last warden of the house, began the construction of a conduit at Boughton,[5] the leaden pipes of which were laid along the river bank.

---

[1] *Scrope and Grosvenor Controversy*, ed. by Sir H. Nicolas (1832), vol. 1, pp. 256, 267–9, 275, 318, 321.

[2] Chetham Soc., 1st ser., vol. 51, p. 7.

[3] Chester Corporation Charters no. 32, quoted in Morris, *Chester in the Plantagenet and Tudor periods*, p. 143 ; see also *The Grey Friars of Chester, ut sup.*, p. 29.

[4] Chetham Soc., 1st ser., vol. 33, p. 8.

[5] Morris, *op. cit.*, p. 282, quoting Harl. MS. 2125 ; *Cheshire Sheaf*, 3rd ser., vol. 8, p. 87.

The Deed of Surrender is dated 15 August 1538 and is signed by the warden and six others.[1] The inventory [2] mentions the quire, vestry, kitchen, brewhouse, buttery and bulting house. The Bishop of Dover, to whom the house was surrendered, made a separate inventory of the buildings which were placed in the custody of Richard Hough, pending a decision as to their disposal. The following items from this document add something to our knowledge of the plan.

" The quere an olde ruffe slated
The steple a sharpe spyar lytyll lede, w^t ij belles in ytt.
The church slated
The northe yle ledyde in certen longe spoutes descendynge to a pane of the cloyster lede into gutters of lede
The south yle ledyd w^t a crosse yle on the same syde ledyde and certen gutters of lede."

The rest of the buildings still stood intact with their doors and gates except those which had been sold to pay the debts. These included " all the pore tables of ye awters in the quere and churche w^t the pachemēte and glasse, w^t the yron in the same quere and churche solde for xlvis. viijd.," " a pore payer of orgeyns 3s. 4d." and " the cellys and parte clossys in the dorter and cellehouse xs." The document concludes with a note that the visitor had refused to recognize divers leases " because ther was crafte in them and ware made off late." [3]

Some further details regarding the site can be gathered from the account of the receiver of the rents of the property in 1539–40. In this, the property which was in the parish of Holy Trinity is stated to comprise

a small toft on the east side of the church with 24 ft. of one " le Aley " held by Ralph Rogerson for 80 years at a yearly rent of 2s. under a lease from the warden, dated 30 April 1538, a close with a stone wall round it on the west of the church and a certain house or chamber built on the east side of the close called the ostrye (guest-house), with a chamber over the common kitchen and another chamber called le Bysshopp chamber held by Ralph Wryne gentleman for a term of 100 years at a yearly rent of 10s. under a lease from the warden dated 10 June 1538.
Two small chambers on the east of the church with a garden

---

[1] *L. and P. Hen. VIII*, vol. 13(2), no. 96(3) ; printed in *The Grey Friars of Chester, ut sup.*, p. 31.
[2] *L. and P. Hen. VIII*, vol. 13(1), no. 1298. Printed in full in *The Grey Friars of Chester, ut sup.*
[3] Mayer MSS., no. 54, quoted in *The Grey Friars of Chester, ut sup.*, p. 33.

called le convent garden held by Thomas Martyn for 60 years at a yearly rent of 2s. 4d. under a lease from the warden dated 6 April 1538.

A house abutting on the dorter on the east part of the farmarye there held by Thomas Pyllyon at a rent of 5s. by a lease dated 1538 (the term is omitted).

An orchard lying on the east of the chancel there held by Fulk Dutton for a term of 80 years at a yearly rent of 3s., under a lease from the warden dated 2 June 1535.

The land and soil of the whole church together with one " le Aley " lying on the south part as disclosed by witnesses per annum 3s. 4d.

The other houses and buildings not demised were valued at 20s. per annum so that the total annual value rental of the site was 45s. 8d.[1]

The evidence afforded by these documents is considered below. A note appended to the entry relating to Thomas Martyn's holding states that in spite of its date his lease was only sealed three days before the actual surrender. In view of the length of the terms and small amount of the rents, coupled with the fact that in at least one case, and probably in all, a premium had been taken on the granting of the lease, it is clear that the last warden, fore-seeing the arrival of the visitor, had endeavoured to dispose of the property on as advantageous terms as possible. These leases, however, were not recognized by the Court of Augmentations and a twenty-one years' lease of the whole site was granted in 1540 to Richard Hough,[2] to whom the custody had already been committed, and in July of the same year he purchased the church and other buildings for the sum of £12 for demolition.[3] On 5 May 1544 the site, together with the site of the Black Friars and White Friars, was sold, subject to Hough's lease, to John Cokkes, citizen and salter of London, for £358 6s. 5½d., and an annual rent of 4s. 7d. reserved to the Crown.[4] Apparently Cokkes had difficulty in obtaining possession from Ralph Wryne, one of the dispossessed lessees, who was alderman and recorder of the city at that time, and some proceedings resulted before the Court of Augmentations which add a little to one's knowledge of the topography of the site.[5]

Its subsequent history does not concern us, but it may be

[1] P.R.O. Ministers' Accounts Hen. VIII, no. 7394.
[2] *The Grey Friars of Chester, ut sup.*, p. 35.
[3] Mayer MSS., no. 57 ; Morris, *ut sup.*, p. 144.
[4] *L. and P. Hen. VIII*, vol. 19(1), no. 610 (12).
[5] P.R.O. Augmentation Proceedings quoted in full in *The Grey Friars of Chester, ut sup.*, pp. 39-42.

added that the surviving buildings appear to have been converted into a dwelling-house early in the seventeenth century, while the property itself ultimately passed by marriage to Sir Thomas Stanley of Alderley, whose name is now preserved in Stanley Street and Stanley Place.

The precinct, which comprised some seven acres, formed a roughly rectangular enclosure bounded by Watergate Street on the south, the city wall on the west, the backs of the houses in Linen Hall Street, formerly Grey Friars Lane,[1] on the east and a line parallel with and slightly south of Bedward Row on the north.[2] The greater part of this area was built over between 1779 and 1783. In the previous year a new Linen Hall, which gave its name to the present street on the east, had been built on the site of the friary buildings in the south-east part of the precinct. This building was demolished many years ago, but its high enclosing walls and some adjoining buildings survived until 1919, when the property was purchased by the Chester Race Company. In the following year the site was cleared and new buildings erected. During the progress of this work several medieval walls were discovered, which add somewhat to our knowledge of the ground plan derived from a rough plan of the site which exists among the Randle Holme MSS. in the British Museum.[3] This latter dates apparently from the middle of the seventeenth century and on it is written in a contemporary hand, "gray friers now Sir William Brereton's house." It shows the church with an aisleless quire and nave apparently with two aisles, thus confirming the evidence of the grant of 1528 referred to above. To the west of the church is a well [4] and from the south-east angle of the nave an alley leads eastward to what must have been the precinct boundary in the present Linen Hall Street. The most remarkable feature of the plan, however, is the position of

[1] Greyfriars Lane was also known as Crofts Lane and at a later date as Lower Lane. It received its present name of Linen Hall Street on the opening of the Linenhall in 1778.

[2] There is a road called " Grey Friars " between Nicholas Street and the city wall to the south of Watergate Street, which has, in the past, led to some confusion as to the site of this house. The name is, however, of modern origin, the road being formerly known as Smith's Walk, and it is actually on the site of the Black Friars' house.

[3] Harl. MS. 2073, fo. 92, reproduced in *The Grey Friars of Chester*, opp. p. 75.

[4] The position of this must be behind the house on the south side of Stanley Place. During the recent excavations an early brick-lined well was found about midway between Stanley Place and Linen Hall Street.

the cloister which is shown at some considerable distance
to the north-west of the church with which it is connected
by a range of buildings running north and south. That
the cloister was on the north side of the house is clear from
the suppression inventory which mentions the north aisle,
" leaded in certain long spouts descending to a pane of the
cloister." The explanation may be that Holme's plan
indicates a small cloister which alone survived at that date
and lay to the north-west of the main cloister, or on the other
hand the draughtsman may merely have exaggerated the
distance between the cloister and the church, which may
well have been separated by an open yard as at London,
Walsingham and elsewhere. In any case it is reasonable
to suppose that the draughtsman would not have shown the
cloister in this manner if it had actually abutted on the
nave. The inventory already quoted affords evidence of
two other important features of the plan of the church
which are not indicated in Holme's survey and had presumably disappeared before his time. The steeple is mentioned as having " a sharpe spyar." It appears as an
isolated structure within a walled enclosure in Speed's
map of Chester in 1610 and in a more imposing form in
Hollar's map of slightly later date. From these views one
is justified in assuming it to have been a lofty building
surmounted by a slender spire like the surviving example
at Coventry. The other feature which calls for particular
note was " the south aisle leaded with a cross aisle on the
same side leaded." The latter was in all probability not a
transept of the ordinary type, but a large transeptal chapel
projecting from the south side of the nave similar to one for
which there is evidence at Llanfaes, and to the numerous
surviving examples in Irish houses of the mendicant
orders.

Unfortunately the excavations carried out in 1920 were
limited to a series of trenches for the laying of drains and
no confirmation of the existence of this chapel appears to
have been found. A trench crossing the site from north to
south, however, revealed a series of cross-walls which were
apparently those of the nave and its aisles and the cloister
and northern range beyond. Another trench disclosed a
considerable section of ashlar wall with a plain splayed
plinth on its northern face. These discoveries, coupled
with the evidence of Holme's plan, point to the church
having been about 200 feet long with a wide aisled nave

extending westward across the site of the present Stanley Street.[1]

Of the domestic buildings very little is known and their positions are for the most part purely conjectural. The property leased to Ralph Wryne, prior to the surrender, comprised a close with a stone wall round it on the west side of the church, with the guest-house built on the east side of the close as well as a chamber over the common kitchen and a chamber called " le Bysshopp chamber." The guest-house was thus probably a detached building to the west or north of the cloister, while the infirmary is referred to as adjoining the dorter. The mention of the Bishop's chamber is interesting, though its position is not indicated. There is, as we have seen, some evidence to suggest that the Bishops of Coventry and Lichfield had an apartment set apart for their use in the Franciscan house at Lichfield, and it seems possible that by virtue of the popular title of Bishop of Chester which the Bishops of Coventry and Lichfield retained throughout the medieval period they had a similar privilege in the Chester house.

The position of the principal gateway can be fixed with some certainty. In 1532 " a howse in the grey frerys lane lying next to the grey frers gate " was granted to the parish of Holy Trinity. Immediately opposite Holy Trinity church on the west side of Linen Hall Street is a piece of land with a warehouse and shop on it which belongs to this day to that parish, and one may therefore identify the site of the friars' gateway as lying immediately to the north where numbers 3–9 Linen Hall Street now stand.

The only portion of the friary buildings now remaining is a section of the precinct wall on the east. It is constructed of red sandstone and extends with some gaps for a distance of about 50 yards along the east side of Linen Hall Place, forming the rear boundary of the properties on the west side of Linen Hall Street. Numerous tiles have, from time to time, been dug up in and near Stanley Street. Eight complete specimens and some fragments which were found in 1830 are now in the Grosvenor Museum. Others found at various subsequent dates are illustrated by Mr. Bennett. The designs include floral and geometric patterns of con-

[1] A plan reproduced in *The Grey Friars of Chester, ut sup.*, indicates the positions of the walls found in 1920, but the conjectural reconstruction of the plan of the church there shown should be disregarded as being highly improbable for a church of the mendicant orders.

siderable variety and originality as well as the two-headed eagle, the leopards of England and single tiles, depicting hounds and rabbits respectively.

(6) GREENWICH [1]

The first English house of the reformed Franciscans or Observants was founded at Greenwich in 1482. This, like the later house at Richmond in Surrey, was a purely royal foundation attached to a royal palace. It was at the personal request of Edward IV, who was possibly influenced in their favour by his sister, Margaret of Burgundy,[2] that friars of the reformed order were brought to England, and the subsequent history of the Greenwich house is largely a record of royal bounty. In January 1481 the King obtained from Pope Sixtus IV a bull authorizing the building of a house with church low bell-tower, bell, cloister, frater, dormitory, gardens and other necessary offices for the perpetual use and habitation of the friars in Greenwich or in some other suitable place in the kingdom.[3] The King then sent to the Vicar-General asking him to select some friars and send them to England to receive the site. Bernard of Lochen or Blochen was appointed the latter's commissary to carry out the transaction. The ceremony of formally handing over possession of the chosen site is minutely described in a notarial instrument prepared by E. Grimely, public notary, and an assistant as a record of the foundation and also in an open letter of Edmund Audley, Bishop of Rochester, setting forth the same events.[4] On Tuesday, 2 July 1482, being the feast of the visitation of the blessed Virgin Mary, James Goldwell, Bishop of Norwich, who acted as the King's representative, received the friars and in the name of the King laid the foundation stone of the future convent with due solemnity. The friars in token of their true and real possession first chanted the Te Deum and then solemnly sang mass.[5] Apart, however, from removing some ancient houses on the site little seems to

[1] A. R. Martin, " The Grey Friars of Greenwich," *Arch. Journ.* vol. 80 (1923), pp. 81–114.
[2] A leaf of an illuminated gradual given by her to the Greenwich friars is in the British Museum (Arundel MS. 71, fo. 9).
[3] Wadding, *Annales Minorum*, vol. 14, p. 264.
[4] Corpus Christi College, Cambridge, MS. 170, fo. 43 (printed in full *Proc. Brit. Acad.*, vol. 10, pp. 466–9). [5] *Ibid.*, fo. 44.

Plate 25

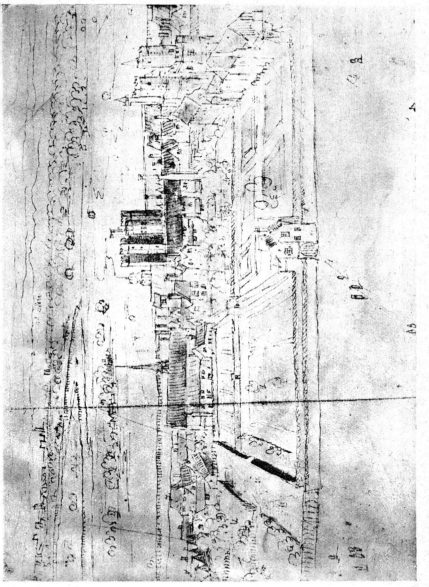

VIEW OF GREENWICH FROM THE SOUTH, SHOWING THE FRIARS' CHURCH TO THE LEFT OF THE PALACE IN 1558

have been done immediately towards erecting the new buildings, probably owing to the inability of the friars to procure the necessary funds from the King. During this period they appear to have used a small chapel dedicated to the Holy Cross and usually referred to as the Rood Chapel which already existed in Greenwich for their services.

Edward IV never lived to see the completion of his plans regarding the new Observant house, and it was not until the accession of Henry VII that any progress was made with the new church. As a result of the friars' petition to the King setting forth their condition and the delay in the completion of Edward IV's intended foundation, Henry granted them a charter dated 14 December 1485 confirming the grant of the site, and " bearing in mind Edward IV's pious intention " he formally founded their convent which was to consist of a warden and twelve brethren at the least.[1] From this time the building of the church proceeded and at some date before 1494 it was consecrated, probably by Thomas Savage, Bishop of Rochester, who issued a decree granting an indulgence to any who should bring to the chapel of All Saints on the day of its dedication alms towards the fabric.[2] The progress of the work can be traced to some extent from contemporary wills. The earliest of these was in 1485, when Richard Tylle of Sellinge in Kent left " to the building of the observance house at Greenwich 100s." [3] Seven years later the church was evidently still unfinished, for in 1493 Elliot Alfons left to the friars 20s. for their " vitaille " or the building of the church.[4] This seems to fix the date of the consecration as 1493 or 1494, as the church had apparently been consecrated before 8 April in the latter year when the Bishop of Rochester authorized any catholic bishop to consecrate " the cemetery and cloister of the religious men friars Donald Gilbert (or Gilberti) guardian of the house of Greenwich and the convent of the same place recently built there." [5]

The later history of the Greenwich friars, whose church

[1] P.R.O. Charters 1 Hen. VII, m. 20. The document is printed in full in *Arch. Journ.*, vol. 23, p. 57 ; see also *Materials, Hen. VII* (R.S.), vol. 1, pp. 216–17.
[2] Hasted, *Hundred of Blackheath* (ed. Drake), p. 86, n. 4. The dedication appears to have been to St. Francis and All Saints. It is referred to as " Saynt Frauncess church " in the will of Philipp Aldewyn in 1528 (Rochester Consist. Ct., vol. 8, fo. 180).
[3] Cant. Consist. Court. Reg. 3 ; *Test. Vet.*, vol. 1, p. 384.
[4] P.C.C. Vox., fo. 27.
[5] Rochester Epis. Reg. T. Savage, fo. 16ᵛ.

witnessed the baptisms of Queen Mary and Queen Elizabeth and such splendid ceremonies as the consecration of Cardinal Pole as Archbishop of Canterbury, does not concern us here. There is no evidence of any considerable building activity subsequent to the completion of the original buildings, and such minor works as were undertaken appear to have been regarded as part of the ordinary upkeep of the palace. The precinct was probably not enclosed by a permanent wall until about 1509, when Henry VII left £200 in his will to the Greenwich friars " for the closing of their gardyne and orcharde with a brikewall." [1]

The Observants were the first to feel the wrath of Henry's resentment for the part they took in opposing his marriage to Anne Boleyn and the Greenwich house was suppressed on 11 August 1534. Some of the friars went apparently unwillingly to conventual houses and others were thrown into prison. For the next twenty years the friary buildings seem to have been put to such occasional use as the needs of the palace demanded. During a brief period in Mary's reign the Greenwich friars were restored to their property, but there is nothing to suggest any renewed building activity, and on the accession of Elizabeth the property again reverted to the crown. Machyn records briefly in 1559, " The XII day of June (*sic*) the frers of Grenwyche whent away." [2]

The site of the buildings consisted of a rectangular strip bounded by the river on the north, the palace buildings on the east, the park on the south and the friars' road which at that date formed the principal approach to the river on the west. It is described in the notarial instrument already referred to as " a certain flat piece of land surrounded by walls in which the game of ball used to be played adjacent to the house or manor of the King together with certain buildings and a plot of land which adjoin the said piece of land and have been bought with the King's money." [3] Henry VII's charter of 1485 describes the site as a certain parcel of land with certain ancient buildings thereon in the town of East Greenwich contiguous to his manor called the King's plot and measuring 12 virgates in breadth and 63 virgates in length. Assuming a virgate here means a rod or pole, the site enclosed an area of 66 by 346½ yards.

---

[1] *Will of Henry VII*, Astle, p. 30.
[2] Camden Soc., vol. 42, p. 204 (the entry appears under July).
[3] *Proc. Brit. Acad.*, vol. 10, p. 469.

Nearly 200 years later when the property was sold during the Commonwealth it was stated to comprise " all these buildings with the appurtenances commonly called or known by the name of the priory buildings (being parcel of that capital messuage commonly called Greenwich house——) lying between the way from the waterside to Greenwich park and the west part of the wall of the great garden otherwise called the common garden with a stillhouse thereunto adjoining and belonging and all that garden with the appurtenances enclosed about with a brick wall and lying to the south of the said buildings commonly called and known by the name of the Privie garden containing from east to west in length 184 foot of assize and in breadth 168 foot of assize be the same more or less with a leaden cistern in the midst thereof and also all that ground whereon the said buildings do stand with the appurtenances and soil thereof containing by estimation 1 acre 2 roods 6 perches be the same more or less." [1]   It is somewhat difficult to reconcile these figures with the earlier ones, but it is clear that the whole property which at one time belonged to the friars was very small.

No remains of the buildings survive, but some idea of their plan and extent can be obtained from the two well-known drawings by Antony van den Wyngaerde made in 1558 just after the final suppression of the house. [2]   These drawings depict the whole of the buildings of the palace from the river and park respectively.   The friars' church appears at the extreme western end of the palace close to the river front, and is shown as a long low building of six bays under a somewhat acutely pitched roof which is continuous throughout its length (Plate 26).   Above and approximately in the middle of the building is a small bell tower surmounted by a light spire.   The view from the park shows the domestic buildings to the south of the church with the garden and orchard extending to the northern boundary of the park where a small gatehouse or lodge gives access into the park (Plate 25).   The size of the church can only be vaguely estimated.   The total distance between the west wing of the palace and the friars' road could not have been more than 250 feet, and as there was apparently an open space between this road and the

[1] P.R.O.   Particulars for sale Commonwealth H. 7, no. 3.
[2] The whole drawings have been reproduced by the London Topographical Society.

west end of the church it seems unlikely that the length
of the latter exceeded at the most 200 feet.   The fact that
the belfry is represented in both views as rising from behind
the ridge of the roof perhaps indicates that the building
was roofed throughout in two spans as in the nave of the
church at Gloucester, though this is by no means certain
as the Observant churches seem to have been generally unaisled.   A passage in an account of the christening of Queen
Elizabeth mentions that " between the quire and the body of
the church was a close place with a pan of fire to make the
child ready in." [1]   This doubtless refers to the " walking-
place " beneath the belfry through which access to the cloister would have been obtained direct from the river.   To the
west of this space and facing the nave was the rood loft
from which friar Elstow is recorded in 1532 to have delivered
an attack on Dr. Curwyn in the King's presence for having
supported   Henry   in   the   question   of   his   divorce.[2]
Wyngaerde's sketch shows a series of six three-light windows
on the north side overlooking the river.   Some very curious
instructions evidently intended for the glass painter who
was to design one of the windows in this church have survived and are now in the British Museum.[3]   The window
in question was probably the great east window which
must have been of considerable size judging from the
number of figures it was to contain.   In the lower portion
were to appear the figures of sixteen kings and saints with
their coats of arms, while above " in ye over fourme and
storie of ye windowe above ye heyar steybarre " were to be
placed a second series of figures.   Henry VII in his robes of
state is included in both series, doubtless in recognition of
him as founder of the convent.
   Of the domestic buildings very little is known.   To
judge from Wyngaerde's drawing, they were on a modest
scale, though from a list of persons " lodged in the friers "
in 1574 [4] the accommodation at that date seems to have been
fairly extensive.   During the Commonwealth the friary
buildings in common with the rest of the palace rapidly
fell into ruin, and when the property reverted to the Crown

---

[1] B.M. Harl. MSS. 3504, fo. 228 ; Stow's *Annals* (1615), p. 568.
[2] Stow's *Annals* (1615), p. 561.   In the previous year the King had
presented the friars with a pulpit for their church (L'Estrange, *Chron.
of Greenwich*, vol. 1, p. 242).
[3] Egerton MSS. 2341 A and B : printed in full in Hasted, *Hundred of
Blackheath* (ed. Drake), p. 86, n. 6.
[4] B. M. Lansdowne MSS. 18, fo. 73, 4.

Plate 26

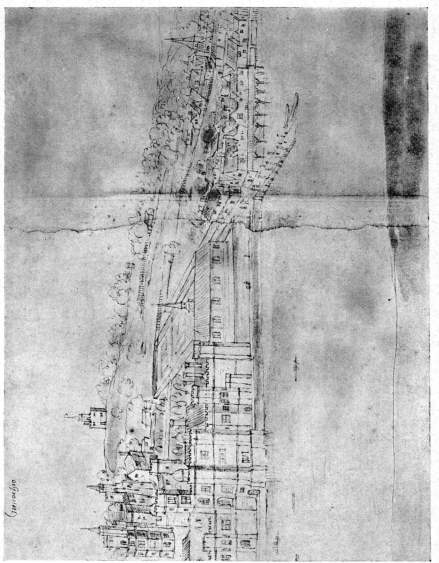

VIEW OF GREENWICH FROM THE NORTH IN 1558, SHOWING THE FRIARS' CHURCH IN THE CENTRE OF THE PICTURE

at the Restoration, Charles II resolved to rebuild the palace on a more magnificent scale. This work involved the demolition of what then remained of the friary buildings, and the first wing of the new palace which was begun in 1664 and now forms the north-west wing of the Royal Hospital stands to-day on their site.

(7) IPSWICH

This house is said to have been founded by Robert de Tiptoft of Bramford, who died in 1298.[1] Several members of this family were buried in the friars' church,[2] and that their descendants regarded themselves as hereditary founders is apparent from a letter written to Thomas Cromwell, on the eve of the suppression, by Thomas, 1st Baron Wentworth of Nettlestead, who had inherited the Tiptoft estates, in which, after referring to the Ipswich Franciscans, he describes himself as " of their founder's blood." [3]

The house was in existence, however, before 1236 as, by an undated deed, which can be assigned to the years 1233–36, Richard, Dean of Coddenham, transferred to the prior and canons of St. Peter at Ipswich certain property on trust for the augmentation and enlargement of the house of Friars Minor there.[4] Very little is known concerning its subsequent history. Robert Farnham, who died in 1319, left two tenements to the friars,[5] and in January 1332 they were licensed to accept from Sir Nicholas Frunceyes, kt., a messuage and toft for the further enlargement of their property [6] and at the same time they were pardoned for having acquired without licence a toft from Geoffrey Poper and a piece of land measuring 50 perches by 7 feet from Sir William de Cleydon, kt.[7] Weever mentions [8] the names of twenty-six persons who were buried in the church as well as the heart burials of Sir Robert Vere the elder and Dame Petronill Ufford. To this list may be added the name of Sir Robert Curson, a prominent Ipswich citizen who desired to be buried at the Grey Friary shortly before the Dissolution, and Sir Richard Wentworth, who in his will

---

[1] Tanner. *Notitia* (1787).
[2] See Weever's *Funeral Monuments* (1631), p. 751.
[3] *L. and P. Hen. VIII*, vol. 13(1), no. 651.
[4] P.R.O. *Cat. Anc. Deeds*, vol. 2, no. A.3292 ; Eccleston, pp. 169–70.
[5] *Hist. MSS. Com. Rep.*, vol. IX, p. 225.
[6] *C.P.R. 1330–34*, p. 247.   [7] *Ibid.*, p. 248.
[8] *Funeral Monuments* (1631), p. 751.

dated 1526 and proved in 1528 desired to be buried " within
the gray freres of Ipswich " and directed his executors to
" make or cause to be made of my soules goodes all the wall
of the north parte of the church of the said gray freres yf
I the said Richard doo not performe the same in my lyfe
time." [1]

The house was perhaps not formally surrendered, as
Lord Wentworth, who regarded himself as its patron by
virtue of his kinship with the founder, finding that the
Warden had been selling the jewels as the only means of
subsistence, purchased the house which consisted of " the
bare site with a garden or two enclosed " for himself for
100 marks. [2]   An inventory [3] was, however, prepared on
7 April 1538 and mentions a holy water stoup and a timber
lectern in the quire, the vestry, among the contents of which
were eighteen hangings for the quire and a lenten veil, the
kitchen, buttery, garner, cheese house, Warden's upper and
nether chambers, " the chamber where the Warden lies,"
the Vice-Warden's chamber, " a house in the dorter " and
" the chamber where the lord Wentworth's servants lay."
The accommodation was thus fairly extensive and the
existence of a special apartment for the Vice-Warden is
unusual.

The only surviving portion of the friary buildings is a
fragment of a wall containing two window arches in the
garden of the corner house on the west side of Friars Road
and the south side of Priory Street.   This wall formed
part of a building of uncertain use which extended northwards across the site of the present Priory Street, and a
further section of the same wall containing three similar
arches was demolished in the middle of last century when
Priory Street was constructed. [4]   On the west side of Friars
Road is a small portion of a wall which may be part of the
precinct wall or possibly later work constructed of old
material.

[1] P.C.C. " Porch," fo. 40.

[2] *L. and P. Hen. VIII*, vol. 13(1), no. 651 ; P.R.O. Ministers' Accounts,
Hen. VIII, no. 3440.   P.R.O., *Cat. of Anc. Deeds*, vol. 3, p. 166 ; no. A.
5346 : Indenture whereby John Hempston the warden, and the Convent
of Grey Friars of Ipswich undertake for 100 marks to make a conveyance
of their house, etc., to Thomas Wentworth knt. lord Wentworth, before
1 April next : 28 March 29 Hen. VIII [1538].

[3] Printed in full in Wodderspoon's *Memorials of Ipswich* (1850), p. 313,
and *Suffolk Arch. Assoc. Original Papers* (1848), p. 14 ; see also *L. and P.
Hen. VIII*, vol. 13(1), no. 699, and vol. 13(2), Appendix 16.

[4] A map dated 1827 in the vestry of St. Nicholas Church contains a
drawing of these five arches intact.

The precinct, which was in the parish of St. Nicholas, occupied most of the land to the west of St. Nicholas Church between Friars Road, formerly called Back Road, on the east, Princes Street on the north and the River Gipping on the west.[1] On the south it probably extended beyond Wolsey Street, but its limit in this direction is uncertain. Most of this area is now built over and Portman Street, James Street, Edgar Street, Priory Street and Cardinal Street are constructed across it. Some evidence as to the buildings formerly occupying the site can, however, be obtained from Ogilby's map of Ipswich in 1674. This shows five principal buildings within the area in question as well as a large house to the south of Wolsey Street and adjoining St. Nicholas Green, which has been conjectured on but slight authority to have been the guest-house of the friary. Ogilby's plan gives the measurements of these buildings, the chief of which appears to have been a structure measuring 102 feet long by 39 feet wide and standing approximately east and west across the middle of the modern Edgar Street.[2] That this building was either the nave of the church or the frater is not unlikely. The remaining buildings were all to the south. Three of these stood north and south at intervals across the line of the present Priory Street and measured respectively 61 feet by 38 feet, 67 feet by 28 feet and 60 feet by 31 feet 6 inches, the easternmost being the one of which a fragment still remains. Slight y farther to the south and parallel with and partly encroaching upon the site of the present Cardinal Street was another building forming three sides of a rectangle and measuring 108 feet 6 inches from east to west and 64 feet from north to south. How far these buildings were of medieval date it is of course now impossible to say, but as a chance excavation may at any time reveal some portion of the friary buildings, it is perhaps useful to refer to the evidence of this plan.

(8) SALISBURY [3]

The Franciscans were introduced into Salisbury between 1225 and 1228 by Richard le Poer, Bishop of Salisbury,

---

[1] This stream now runs in a sewer and its bed has been built over.
[2] For a plan showing the approximate position of these buildings based on Ogilby's map, see *Suffolk Arch. Inst.*, vol. 9 (1897), p. 373.
[3] A. G. Little, " The Grey Friars of Salisbury," *Wiltshire Archæol. Magazine*, vol. 47, pp. 36–54, 1935.

who granted them the site to the east of the Cathedral church which they retained until the Dissolution.[1] The progress of the buildings can be followed from the periodical grants of materials.   In March 1230 the friars received five oaks for timber to help in building their houses,[2] and in the following year two old oaks to make shingles for covering their church and fifty " copulas " for the fabric and work of the church,[3] while the foresters of Savernake and Chute were ordered not to hinder any persons having woods in the forest who should wish to help the Friars Minor with timber for a like purpose.[4]   In September 1233 the King gave five more oaks to make shingles for roofing their chapel,[5] and in January 1234 timber from Clarendon and Chute forests " ad stalla fratrum minorum Sarum' facienda et ad scindulas faciendas ad cooperiendum id quod restat cooperiendum de ecclesia sua." [6]   In the following May there is a further grant of timber for the stalls, " unless they have already had it." [7]   Finally, in December 1252 the site was enclosed by pales, sixteen cartloads being provided for that purpose by the King.[8]

The original area appears to have been very cramped [9] and, in July 1280, the friars were licensed to receive from friends any adjoining houses or areas for its enlargement.[10] A fresh building period seems to have begun about 1290, and in February 1291 the Sheriff of Wiltshire was ordered to deliver to Friar Salomon of this house the stones of the cellar which had been the treasury of the great church in the castle at Old Sarum, " for the profit of the house of Friars Minor of Salisbury." [11]   This probably indicates the replacement of the original wooden church by a stone one. At the same time the area was surrounded by a fence of thorns and brambles.[12]

A third period of building activity began in 1350, immediately after the Black Death, when the King granted pro-

[1] *Charters, etc., illustrating the History of Salisbury* (R.S.), 1891, p. 269 ; Worcester, *Itin.* pp. 81–2 ; Leland, *Itin.*, vol. 1, p. 260.
[2] *C. Lib. R.*, vol. 1, p. 171 ; *C.C.R. 1227–31*, p. 310.
[3] *C.C.R. 1231–34*, pp. 43, 45.   " Copula " may mean a split tree-trunk.
[4] *C.P.R. 1225–32*, p. 467.
[5] *C. Lib. R.*, vol. 1, p. 230 ; *C.C.R. 1231–34*, p. 260.
[6] *C.C.R. 1234–37*, p. 370.   [7] *Ibid.*, p. 414.
[8] *C.C.R. 1251–53*, p. 297.
[9] P.R.O. Ancient Correspondence, vol. XXII, p. 131.
[10] *C.P.R. 1272–81*, p. 392.
[11] *C.C.R. 1288–96*, p. 82 ; *Cal. Chancery Warrants*, vol. 1, p. 30 ; cf. will of Nic. Longespee, in *E.H.R.*, vol. 15 (1906), p. 525.
[12] Salisbury City Documents,

tection for two years for carpenters, masons and other
workmen hired by the guardian of the Friars Minor of
Salisbury for the repair of their church and houses of the
dwelling-place there.[1] Seven years later the site was
enlarged by the acquisition of a messuage and toft in Salisbury.[2] In 1367 a bull of Pope Urban V licensed the Friars
Minor to receive a messuage adjacent to their dwelling worth
40s.[3] a year.

In 1393 an important provincial chapter was held at the
Salisbury house at which Richard II, and his Queen, Anne,
attended in state.[4] The recorded burials are few and furnish
little information concerning the church. The earliest is
that of Ralph de Monthermer in 1325.[5] In 1407 Richard
Fromee desired to be buried in the conventual church of the
Friars Minor in Salisbury.[6] In 1485 Robert Ryngeborn,
armiger, directed that he should be buried in the chapel of
St. John within this church.[7] Henry Cheyny (1502),[8]
Thurstan Chaydok of Norton (1513)[9] and Thomas Lamberde,
armiger (1509),[10] also provided in their wills for burial in the
Grey Friars' church, the latter " near to the burial of William
Lamberde." During the fifteenth century the number of
friars, which had been twenty in 1243[11] and about twice
that number in 1290,[12] declined considerably and the records
at the time of the suppression show that early in the sixteenth century parts of the buildings had been let out as
lodgings to private individuals.

The deed of surrender is dated 2 October 1538 and is
signed by ten friars.[13] The inventory[14] mentions the high
altar and " a table of imagery " in the quire, four altars—one
alabaster—in the church (i.e. the nave), two bells in the
steeple—one " a fair bell "—the vestry, frater, parlour and
hall. In a separate survey of the lead it is recorded, " The

[1] *C.P.R. 1350-54*, p. 445.
[2] *C.P.R. 1354-58*, p. 588 ; P.R.O. Inq. ad quod damnum 321/13.
[3] *C. Pap. L.*, vol. 4, p. 64 ; *Bull. Franc.*, vol. 6, p. 413. It was part
of the property referred to in the Inq. a. q. d. 321/13, and 303/2.
[4] *Eulogium Histor.* (R.S.), vol. III, p. 369 ; P.R.O. Exch. Accounts,
402/10.
[5] Worcester, *Itin.*, p. 81.   [6] P.C.C. " Marche," fo. 110b.
[7] P.C.C. " Logge," fo. 103.   [8] P.C.C. " Blamyr," fo. 104b.
[9] P.C.C. " Fetiplace," qu. 18.   [10] P.C.C. " Bennett," qu. 19.
[11] *Rôles Gascons*, ed. Michel, vol. 1, no. 1969.
[12] P.R.O. Exch. Accts. 352/18 ; *ibid.*, 387/9 ; Chancery Miscell. 4/2 ;
ibid., 4/4 ; B.M. Add. MSS. 7965, fo. 7 ; Cotton MSS. Nero CVIII, fo. 201.
[13] *L. and P. Hen. VIII*, vol. 13(2), no. 518.
[14] Printed in full in *Wilts Arch. Mag.*, vol. XXX, pp. 30-2 ; see also
L. and P. Hen. VIII, vol. 13(2), no. 518.

church all leaded the upper parte of the steple leade, a gutter between the quere and the batilment a grete cloyster and all iiij panes leade." [1]   The hall which is mentioned as distinct from the frater was, no doubt, the common hall which was used for guild meetings between 1450 and 1533.[2]   Charles Bulkeley offered £100 for a grant of the site.   On 21 September 1538 he had written to Cromwell : " I beg your favour to get me the house of the Grey Friars in Salisbury which is like to be soon in the Kings hands.   I have had lodging in it this 20 years at 26s. 8d. a year which is all the yearly profits they receive within the precincts of the house." [3]   Bulkeley was only successful, however, in procuring a lease of the property, though it is probable that he demolished the church and converted the buildings into a residence.   The reversion on this lease was sold in 1544 to John Wrothe [4] and the property passed about 1600 into the possession of William Windover.

What remains of the friary is now incorporated in Windover House on the south side of St. Ann Street.   The friars' property doubtless stretched down to the River Avon on the south, but its exact extent cannot now be ascertained.

In William Naish's plan of Salisbury in 1716 [5] a roughly rectangular enclosure measuring approximately 500 feet from east to west and 400 feet from north to south is shown to the south of the houses in St. Ann's Street.   It was entered at the north-west corner by the lane now called Friary Lane and may have represented the area originally occupied by the principal buildings of the friary.   Some confirmation that the church stood in this part of the site is afforded by the fact that a number of burials are said to have been found in this area, most of which apparently came from the immediate vicinity of the large brewery building behind Windover House.   The surviving medieval buildings are situated to the north of this area and clearly formed no part of the main claustral ranges.   They comprise the rear portion of Windover House, the front part of which is probably of early seventeenth-century date with later additions (see Fig. 17).   At the south-east corner,

[1] P.R.O. E. 36/153.   [2] Salisbury City Documents.
[3] *L. and P. Hen. VIII*, vol. 13(2), no. 403.   See also P.R.O. Ministers' Accounts, Hen. VIII, no. 7047.
[4] *L. and P. Hen. VIII*, vol. 19 (2), no. 340 (36) ; P.R.O. Partic. for grants Hen. VIII, no. 1262.
[5] Reproduced in *Archæologia*, vol. 68, at p. 126.

however, is a small timber-framed hall about 20 feet square and 25 feet high, with an open timber roof of two bays carried on a single hammer beam truss now hidden by a later ceiling. In the centre of the roof are indications of

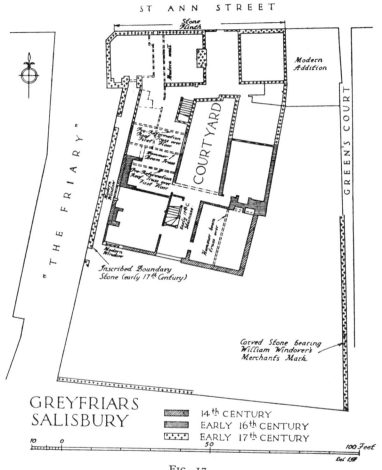

FIG. 17.

a former opening or louvre for the emission of smoke from a central fire. The west end and apparently also the east are of solid timber framing and there are no indications of original windows or doors surviving.

A second medieval structure occupies the south-west

corner of the present house and is separated from the hall just described by a passage some 10 feet wide containing a seventeenth-century staircase. This building is placed north and south and is divided into two storeys. There is again no indication of original doors or windows and the roof has been largely reconstructed though some part of it is probably original. How far this building extended northward is somewhat difficult to determine as the present divisions on the ground floor do not correspond with the roof trusses above. The northern end may be of somewhat later date, as considerable alterations seem to have been undertaken early in the sixteenth century when the two massive brick fireplaces with stone chimney-pieces on the west side were presumably inserted.[1]

There is very little from which to fix the date of these two buildings though the roof over the small hall which is the best-preserved feature may well date from the fourteenth century. That they were in fact erected on the site of the property acquired in 1356 and 1367 seems not improbable as the friars may not originally have owned any frontage to St. Ann Street. As to the use to which they were put it is only possible to conjecture. Their proximity to the main precinct gateway, which presumably stood at the north end of the lane known as Friary Lane facing Brown Street, suggests that they may have served as the guest house of the friary. On the other hand the guardian's lodging not infrequently included a small hall, and the fact that the buildings formed a compact group apparently detached from the main cloister makes this a possible alternative.[2]

(9) SHREWSBURY

The origin of this house is described in some detail by Eccleston, who states that " At Shrewsbury the lord king gave the friars a site and a certain burgess by name Richard Pride built them a church and thereafter one Laurence Cox

---

[1] During a recent rebuilding of the southernmost of the two fireplaces, necessitated by a subsidence, it was found that this had been built on a filled up surface well about 6 feet square lined with neatly squared blocks of chalk.

[2] I am indebted to Mr. J. L. Lovibond, the present owner of the property, for kindly allowing me to inspect the buildings.

other offices." [1] The latter buildings were evidently on a somewhat imposing scale for this period, as Eccleston records that William of Nottingham, the provincial minister, " out of zeal for poverty," ordered Laurence Cox to remove the stone walls of the dormitory and make mud walls, which he did " with great devotion and sweetness and very great expense." [2] The records of the royal grants fix the date of these events with certainty. On 30 October 1245 the King ordered that a sufficient and suitable site in Shrewsbury should be assigned to the friars for the building of their church and for their accommodation, [3] and in the following February the Sheriff of Shropshire was ordered to give them full possession of the site [4] and to hand the sum of £25 to the proctor of their house " to acquit " the place bought for their use. [5] On 28 September 1246 the bailiffs of Shrewsbury were ordered to give them another £10 to buy their place. [6] The site thus acquired lay outside the walls to the southeast and extended down to the river. It was thus cut off from the town, and accordingly in July 1246 the friars were licensed to construct a gate in the town wall for obtaining access to their property. [7] This gate was enlarged to allow of the passage of carts in 1267. [8]

The church was still in course of construction in April 1251, when the King gave fifty " quarters " of limestone to the friars " ad fabricam ecclesie sue," [9] and there is no hint as to when it was completed. The original site never appears to have been enlarged apart from the grant in 1371 of a certain plot for making a staindelfe (stone quarry) for the use of the friars, [10] and at the Dissolution it comprised only some 3 or 4 acres. On 21 May, 1463 Richard Fitzjohn, a friar of this house, was granted by the Minister-General, as a reward for his services in his old age, a chamber with a cell, fireplace (*camino*), garden and other places for his use and habitation in the Shrewsbury house. [11] The grant of 1371 probably indicates that some building was then in contemplation, but it is not until the eve of the suppression that there is any definite mention of further work on the site.

[1] Eccleston, pp. 28–9 ; trans. (ed. Salter), p. 31.   [2] *Ibid.*
[3] *C.C.R. 1242–47*, p. 367.   [4] *Ibid.*, p. 392.
[5] Liberate Roll, 30 Hen. III, m. 18.
[6] Ibid., m. 3 ; cf. ibid., 31 Hen. III, m. 4, for a further grant of money.
[7] *C.C.R. 1242–47*, p. 445.   [8] *C.P.R. 1266–72*, p. 113.
[9] *C.C.R., 1247–51*, p. 435. Cf. Lib. R., 33 Hen. III, m. 6 (1248–49), 40 quarters of lime for their buildings.
[10] Owen and Blakeway, *History of Shrewsbury*, vol. 2 (1825), p. 460.
[11] *C. Pap. L.*, vol. 12, p. 183.

Dr. Duffield, the guardian at that time, appears to have carried out repairs to the convent granary, then in ruins, towards the cost of which work the Corporation granted 10 marks in 1520.[1] Nine years later the guardian appealed for a further grant and received 33s. 4d.[2]

Of persons buried in this house the most important were probably John de Charlton, first Earl of Powys, who died in 1353,[3] and Lady Hawyse, his wife, who predeceased him and is said to have been a great benefactor to this house. The great east window of St. Mary's church, Shrewsbury, contains some fourteenth-century glass depicting a Tree of Jesse, which is said to commemorate the Powys family, and on this account it is often stated to have been removed from the Grey Friars' church, though there appears to be nothing to substantiate this tradition.[4] By his will, dated 1473, and proved in 1476, Robert Gryme, citizen and grocer of London, directed that he should be buried " in the freres mynours in Shrewsbury on the ryght side of my fader," and he left a sum of money for his burial and " to every priest of the said place 20d." [5]

The house was surrendered to the Bishop of Dover in August 1538, when he reported that, unlike the Black Friars in the same town, who appear to have resisted, the Grey Friars had sold everything and were glad to give up. He describes their property as " a proper house . . . no rentts but ther howse and abowte iij or iiij acores of eryabull londe lyeynge to yt." [6] Edmund Cole and Adam Mytton were placed in charge of what goods were left and the inventory [7] prepared by them mentions a table of alabaster on the high altar, a fair old lectern of timber and a parclose of timber, the lower vestry and high vestry, the kitchen, the hall, the chamber, the frater and two boxes " with

[1] *Hist. MSS. Com.*, 15th Report, Appendix X, p. 32.
[2] *Hist. MSS. Com.*, 15th Report, Appendix X, p. 48 ; Owen and Blakeway, *op. cit.*, vol. 2, p. 463.
[3] See *D.N.B.* and G.E.C.'s *Complete Peerage*, Vol. 3 (1913), p. 160. Another member of the family, Griffin de Charlton, Prebendary of Hereford, desired to be buried in the chancel of the Friars Minor of Salop, " behind the lectern where the Epistle is read," in 1385 : *Heref. Epis. Reg.*, J. Gilbert, p. 66.
[4] According to another tradition this glass was removed from the friars' church and placed in the old church of St. Chad, and on the latter's destruction in- the eighteenth century was transferred to its present position.
[5] P.C.C. " Wattys," fo. 190 (formerly qu. 25).
[6] Wright, *Suppression*, p. 205.
[7] Printed in full in *Shropshire Arch. Soc.*, 3rd Ser., vol. 5, pp. 384–6.

Plate 27

A. GREY FRIARS, SHREWSBURY, REMAINS OF A SUBSIDIARY BUILDING
FROM THE SOUTH

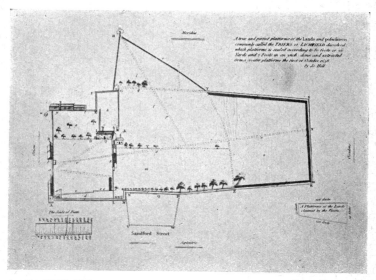

B. GREY FRIARS, LICHFIELD. 17TH-CENT. PLAN OF THE PRECINCT

evidences." The site with " the Walnoott orchard," [1] was granted in 1544 to Richard Andrews and sold to Roger Lewys, alias Pope, of Shrewsbury, Draper, in August, 1544. [2] The only surviving portion of the friary buildings belongs to a subsidiary structure of uncertain use, and is now incorporated in some cottages on the river bank, close to the modern Grey Friars' footbridge. The building, which is apparently of early sixteenth-century date, is constructed of the local red sandstone and on its southern side contains three windows, each of three lights, with somewhat depressed external arches (Plate 27A). To the east of these is an original buttress and on the north side of the building a plain doorway. The upper part of the structure is entirely modern. Part of the precinct walls could be traced in an adjoining meadow in 1825, but this has now disappeared.

(10) WORCESTER

This house was already in existence in 1231 and perhaps as early as 1226. [3] Eccleston states that its first custodian, Robert of Leicester, was "always devoted to the highest simplicity and brought many men into the order." [4] The position of the original site is unknown, but it was apparently within the walls as, in October 1231, the bailiffs of the city were ordered to enlarge the postern in the wall before the house of the Friars Minor and to make them a more convenient way for bringing in firewood and other necessaries. [5] While Albert of Pisa was provincial minister (1236–39) the friars moved to a new site outside the walls, [6] and in April 1246 they were licensed to have a postern in the city wall "if it be not to the danger of the city." [7] The progress in the erection of buildings appears to have been remarkably slow if one may judge from the periodical grants of oaks fit for timber which occur in 1256, [8] 1257, [9] 1276 [10] 'and 1282, [11] though the fact that a

[1] P.R.O. Ministers' Accounts, Hen. VIII, no. 7444.
[2] *L. and P. Hen. VIII*, vol. 19(ii), no. 166 (82), p. 87.
[3] *V.C.H. Worcestershire*, vol. 2, p. 169. The statement there that Adam Marsh entered the Order not later than 1230 is incorrect. Dr. Little has pointed out to me that he entered the Order in 1232 : see *Arch. Franc. Hist.*, vol. XIX, p. 833.
[4] Eccleston, p. 45.   [5] *C.C.R. 1227–31*, pp. 566–7.
[6] *Eccleston*, p. 55 ; trans. (ed. Salter), p. 62.
[7] *C.C.R. 1243–47*, p. 417.
[8] *Ibid. 1254–56*, p. 346.   [9] *Ibid. 1256–59*, p. 96.
[10] *Ibid 1272–79*, p. 311.   [11] *Ibid 1279–88*, p. 145.

provincial chapter was held there in 1260 indicates that some buildings were finished by that date.[1] The church is not mentioned until 1268, when William Beauchamp, the father of the first Earl of Warwick, directed that he should be buried in the church of the Friars Minor at Worcester and that a horse completely harnessed with all military caparisons should precede his corpse.[2] On Sunday following the feast of St. Francis 1282 the Bishop celebrated Mass in the Grey Friars' church and supplied food to all the brethren.[3] There were thirty-four friars here in 1301.[4]

This house appears to have been favoured as a place of burial, a fact which occasionally involved the friars in unseemly disputes with the monks of Worcester such as that which arose over the burial of Henry Poche in 1290.[5] Occasionally these records throw a little light on the plan and arrangement of the church. For instance, in 1290, Sir Nicholas de Muthon or Mitton, after directing that he should be buried at Bredon, left his heart to be buried " in the place of the Friars Minor of Worcester and with his heart £40 for the fabric of six altars in the same place." [6] William Beauchamp, 1st Earl of Warwick, who died 9 June 1298, desired to be buried in the quire of the church of the Friars Minor, " if I die within the compass of the four English seas," and he gave to the place where he should be buried two great horses, namely those which at his funeral should carry his armour, and £200 for solemnizing his funeral.[7] The Earl died in England and this windfall accordingly came to the Worcester friars. The monkish annalist lost no time in recording the incident from his point of view when he wrote " at length on 22 June the friars having got hold of the body of so great a man like conquerors who had obtained booty paraded the public streets and made a spectacle for the citizens : And so they buried him in a place where no one had yet been interred in which in winter-time he will be said to be drowned rather than buried where

[1] *Ann. Mon.* (R.S.), vol. 4, p. 446.
[2] *Test. Vet.*, vol. 1, p. 50 ; *Worc. Epis. Reg. Giffard* (Worc. Hist. Soc.), pp. 7–9. He mentions " my chapel without the city of Worcester near unto that house of Friars which I gave for the health of my soul," etc., but there is nothing to show that this ever became part of the friars' property.
[3] *Worc. Episc. Reg. Giffard* (Worc. Hist. Soc.), p. 165.
[4] Brit. Mus. MS. Add. 7966 A., fo. 25.
[5] *Ann. Mon.* (R.S.), vol. 4, pp. 499–500, 502–3, 504.
[6] *Worc. Epis. Reg. Giffard, op. cit.*, pp. 388–90.
[7] *Test. Vet.*, vol. 1, p. 52. Several other members of the Earl's family were buried here.

I have once seen herbs growing." [1]   The latter part of
this account of an eyewitness is of particular interest as it
not only implies that the site was low-lying and damp,
but suggests that the building where the burial took place,
which according to the Earl's will was the quire of the
friars' church, had been built on an unoccupied site within
the memory of the writer.   Assuming that the directions
in the Earl's will were carried out and that the Worcester
annalist is speaking literally, the inference is therefore
strong that a new quire had been added to the earlier church
not many years before, and it is just possible that the Mass
celebrated by the Bishop of Worcester in 1282 may have
marked a dedication ceremony.

Bequests to this house are numerous and sometimes of
substantial amounts, but they afford no information regarding the buildings.   Prior to 1322 the site had apparently
been enlarged, as Edward II in that year confirmed the
friars in their property including the areas for its enlargement given " by our ancestors and others." [2]   In September
1483 Richard III granted a meadow called Digley, " lying
under the castle," to Friar Thomas Jonys of the Worcester
friary during pleasure,[3] but this was presumably in the
nature of a personal grant.   In the following December the
King granted to Master Peter Webbe, S.T.P. Warden, and
the Friars Minor of the house of St. Francis in Worcester
his moiety in the manor of Perry by Worcester, a mill under
the Castle called Frogge Mill and a street adjoining to
hold during the minority of Edward Earl of Warwick at an
annual rent of £6.[4]   In May 1485 this rent was remitted
" because the dormitory of their house which was ruinous
fell down on the evening of St. Laurence's day " [5]
(10 August).

A few years before the Suppression the state of affairs in
this house appears to have been far from satisfactory.   One
of the friars who calls himself doctor was charged with being
a procurer of young women to vice, and about 1535 the
house is described as " more like a house of vicious and
incontinent living than a religious place." [6]   Such charges
are so rare against houses of the mendicant orders that
their occurrence is worthy of note.

[1] *Ann. Mon.* (R.S.), vol. 4, p. 537.
[2] *C.P.R. 1321–24*, p. 50.   [3] *Ibid. 1476–85*, p. 461.
[4] *Ibid. 1476–85*, p. 414.   [5] *Ibid.*, p. 523.
[6] *L. and P. Hen. VIII*, vol. 9, no. 1109.

The house was surrendered on 4 August 1538 [1] and the inventory [2] mentions the dormitory, the " custeres " (? custodian's) chamber, the minister's chamber, kitchen, brewhouse and buttery, in the quire a pair of organs and a frame for the sepulchre and two bells in the steeple.   In addition to these buildings there was probably a building set apart as a library, as the friars appear to have possessed a number of theological books. [3]   The Bishop of Dover reported to Cromwell that " the Grey Friars is a fair house well builded with not above 40s. a year in orchards and gardens, two aisles (yelys) leaded, the rest tile and slate." [4]   On 5 October 1538 the city authorities applied to Cromwell for a grant of this house and that of the Black Friars " for the maintenance and defence of the city and amendment of the walls and bridge now being in ruin and decay.   The stone of the said houses is very meet for the purpose." [5]   In the following January they stated that these houses " are set in two barren sides where is no defence but the said houses joined to the walls," and again in March, they recommend that " the churches should be pulled down to make towers and ' fortytudes ' in the walls," [6] in which suggestion they were supported by Bishop Latimer. [7]   Accordingly, on 9 December 1539, the two friars' houses with the churches, steeples, and churchyards and 20 messuages, lands, etc., in the city and in the parishes of Powick, Warmedon and Severn Stoke belonging to the said houses were sold to the city for £541 0s. 10d. to be held at an annual rent of 26s. 8d. [8] The grant does not distinguish between the properties of the two houses, but there seems to be no other evidence that the Grey Friars owned any property apart from their actual precinct.   A survey of their property appears to have been made by Robert Burgoyne, but unfortunately does not seem to have survived. [9]   The superfluous buildings were sold [10] and the City Chamberlains' accounts [11] contain

[1] *L. and P. Hen. VIII*, vol. 13(2), no. 32.
[2] *Ibid.*, vol. 13(1), no. 1513(2) ;   printed in *Assoc. Archit. Soc. Rep.*, vol. 11, pp. 307–08.
[3] Two volumes belonging to it are in the B.M., one in Worcester Cathedral Library and another at Cambridge.
[4] *L. and P. Hen. VIII*, vol. 13(2), no. 49.   *Ellis Original Letters*, 3rd ser., vol. III, p. 189.
[5] *L. and P. Hen. VIII*, vol. 13(2) no. 540.
[6] *Ibid.*, vol. 14(1), nos. 102 and 543.
[7] *Ibid.*, vol. 13(2), no. 543.   [8] *Ibid.*, vol. 14(2), no. 780(9).
[9] B.M. Add. MS. 11041, fo. 30.
[10] P.R.O. Ministers' Accounts, Hen. VIII, no. 230.
[11] Quoted in *Assoc. Archit. Soc. Trans.*, vol. 31 (1911), pp. 268–9.

many entries relating to these transactions. The following items are of special interest.

> The chapter-house sold to Thomas Evett for £10 and another house for 48s. 4d.
> Thomas Haywode bought the steeple for 10s.
> The parson of All Hallows gave £3 for the church ruffe (roof).
> Four glass windows 4s.
> The sanctus bell 15s.
> 1 cwt. of lead 5s.

The sales proceeded for some years and among the later entries are—" a wall in the body of the grey freres church was sold to Thomas Solley for 40s." Thomas Carter for one cloyster 13s. 4d., Thomas a'Flete for Guy's Hall £24.[1] Paid for making a new gate at the old Grey Friars for lockes, hinges, etc., 12s. 4d. Paid for making a new bridge at the late Grey Friars, 5s.

Nothing now remains of the buildings although a considerable portion of these survived until the latter part of the eighteenth century. The site is on the east side of Friar Street, where Laslett's almshouses now stand.[2] In 1782 the great hall or refectory was part of the city gaol and, according to Nash,[3] contained the arms of several benefactors to the friary, including those of Throgmorton, Besford, Russel, Hodyngton, Bridges and an unidentified coat bearing 3 crescents argent. Green[4] adds the further note in 1788, apparently in reference to this building, " that the wainscoting . . . is ornamented above the carvings in which the instruments of the Passion are represented inscribed B.V. and on some I.H.S. whilst others have the plume of feathers . . . between the initials E.P." He also observed, " this building is the most entire remains of an ancient religious house of any in the city; not a room has been changed . . . It is encompassed by the ancient city walls; the embrasures are stopt up but are everywhere discernable." It is probable that the building here described was identical with Guy's Hall, which was sold for £24 after the suppression, as the amount paid for the latter building shows it to have been of more than usual importance. It

---

[1] The name suggests that it may have been built by Guy de Beauchamp, Earl of Warwick, who died 1315, and whose family were great benefactors of the friary.
[2] These were erected in 1868 and rebuilt in 1911.
[3] *History of Worcestershire*, vol. 2 (1782), Appendix, p. cli.
[4] *Ibid.*, vol. 1 (1788), p. 243.

is greatly to be regretted that no plan or view of it or of any portion of the medieval buildings appears to have survived. Immediately to the north of the site of these buildings is a two-storeyed timber building, facing Friar Street, with a gable at either end and a gateway in the middle over which is a window of twelve lights. It is probably of late fifteenth-century date and has been described as the refectory or guest-house of the friary.[1] It appears, however, to be a typical example of a wealthy merchant's house of the period and was certainly no part of the ordinary domestic buildings of the friary, though it may possibly have, at one time, belonged to the friars.

[1] *Assoc. Archit. Soc. Trans.*, vol. 31 (1911), pp. 243–70, where this building is described and illustrated in detail.

CHAPTER V

HOUSES OF FRANCISCAN NUNS

No account of Franciscan building would be complete without some reference to the nuns' houses and the special problems to which they give rise. Unfortunately the surviving remains of the English nunneries belonging to the mendicant orders are practically confined to a single building of the Franciscan abbey at Denny and some foundations of the Dominican priory at Dartford,[1] so that it is impossible to say how far if at all the distinctive features of the friars' buildings were adopted in the nuns' houses.

In many respects the conditions under which the nuns lived and which doubtless influenced their buildings were totally different from that of the friars. In nothing was this more marked than on the question of the ownership of property. The austerities of the nuns' Rule of 1219 and the importance it laid on the enclosed life made some relaxation of the theory of absolute poverty inevitable almost from the first. Not only were permanent houses essential but the inability of the nuns to collect alms except with the assistance of the Friars Minor or other proxies led to the abandonment of mendicancy at a very early date. Consequently the possession of corporate property was allowed both in the Rule of 1247 and in those of 1263,[2] and although St. Clare, in her own Rule of 1253, attempted to restrict it to the area of the precinct there is ample evidence to show that at the time of the introduction of the order into England the practice as to the ownership of property among the Franciscan nuns differed in no essential respect from that of the Benedictine nuns or of

---

[1] *Arch. Journ.*, vol. 83 (1924), pp. 67–85 (with plan).

[2] These were the Isabella Rule which was originally intended exclusively for the house at Longchamp near Paris and another of the same date drawn up by Urban IV for the use of the whole order. Only the members of that branch of the order which followed the Isabella Rule, to which all the English houses belonged, were strictly called Minoresses, those who followed the Urbanist Rule being described as of the order of St. Clare or Claresses.

the earlier orders generally. The Minoresses nevertheless remained among the strictest of the medieval nuns and there is certainly nothing to suggest that in their buildings there was any greater departure from the rule of poverty than was common to the mendicant orders generally. Indeed so far as their churches were concerned it is unlikely that these ever attained a size comparable with those of the friars. The wide aisled naves of the friars' churches were of course uncalled for in a community where there was no facility for preaching, and like the churches of the earlier nunneries it is probable that those of the mendicant nuns were generally planned as aisleless rectangles with a single altar. There is some evidence that the Dominican church at Dartford was of this type though the remains at Denny indicate that the fully aisled quire was not unknown.

Of the domestic buildings in the English houses of Minoresses very little can be said. Provision had usually to be made for the accommodation of a small staff of chaplains chosen from those friars minor who were in priests' orders,[1] but the building set apart for this purpose would doubtless have been separated from the main claustral block. Apart from the possible existence of an open court between the church and the cloister at Denny there is nothing to show how far the peculiarities of the friars' buildings were copied in the nunneries, but it is interesting to note that at Denny the refectory is of one storey and not, as generally in the friars houses, placed on the upper floor.

Of the three English houses of Franciscan nuns only two have left any trace above ground. These will now be described.

(1) DENNY

HISTORY

The history of Denny Abbey is peculiar and of particular interest as it not only concerns what are the only substantial architectural remains of the order of St. Clare now surviving in this country, but also affords the only instance of an

---

[1] The Isabella Rule, unlike that of Urban IV, expressly provides for this arrangement.

existing monastic site being converted to Franciscan uses.[1]
Although there were, as we have seen, Franciscan women in
England apparently as early as 1250,[2] it was not until the
close of the thirteenth century that the first permanent
houses of the second order of St. Francis were established on
English soil. The sites of the first two foundations were at
Waterbeach, in which parish the later site at Denny is
situated, and in London just outside the city walls in the
district which became known as the Minories. In order to
understand the history of Denny it will be necessary to
refer briefly to the original foundation at Waterbeach from
which the nuns of Denny were transferred. As early as
1281 a papal bull makes mention of " the church of the
enclosed sisters without the walls of London of the Order
of St. Clare " and the church of the same order at Waterbeach,[3] but it has been shown [4] that in both instances this
reference was premature. The circumstances connected
with the foundation of Waterbeach are set out in some
detail in the contemporary annals of the neighbouring
Augustinian priory of Barnwell. It is there stated that at
Ascension-tide in 1294 four sisters of the Order of Friars
Minor came from France to the church and many other
buildings which Denise de Munchensey had been preparing
for them for the last year at Waterbeach.[5] It is probable
that the foundress had contemplated the establishment of
this house for some time, as on 1 August 1281 she had
obtained a licence from the King to grant her manor of Waterbeach to found a religious house there,[6] a fact which doubtless
accounts for its premature mention referred to above. The
date given by the Canons of Barnwell is, however, confirmed
by the fact that licence for the grant of the manor of Waterbeach to the new foundation is dated 3 March 1294, and
refers to the nuns as about to be brought from beyond the
seas.[7] On 13 March 1296 a papal bull granted a rule to the

[1] Cf. the case of the Carmelites of New Shoreham, Sussex, who acquired
from the Knights Hospitallers the buildings of the dissolved order of
Templars there. When this property was overwhelmed by the sea at
the end of the fifteenth century the friars removed into the buildings of
the suppressed alien priory at Sele in the parish of Breeding.
[2] See p. 4. [3] *Bull. Franc.*, vol. 3, p. 471.
[4] A. F. C. Bourdillon, *The Order of Minoresses in England* (B.S.F.S.)
(1926), p. 13.
[5] *Ecclesie de Bernewelle Liber Memorandorum*, ed. J. W. Clark, p. 214.
The Canons of Barnwell strenuously opposed the intended foundation,
ibid., p. 135.
[6] *Cal. Chart. Rolls*, vol. 2, p. 254.
[7] *C.P.R. 1292–1301*, p. 63.

houses at London and Waterbeach,[1] and it is significant
that this is stated to be that which was followed at the
Monastery of the Humility of the B.V.M. at Longchamp,
near St. Cloud, Paris. As Miss Bourdillon has shown,[2]
the fact that "Jeanne I de Nevers" appears in a list of
abbesses of Longchamp from March 1289 to April 1294,
while the first abbess of Waterbeach was Joan of Nevers,
makes it practically certain that these were the same person
and that Longchamp was the mother house of Waterbeach.
Denise de Munchensey, the foundress of Waterbeach, was
the daughter and heiress of Nicholas de Anesty, and at the
time of the foundation widow of Warine de Munchensey.
By him she had an only son, William, who predeceased
his mother, leaving an only daughter, Denise, who married
Hugh de Vere, and died without issue in 1314. In 1296
Hugh de Vere obtained a licence for Denise I to assign the
church of Ridgwell in Essex to the newly founded house,[3]
and subsequent gifts from other donors included land in
Biddenham in Bedfordshire with the advowson of the
church, and two messuages in Cambridge.[4] In 1311 Hugh
de Vere and his wife, who are described, by virtue of the
latter's descent from Denise I, as founders of the house,
were authorized to enter Waterbeach twice a year with a
retinue.[5]

The history of the foundation of the abbey of Denny
with which we are here primarily concerned is also that of
the decline and final extinction of Waterbeach. The plan
owed its origin to Mary de St. Pol,[6] the widow of Aymer de
Valence, Earl of Pembroke, whose mother, Joan, was a
daughter of Warine de Munchensey by his first wife. She
was thus connected by marriage with the foundress of the
house at Waterbeach, and on the death of Denise, the wife of
Hugh de Vere, in 1314, inherited her extensive estates
including the advowson of the abbey of Waterbeach.[7]
Her interest in the Minoresses can thus be explained, but
there is at first no evidence of her intention to establish a
new house. In 1327 the property of the Knights Hospitallers
at Denny, which had reverted to the Crown in 1324 after

[1] *Bull. Franc.*, vol. 4, p. 385.
[2] *The Order of Minoresses in England, ut sup.*, pp. 17–18.
[3] *C. Pap. L.*, vol. 1, p. 566 ; *C.P.R. 1292–1301*, p. 190.
[4] *The Order of Minoresses in England, ut sup.*, p. 96.
[5] *C. Pap. L.*, vol. 2, p. 82.
[6] Hilary Jenkinson, "Mary de Sancto Paulo," *Archæologia*, vol. 66 (1915), pp. 401–46.   [7] *C.C.R. 1323–27*, p. 268.

they had been in possession for ten years, was granted to Mary de St. Pol for life,[1] but it was not until 8 April 1336 that she obtained a grant of the manor in fee.[2] Four days later she was licensed to alienate this property to the nuns of Waterbeach,[3] but it seems uncertain whether this was carried out, as in April 1339 a further licence was granted authorizing her to transfer the community of Waterbeach to new buildings at Denny which she was to construct, since the old abbey was said to be situated in a place "straight low and bad and otherwise insufficient."[4] Katherine de Bolwyk was at this time Abbess of Waterbeach and it appears that it was largely as a result of her entreaties that Mary de St. Pol resolved on the transfer.[5] The existing buildings at Denny were accordingly adapted to accommodate the new community and, by February 1342, the abbess and some of the sisters had been moved from Waterbeach to Denny.[6]

The fact that a portion of the buildings already existing at Denny was retained makes it desirable to refer briefly to their earlier history. A small house of Benedictine monks had been established there in 1160 as a cell of the Abbey of Ely. In the following century the property passed into the hands of the Knights Templars, who ejected the monks and remained in possession until the suppression of their order in England in 1314, when it reverted to the Crown, and was granted to the Knights Hospitallers with most of the rest of the property of the Templars. As already stated, it again reverted to the Crown in 1324.

As we have seen, a number of the sisters were left behind at Waterbeach on the original transfer and the two houses continued to exist side by side for some years, the older house being nominally under the control of their Abbess at Denny. The arrangement was, however, obviously untenable and, in 1346, Mary de St. Pol was licensed to unite the two houses by finally suppressing that at Waterbeach.[7] The nuns of Waterbeach, who, with some justification, appear to have regarded their house as the mother house of Denny, strongly opposed this proposal and refused to move, but instead "rashly chose another abbess"[8] and proceeded to receive new members into their community.[9] The opposi-

---

[1] *C.P.R. 1327–30*, p. 27.
[2] *Ibid. 1334–38*, p. 250.
[3] *Ibid.*, p. 248.
[4] *Ibid. 1338–40*, p. 242.
[5] *Ibid. 1350–54*, p. 72.
[6] *Ibid. 1340–43*, p. 381.
[7] *Ibid. 1345–48*, p. 119.
[8] *C.C.R. 1349–54*, p. 237.
[9] *C. Pap. L.*, vol. 3, p. 433; *Bull. Franc.*, vol. 6, p. 253.

tion was, however, ineffectual as, in 1349, Mary de St. Pol obtained a Papal mandate ordering the Bishop of Hereford to compel the delinquent nuns to obey their abbess,[1] and by 1351 it is recorded that " having been forcibly transferred by the abbess to the number of twenty they have now except three or four consented to remain under her obedience " at Denny.[2] The deserted buildings at Waterbeach, of which nothing now remains, above ground, were probably of small extent, as in 1349 the Pope authorized the Provincial Minister to receive them " wherein can be placed twelve friars." [3] This proposal, which is referred to again in the following year when the King requested the Minister-General to compel brethren of the order to reside there,[4] never seems to have been carried out. The buildings presumably gradually fell into ruin, and in 1359 the Pope licensed the removal of the bodies from twelve graves at Waterbeach to Denny.[5]

Of the later history of Denny not much is recorded apart from the names of the abbesses and some of the nuns.[6] Gifts of property, however, were numerous and included the manor of Strood in Kent and the Cambridgeshire manors of Eye and Histon, in addition to the advowsons of five churches and some 150 acres of neighbouring land.[7] Unlike the London house, however, Denny was not a particularly wealthy foundation and in the middle of the fifteenth century appears to have been in some financial difficulties.[8] In 1535 the annual value of their property is given as £174,[9] which probably excludes the demesne, as three years later the net value is stated to be £251 3s. 11d.[10] In 1360, at the request of Mary de St. Pol, Denny was granted exemption from payment of all subsidies and taxes,[11] and in the following year the foundress granted the patronage of the

[1] *C. Pap. L.*, vol. 3, p. 285 ; *Bull. Franc.*, vol. 6, pp. 223–4 ; for Mary de St. Pol's petition to the Pope, see *C. Pap. Pet.*, vol. 1, p. 160.
[2] *Bull. Franc.*, vol. 6, p. 253 ; *C. Pap. L.*, vol. 3, p. 433.
[3] *Bull. Franc.*, vol. 6, pp. 223–4 ; *C. Pap. L.*, vol. 3, p. 285.
[4] *C.C.R. 1349–54*, p. 237.
[5] *C. Pap. L.*, vol. 3, p. 605.
[6] See list in *The Order of Minoresses in England, ut sup.*, Appendix I.
[7] *Ibid.*, Appendix II, where the references to these grants are set out.
[8] A letter on this subject from Joan Keteryche, Abbess of Denny, to her kinsman John Paston and dated 1459 is printed in Camden's *Britannia*, vol. II, pp. 142–3, and in A. F. C. Bourdillon, *op. cit.*, p. 30.
[9] *Val. Eccles.*, (R.C.), vol. 3, p. 499.
[10] P.R.O., Rentals and Surveys, 6/6.
[11] *C. Ch. R.*, vol. 5, p. 168.

Abbey to Edward III,[1] in gratitude for which compliment the King in 1368 gave the Abbey another charter conferring on it additional privileges including a right of independent election of its Abbess.[2] The house had been already exempted from episcopal jurisdiction in 1343,[3] so that it was now in an unusually favoured position.

The number of sisters in the house no doubt varied considerably from time to time. When the remaining twenty nuns from Waterbeach were transferred to Denny there was probably some overcrowding, which would have been relieved some fourteen years later by the transfer of thirteen nuns to the new house at Bruisyard. The normal number at Denny does not appear to have exceeded about twenty-five,[4] in addition to which there were, of course, as in all houses of this order, at least one and usually several resident Franciscan chaplains, for whom special accommodation must have been provided.

Denny, and its daughter house at Bruisyard in Suffolk,[5] came within the Act of 1536 for the suppression of the smaller monasteries, being valued at less than £300 a year, but both received special exemptions.[6] This respite lasted only for three years, for in 1539 all three houses of minoresses were dissolved. The deed of surrender of Denny has not survived and there is no evidence of the number of nuns in the house at that date. There is some evidence to suggest that the community at this time was divided in its attitude to the march of events. Dr. Thomas Legh, one of the Crown Commissioners, states in a letter to Cromwell, dated 30 October 1535, that " at Denny there we found half a dozen of full (*sic*), most instantly desired with weeping eyes to go forth, amongst whom is a fair young woman sister to Sir Gyles Strangwise, which was and is married to one Ryvel, a merchant ventrer of London with whom she had four children and now moved of scruple of conscience, as she saith, desireth most humbly to be dismissed and restored

---

[1] *C.P.R. 1361–64*, p. 134 ; *C.C.R. 1360–64*, p. 404. Mary de St. Pol died in 1376. In her will she desired to be buried at Denny, " being clothed in the habit of that order," and left a ring to the King, " hoping that he will assist her poor house of Denny " (*Cal. of Wills enrolled in the Court of Hustings*, ed. R. R. Sharpe, vol. 2, p. 194).

[2] *C. Ch. R.*, vol. 5, p. 168.

[3] *C. Pap. L.*, vol. 3, p. 68 ; *Bull. Franc.*, vol. 6, no. 176.

[4] A. F. C. Bourdillon, *op. cit.*, p. 25.

[5] Founded between April 1364 and October 1367. It was the only other house of the order in England as the proposed foundation at Kingston-upon-Hull never materialized.

[6] *L. and P. Hen. VIII*, vol. 11, no. 385 (35), for Denny.

to her husband. And so by this ye may see that they shall not need to be put forth but that they will make instance themselves to be delivered." [1] A later tradition [2] on the other hand states that the last abbess, Elizabeth Throckmorton, retired with two or three of her nuns to her family at Coughton Court in Warwickshire and there continued to lead a conventual life until her death in 1547.[3]

The site of the abbey with its scattered properties was granted in 1539 to Edward Elrington of Wythington in Essex.[4] In 1544, however, he exchanged it for other property [5] and the later history of the site is obscure.[6]

DESCRIPTION

The site of the abbey lies in the valley of the Cam about 7 miles to the north-east of Cambridge and to the right of the road to Ely.

It is surrounded by a complicated series of double ditches which seem to have enclosed the precinct on all sides. The only important parts of the buildings now surviving are the nave, transept and central tower of the Norman church and a long aisleless apartment now used as a barn, which was apparently the nuns' refectory. The remains of the church are incorporated in the present farmhouse and are consequently considerably obscured by modern walls and partitions. The arches of the central tower and the two arms of the transept, however, are still more or less intact, together with part of the walls and arcading of the nave. The aisles of the nave have gone, but it is clear that the original Norman church consisted of a short aisled nave with transept and central tower and an aisled quire probably not more than three bays in length. The latter was entirely demolished in the middle of the fourteenth century when Mary de St. Pol erected in its

[1] Ellis, *Original Letters*, 3rd series, vol. 3, p. 119. See also *L. and P. Hen. VIII*, vol. 9, pp. 651 and 694.
[2] B.M. Add. MSS. 5833, p. 180 (Cole MSS.).
[3] A brass inscription to her memory in which she is described as " Dame Elizabeth Throckmorton last Abbess of Denye " is in the parish church at' Coughton. A sixteenth-century Dole gate reputed to have come from Denny Abbey is still preserved at Coughton (*Camb. Antiq. Soc.*, vol. 29, pp. 72–5).
[4] *L. and P. Hen. VIII*, vol. 14(2), no. 435(49) ; see also P.R.O. Ministers' Accounts Hen. VIII, no. 7295. The grant included the bell tower and churchyard.
[5] P.R.O. Augm. Off. Deeds of Purchase and Exchange, D. 23.
[6] Robert Masters, *A Short Account of the Parish of Waterbeach* (1795), W. K. Clay, *History of the Parish of Waterbeach* (1859), pp. 120–132.

Plate 28

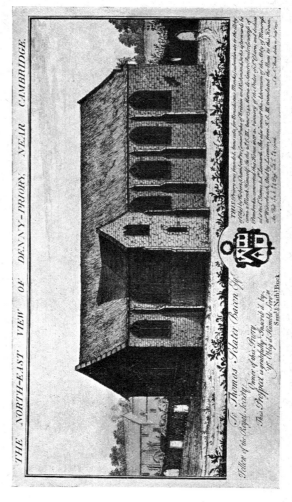

DENNY ABBEY FROM THE NORTH-EAST.   BUCKS' VIEW, 1730

place a large aisled quire to serve as the nuns' church. Nothing has survived of this building save the western respond of its north arcade, which is constructed against the filling of the original arch opening from the transept into the Norman quire aisle. The corresponding respond on the south side, which is shown in several old views of the building,[1] remained *in situ* until the early part of last century,[2] and their position indicates with reasonable certainty that the new quire extended to the full width of the twelfth-century transept. Its length is less certain though James Essex, the Cambridge architect who carried out entensive alterations to the house in 1773 and made a rough plan of the medieval buildings,[3] assumed probably rightly that the wall, bounding the enclosure at the back of the house on the east, marked the eastern limit of the fourteenth-century quire. This would allow for a length of 94 feet and suggests a quire of six bays as indicated on the accompanying Plan (Fig. 18). How far the Norman church remained in use after the nuns had entered into occupation must remain uncertain. The tower no doubt continued to serve as a belfry, but apart from a narrow opening in the east wall of the north transept, which may date from this period, there is no evidence that the transepts were open to the quire aisles after the Norman arches had been blocked, and it seems probable that the western part of the church was screened off and served as little more than an ante-chamber to the quire which formed the nun's church.

The new domestic buildings of the nunnery were placed to the north of the new quire. When Essex made his plan a considerable part of these seems to have been standing and the general layout, shown on the accompanying Plan is based on his drawing. The most noticeable feature is the exceptionally wide open space intervening between the quire and the cloister. It is not always clear from Essex's description [4] how far the walls he shows were actually visible

[1] B.M. Add. MSS. 6768, p. 228, and 6757B, fo. 41 ; see also Bucks' view and a view in Masters' *Short Account of Waterbeach, ut sup.*

[2] It was removed about 1814, divided into two and set up as part of a gateway adjoining the main road, where it still remains.

[3] B.M. Add. MSS. 6772, fo. 180^v ; Lysons made fair copies of this plan (B.M. Add. MSS. 9461, ff. 38^v–39) which however do not add any further details. Lyson's plan is reproduced on a small scale in his *Magna Britannia* and also in Clay's *History of Waterbeach, ut sup.*, p. 133.

[4] For his notes on Denny Abbey see B.M. Add. MSS. 6761, ff. 9–14, and 6772, ff. 179–180.

and how far they were conjectural, but the fact that an open court in this position, though on a less extensive scale, was, as we have seen, a common feature of the friars' houses, points to the probable accuracy of his plan. The

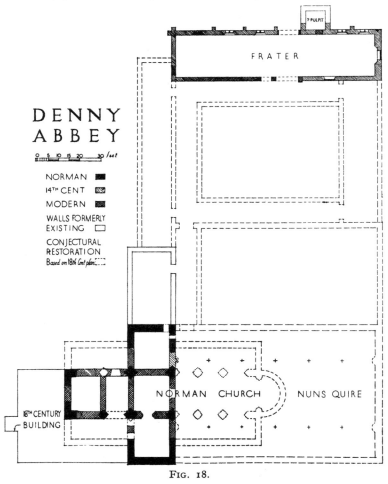

DENNY
ABBEY

0 5 10 15 20   30 feet

NORMAN ▆
14ᵀᴴ CENT ▨
MODERN ▨
WALLS FORMERLY EXISTING ☐
CONJECTURAL RESTORATION
Based on 18th Cent plan

? PULPIT

FRATER

NORMAN CHURCH

NUNS QUIRE

18ᵀᴴ CENTURY BUILDING

FIG. 18.

presence of this arrangement at Denny if it could be proved by excavation would be of considerable interest as an indication of the deliberate adoption of a feature peculiar to the friars' houses for which, in the absence of remains, there is otherwise very little evidence in the nunneries.

To the north of the Norman transept there was in Essex's time a half-timbered building of two storeys with a modern attic above and a door with a two-centred head opening into the passage leading to the cloister. This has now disappeared but it is shown in several views and apparently dated from before the suppression.[1]

The only other part of the buildings now remaining is the refectory already mentioned. It is situated about 120 feet to the north of the site of the quire and seems to have formed the northern range of the cloister. The building which appears as a prominent object in the foreground of the brothers Buck's view in 1730 (Plate 28) is 94 feet long and 22 feet wide and of mid-fourteenth-century date. It is of one storey only, and was lit originally by six windows on the north side, each of two trefoiled lights with a quatre-foil in the head, but one of these has been destroyed by the insertion of a modern doorway. On the south side only one window survives, the greater part of the wall adjoining the cloister having been rebuilt. The east window is now blocked but it is shown in Buck's view as of four lights with a quatrefoil in the head. On either side appears a small trefoiled window and in the gable end above a quatre-foil opening. According to Essex there was a similar window at the west end and he also mentions " a recess for the laver " in the middle of the west wall. Elsewhere he describes the walls as " wainscoted part of their height and the rest plastered and painted in imitation of tracery." [2] On the north side there was formerly a small projecting building of two storeys, which is shown intact in Buck's view, and was probably connected with the frater pulpit. The small door by which it was approached from the main building still survives, though now blocked up.

(2) LONDON

(MINORIES)

As already mentioned in connection with Denny Abbey, " the church of the enclosed sisters without the walls of London of the Order of St. Clare " is referred to in conjunction with the church of the same order at Waterbeach

---

[1] Essex refers to it as the Abbesses lodging, but there seems to be no evidence for this.

[2] B.M. Add. MSS. 6761, fo. 13.

in a Papal bull as early as 1281.[1] In both instances, however, the reference was premature and in the case of London
it was not until 1293 that a site was provided for the new
house. On 18 June in that year Edmund, Earl of Lancaster, the King's brother, was licensed to assign a plot of
land in the parish of St. Botolph without Aldgate, which
he had by the gift of Master Thomas de Bredstrete, to the
minoresses who are stated to be " about to be brought into
England by his consort, Blanche, Queen of Navarre."[2]
From this it would appear that Thomas de Bredstrete
actually provided the site, though the Queen of Navarre
may be regarded as the foundress, as it is certainly to her
influence that the establishment of the nuns in London
must be attributed.

They had already arrived in London by August 1294
when the King took the new house, later to be known as the
Abbey of the Grace of the Blessed Virgin, under his special
protection.[3] The Earl of Lancaster was its earliest and
principal benefactor,[4] and in 1294 and 1295 bestowed on the
nuns several properties, including the advowson of Hartington Church, Derbyshire.[5] Subsequent gifts of rents and
property from other sources are very numerous, and the
London house became by far the wealthiest of the houses
of minoresses in England. Between 1321 and 1512 no less
than twenty-five such acquisitions, including two manors
and several advowsons in nine different counties, are recorded.[6] In spite of this, however, there appears to be
no record of any extension of the actual precinct, nor is there
any definite mention of the erection of buildings.

In 1402 the Abbot of Westminster received a Papal
mandate to inquire into an allegation of the Abbess of the
Minories that " a certain temporal lady," who had come
into the possession of a house near to the nuns' church
formerly belonging to Thomas, Earl of Gloucester, had
presumed, " to the inconvenience and disturbance of the
nuns," to make use of a door which had been constructed
by the late Earl with the consent of the then abbess for the

---

[1] *Bull. Franc.*, vol. 3, p. 471.
[2] *C.P.R. 1292–1301*, p. 24.   [3] *Ibid.*, p. 86.
[4] His heart was buried in the Nuns' church (B.M. Lansd. MSS. 205,
ff. 21–3).
[5] *C.P.R. 1292–1301*, p. 170.
[6] For a list of these benefactions see A. F. C. Bourdillon, *The Order of
Minoresses in England* (1926), Appendix II. The property of this house
excluding the precinct was valued at £318 13s. 6d. yearly in 1535 (*Val.
Eccles.*, vol. 1, p. 397).

purpose of entering the church from his house.[1] The abbot was authorized to consent to the nuns sealing up the said door if the facts were as stated, but the finding is not recorded. In 1423 Lucy, Countess of Kent, left money to establish a perpetual chantry in the nuns' church,[2] and this is of interest, as two years previously she had dated a deed " in hospitio meo infra monasterium monialium Sancte Clare extra muros Lond.," [3] from which it would appear that she had a permanent residence in the nunnery.[4] A later instance of the same practice occurs in 1488 when Margaret, Duchess of Norfolk, paid a rent of £10 for " the great house " within the precinct.[5] This was probably the same building as the " great palace " occupied by the Countess of Kildare in 1538.[6] These entries indicate that the domestic buildings were extensive.

Henry le Walys, Lord Mayor of London, who died in 1302, desired to be buried in the chantry chapel which he had founded in the nuns' church.[7] Among others to be buried there was Elizabeth de Burgh, Lady of Clare, who died in 1360,[8] Agnes Mortimer, widow of Laurence Hastings, Earl of Pembroke, who died in 1369 ; [9] Jane, wife of Sir Humphrey Talbot, who in 1505 desired to be buried in the church of the Friars Minors without Aldgate and directed that " a convenient stone be laid over my sepultre on which shall be made the picture of a dead corpse in his winding sheet, with my arms and my husband's engraven thereon." [10] Elizabeth, Duchess of Norfolk, by her will dated 1506 directed that she should be buried " in the nuns' quire of the Minories without Aldgate nigh unto the place where Anne Montgomery is buried." [11] In 1515, Margaret, widow of Edmund de la Pole, Duke of Suffolk, also desired to be buried here with her husband.[12] In 1510-11 Henry

---

[1] *C. Pap. L.*, vol. 5, p. 544.
[2] *Test. Vet.*, vol. 1, p. 205. She was sister of Barnabo Visconti, duke of Milan, widow of Edmund Holland, earl of Kent, who died 1408.
[3] *Rot. Parl.*, vol. 4, p. 145a.
[4] The rule itself authorizes this and the practice seems to have been common. There are also several references to male and female holders of corrodies in this house (Bourdillon, *op. cit.*, pp. 65-7).
[5] P.R.O. Ministers' Accounts Hen. VII, no. 395.
[6] P.R.O. Rentals and Surveys, 955 ; Ministers' Accounts Hen. VIII, no. 2396.
[7] *Chron. Ed. I and II* (R.S.), vol. 1, p. 128.
[8] Nichols' *Royal Wills* (1780), p. 22 ; *Test. Vet.*, vol. 1, p. 56.
[9] *Test. Vet.*, vol. 1, p. 87.
[10] *Ibid.*, vol. 2, p. 471.
[11] *Ibid.*, p. 483.
[12] *Ibid.*, p. 530.

T

VIII had given 40 marks to the Abbess for the profession of Elizabeth their daughter as a nun in that house.[1]

A serious fire seems to have occurred in the precinct in 1519, but except for the fact that the citizens of London contributed 300 marks (£200) to complete the rebuilding which became necessary [2] there is no record of precisely what damage resulted. A grant in the same year of £200 from the King " towards the building of the minories " [3] probably also refers to this disaster. That further extensive building operations immediately preceded the suppression may be inferred from the fact that in 1538 Alice Lupsett was granted a corrody in consideration of the large sums of

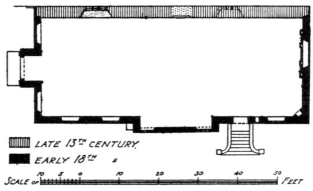

LATE *13 TH* CENTURY

EARLY *18 TH* ,,

SCALE or ░░░░░ FEET

FIG. 19.—The church of the Holy Trinity, Minories.

money which she had spent on the repairing and rebuilding of the Minories.[4]

The house was suppressed on the Monday after Palm Sunday 1539, and in the same year the site and buildings were, in exchange for an episcopal palace at Temple Bar, granted to John Clerk, Bishop of Bath and Wells and Master of the Rolls, whose successor in the bishopric of Bath and Wells converted the buildings into a new town house. The property was exchanged by Bishop Barlow soon after 1548 with the Duke of Somerset for other property and passed to the Duke's brother, Lord Seymour, on whose attainder it reverted to the Crown. In 1552 it was granted

---

[1] *L. and P. Hen. VIII*, vol. 2, nos. 1446 and 1450.
[2] *V.C.H. London*, vol. I, p. 519.
[3] *L. and P. Hen. VIII*, vol. 3(2), no. 1536.
[4] P.R.O. Augm. Off. Misc. Bks., vol. 100, p. 359.

to Henry, Duke of Suffolk, by the name of " the Minory
House," and in 1563 was repurchased by the Crown for
" a storehouse for armour and habiliments of war." [1]
The precinct, which comprised about five acres, was on
the east side of the Minories and was represented by the
extramural parish of Holy Trinity, Minories, prior to the
latter being reunited with St. Botolph's parish in 1899.
The church of Holy Trinity is referred to by Stow in 1603
as a small parish church for the inhabitants of the close,[2]
which was evidently at that date clearly defined. It
appears to have been the building referred to in 1541 as
the chapel of the Bishop of Bath's house in the Minories,
Aldgate,[3] and there can be little doubt that it was a portion
of the Nuns' church which was retained at the Dissolution.
The building which stands at the east end of St. Clare Street,
Minories was rebuilt in brick in 1709,[4] but the north wall
(Fig. 19) is of medieval date, and is the sole remaining
fragment of the conventual church. It is constructed of
rubble, now plastered internally, and contains a large
window with a two-centred head probably of late thirteenth-
or early fourteenth-century date, which is now blocked and
invisible. A second blocked window farther east is probably
of seventeenth-century date. A portion of the domestic
buildings of the nunnery appears to have survived until
they were destroyed in a fire in the precinct in 1797. Some
early foundations are said to be still preserved beneath the
houses on the south and east sides of Haydon Square.[5]

[1] E. M. Tomlinson, *History of the Minories*, pp. 80–119.
[2] Stow's *Survey* (ed. Kingsford), vol. 1, p. 126. On the authority of a
deed of 1303 Stow states that the length " of the abbey contained 15
perches and 7 feet near unto the Kings street or highway " (*ibid.*).
[3] *History of the Minories, ut sup.*, p. 105.
[4] *R.C.H.M. London*, vol. 5, p. 82. The church is now used as a parish
hall.
[5] *Archæologia*, vol. 15 (1806), p. 92.

APPENDIX I

LIST OF BURIALS IN THE GREY FRIARS' CHURCH AT COVENTRY

British Museum, Harleian MS. 6033, ff. 17-19 (formerly ff. 55-7).

Coventree.

Nomina Fundator' fr'm Minor'.

PRIMUS, Ranulphus Comes Illustris Cestriae, d'ns de Cheylesmour, cum d'na Clementia Consorte sua, qui dn's Radulphus obiit 1232.

Secundus, Hugo de Albaneyo Comes Arrundelliae.

Tertius, d'ns Rogerus de Monte Alto, qui jacet in choro coram magno Altari in medio cum d'na Cecilia Consorte sua, filia d'ci Co'itis Ranulphi, qui jacet in medietate a sinistris ejus.

Joh'es de Monte Alto filius ejus.

Rob'tus de Montealto filius junior germanus p'd'ci Joh'is.

D'ns Rogerus de Monte Alto, filius senior p'd'ci d'ni Rob'ti, cum d'na Johanna Consorte sua, filia d'ni Rogeri de Clifford.

It'm, d'na Isabella, consors d'ni Rob'ti de Monte Alto junioris, filia d'ni Rogeri de Clifford.

It'm, d'ns Thomas Hastang, miles strenuissimus et d'na Elizabeth uxor' sua jacent ex p'te boreali.

Nomina alior' amicor' sepultor' in Choro in infimo gradu presbiterarij.

Will'mus Rivell.—D'na Alicia Rivel mater ejusdem.—D'na Johanna de Chaunceus.—D'na Margareta de Braundeston, d'na de Capworth. —Emma, d'na de Wappenbury.—Guido de la greene.—Cor d'ni Thome de Bray.—Cor d'ni Ricardi de Amundevill.—Robertus de Stone et Matild' uxor ejus.—D'na Joh'es de Odyngsels, miles quond' d'ns de Longichunt'. —D'ns Nicolaus Hastang, rector de Estlemingt' eccl'ie.—D'na Alionara West.—D'na Beatrix de Bishoppdon.—D'na Margareta de Hardeshull. —Agnes, filia D'ni de Bradesto,'

In Capella d'nor' de Hasting. c. penbrok sepel '.

D'ns Henricus Hastings, cum d'na Joh'na, Consorte sua, filia d'ni, Will'mi de Cantelupe, Et e'pi Heref', S. Th. soror.'—D'ns Johes de Hastings, filius eor' cum dna' Isabella, Consorte sua, filia d'ni Will'mi de Valencio, co'it's Penbrok et Weford.—D'na Johanna de Huntingfeild, filia p'd'ci Joh'is et Isabelle.—Rob'tus de Shottesbroke, armiger, strenuissimus et ejusd'm d'ni Henrici (Hastings) quondam vexillator, et postea seneschallus. —D'na Lora de Latimer, filia d'ni Henrici supradc'i.—Edmundus de Segrave, filius d'ni Johis de Segrave.

Nomina alior' qui jacent infra d'ca' eccl'iam.

Thomas, filius Will'mi Boteler de Werinton baronis.—Joh'a filia d'ni Will'mi Bagott, milit'.—D'ns Nicolaus Pecche, miles.—D'ns Robertus de Verton, senior, et miles, cum d'na Margareta, uxor' sua.—Isabella Otteley.—Joh'es de Clifton et Lucia uxor ejus.—Alicia de Draycote.— Galfridus de Whitteleye.—D'ns Joh'es de Solneye, miles.—D'na Maryona de Burmyngham.—D'na Alicia de Welles.—Henricus de Vernoye, fundator duor' locor' fr'um in hib'nia.—Johanna de Sackevile, quondam domicilla d'ne de Segrave.—Will'mus de Aubeneye, quondam d'ns de Hasthull.— Rob'tus de Sheppey, et matild', uxor ejus.—Rad'us Hunte.—Henricus Dodenale.—Adam Botenere, maior.—Agnes Michell, mater Adae (Botener).—Joh's Maxstocke, et Alicia, uxor ejus.—Alicia, uxor Ranulphi Damet.—Will'mus Horne.—Joh'es Pomfrett Ball', et Agnes, uxor.— Thomas Parker.—Johanna Bowdy.—Philippus Corley, et Isabella, uxor ejus.—Adam Makehayte.—Symon de Shepeye, et Margareta, uxor.—

Robertus Spencer, et Isabella uxor.—Joh'es Spencer, filius Rob'ti.—
Joh'es Multon.—Nicolaus Oxborowe.—Joh'es Marchall, et Margaretta
uxor.—Rob'tus Koke, et Juliana uxor, et Joh'es, filius eor'.—Isold Belvile.
—Joh'es de Toneworth, mortuus apud Burgavenny.—Hugo de Melton.
—Joh'es de Toltham.—Henricus de Dancaster.—Ric'us le Latymer.—
Alionara de Stoneleye.—Isabella Leycester.—Robertus Rydewale.—Ric.
Lateuer.—Rogerus Box.—Agnes Sampson.—Thomas le Waydir.—Agnes
le Spicer.—D'ns Joh'es de Langford, miles et Constabularius de Kenel-
worth.—Rob'tus Dowbrugg, et Alicia uxor.—Henricus Verney, et Alicia
uxor.—Joh'es Verdun, miles.—Joh'es Rotener.—Rogerus Bray, et Emma
uxor.—Thomas Bray, filius Rogeri, cum filiis et filiab'.—Will'mus Wednis-
bury, et Alicia uxor.—Thomas de Clendon.—Isabella Glym.—Joh'es
Exton.—Adam Rotener et Alicia.—Joh'es Manby et Marger'.—Galfrid'
de Langley, Matildis consors ejus.—D'na Margareta de Pinkenye.
—Will'mus de Beuler.—Walterus de Langley, filius p'fat' Galfrid.—
Joh'es de Langley.—Isabella de Hull.—Ric' Shypton, cum Marya Cons'.
—Sara, uxor Rob'ti de Stokes.—Henricus de Ballard, et Agnes.—Ricardus
de Weston, et Alicia.—Joh'es de Cleibreok.—Joh'nes de Mynoth.—
Alexander de Filongelyes, et Ric' Dubber, et Beatrix.—Joh'es Hunt.
—Agnet' Marstock.—Eliena Corby.—Henricus Yginton, sacre the'.—
Joh'es Wychard,[1] et Alicia.—Joh'es Knyte.—Juliana, quond' d'na de
Hasthull.—Rob't Fachaw cum Felicia uxor sua qui dedit fontem de
dodmanswell.—Rogerus de Monte alto, Junior.—Symon Colushull.—
Alicia de Wyldshire.—Juliana de Assefleye.—Juliana de Wylenhale.—
Symon de Tolham.—Henricus de Paylenton, et Alicia uxor.—Amicia
uxor Symonis Chyld.—Will'mus Lutemon.—Thomas Celer, et Petrus
filius.—Will'mus Path.—Joh'es de Eton.—Walterus Tynell, et Walterus
filius.—Ricus de Rockingham.—Rogerus Camerarius D'ni Thome Blunt.
—Ranulphus Palmer, Benefactor magnus, cum uxor '.—Joh'es Warde,
Primus Maior Coventrie.

---

[1] Alice Wyschard, by will, dated 1401, bequeaths 6s. 8d. to the Friars
Minors, in Coventry, and directs her body to be buried there.

APPENDIX II

DESCRIPTION OF THE HASTINGS CHAPEL IN THE GREY FRIARS' CHURCH AT COVENTRY.

Stevens's supplement to Dugdale's " Monasticon," vol. I (1722), p. 138.
Translation from a Manuscript in French formerly in the possession of Sir Simon D'Ewes.

In the chapel of the Friars Minors of Coventry, called " Hastings Chapel," is a window in the north part, on which is a scutcheon of the arms of Hastings ; the second part, or and sinople, charged with a lion rampant, gules, the third, azure, three garbs of cummin, or, bound about the middle, gules. On a window in the east are the arms of Hastings, of Cantelow, and of Valence. On another window in the east are the arms of Hastings and azure, six lioncels argent and De la Spencer.

Item on another window in base are the arms 'of Hastings and of Huntingfeld, viz. or, a fess gules between three torteaux argent. In the second is Hastings, and argent, two bars, gules, with a label of Valence. In the third are the arms of Hastings, and the fourth is, gules, an eagle argent and beaked or.

And there are buried two knights, viz. Sir Henry de Hastings, and Joanna, the daughter of Sir William de Cantelow and sister to Thomas of Hereford, the Bishop ; and near him lies the said Joanna, with the arms of Hastings and Cantelow ; the other knight is where the arms of Hastings are with those of Valence, his name was John de Hastings, and near him lies Dame Isabel of Valence, with the arms of Hastings, and by the said Isabel lies Dame Joanna Huntingfeld, daughter to Sir John de Hastings and Isabel of Valence, in a gown powdered with the arms of Hastings, and or, a fess, gules ; and on her mantle over the same is argent, two fesses gules, and on her sleeves the arms of Valence. And there is a pillow under her head on which are the arms of Hastings and Huntingfeld, four times, viz. or, a manche gules, and or, a fess gules, and three torteaux argent.

On the table was writ—Sir Henry de Hastings, with the Lady Joanna his wife, the daughter of Sir William de Cantelow and sister of St. Thomas of Hereford ; and Sir John de Hastings their son, with the Lady Isabella his wife, daughter of Lord William de Valence, Earl of Pembroke and Wexford, buried in the habit of the Friars Minors ; John died 9 March 1312, and Isabella 3 October 1305, on whose right lies the Lady Joanna de Huntingfeld, daughter to the aforesaid John and Isabella.

Robert de Shotebroke, a most valiant esquire, once standard bearer to the said Sir Henry, and afterwards his steward.

And there lie John, Edmund, and Henry, sons to Sir William de Hastings, the son of Sir John de Hastings ; and John Huntingfeld, the son of William de Huntingfeld and the Lady Joanna, his wife.

APPENDIX III

SURVEY OF THE GREY FRIARS AT BABWELL

Public Record Office. State Papers Domestic ; Suppression Papers, vol. iii, no. 129.

Babwell.—A Estimacion of the Leade Sometyme remayning Apon the Chirche and diverse other buyldinges of the late Frerye of Babwell nyghe Burye As Appereth by the walles ther yett Remayning As hereafter Folowith :

That is to saye

Firste the Churche conteyneth in lenght by estimacion 167 Foote and the sparre on the onsyde 25 foote whiche is in bredeth 50 foote and so by estimacion conteynyd . 28½ Fodder

Item the twoo Iles of the same conteyneth every of theme 88 foote in lenght And the sparre of eyther of theyme in on hole lenght 17 foote And so by estimacion conteyned . . 10 fodder

Item the Cloyster of the same conteynith in lenght being fowre sware [? square] 352 foote And the sparre in on lenght 12 foote And by estimacion conteyned . . . . 14 fodder

Item the Cloyster Frome the Fratrye to the Kechyn conteynith by estimacion in lenght 79 foote And the sparre in one hole lenght 10 foote And conteyned by estimacion . . 3 fodder

Sum Totall of the seyd Fodders

55½ Fodders

[Here follows an account of the fate of the 4 bells.]

APPENDIX IV

LIST OF ENGLISH FRANCISCAN HOUSES ARRANGED
UNDER THEIR CUSTODIES

THE division of a Franciscan province into custodies had its counterpart in the " visitations " of the Dominican province and the " distinctions " of the Carmelite province.[1] In England the Dominican and Carmelite provinces comprised four visitations and four distinctions respectively, and there is some grounds for believing that the English Franciscan province was also originally composed of four custodies. This arrangement, however, if it ever existed cannot have lasted long, as Eccleston mentions the custodies of London, Oxford, Cambridge, York, Salisbury and Worcester, and implies the existence of a seventh with its headquarters at Hereford. The custody of Salisbury subsequently became absorbed in that of London, while the headship of the custody of Hereford was transferred to Bristol and a new custody of Newcastle was formed out of that of York. The dates of these changes are unknown, but they were certainly effected before and probably long before 1331, when the official list of provinces with their custodies and houses was drawn up for the General Chapter of the Order held at Perpignan in that year.[2] This list shows fifty-eight houses in the English province at that date divided into the seven custodies which were retained until the Dissolution. Of these fifty-eight houses five—Berwick, Roxburgh, Haddington, Dundee and Dumfries—are included in the custody of Newcastle although they had been actually transferred to the newly formed vicariate of Scotland in 1329. The short-lived houses at Romney and Durham are of course omitted as they had then ceased to exist, while Walsingham, Ware, Aylesbury and Plymouth had not yet been founded.

The total number of houses in the English province at the time of the suppression, excluding the three Observant houses at Greenwich, Richmond and Newark, and the nunneries at Denny, Bruisyard and London, which were always separately governed, was thus fifty-seven [3] grouped in seven custodies as follows :

1. Custody of London :
   London, Salisbury, Canterbury, Winchelsea, Southampton, Lewes, Winchester, Chichester, Ware.
2. Custody of Oxford :
   Oxford, Reading, Bedford, Stamford, Nottingham, Northampton, Leicester, Grantham and probably Aylesbury.
3. Custody of Bristol :
   Bristol, Gloucester, Hereford, Carmarthen, Cardiff, Bridgwater, Exeter, Dorchester, Bodmin, and probably Plymouth.

---

[1] See A. G. Little, " The Administrative Divisions of the Mendicant Orders in England," *E.H.R.*, vol. 34, pp. 205–9.

[2] Printed by Dr. Little in *Studies in English Franc. Hist.*, p. 236.

[3] This figure includes the three houses at Canterbury, Southampton and Newcastle which had been transferred to the Observants in 1498 but are included under their conventual custodies for convenience.

4. Custody of Cambridge :
    Cambridge, Norwich, Bury St. Edmunds, Lynn, Yarmouth,
    Ipswich, Colchester, Dunwich, Walsingham.
5. Custody of Worcester :
    Worcester, Coventry, Lichfield, Stafford, Preston, Shrewsbury,
    Chester, Llanfaes, Bridgnorth.
6. Custody of York :
    York, Lincoln, Beverley, Doncaster, Boston, Grimsby, Scar-
    borough.
7. Custody of Newcastle :
    Newcastle, Richmond (Yorks), Hartlepool, Carlisle.[1]

THE OBSERVANT PROVINCE

England was constituted a separate province of the Ultramontine
Family of the Observant order at the General Chapter at Malines on
19 May 1499, prior to which it had been governed by a commissary of
the Vicar-General. The six Observant houses which ultimately composed the province were Greenwich, Richmond (Surrey), Newcastle,
Canterbury, Southampton [2] and Newark. The house in Guernsey founded
in 1486 was incorporated in the province of France from the first.

SCOTLAND

It may be convenient to add here a list of the Scottish houses, as
these, though outside the scope of the present work, at various dates
formed part of the English province. The English province was divided
into two provinces of England and Scotland (the latter including Northern
England) about 1230–33, but this arrangement lasted only till 1239, when
the undivided English province was restored, the Scottish houses being
then or soon afterwards incorporated in the custody of Newcastle.[3] The
Scottish friars struggled against their subordinate position.[4] It is doubtful
whether the letter of Pope Alexander IV instructing the General Chapter
in 1260 to institute a provincial minister in Scotland is genuine ;[5] it
certainly had no result. But the Scottish friars succeeded with the support
of the general minister in forming themselves into a vicariate independent
of the custody of Newcastle in 1278.[6] In 1296 they admitted that the
Vicariate was part of the English province and in some respects subject
to the English provincial minister.[7] In 1329 the Scottish vicariate was
completely separated from the English province and made directly de-
pendent on the general minister.[8] In the list of custodies and houses of
the English province drawn up for the general chapter of Perpignan in

---

[1] Berwick is omitted as it was usually regarded as one of the Scottish
houses.
[2] Dr. Little points out to me that his former suggestion (*Proc. of Brit.
Acad.*, vol. 10, p. 464), that at Southampton the conventuals and observants
formed independent communities which existed separately until the Dissolution, is an error due to a misunderstanding of the records (see P.R.O.
Ministers' Accounts Hen. VIII, no. 7407). The Southampton Observants
seem to have escaped suppression in 1534 by taking the oath of succession.
—*Letters of Stephen Gardiner*, ed. J. A. Muller, 1933, p. 56.
[3] Eccleston, pp. 50–2.
[4] Eubel, *Bullarii Franciscani Epitome et Supplementum* (1908), p. 268 :
Moir Bryce, *Scottish Grey Friars* (1909), vol. 1, pp. 9–10 ; vol. 2, p. 275 ;
Golubovich, *Biblioteca Bio-Bibliografica della Terra Santa*, vol. 2 (1913),
p. 223.
[5] *Archiv. Franc. Hist.*, vol. 24, pp. 315–16 (extracts from the Register
of the Franciscan Order in Scotland).
[6] *Ibid.*, p. 325.   [7] *Lanercost Chronicle*, p. 265.
[8] Little, *Studies in Engl. Franc. Hist.*, p. 236.

1331 the Scottish houses were included in the custody of Newcastle, though they appeared also in the same lists as an independent vicariate.[1] In 1359 the decision of 1329 was reversed and the vicariate reunited to the English province,[2] but it continued to exist as a vicariate [3] and is represented as such in the list of provinces drawn up at Ragusa in 1385, though it is not mentioned in the almost contemporary list in the *Liber de Conformitate* of Bartholomew of Pisa.[3] The great schism(1378–1417), when the kingdoms of England and Scotland took opposite sides and adhered to rival popes, severed relations between the English province and the Scottish vicariate, and it does not appear that any constitutional connection between the two communities was ever re-established. The eight conventual houses of the Scottish vicariate are given below with the approximate dates of their foundation :

Berwick (*c.* 1244), Roxburgh (*c.* 1232–34), Haddington (*c.* 1242), Dumfries (*c.* 1262), Dundee (*c.* 1284), Lanark (1328–29), Inverkeithing (*c.* 1346), Kirkcudbright (1455–56).

The Observants arrived in Scotland about 1447 and a separate Scottish province of the Observant order was sanctioned at the General Chapter held at Monte Lucido in 1467 and confirmed three years later. The nine houses which were ultimately comprised in it were :

Edinburgh (1447), St. Andrews (*c.* 1458), Perth (*c.* 1460), Aberdeen (1461–69), Glasgow (1472), Ayr (*c.* 1474), Elgin (1479), Stirling (*c.* 1484) and Jedburgh (1513).

---

[1] *Chron. XXIV. Generalium* in *Analecta Franciscana*, vol. 3 (1897), pp. 557–8.

[2] *Cal. Pap. L.*, vol. 4, p. 216.

[3] Both lists are given in Golubovich, *op. cit.*, pp. 254, 257.

APPENDIX V

LIST OF FRANCISCAN HOUSES IN ENGLAND AND WALES

(with bibliographical references and approximate dates of foundation)

THE majority of the papers referred to in the following list deal primarily with the historical aspect of the different houses. Most of the articles which contain architectural or topographical descriptions of any value have already been referred to in the footnotes to the preceding pages, but for convenience of reference they are again included here. Wherever a plan accompanies an article, the fact has been noted. Historical accounts of all the English Franciscan houses except Bodmin, Bridgnorth, Cambridge, Chester, Denny, Exeter, Leicester, Lichfield, Newcastle-on-Tyne, Plymouth, Salisbury, Shrewsbury, Stafford and Waterbeach have appeared in the *Victoria County History*. These are not referred to below, but wherever a house has been described in the topographical sections of that work the appropriate reference is given.

Wherever possible, the date of publication of each work referred to has been stated, as many of the earlier articles have been largely superseded by later discoveries. Where more than one reference is given, the first is generally the principal source of information on the topography and architecture of the house in question. For books dealing with the English Franciscan Province generally, reference should be made to the bibliography at page xxi. An asterisk denotes that there are surviving remains.

AYLESBURY (BUCKINGHAMSHIRE). 1386–87.
> Inventory of the Historical Monuments Commission, Buckinghamshire, vol. 1 (1912), p. 31.
BABWELL (see Bury St. Edmunds).
BEDFORD (BEDFORDSHIRE). *Before* 1238.
> Victoria County History, Bedford, vol. 3, p. 22.
> Lysons Magna Britannia, vol. 1(1), p. 48.
> T. A. Blythe, History of Bedford (*c.* 1860), p. 34.
> Beds. Notes and Queries, vol. 1, p. 351.
BERWICK (NORTHUMBERLAND). *c.* 1244.
> (Originally in the English Province but subsequently transferred to the Vicariate of Scotland.)
> W. Moir Bryce. The Scottish Grey Friars, 2 vols. *passim.*
BEVERLEY (YORKSHIRE, EAST RIDING). *Before* 1267.
> (Transferred to later site *c.* 1297.)
> L. M. Goldthorp, "The Franciscans and Dominicans in Yorkshire," Yorks. Arch. Soc. Journ., vol. 32 (1935), pp. 291–8.
> Geo. Poulson, Beverlac or the Antiquities and History of Beverley (1829), pp. 770–3.
> Collectanea Topographica et Genealogica, vol. IV (1837), pp. 129–31.
BODMIN (CORNWALL). *c.* 1239.
> Sir John MacLean, F.S.A. The Parochial and Family History of the Deanery of Trigg Minor Cornwall, vol. 1 (1873), pp. 186–93.
> A Complete Parochial History of the County of Cornwall, vol. 1 (1867), pp. 91–2.
> G. Oliver, Monasticon Dioecesis Exoniensis (1846), pp. 17–18, 412.

Suppression Inventory printed in Journal of the Royal Institute of Cornwall, vol. 8 (1886), pp. 24–6.

BOSTON (LINCOLNSHIRE). *Before* 1268.

P. Thompson, Collections for a Topographical and Historical Account of Boston (1856), pp. 112–13.

BRIDGNORTH (SHROPSHIRE). *c.* 1244.

Paper and illustrations by Rev. Prebendary Clark-Maxwell, F.S.A., in Transactions of Shropshire Arch. and Nat. Hist. Society— 4th series, vol. XI, part 1, pp. 49–66 (1927).

Suppression inventory printed in *ibid.*, 3rd series, vol. V, pp. 378–9 (1905).

G. Bellett, The Antiquities of Bridgnorth (1856), pp. 87–97.

BRIDGWATER (SOMERSET), *c.* 1245.

Archæological Journal, vol. 43 (1886), p. 299 (note).

Collinson, History of Somerset (1791), vol. III, pp. 80, 306 and 385.

A. H. Powell, The Ancient Borough of Bridgwater (1907), pp. 78–93.

BRISTOL (GLOUCESTERSHIRE). *Before* 1230.

G. E. Weare, A Collectanea relating to the Bristol Friars Minors and their Convent (1893), plan and illustrations.

Archæological Journal, vol. 43 (1886), p. 298 (note).

British Arch. Assoc. Trans., new series, vol. 32, pp. 139–40 (note).

W. Barrett, History of Bristol (1789), pp. 399–400.

BRUISYARD (SUFFOLK). *c.* 1364–7 NUNNERY.

A. F. C. Bourdillon, "The Order of Minoresses in England," Brit. Soc. Franc. Studies, vol. XII (1926), pp. 22–5, etc.

BURY ST. EDMUNDS (SUFFOLK). 1257.

(Removed in 1265 to Babwell outside the town.)

J. Carter, Ancient Architecture of England, part II (1807), plate VIII (*c*), (view of gateway dated 1786).

CAMBRIDGE (CAMBRIDGESHIRE). *c.* 1225.

J. Willis Clark, The Architectural History of the University of Cambridge, vol. I (1886), pp. 723–36 and *passim*.

* CANTERBURY (KENT). 1224. *Observant after* 1498.

Charles Cotton, " The Grey Friars of Canterbury," British Soc. of Franciscan Studies, extra series, no. 2 (1924), illustrations and plan.

A. G. Little, " The Grey Friars of Canterbury," Arch. Cant., vol. 34 (1920), pp. 79–91.

Arch. Journal, vol. 86 (1929), p. 286 (note and plan).

Somner's Antiquities of Canterbury, edit. Bateley (1703), part I, pp. 54–7.

CARDIFF (GLAMORGAN). *c.* 1280.

A. W. Clapham, " The Architectural Remains of the Mendicant Orders in Wales," Arch. Journal, vol. 84 (1927), pp. 98–9.

C. B. Fowler, Excavations on the Site of the Grey Friars' Monastery, Cardiff (1896).

R. C. Easterling, " The Friars of Wales," Arch. Cambrensis, 6th series, vol. 14 (1914), pp. 340–1.

Suppression Inventory printed Arch. Cambrensis original documents, 1870.

J. M. Cronin, Cardiff Grey Friars (1924), illustration and plan, 35 pp.

Arch. Camb., 6th series, vol. 1 (1900), p. 72 (plan).

CARLISLE (CUMBERLAND). 1233.

Samuel Jefferson, The History of Antiquities of Carlisle (1838), pp. 139–42.

CARMARTHEN (CARMARTHENSHIRE). *Before* 1284.

A. W. Clapham, " The Architectural Remains of the Mendicant Orders in Wales," Arch. Journal, vol. 84 (1927), p. 99.

R. Com. Hist. Mons. Wales, vol. V, Carmarthen, p. 259.

R. C. Easterling, " The Friars of Wales," Arch. Camb., 6th series, vol. 14 (1914), pp. 345–6.

Suppression inventory printed in Arch. Camb. Original Documents (1870), p. xxxix.

CHESTER (CHESHIRE). *c.* 1238.

    J. H. E. Bennett, " The Grey Friars of Chester " in Journ. of Chester Arch. Soc., vol. 24, part 1, pp. 5–85 (1921) (site plan and illustrations).

* CHICHESTER (SUSSEX). *c.* 1240. *Transferred to later site* 1269.

    W. V. Crake, Sussex Arch. Coll., vol. 51, pp. 14–36 (1908).

    Victoria County History, Sussex, vol. 3 (1935), p. 80, illustrations and plan.

    E. B. Poland, The Friars of Sussex (1928), pp. 65–73.

    F. Grose, The Antiquities of England and Wales, vol. 1 (illustration).

    The Topographer, vol. 1, p. 215.

    Suppression inventory printed in Sussex Arch. Coll., vol. 44, pp. 71–2 (1901).

    Knight's Old England, vol. 1 (1845), no. 1105.

COLCHESTER (ESSEX). *Before* 1237.

    P. Morant, History and Antiquities of the County of Essex, vol. 1 (1768), pp. 151–2.

    Thos. Cromwell, History of the Borough of Colchester, vol. 1 (1825), p. 213.

    T. Wright, History of the County of Essex, vol. 1 (1836), p. 317.

* COVENTRY (WARWICKSHIRE). *c.* 1234.

    W. G. Fretton, " Memorials of the Franciscans or Grey Friars' of Coventry," Birmingham and Midland Institute, vol. IX (1878–79), pp. 34–53 (plan).

    T. Sharp, Antiquities of Coventry (1871), pp. 196–209.

    Archæologia, vol. 43 (1871), p. 204 (note).

    A. G. Little, Studies in English Franciscan History (1917) pp. 225–8.

    B. Poole and W. F. Taunton, Coventry, its History and Antiquities (1870), pp. 19–21 and 220–1.

    W. Reader, History and Antiquities of Coventry (N.D. *c.* 1810), pp. 159–63.

    W. Dugdale, The Antiquities of Warwickshire (1765), pp. 119–22.

    W. Reader, Coventry MSS. in Coventry Public Library.

* DENNY (CAMBRIDGESHIRE). 1342 NUNNERY. (*See also* WATERBEACH).

    Bourdillon, " The Order of Minoresses in England," Brit. Soc. Franc. Studies, vol. XII (1926) *passim*.

    E. A. B. Barnard, " A Sixteenth-century Dole Gate from Denny Abbey," Camb. Antiq. Soc., vol. 29 (1928), pp. 72–5.

DONCASTER (YORKSHIRE, WEST RIDING). *Before* 1284.

    F. R. Fairbank, F.S.A. " The House of Grey Friars, Doncaster," Yorks. Arch. Soc., vol. XII (1893), pp. 481–6 (site plan).

    L. M. Goldthorp, " The Franciscans and Dominicans in Yorkshire," Yorks. Arch. Soc. Journ., vol. 32 (1935), pp. 298–303.

DORCHESTER (DORSET). *Before* 1267.

    J. Hutchins, History and Antiquities of Dorset (3rd edit., 1864), vol. II, pp. 364–6.

* DUNWICH (SUFFOLK). *Before* 1277. *Transfer to later site* 1289.

    Thomas Gardner, Historical Account of Dunwich (1754), pp. 59–61.

    A. Suckling, The History and Antiquities of Suffolk, vol. 2 (1848), pp. 282–5 (illustrations).

DURHAM (DURHAM). *c.* 1239.

    (This house was only in existence for a few years.)

EXETER (DEVON). *c.* 1240. *Transferred to later site c.* 1300.

    A. G. Little and R. C. Easterling, " The Franciscans and Dominicans of Exeter " (History of Exeter Research Group Publications, no. 3, 1927), pp. 12–30.

    Suppression Inventory printed in Exeter Dioc. Arch. Soc. Trans., 2nd series, vol. II, p. 268.

* GLOUCESTER (GLOUCESTERSHIRE). *c.* 1231.
   Paper and plan by V. M. Dallas in Bristol and Glouc. Arch. Soc. Trans.,
     vol. 54, pp. 117–27 (1932).
   Paper by Rev. W. A. Silvester Davies in Bristol and Glouc. Arch. Soc.,
     vol. 13 (1888), pp. 173–87.
   Note by Sinclair Baddeley in Proc. Cotteswold Naturalists Field Club,
     vol. 19, part 3, p. 203 (1917).
   T. D. Fosbrooke, History of Gloucester (1819), pp. 148–9 (illustration).
   J. Smyth, Lives of the Berkeleys (ed. Maclean), vol. II (1885) *passim.*
   Stukeley Itinerarium Curiosum (1776), plate 4 facing page 67 (wrongly
     called Whitefriars).
   Gentleman's Magazine 1860, p. 259.
   Suppression inventory printed in Bristol and Glouc. Arch. Soc. Trans.,
     vol. 13, p. 184.
GRANTHAM (LINCOLNSHIRE). *Before* 1290.
   B. Street, Historical Notes on Grantham (1857), pp. 44–7.
GREENWICH (KENT). 1482. *Observant.*
   Paper and plan by A. R. Martin in Arch. Journal, vol. 80, pp. 81–114
     (1923).
   A. G. Little, "The Introduction of the Observants into England,"
     Proc. Brit. Acad., vol. X, pp. 455–71 (1922).
   Hasted History of Kent: Hundred of Blackheath (ed. Drake), 1886,
     pp. 86–8.
   Archæological Journal, vol. 23 (1868), pp. 54–7.
GRIMSBY (LINCOLNSHIRE). *c.* 1240.
   G. Oliver, Monumental Antiquities of Grimsby (1825), pp. 108–10.
HARTLEPOOL (DURHAM). *Before* 1239.
   Victoria County History Durham, vol. III (1928), p. 264 and plate
     opp. p. 266.
   Cuthbert Sharp, History of Hartlepool (1816), pp. 115–120.
   Robert Surtees, History of . . . Durham, vol. 3 (1828), p. 119.
HEREFORD (HEREFORDSHIRE). *c.* 1228.
   John Duncumb, Collections towards the History and Antiquities of
     the County of Hereford, vol. 1 (1804), pp. 376–81.
   M. R. James, "The Library of the Greyfriars of Hereford," Brit.
     Soc. Franc. Studies, Collectanea Franciscana, vol. I (1914),
     pp. 114–23.
* IPSWICH (SUFFOLK). *Before* 1236.
   B. P. Grimsey, "The Grey-Friars Monastery Ipswich," Suffolk
     Arch. Institute, vol. 9 (1897), pp. 373–8 (site plan).
   John Wadderspoon, Memorials of Ipswich (1850), pp. 313–19,
     where the Suppression inventory is printed.
   Paper on "Religious Houses in Ipswich," Arch. Journ., vol. 56
     (1899), pp. 232–8 *passim.*
   J. Weever, Funeral Monuments (1631), p. 751 (for list of burials).
   Suppression Inventory printed in Suffolk Arch. Assoc. Original
     Papers (1848), p. 14.
LEICESTER (LEICESTERSHIRE). *Before* 1230.
   J. Nichols, History and Antiquities of the County of Leicester, vol. I,
     part I (1815), pp. 297–9.
   Derbyshire Arch. Soc., vol. V (1883), pp. 157–61.
   J. Throsby, History of Leicester (1791), pp. 290–1.
LEWES (SUSSEX). *c.* 1240.
   J. W. Horsfield, History and Antiquities of Lewes (1824), vol. I,
     pp. 282–3.
   E. P. Poland, The Friars of Sussex (1928), pp. 87–94.
LICHFIELD (STAFFORDSHIRE). *c.* 1237.
   Thomas Harwood, The History and Antiquities of Lichfield (1806),
     pp. 480–8 (plan).

S. Shaw, The History and Antiquities of Staffordshire, vol. 1 (1798), pp. 320–2.

P. Anthony, Ancient Friary of Lichfield. Franciscan Annals, July, 1910, pp. 202–6.

* LINCOLN (LINCOLNSHIRE). *c.* 1230.

A. R. Martin, " The Grey Friars of Lincoln," Arch. Journal, vol. 92 (1936), pp. 42–63, plans and illustrations.

J. S. Padley, Selections from the Ancient Edifices of Lincolnshire (1851), (plan and illustrations).

Henry Bond, " The Greyfriars of Lincoln " (printed in the Catalogue of the Lincoln Health Exhibition 1899, 25 copies reprinted).

E. Mansel Sympson, " The Greyfriars of Lincoln," Lincs. Notes and Queries, vol. 7, no. 59, pp. 193–202 (July 1903).

W. Watkins & Son, Report on the Structure (see 13th Annual Report of Art and Industrial Exhibition, 1906).

LLANFAES (ANGLESEY). 1237.

A. W. Clapham, " The Architectural Remains of the Mendicant Order in Wales," Arch. Journal, vol. 34 (1927), pp. 100–1 (plan).

Arch. Camb., 3rd series, vol. I, p. 76 (plan).

R. C. Easterling, " The Friars in Wales," Arch. Camb., 6th series, 14 (1914), pp. 331 and 342–5.

C. R. Hand, " Llanfaes Friary and its Mystery Monuments," Arch. Camb., vol. 79 (1924), pp. 125–88.

Suppression Inventory printed in Arch. Camb. Original Documents (1870), p. xliii.

LONDON. NEWGATE, 1224.

E. B. S. Shepherd, " The Grey Friars Church in London," Arch. Journal, vol. 59 (1902), pp. 248–53, plans.

E. B. S. Shepherd, " The Church of the Friars Minors in London," London Topographical Society, vol. II (1903), pp. 29–35.

C. L. Kingsford, " The Greyfriars of London," 1915 (Brit. Soc. of Franc. Studies, vol. VI).

C. L. Kingsford, " Additional Material for the History of the Grey Friars, London," 1922. (Brit. Soc. Franc. Studies, vol. X. Collectanea Franciscana, vol. II, pp. 61–149.)

G. H. Birch, " Greyfriars," St. Paul's Ecclesiological Society Trans. vol. III (1895), pp. 101–4.

M. B. Honeybourne, " The Precinct of the Grey Friars," London Topographical Record, vol. 16 (1932), pp. 9–51. Plans.

The Builder, 22 December 1855, p. 619. (Note on a discovery in Newgate Street relating to the Grey Friars.)

J. E. Price, " On Recent Discoveries in Newgate Street," illustrations. London & Middlesex Arch. Soc., vol. V (1881), pp. 403–24.

Philip Norman, " On an Ancient conduit head in Queen Square, Bloomsbury " (Archæologia, vol. 56, part 2, 1899), pp. 251–66.

Philip Norman and E. A. Mann, " On the White Conduit Chapel Street, Bloomsbury, and its connection with the Grey Friars water system," Archæologia, vol. 61 (1909) pp. 347–56. Plans.

Philip Norman, " Christ Church Newgate," St. Paul's Ecclesiological Society's Transactions, vol. 7 (1911–15), pp. 32–6.

London and Middlesex Arch. Soc., vol. 4, pp. 420–3.

Proc. Soc. Antiquaries, vol. 21 (1906), pp. 12–21.

A. W. Clapham and W. H. Godfrey, Some famous Buildings and their Story (N.D.), p. 250 (plan).

Stow's Survey of London (ed. Strype), vol. I, book 3, pp. 129–134; (ed. Kingsford), vol. I, pp. 316–22.

Maitland, History of London (1756), vol. II, p. 1316.

J. G. Nichols (editor), " A Chronicle of the Grey Friars in London " (Camden Society, vol. 31, 1852).

Greyfriars Chronicle, Monumenta Franciscana (Rolls Series), vol. II.

Trollope, History of Christ's Hospital (1833), *passim*, illustrations.
E. H. Pearce, Annals of Christ's Hospital, 2nd edit. (1908), pp. 56–8.
C. J. Sisson " Grafton and the London Greyfriars," Bibliographical Soc. The Library, 4th series, vol. XI (1930), p. 124.
Wren Society, vol. XI (1934) (Christ's Hospital, Newgate Street), pp. 60–80 and plates 47–8.
LONDON. MINORIES. 1293. NUNNERY.
R. Com. Hist. Mons. England. London, vol. V (1930), p. 72 (plan).
E. M. Tomlinson, History of the Minories, London (1907), pp. 11–79.
A. F. C. Bourdillon, "The Order of Minoresses in England," 1926 (Brit. Soc. Franc. Studies, vol. XII) *passim*.
H. Fly, "Some Account of an Abbey of Nuns formerly situated in the Street now called the Minories," Archæologia, vol. 15 (1806), pp. 92–113.
* LYNN REGIS (NORFOLK). *c.* 1230–40.
Archæological Journal, vol. 89 (1932), pp. 335-6 (note and plan).
Blomefield, History of Norfolk, vol. VIII (1808), p. 526
Storer and Greig's Topographical Cabinet vol. 3 (1808).
NEWARK (NOTTINGHAMSHIRE). 1507. *Observant.*
Brown's History of Newark (1904), p. 42.
NEWCASTLE-ON-TYNE (NORTHUMBERLAND). *Before* 1237. *Observant after* 1498.
J. Brand, History of Newcastle-on-Tyne (1789), vol. I, pp. 331–7.
NORTHAMPTON (NORTHAMPTONSHIRE). 1225.
R. M. Serjeantson, History of the Six Houses of Friars in Northampton, (1911), pp. 1–25.
Victoria County History, Northamptonshire, vol. III (1930), p. 58.
Sir H. Dryden, " The Grey Friars of Northampton," Assoc. Arch. Socs. Rep. (1887–88), pp. 121–4.
NORTHAMPTON (NORTHAMPTONSHIRE). *c.* 1252. NUNNERY.
This house, which only survived for a few years, may not have been strictly of the Second Order of St. Francis.
NORWICH (NORFOLK). 1226.
Blomefield, History of Norfolk, vol. IV (1806), pp. 106–16.
British Arch. Assoc., vol. 30, part 1 (1924), p. 139 (note on burials discovered).
Kirkpatrick, Religious Orders of Norwich (1845), pp. 104–9.
NOTTINGHAM (NOTTINGHAMSHIRE). *c.* 1230.
John Blackner, The History of Nottingham (1815), pp. 133–4.
F. W. Wadsworth, "Extracts from wills relating to the Grey Friars, Nottingham," Thoroton Society, vol. 22 (1918), pp. 79, 108–11.
OXFORD (OXFORDSHIRE). 1224.
A. G. Little, " The Grey Friars in Oxford " (1892) (Oxford Historical Society, vol. 20).
A. Wood, Survey of the Antiquities of the City of Oxford (ed. A. Clark), 1889–90.
The Suppression inventory is printed in " The Grey Friars in Oxford," *ut sup.*
Mgr. A. Barnes, English Life, July 1924.
A. G. Little, " The Franciscans at Oxford," Brit. Soc. Franc. Studies Extra Series, vol. I (1912), pp. 71–87.
" The Franciscan School at Oxford in the Thirteenth Century," Arch. Franc. Hist., vol. 19 (1926), pp. 803–73.
PLYMOUTH (DEVON). 1383.
Llewellynn Jewitt, A History of Plymouth (1873), pp. 494–6.
R. N. Worth, History of Plymouth (1890), p. 230.
G. Oliver, Monasticon Dioecesis Exoniensis (1846), p. 157.
PRESTON (LANCASHIRE). *c.* 1260.
H. Fishwick, History of the Parish of Preston (1900), pp. 198–203.

U

* READING (BERKSHIRE). 1233. *Transfer to new site c.* 1286.
Paper and plan in Arch. Journal, vol. III (1846), pp. 141–8.
Victoria County History, Berkshire (1923), vol. 3, pp. 374–5 (plan).
Chas. Coates, History of and Antiquities of Reading (1802),
pp. 299–309, and appendices 2–4.
Paper by F. W. Albury in Newbury District Field Club. Trans.,
vol. 2 (1878), pp. 212–17.
John Man's History of Reading (1816), pp. 289–96 and plate 17.
Grey Friars Church, Reading. Circulars and Appeals relative to the
restoration (reprinted for private circulation, 1874), 20 pp.
Rev. Chas. Hole, The Life of the Rev. and Ven. William Whitmarsh
Phelps, vol. II (1873), pp. 214–20, 230–1, 235–7 and 286, with
photograph of the church before restoration opp. p. 393.
J. Doran, The History and Antiquities of the Town and Borough
of Reading (1835), pp. 100–12.
William Fletcher, Reading Past and Present (1839), pp. 44–6.
Reminiscences of Reading by an Octogenarian (N.D.) (*c.* 1885),
pp. 50–1. View before restoration opposite p. 51.
RICHMOND (SURREY). 1500. *Observant.*
R. Crisp. Richmond and its inhabitants from the Olden Time (1866),
pp. 126–9 (with illustration from an old view).
Victoria County History, Surrey, vol. III (1911), p. 537, and plate
opposite p. 540.
* RICHMOND (YORKSHIRE, NORTH RIDING). 1257–58.
Victoria County History, North Riding, vol. I (1914), pp. 31–2 (plan).
Christopher Clarkson, History and Antiquities of Richmond (1821),
pp. 214–23 (illustration).
L. M. Goldthorp, " The Franciscans and Dominicans in Yorkshire,"
Yorks. Arch. Soc. Journ., vol. 32 (1935), pp. 303–10.
T. D. Whitaker, History of Richmondshire, vol. I (1823), pp. 98–9,
with plate by J. Pye after J. Buckler (1819)
Henry Lawrance, Short History of the Grey Friars of Richmond (N.D.)
(*c.* 1908).
F. Grose, The Antiquities of England and Wales, vol. 4 (illustration).
ROMNEY (KENT). *c.* 1241.
This foundation lasted some 40 years : Archæol. Cantiana., vol. 46
(1935), p. 29.
* SALISBURY (WILTSHIRE). *Before* 1230.
A. G. Little and J. Lovibond, " The Grey Friars of Salisbury," Wilts.
Arch. and Nat. Hist. Mag., vol. 47 (1935), pp. 36–54 (illustration
and plan).
Suppression inventory printed in Wilts. Arch. and Nat. Hist. Mag.,
vol. 30, pp. 30–33.
SCARBOROUGH (YORKSHIRE, NORTH RIDING). *c.* 1239.
J. B. Baker, The History of Scarborough (1882), pp. 125–8.
L. M. Goldthorp, " The Franciscans and Dominicans in Yorkshire,"
Yorks. Arch. Soc. Journ., vol. 32 (1935), pp. 310–19.
The History of Scarborough, edit. Arthur Rowntree (1931) *passim.*
Collectanea Topog. et Gen., vol. IV (1837), p. 132.
* SHREWSBURY (SHROPSHIRE). 1245.
Canon A. J. Moriarty, " The Greyfriars of Shrewsbury," Shropshire
Arch. and Nat. Hist. Soc., 4th series, vol. 12, part 1 (1929), pp. 75–84.
Owen and Blakeway, History of Shrewsbury (1825), vol. II, pp. 460–4
(view).
Suppression inventory printed in Shropshire, Arch. Soc., 3rd series,
vol. 5 (1905), pp. 384–6.
SOUTHAMPTON (HAMPSHIRE). *c.* 1235. *Observant after* 1498.
T. S. Davies, History of Southampton (1883), pp. 444–8.
STAFFORD (STAFFORDSHIRE). *Before* 1277.
F. A. Hibbert, Monasticism in Staffordshire, 2nd edit. (1910) *passim.*

List of Franciscan Houses in England and Wales 285

F. A. Hibbert, The Dissolution of the Monasteries in Staffordshire (1910) *passim.*

STAMFORD (LINCOLNSHIRE). *c.* 1230.
F. Peck, Antiquarian Annals of Stamford, vol. VIII, p. 55.
The History of Stamford (pub. John Drakard 1822), pp. 189–94.

* WALSINGHAM (NORFOLK). 1347.
A. R. Martin " The Grey Friars of Walsingham," Norfolk and Norwich Arch. Soc., vol. 25 (1934), pp. 227–71 (plans and illustrations).
Blomefield, History of Norfolk (1808), vol. IX, p. 281.

* WARE (HERTFORDSHIRE). *c.* 1350.
R. Com. Hist. Mons. England Herts. (1910), p. 228.
Victoria County History, Herts., vol. 3 (1912), pp. 382 and 392.
R. Walters, " Ware Priory," East Herts Arch. Soc., vol. I, part 1, (1901), pp. 39–43.
G. R. Owst, " The Franciscans in Hertfordshire," St. Albans and Herts, Architectural and Arch. Soc. Trans. (1925), pp. 108–28.
The Builder, vol. VII, p. 342 (21 July, 1849).

WATERBEACH (CAMBRIDGESHIRE) 1294. NUNNERY. *(Finally transferred to Denny in Waterbeach parish in 1351.)*
A. F. C. Bourdillon, The Order of Minoresses in England, 1926 *passim.*
Robert Masters, A Short Account of the parish of Waterbeach (1795).
W. K. Clay, History of the parish of Waterbeach (1859), pp. 91–138.

* WINCHELSEA (SUSSEX). *Before* 1242. *(Town destroyed 1287. Removed to new Town 1291.)*
W. D. Cooper, History of Winchelsea (1850), pp. 144–9 (illustrations).
E. P. Poland, The Friars in Sussex (1928), pp. 77–84 (illustrations).
F. Grose, The Antiquities of England and Wales, vol. 3 (illustration).

WINCHESTER (HAMPSHIRE). *c.* 1237.
Archæologia, vol. 43 (1871), p. 246 (note).
Suppression inventory in Victoria County History, Hampshire, vol. 2, pp. 191–2.

WORCESTER (WORCESTERSHIRE). *c.* 1225–30. *(Original site inside the city. Removed to new site outside c. 1236–39.)*
L. Sheppard, " The Franciscans or Grey Friars of Worcester," Assoc. Arch. Socs., vol. 31 (1911), pp. 243–70 (plans and illustrations).
Suppression inventory printed in Associated Arch. Socs. Reports, vol. XI (1872), pp. 307–8.
Victoria County History, Worcester, vol. 4, p. 392.
Valentine Green, History of Worcester, vol. I (1788), p. 243.
Treadway Nash, History of Worcestershire, vol. II (1782), Appendix, p. cli.

* YARMOUTH (NORFOLK). *Before* 1271.
J. Bately, and H. Olley " Recent discoveries on the site of the Grey Friars, Great Yarmouth," Norfolk and Norwich Arch. Soc., vol. 13, part I (1896), pp. 21–32 (plan and illustrations).
Henry Swinden, The History and Antiquities of Great Yarmouth, (1772), pp. 734–5.
The History of Great Yarmouth, by Henry Manship, ed. C. J. Palmer (1854), pp. 418–25.
C. J. Palmer, The Perlustration of Great Yarmouth, vol. II (1874), pp. 128–9.
F. R. B. Howards, " The Grey Friars Cloisters, Great Yarmouth," Brit. Arch. Assoc. Journ., vol. 31, part I (1925), pp. 107–9.

YORK (YORKSHIRE). *c.* 1230.
F. Drake, Eboracum or the History and Antiquities of the City of York (1736), pp. 282–3.
L. M. Goldthorp, " The Franciscans and Dominicans in Yorkshire," Yorks. Arch. Soc. Journ., vol. 32 (1935), pp. 269–91.
William Hargrove, History and Description of . . . York (1818), vol. 2, pp. 210–16.

INDEX

Germany, 40. *See also* Lübeck
Gethen, Hugh, 85
Giffard, Walter, Abp. of York, 218
Gifford, George, 72
" Giffs," the, 189
Gilbert(i), Donald, guardian at Greenwich, 235
Gilbertines, the, 30 n.
Gille, Alan, 186
Gipping, River, 241
Glasgow, Observant house at, 277
Gloucester, Dominican house at, 33, 37
— Franciscan house at, 275, 281 ; history, 82–5 ; description, 8, 13, 14, 22, 36, 85–9, 238
— Margaret, Countess of, 180 ; Thomas, Earl of, 266. *See also* Clare
— *see* Alexander of
Glym, Isabella, 272
Glyndwr, Owen, 160, 173
Godewyn, William, 220
Godwin, E. W., 225
Goldsmith, *see* Thomas le
Goldwell, James, Bp. of Norwich, 234
Goodsall, R. H., 49 n.
Gornay, Gourney, Matthew, 213 and n. ; Alice his wife, 213
Gorringe, G., 57
Gostwick, Gostwikke, Mr., 155. *See also* Gostwyk
Gostwyk, John, 156 ; Joan his wife, 156. *See also* Gostwick
Gourney, *see* Gornay
Gower, Ralph, 121, 122
Gradely, Grately, Robert, 219
Grafton, Richard, 188
Grandison, John de, Bp. of Exeter, 205, 206 ; Otho de, 156 n.
Grant, J. P., 162
Grantham, Franciscan house at, 12, 275, 281
Grately, *see* Gradely, Robert
Grays Inn Road, London, 202 n.
Great Chamber, the, *see* Bishops Lodging, the, Lichfield
Green, Jeremy, 221 ; Valentine, *cited*, 253
greene, *see* Guido de la
Greenwich, Observant house at, 24, 234–9, 275, 276, 281 ; guardian of, *see* Gilbert(i), Donald
Gregory IX, Pope, 218
Gregory de Rokesley, Mayor of London, 178
Gregory, Thomas, 72
Grene, Richard, 128, 129 n.
" grette fryers close," Cardiff, 161

Grey, Robert, 80, 127
Grey Friars Churchyard, the, Coventry,· 73
Grey Friars' footbridge, Shrewsbury, 249
Grey Friars' Gate, Coventry, 74
Grey Friars Lane, Canterbury, 53 ; Coventry, 74. *See also* Linen Hall Street, Chester
Grey Friars (Christ Church) passage, London, 182 and n., 193
Grey Friars Road (Smith's Walk), Chester, 231 n.
Grey Friars Road, Lynn Regis, 103
Grimely, E., 234
Grimm, S. H., 97, 147 n.
Grimsby, Franciscan house at, 9, 276, 281
Grose, *cited*, 58
Grosseteste, Robert, Bp. of Lincoln, 7 n., 8, 35 and n., 226
Grosvenor, Robert, of Hulme, 227 ; Robert, 118. *See also* Scrope v. Grosvenor, law suit of
Grosvenor Museum, Chester, 233
Gryme, Robert, grocer, 248
Guernsey, Observant house at, 276
Guido de la greene, 271
Guildhall, Chichester, 57
Gunter, James, 161
Guy's Hall, Worcester, 253
Gwyn, Thomas, guardian at Cardiff, 161

Hackington, anchoress at, *see* Beaumont, Loretta, widow of Robert de
Haddington, Franciscan house at, 275, 277
Hall, Thomas, 210
Hallam, Richard, 197
Ham Hill stone, 215, 217
Hanchurche meade, Bedford, 156
Hardeshull, *see* Margaret de
Hardwen, John, draper, 68
Hardwick (Norfolk), 102
Harpur, John, Lord of Ruyssheale, 171
Harrington, Thomas, 68
Harris, John, warden at Bridgwater, 213
Harrold, Nunnery of, 154
Hartington Church (Derbs.), 266
Hartlepool, Franciscan house at, 276, 281
— *see* Arthur de
Harwood, T., *cited*, 164, 168 n., 171
Hastang, Nicolas de, 271 ; Sir Thomas, and Elizabeth his wife, 271